PITT LATIN AMERICAN SERIES

Ascent to Bankruptcy

Financing

Social Security

in Latin America

Carmelo Mesa-Lago

UNIVERSITY OF PITTSBURGH PRESS

Published by the University of Pittsburgh Press, Pittsburgh, Pa.,
15260
Copyright © 1989, University of Pittsburgh Press
All rights reserved
Baker & Taylor International, London
Manufactured in the United States of America

Library of Congress Cataloging-in-Publication Data

Mesa-Lago, Carmelo, 1934–
    Ascent to bankruptcy : social security financing in Latin America
    / Carmelo Mesa-Lago.
    p.   cm.—(Pitt Latin American series)
    Includes index.
    ISBN 0-8229-3600-3
    1. Social security—Latin America—Finance—Case studies.
2. Social security—Latin America—Finance. I. Title. II. Series.
HD7130.5.M44   1989
368.4'01'098—dc20   89-35475
                                                        CIP

Contents

Tables

Acronyms

AFP	Administradoras de Fondos de Pensiones = Administrators of Pension Funds (Chile)
ANAP	Asociación Nacional de Agricultores Pequeños = National Association of Small Farmers (Cuba)
APRA	Alianza Popular Revolucionaria Americana (Peru)
BID	Banco Interamericano de Desarrollo = IDB
BPS	Banco de Previsión Social = Social Insurance Bank (Uruguay)
BSE	Banco de Seguros del Estado = State Insurance Bank (Uruguay)
CANAEMPU	Caja Nacional de Empleados Públicos y Periodistas = Civil Servants' and Journalists' Fund (Chile)
CCAF	Consejo Central de Asignaciones Familiares = Central Board of Family Allowances (Uruguay)
CCSS	Caja Costarricense del Seguro Social = Costa Rican Social Insurance Fund
CDR	Comités de Defensa de la Revolución = Committees for the Defense of the Revolution (Cuba)
CEE	Comité Estatal de Estadísticas = State Statistical Committee (Cuba)
CELADE	Centro Latinoamericano de Demografía = Latin American Center for Demography
CEPAL	Comisión Económica para América Latina = ECLA

CETSS	Comité Estatal de Trabajo y Seguridad Social = State Committee of Labor and Social Security (Cuba)
CIEPLAN	Corporación de Investigaciones Económicas para América Latina = Corporation for Economic Research on Latin America
CIESS	Centro Interamericano de Estudios de Seguridad Social = Interamerican Center of Social Security Studies
CIESU	Centro de Informaciones y Estudios del Uruguay = Center for Information and Studies of Uruguay
CLAEH	Centro Latinoamericano de Economía Humana = Latin American Center of Humanist Economy (Uruguay)
COPLAMAR	Coordinación General del Plan Nacional de Zonas Deprimidas y Grupos Marginados = General Coordination of the National Plan for Deprived Zones and Marginal Groups (Mexico)
CPISS	Comité Permanente Interamericano de Seguridad Social = Interamerican Permanent Committee on Social Security
DGSS	Dirección General de Seguridad Social = General Division of Social Security (Uruguay)
EAP	Economically active population
ECIEL	Estudios Conjuntos sobre Integración Económica Latinoamericana = Joint Studies on Economic Integration of Latin America
ECLA	United Nations Economic Commission for Latin America = CEPAL
EMPART	Caja de Empleados Particulares = Social Insurance Fund for Private (White Collar) Employees (Chile)
FMC	Federación de Mujerers Cubanas = Federation of Cuban Women (Cuba)
FONASA	Fondo Nacional de Salud = National Health Fund (Chile)
GDP	Gross domestic product
GSP	Global social product (Cuba)
IDB	Inter-American Development Bank = BID

ILO	International Labour Office/Organization
ILPES	Instituto Latinoamericano de Planificación Económica y Social = Latin American Institute of Economic and Social Planning
IMSS	Instituto Mexicano del Seguro Social = Mexican Institute of Social Insurance
INE	Instituto Nacional de Estadística = National Institute of Statistics (Chile and Peru)
INEGI	Instituto Nacional de Estadística, Geografía e Informática (Mexico)
INS	Instituto Nacional de Seguros = National Insurance Institute (Costa Rica)
INTAL	Instituto para la Integración de América Latina = Institute for the Integration of Latin America
IPC	Income Per Capita
IPEA	Instituto de Planejamento Economico e Social = Institute of Economic and Social Planning (Brazil)
IPSS	Instituto Peruano de Seguridad Social = Peruvian Social Security Institute
IRIC	Impuesto sobre Remuneración de Industria y Comercio = Income Tax on Industry and Commerce
ISAPRE	Institutos de Salud Previsional = Health Insurance Institutes (Chile)
ISSA	International Social Security Association
ISSSTE	Instituto de Seguridad Social y Servicios de los Trabajadores del Estado = Social Security Institute of Civil Servants (Mexico)
JUCEPLAN	Junta Central de Planificación = Central Planning Board (Cuba)
MINFAR	Ministerio de las Fuerzas Armadas = Ministry of Armed Forces (Cuba)
MININ	Ministerio del Interior = Ministry of Interior (Cuba)
MINSAP	Ministerio de Salud Pública = Ministry of Public Health (Cuba)

MPS	Material Production System (Cuba)
MS	Ministerio de Salud = Ministry of Health
MSP	Ministerio de Salud Pública = Ministry of Public Health
ODEPLAN	Oficina de Planificación Nacional = National Planning Office (Chile)
OEA	Organización de Estados Americanos = Organization of American States
OECD	Organization for Economic Co-Operation and Development
OISS	Organización Iberoamericana de Seguridad Social = Iberomamerican Organization of Social Security
OPP	Organos de Poder Popular = Organs of People's Power (Cuba)
PAHO	Pan-American Health Organization
PEMEX	Petróleos Mexicanos = Mexican State Oil Enterprise
PREALC	Programa Regional de Empleo para América Latina y el Caribe = Regional Program on Employment for Latin America and the Caribbean
SDPE	Sistema de Dirección y Planificación de la Economía = System of Economic Direction and Planning (Cuba)
SERMENA	Servicio Médico Nacional = Employees (White Collar) National Medical Service (Chile)
SNA	System of National Accounts
SNDIF	Sistema Nacional de Desarrollo Integral de la Familia = National System of Comprehensive Family Development (Mexico)
SNS	Servicio Nacional de Salud = National Health Service (Chile)
SNSS	Sistema Nacional de Servicios de Salud = National System of Health Services (Chile)
SPP	Secretaría de Programacíon y Presupuesto = Secretary of Programming and Budget (Mexico)
SSA	Secretaría de Salubridad y Asistencia = Secretary of Sanitation and Welfare (Mexico)

SSE	Social Security Expenditures
SSS	Servicio de Seguridad Social = Social Insurance Service (Chile)
UN	United Nations
UNICEF	United Nations Children's Fund
UNPD	United Nations Program for Development
USAID	United States Agency for International Development
VAT	Value-added tax
WHO	World Health Organization

Introduction

IN THE LAST hundred years social insurance has advanced notably in many Latin American countries and has played a crucial role both in preventing loss of income of the head of household due to social risks and in the development of curative medicine. Programs have existed in Latin America since the end of the nineteenth century to protect civil servants and members of the armed forces and since the beginning of this century to protect groups of workers in strategic sectors, such as public utilities. The year 1984 marked the seventieth anniversary of the first hemispheric laws to insure workers against occupational accidents and diseases in Uruguay and the sixtieth anniversary of laws providing insurance for old age, disability, death, and non–work-related diseases in Chile. These pioneering countries preceded the United States in introducing such programs and even today surpass the United States in health-maternity insurance, family allowances and some other programs. In terms of social security, as in other areas, Latin America is a leader in the Third World.[1]

But the region has not seen uniform progress in the area of social security and faces serious problems even in the most advanced countries. Although various countries have achieved universal population coverage, if one excludes Brazil (which contains more than half of the insured population of Latin America), the total coverage in the region does not reach 43 percent, and in the majority of the countries, it is less than 25 percent. There are also significant inequalities in the coverage of occupational categories, economic sectors, and geographic areas. In many countries the cost of social security in relation to economic capacity seems excessive. At the beginning of the 1970s, the cost of social security in the two pioneer countries reached 14 percent and 17 percent of gross domestic product, (GDP), a proportion exceeded in the world at that time only by the most industrialized nations of Europe. In 1980 social security costs neared or surpassed 10 percent of GDP in five countries, a figure similar to those for Japan (10.9 percent) and the United States (12.7 percent). In the 1960s, the social security systems of the pioneer countries suffered from an actuarial disequilibrium and, at times, a financial one that increased in the 1970s and has been further complicated by the economic crisis of the current decade.

Latin American history suggests that social security is like a staircase that leads to an abyss: as the coverage of risks and population rises, so does the financial disequilibrium that seems to end in crisis. In an attempt to resolve the situation, several Latin American countries has restructured their social security system: the nationalization of the Cuban system and the privatization of the Chilean one represent the most drastic, albeit opposite, global reforms.

The above account makes plain the economic importance of social security. In addition, the method of financing can affect the substitution of labor by capital, the generation of savings and investments, and the distribution of income. In spite of social security's importance, only recently have several international and regional development agencies begun to carry out economic studies of it in Latin America and to include the field in some country studies.

The United Nations Economic Commission for Latin America (ECLA), acknowledging the close relation between social security and development, decided to undertake the research on which the present book is based. I subsequently carried it out between August 1983 and June 1984. My work encompassed all twenty countries of Latin America. The non-Hispanic Caribbean was excluded because the development of social security there has followed a different historical trajectory and models different from those of Latin America. A questionnaire used to collect information was answered in all twenty Latin American countries. In addition, I compiled data from statistical yearbooks, accounting reports, and technical publications. Six countries were selected for in-depth case studies: Costa Rica, Cuba, Chile, Mexico, Peru, and Uruguay. I collected additional material in all of these countries and conducted field research in Chile, Mexico, and Peru during the year of study. I had previously conducted research in Costa Rica, Cuba, and Uruguay.

Chapter 1 describes the development of Latin American social security and ranks the countries according to a set of eleven variables. It also discusses current problems faced by the region with regard to organization, coverage of population and social risks, financing, benefits, and cost of social security as well as its impact on savings, employment, and income distribution. Chapters 2 through 7 analyze the six case studies. These cases were selected from the top and middle groups in social security development and were chosen to represent different economic systems and social security policies. Each case study reviews the historical evolution of social security as well as current structures, problems, and policies. Chapter 8 sets forth conclusions and recommendations.

For the sake of simplicity I use the term "social security" (rather than "social insurance") to encompass five principal programs: occupational risks (health care and cash benefits for work-related accidents and diseases), old age, disability, and survivors' pensions (also seniority and unemployment pensions in some countries), health care and cash benefits for maternity and non–work-related accidents and diseases, family allowances, and unemployment compensation. Also, social security frequently includes additional benefits (for example, funeral aid, personal and mortgage loans, and day care centers), plus social welfare programs (for example, noncontributory health care and pension programs for low-income groups).

Technically speaking, the majority of Latin American countries either have compulsory social insurance programs or are between the social insurance stage and the more advanced stage of social security. These are two different concepts of social protection. Only a few countries have systems with characteristics more typical of social security than of social insurance. Social insurance, introduced by Chancellor Bismarck of Germany in the 1880s, derives from the employment relationship and has the following features: (1) separate programs for different social risks (especially occupational risks, pensions, and health care); (2) coverage of the employed, salaried labor force, especially urban; (3) three-part wage contributions (made by the insured, the employer, and the state); (4) benefits directly related to contributions; and (5) full capitalization methods of financing.

Social security, which began with Sir William Beveridge's report at the beginning of the 1940s and was strongly influenced by Keynesianism, reflects a series of new principles that promote: (1) the unification, under one single administrative or coordinating agency, of the diverse programs of social insurance, along with social welfare, health care (integrating preventive and curative medicine), employment programs, and family allowances (principle of unity); (2) the standardization of legal conditions for entitlement and the elimination of unjustifiable inequalities among the insured (principle of equality); (3) total coverage of the population, regardless of employment status (principle of universality) and for all social risks (principle of completeness); (4) financing by means of taxation, the provision of minimum but sufficient benefits—not related to contributions—and the progressive redistribution of income (principle of solidarity); and (5) the use of the pure assessment financing method.[2]

The book would not have been possible without the interest and support offered by Enrique Iglesias, then executive secretary of ECLA, and by Andres Bianchi, director of ECLA's Division of Economic Development. Also important were the help and suggestions of other officials in the same division and others in ECLA, ILPES, and CELADE: Joseph Ramos, Guillermo Munt, Enrique de la Piedra, Carlos Diaz de la Guardia, Adolfo Gurrieri, Francisco Leon, Oscar Altimir, Ruben Katzman, Carmen Arretx, and Jose Pujols. Particularly valuable was the detailed criticism of the first version of the study, *El desarrollo de la seguridad social en America Latina* (Santiago: ECLA, 1985), made by Giovanni Tamburi, chief of the Social Security Division of the International Labour Organization. I alone am responsible for the statements made on these pages. The first version, published in Spanish by ECLA, was translated by my research assistant Katherine MacKinnon Scott, and I thoroughly revised the translation. Martha Arredondo, administrative secretary of the Center for Latin American Studies, did all the typing and corrections. Marcia Brubeck did the excellent editing of the manuscript.

The support of the Latin American countries was essential for the successful completion of the book. It would be impossible to mention here all the people who cooperated in supplying information, statistics, and comments. This volume is dedicated to them with the hope that it will contribute to the improvement of social security in the region.

Ascent to Bankruptcy

1

The Evolution of Social Security in Latin America: Its Problems and Relationship with Development

HISTORICAL EVOLUTION

SOCIAL SECURITY IN Latin America has evolved following two basic forms, the stratified and the relatively unified.

The Pioneer Countries and Stratification

In Chile, Uruguay, Argentina, Cuba, and Brazil, a small group that includes Latin America's most developed countries, the social security system started early, in the 1920s, but in a gradual and fragmented manner that created a multiplicity of administrative institutions. Each institution protected a different occupational group by means of independent subsystems, each with its own legislation, administration, financing, and benefits. The state supported these subsystems financially through specific taxes or direct budgetary allocations. The subsystems gradually incorporated broader occupational groups or labor sectors as well as their dependents but generally with less generous benefits and stricter entitlement conditions. The subsystems appeared in roughly the following order: the armed forces, civil servants, and teachers; blue- and white-collar workers in transportation, energy, banking, communications, and other public utilities; and much later the bulk of urban white- and blue-collar workers (often separated into two large groups); and last agricultural workers, the self-employed, small farmers and entrepreneurs, and domestic servants. This type of evolution resulted in a stratified social security system that assumed a pyramidal structure, with relatively small groups of insured protected by privileged subsystems at the apex and center and the majority of the population covered by poorer subsystems at the base.

The explanatory theories of social security evolution implicate economic development[1] and the diffusion or demonstration effect generated by international organizations and pioneer countries as basic causes.[2] But these theories do not explain stratification. In the last decade an important debate has

3

arisen concerning the two principal instigating forces of this phenomenon: pressure groups and the state. The above-mentioned occupational groups base their power on the tenancy of arms, the administration of the government, the scarcity of their skills in the labor market, and their organization in trade unions. They exert pressure on the state—allied with political parties—to obtain social security concessions. Studies of various countries in the region show that generally the greater the power held by a pressure group, the more social security concessions received, in terms of earlier and wider coverage, more generous benefits, and more advantageous financial means.[3] The state may not only be on the receiving end of pressure from the groups but may also exercise its initiative, using social security as an instrument to coopt, neutralize, and control these groups in order to maintain the status quo.[4] These pressure groups typically play a dominant role in the evolution of social security in populist, democratic-pluralist political systems such as those in Chile and Uruguay during the first seven decades of the twentieth century. In political systems that are populist but authoritarian with corporatist characteristics, for example Brazil under Getúlio Vargas and Argentina under Juan Perón, the state is more likely to play the predominant role in social security evolution. In practice the two forces (pressure groups and the state) have functioned together in both types of political systems, so that it is difficult at times to determine which force has predominated.[5]

As the pioneer countries advanced in economic development, urbanization, trade union organization, and political mobilization, groups lacking social security protection developed sufficient power to obtain coverage either within already existing subsystems or within a subsystem of their own. In several countries, these groups were even capable of obtaining certain benefits that had been reserved for the privileged subsystems, so that what I have called "massification of privilege" resulted. The cost of universalizing coverage, combined with generous benefits and liberal entitlement conditions, became excessive and brought about the final disequilibrium of many subsystems. Social security reform, fostered by national and international technical studies, prescribed the unification and standardization of the subsystems as well as the elimination of costly privileges. But the power of the pressure groups was such that the state was forced to postpone the needed reforms, often for decades. The institutional crisis suffered by these countries in the 1960s and 1970s strengthened the power of the state against pressure groups (groups that in many cases were demobilized or had their power significantly curtailed) and facilitated the process of social security reform.[6] A few countries (for example, Cuba and Brazil) unified practically the entire system; other countries (for example, Argentina and Uruguay) established a centrally unifying or coordinating agency that grouped different institutions, giving each a uniform system; finally, one country (Chile) introduced some standardization measures and eliminated privileges in the old social security system but also created a new system strongly influenced by private insurance, which favors individuality and multiplicity.

Countries with Relatively Unified Systems

The second form of social security evolution arose in countries with principal systems that had been established since the beginning of the 1940s. These nations were influenced by new trends in the literature emanating from the International Labour Organization (ILO) and the Beveridge report and attempted to avoid the problems that the pioneer nations had encountered. Several of these countries were, at that time, relatively developed (for example, Mexico), but the majority lacked industrial development, and in practically all of them, the rural sector predominated over the urban sector. In these countries a general administrative agency was created and charged with implementing the eventual coverage of the total population even though such coverage was initially circumscribed, extending only to the capital and principal cities. In the more-developed nations of this second group (for example, Colombia, Costa Rica, Mexico, Paraguay, Peru, and Venezuela), however, several social security institutions protecting the most powerful pressure groups—such as the armed forces, civil servants, teachers, and energy and railroad workers—existed prior to the creation of the general administrative agency. Furthermore, in several countries (Mexico and Costa Rica are examples) after the creation of the general administrative agency, exceptions were made with the object of establishing separate subsystems for certain groups, usually in the public sector. But these groups are generally small and (apart from the armed forces and civil servants) represent a small percentage of the population in relation to that covered by the general agency. In any event, even though a certain degree of social security stratification is evident in several of these countries, it has never approximated the level apparent in the first group. The late appearance of social security in this second group, as well as its relative unity and standardization and its lower risk and population coverage, has generally kept these systems from encountering the administrative and financial problems experienced by the first group. Drastic reforms have thus not been necessary. Nevertheless, the countries at the head of this group (those with the highest coverage, a growing maturation of pension programs, and highest costs) are beginning to suffer the financial problems typical in the first group. In this sense, Costa Rica is the most pressing case. Because its population coverage rapidly increased during the 1960s and 1970s, Costa Rica almost left the second group. Furthermore, even though its pension program has not fully matured, its social security costs resemble those of the countries in the first group.

Countries in Which Social Security Appeared Late

Finally we can identify a third group of countries that also have social security systems that are relatively unified, but to a greater degree than those of the second group. These are the least-developed countries of the region: Central America (with the exception of Costa Rica and Panama) and the Latin American Caribbean (with the exception of Cuba). In this third group, social security generally did not appear until the 1950s and 1960s; the general administrative agency covers practically all insured (even though the armed forces, and in some cases civil servants, have separate subsystems); and population coverage is very low and often confined to the capital and most populated cities. These countries do not usually face financial difficulties in the short and medium range, and their principal problem is to expand population coverage.

ORGANIZATIONAL STRUCTURE

Today, in the wake of the administrative reforms of the last two decades, social security systems in Latin America show greater similarity in degree of administrative unity, inasmuch as total or partial unification in the pioneer nations has significantly reduced stratification (except in Chile). Nonetheless, many systems need to merge the privileged subsystems further and to integrate or at least coordinate their health policies.

The administration of the general social security systems is entrusted to autonomous institutions in fifteen countries, to ministries or state agencies in four countries (Argentina, Brazil, Cuba, and Uruguay), and to a combination of state agencies and private corporations in Chile. The administrative agency or ministry always administers the general pension program, but the majority of the countries have separate subsystems for the armed forces and civil servants and in some cases for other powerful occupational groups. The workmen's compensation program is usually managed by the agency or ministry, but in a few countries (Costa Rica and Uruguay), an independent state agency has a monopoly on this program; in the others, private insurance or mutual aid societies operate them, supervised by the general agency or ministry. The agency/ministry administers the family allowances program with autonomous funds supervised by a state agency.

The administration of the health-maternity program is more complex. There are three health care systems: (1) direct, in which the agency/ministry operates all facilities and hires the staff; (2) indirect, in which the agency/ministry does not have its own facilities and subcontracts with other agencies and public and private personnel; and (3) mixed, in which the agency/ministry has its own facilities and personnel, but these are not sufficient and hence must subcontract with other services. The pure form of the direct system exists in Cuba and Nicaragua (where the ministry of health operates all services) and in Costa Rica and Panama (where the services of the social security agency and the ministry of health are highly integrated and operated by the former). The indirect system in its pure form does not exist in Latin America. The most common system is the mixed one, which functions in the rest of the countries. In Mexico, two principal administrative agencies provide health care (covering salaried workers from the private sector and the federal government), but they subcontract with other suppliers in some geographic areas. In Colombia, Ecuador, and El Salvador, the administrative agency covers a small percentage of the population, while the great majority is cared for in the facilities of the ministry of health. In Bolivia, Brazil, Guatemala, and Venezuela, the administrative agency lacks sufficient services and thus subcontracts with other public and private suppliers. In Argentina, Chile, Peru, Uruguay, and the Dominican Republic, the insured can to some extent choose among the services supplied by the administrative agency, the ministry of health, and/or private entities. (Argentina and Uruguay have an important sector of mutual aid societies and medical cooperatives, whereas in Chile there is an incipient but growing private sector.) In practically all of the countries, the armed forces have their own facilities (sometimes separated by branches), and several countries have powerful occupational groups (for example, the petroleum industry) that also have their own services. Finally, in the majority of the countries the curative medicine supplied by social security and that provided to the noninsured population by the ministry of health and other social welfare or private charity organizations are clearly separated.

The persistence of a plethora of administrative agencies in social security usually adds to inefficiency, increases administrative costs, makes it difficult to maintain a single registry, hampers efforts at control and inspection, and facilitates evasion. It also makes it difficult to provide continuity for the insured (that is, it is necessary to combine accumulated times of service under various employers) and fosters privilege and irritating inequalities. International and regional technical organizations have recommended that social security be unified—in health at least the integration or coordination of services—but efforts to bring about unification have often been blocked by pressure groups.

COVERAGE OF RISKS AND POPULATION

Coverage of Risks

Social security coverage of risks has evolved gradually, as table 1 shows, and with some exceptions, coverage always depends on employment. Ac-

TABLE 1

HISTORICAL EVOLUTION OF SOCIAL SECURITY COVERAGE
OF RISKS IN LATIN AMERICA, 1922–1982

Program	No. of Countries with Risk Coverage Programs						
	1922	*1932*	*1942*	*1952*	*1962*	*1972*	*1982*
Occupational risks	10	15	17	20	20	20	20
Health-Maternity	0	1	7	13	17	18	20
Old age, disability, and survivors	0	2	7	12	14	19	20
Family allowances	0	0	0	1	5	6	7
Unemployment	0	0	0	1	3	4	5

Source: Alfredo Mallet, "Evolución y perspectivas de la seguridad social en América Latina," *Seguridad social* 21:77–78 (September–December 1972): 256–61; and U.S. Social Security Administration, *Social Security Programs throughout the World, 1981* (Washington, D.C.: SSA, 1982).

cording to the theory of employer responsibility, the first category to be covered was occupational accidents and diseases. The second was nonoccupational accidents and diseases and maternity care, but as with the first, coverage was still conditional on employment. Thus maternity care was initially provided only to female employees, although it was later extended to include the insured's wives, and disease coverage was offered to dependents. At almost the same time, old age and disability pensions were introduced and a little later survivors' pensions. At the beginning of the 1980s, these three programs were in effect in all Latin American countries, even though universal population coverage existed in only a minority of them. The last programs to appear—and they did so in a few countries—relate to family allowances and unemployment subsidies. Family allowances programs exist in Argentina, Bolivia, Brazil, Chile, Colombia, Costa Rica, and Uruguay, and unemployment subsidies exist in Argentina, Brazil, Chile, Ecuador, and Uruguay. In general, risk coverage has expanded far more rapidly than has population coverage. The reason is that vertical expansion has been given priority over horizontal expansion. Frequently, a minority of the population is covered against all risks, while the majority of the population has no protection at all.

Legal and Statistical Coverage of the Population

It is important to distinguish between legal and statistical population coverage. The first is prescribed by law but is not always enforced; the second reflects estimates of the population covered, and while these estimates are more representative of reality, they are not always reliable.

The health-maternity program generally has the broadest legal coverage, although in half of the countries it extends only to the employed labor force (and in some cases only to the salaried segment). In the other half—usually in the civil service, industry, mining, commerce, and financial services— only some employees are eligible. Nevertheless, in Cuba all residents are legally covered, while in Chile and Costa Rica all of the population is covered except the nonworking segment with high income. In contrast, in the remaining Central American countries legal coverage is normally limited to the capital and the most important cities. Only six countries protect self-employed workers by law, but in almost all countries, the law covers dependents of the insured (usually the wife—or the common-law wife—and children) and pensioners. In summary, where legal coverage is concerned, in the majority of countries those insured are salaried urban workers (and their closest dependents), while the self-employed, agricultural workers, and domestic servants (as well as the unemployed) and their dependents are not covered by social security. Moreover, in one-fourth of the countries—those that are least developed—coverage is limited to the capital and the most important cities.

The problems associated with statistical estimations of social security coverage in Latin America are legion. A recent report of the ILO on Brazil, for example, acknowledged that available health data were so speculative as to make the margin of error incalculable. There was no registry of the insured, and data on contributions were so riddled with error that they could not be used in lieu of registration data.[7] In countries with several administrative agencies, it is difficult if not impossible to estimate the total coverage; there are statistics for the bigger institutions but not the smaller ones. In Mexico, for example, it is easy to obtain coverage figures from the two principal administrative agencies (which cover salaried workers in the private sector and in the federal government), but it is very difficult to obtain these figures from the institutions and hospitals that cover the armed forces and other small groups. Coverage statistics published by international and regional organizations frequently refer to the bigger institutions and thus underestimate total coverage.

Table 2 shows the total coverage in those countries that have several agencies and have been included among the six case studies, but in the case of countries for which in-depth studies could not be done (such as Colombia, Paraguay, and Venezuela), only coverage by the general agency is shown. Another problem occurs in Argentina and Uruguay, where health services are largely supplied by mutual aid societies, medical cooperatives, and private clinics, whose figures are very difficult to obtain. In the case of pension programs, on the other hand, overestimation sometimes occurs; because there are a number of institutions, double or triple coverage is possible (for example, in Uruguay). In recent years, however, this phenomenon has been largely

TABLE 2

TOTAL POPULATION AND EAP COVERED BY SOCIAL SECURITY
IN LATIN AMERICA, 1980

	Total Population (thous.)	Total Insured (thous.)	Coverage (%)	Distri- bution (%)	EAP (thous.)	Active Insured (thous.)[b]	Coverage (%)	Distri- bution (%)
Argentina	28,237	22,278	78.9	10.3	10,690	7,391	69.1	10.5
Bolivia	5,570	1,412	25.4	0.7	1,754	324	18.5	0.5
Brazil	121,286	116,800	96.3	54.1	40,292	38,523	95.6	54.6
Chile	11,104	7,418	67.3	3.5	3,788	2,337	61.7	3.3
Colombia[c,f]	25,247	2,925	11.6	1.4	8,477	1,900	22.4	2.7
Costa Rica	2,279	1,733	76.0	0.8	770	526[a]	68.3	0.7
Cuba[d]	9,724	9,724[g]	100.0[g]	4.5	3,618	3,364[g]	93.0[g]	4.8
Dominican Republic	5,558	440[h]	7.9	0.2	2,019	283[h]	14.0	0.4
Ecuador	8,021	636	7.9	0.3	2,393	555	23.2	0.8
El Salvador	4,797	300	6.2	0.1	1,611	187	11.6	0.3
Guatemala[d]	7,480	1,064	14.2	0.5	2,314	767	33.1	1.1
Haiti	5,809	44[h]	0.8	0.0	2,815	44[h]	1.6	0.1
Honduras[e]	3,955	288	7.3	0.1	1,172	156	14.4	0.2
Mexico	69,393	37,056	53.4	17.2	19,423	8,158	42.0	11.6
Nicaragua	2,771	253	9.1	0.1	773	146	18.9	0.2
Panama	1,956	985	50.3	0.4	701	319	45.6	0.4
Paraguay[f]	3,168	575	18.2	0.3	1,077	151	14.0	0.2
Peru	17,295	3,016	17.4	1.4	5,719	2,142	37.4	3.0
Uruguay	2,908	1,993	68.5	1.0	1,123	912	81.2	1.3
Venezuela[f]	15,024	6,790	45.2	3.1	4,723	2,350	49.8	3.3
Latin America	**352,774**	**215,730**	**61.2**	**100.0**	**115,252**	**70,535**	**61.2**	**100.0**
Latin America[i]	**231,488**	**98,930**	**42.7**	**45.9**	**74,960**	**32,012**	**42.7**	**45.4**

Source: Total population and EAP from CELADE, *Demographic Bulletin* 15:29 (January 1982), and 17:33 (January 1984), except those for Cuba, from the 1981 census. Number of insured is based on countries' responses to the ECLA questionnaire and statistical yearbooks and accounting reports with author's adjustments.

a. In the program of health/maternity.
b. In pension programs.
c. 1979.
d. 1981.
e. 1982.
f. Excludes various insured groups.
g. Because of the lack of statistical data, an estimate was based on legal coverage.
h. Gross estimate.
i. Excluding Brazil.

reduced. In many countries, health care coverage of dependents (an extremely important group, as it is the largest) is calculated by using an estimated ratio of dependents to insured. Small changes in the ratio can produce significant decreases or increases in coverage. Thus the coverage of the economically active insured population (EAP) is generally more reliable than that of the total population. Finally, there are problems of comparison. For instance, in table 2 the figures for Cuba refer to legal coverage because statistical data are not published. Countries with only one administrative agency, namely the ministry of health (for example, Nicaragua), provide total figures for coverage. Conversely, other countries—even with highly integrated health systems—report the coverage of the principal social security agency but not that of the ministry of health and, at times, not even that of the indigent population covered by that agency (for example, Costa Rica).

Despite the above-mentioned deficiencies, table 2 presents the most reliable, comparable, and recent (1980) coverage figures yet published. If we use pension coverage of the EAP as a basis, the countries may be ranked as follows: 75–100 percent in Cuba (legal coverage), Brazil, and Uruguay; 50–74 percent in Argentina, Costa Rica, Chile (in these nations the coverage is higher if welfare pensions are included), and Venezuela; 25–49 percent in Panama, Mexico, Peru, and Guatemala; and 1–24 percent in Ecuador, Colombia, Nicaragua, Bolivia, Honduras, Paraguay, Dominican Republic, El Salvador, and Haiti. If we use health coverage as a base, the countries rank as follows: 75–100 percent in Cuba, Brazil, Argentina, and Costa Rica; 50–74 percent in Uruguay, Chile, Mexico, and Panama (if coverage of indigents and services provided by mutual aid societies is included, Uruguay and Chile would probably be in the first group); 25–49 percent in Venezuela and Bolivia; and 1–24 percent in Paraguay, Peru, Guatemala, Colombia, Nicaragua, Ecuador, the Dominican Republic, Honduras, El Salvador, and Haiti. In general, coverage is higher in the most-developed countries with the oldest social security systems; also, in these countries, total population coverage is higher than coverage of the EAP because the number of pensioners and dependents entitled to health protection is proportionally much greater than in the less-developed countries with newer systems.

The penultimate line of table 2 presents an estimate of total coverage in Latin America, showing 61 percent for the total population and the EAP. Certainly, Latin America stands at the head of the developing nations in this regard. In addition, a group of Latin American countries exhibits levels of coverage similar to those in the developed nations. Coverage has expanded rapidly in the pioneer nations and in a few countries of the intermediate group. If we take into account protection of the indigent population in health care and pensions, in these countries coverage is almost universal. But in most of Latin America social security coverage is very low and its expansion is blocked by structural barriers. A more precise analysis of table 2 shows that total coverage in the region is strongly influenced by the very high coverage in Brazil, a country that contains more than half of the insured. Inasmuch as the figures for Brazil need to be more precise, probably total coverage in Latin America is overestimated. When Brazil is excluded from table 2 calculations (see the last line in the tables), the percentage of coverage in Latin

America falls to less than 43 percent of both the total population and the EAP. Furthermore, in half the countries, coverage is less than 25 percent.

Inequalities in Population Coverage

To the problem of overall low population coverage we must add—in the case of most countries—the problem of inequalities in the extent of coverage among occupational groups, economic sectors, and geographic areas. Coverage tends to correlate positively with income, labor skills, and the power of pressure groups. Investigations carried out in seven countries (Argentina, Chile, Costa Rica, Cuba, Mexico, Peru, and Uruguay) show that historically coverage for different occupational groups varies, to a great degree, with the power of these groups; a gap of almost 200 years separates the first and last groups to obtain pension coverage. Coverage for the armed forces and civil servants was instituted between early 1800s and the early 1900s; for teachers, between the 1880s and the 1930s; for police, between the 1890s and the 1940s; for the labor aristocracy (in public utilities, banking, and the merchant marine) between the 1910s and the 1940s; for the bulk of the urban labor force (white- and blue-collar workers) between the 1920s and the 1940s; for agricultural workers between the 1930s and the 1950s; for domestic servants between the 1930s and the 1970s; and for self-employed workers between the 1930s and the 1970s.[8] It must be remembered that in these countries all these groups are covered, although significant differences in the degree of coverage still exist today despite trends in most nations toward universality, unification, and standardization. The differences noted are much more prominent in the countries where total coverage is low because the majority of the population is excluded from the social security system. A recent analysis of Brazil also shows a positive correlation between the degree of coverage on the one hand and labor skills or status and income on the other: unemployed, unskilled workers (especially in agriculture and self-employment) and individuals with the lowest income exhibit lowest coverage.[9] Information for 1979–81 from four countries (Chile, Colombia, Costa Rica, and Mexico) indicates that the highest coverage of the EAP by economic sector occurs in public utilities (75–100 percent), manufacturing (51–90 percent), and transport and communications (34–71 percent), whereas the lowest is found in agriculture (4–59 percent; Chile and Costa Rica—the countries with nearly universal coverage—exhibit the highest percentages).[10] Finally, 1979–81 information from six countries (Chile, Costa Rica, Guatemala, Mexico, Panama, and Peru) on the geographic extent of coverage proves that the most-developed states/provinces/departments (those that are most industrialized, unionized, and urbanized and that have a greater percentage of salaried workers and higher per capita income) have significantly greater coverage than the least-developed states/provinces/departments (those that are most agricultural, least unionized, most rural, and with a greater percentage of self-employed workers and lower per capita income). The total range of geographic coverage fluctuates from 54 percent to 100 percent in Costa Rica, 39 percent to 95 percent in Chile, 0.2 percent to 33 percent in Guatemala, 5 percent to 100 percent in Mexico, 13 percent to 73 percent in Panama and 3 percent to 27 percent in Peru. With one exception, the province/state/department where the capital city is located has the highest coverage.[11] In summary, the neediest groups (including the critically poor sector) lack social security protection in the great majority of the countries. The key issue is finding the best way to expand coverage to these groups.

Structural Factors That Facilitate/Hinder Expansion

Various specialists have observed that the Bismarckian model of social insurance has been unable to function adequately in Latin America because the labor force there differs in composition from that of Europe. In the latter, salaried urban workers represented a larger part of the labor force, whereas in Latin America the labor force consists mostly of agricultural workers and the self-employed.[12] In the reformed Bismarckian model, social security is financed by contributions from the worker and the employer that are based on the salary of the worker. The self-employed worker in Latin America cannot afford to pay the employer's contribution, and low-income agricultural workers who tend to be migratory and to change employers frequently are difficult to identify.

The first segment of table 3 shows that, in the most-developed nations in the area, salaried workers constitute anywhere from 63 percent to 89 percent of the labor force (for example, Argentina, Brazil, Chile, Costa Rica, Cuba, Panama, Uruguay, and Venezuela), and less than one-third of the labor force consists of either self-employed or unpaid family workers. For this reason the Bismarckian social insurance model has been able to function and expand coverage in these countries. In contrast, in the remaining countries for which we have data (Bolivia, Ecuador, Guatemala, Haiti, Honduras, Paraguay, and Peru), from 48 percent to 50 percent of the labor force consists of self-employed or unpaid family workers (and a similar proportion works in agriculture). Precisely these countries have the lowest social security coverage. As an obvious result, it is very difficult using the Bismarckian model to expand coverage to those outside the salaried labor force.

The second segment of table 3 presents the distribution of the labor force by sectors following the method of The Programa Regional de Empleo para America Latina y el Caribe (PREALC). In the majority of countries, when the percentage of the EAP in the urban-formal sector is compared with the percentage of the EAP covered by social security, a marked relationship between the two is evident. A few countries have been able to extend coverage somewhat beyond the urban-formal sector, either because these countries have a relatively modern and unionized rural sector (Costa Rica and Chile) or

TABLE 3
DISTRIBUTION OF THE LABOR FORCE IN LATIN AMERICA CIRCA 1980
(PERCENT)

	By Occupational Category[a]			By Sector[b]			
				Urban		Rural	
	Salaried	Self-employed	Unpaid Family Worker	Formal	Informal	Modern	Traditional
Argentina	71.5	25.2	*	65.0	19.4	8.8	6.3
Bolivia	38.2	48.9	9.2	17.9	23.2	5.2	50.9
Brazil	65.3	27.0	5.1	45.2	16.9	9.8	27.6
Chile	66.7	25.3	3.6	54.1	20.1	14.0	8.8
Colombia	**	**	**	42.6	22.3	15.8	18.7
Costa Rica	75.2	19.6	3.9	52.9	12.4	19.6	14.8
Cuba	88.8	5.4	0.3	**	**	**	**
Ecuador	51.7	39.3	8.9	22.7	25.4	13.7	37.9
El Salvador	58.0	28.2	10.9	28.6	18.9	22.3	30.1
Guatemala	47.2	42.5	6.7	26.7	17.8	22.3	33.1
Haiti	16.6	59.4	10.4	**	**	**	**
Honduras	45.4	33.3	14.6	**	**	**	**
Mexico	**	**	**	39.5	22.0	19.2	18.4
Panama	63.3	23.2	3.6	45.3	20.9	9.1	24.6
Paraguay	36.7	41.2	11.6	**	**	**	**
Peru	41.8	39.8	8.4	35.0	23.8	8.0	32.0
Uruguay	69.4	23.8	2.0	63.3	19.0	9.5	8.0
Venezuela	64.1	26.5	3.1	62.6	16.4	4.4	15.1

Sources: The first distribution is based on ILO, *Yearbook of Labor Statistics, 1980* to *1984* except Cuba from CEE, *Encuesta demográfica nacional de 1979* (Havana: CEE, 1981). The second distribution is from PREALC, (Geneva: ILO, 1981–1985), *Dinámica del desempleo en América Latina,* Estudios e Informes de CEPAL, no. 10 (Santiago: CEPAL, 1981), p. 16.

   a. Excludes a small percentage of nonclassified workers. Data are for years other than 1980 in Bolivia (1976), Chile (1978), Cuba (1979), Ecuador (1974), Guatemala (1981), Haiti (1982), Honduras (1977), Peru (1981), and Uruguay (1975).
   b. Excludes a small percentage in mining.

*Not applicable.

**Not available.

because, despite the presence of an important rural-traditional sector, new means of financing have been created so that the urban sector sustains the expansion of coverage to the rural areas at least in part (Brazil). In Colombia and Venezuela, social security coverage is substantially smaller than in the urban-formal sector, indicating that these countries—especially Venezuela, with its relatively abundant natural resources—can make a greater effort to extend coverage even within the narrow limits of the Bismarckian model. Only two countries, Brazil and Uruguay, have social security coverage that surpasses the sum of the urban-formal and rural-modern sectors; this indicates the difficulties that hinders the extensions of coverage to the urban-informal and rural-traditional sectors. In these two sectors we find self-employed and unpaid family workers who are typically underemployed and with low income, so that it is difficult for them to finance their coverage themselves.

It seems unlikely that social security coverage will rapidly expand in many countries in the near future as a result of the natural growth of the formal-modern sector. In 1950–80 the urban-formal sector grew by more than 14 percentage points in the region, but the rural-modern sector declined by almost 10 percent. The formal sector did not grow enough to absorb the increase in the labor supply plus the intense rural-urban migration and preexisting under-employment. Capital-intensive methods of production do not contribute to greater labor absorption. In the same period the informal-traditional sectors in the region fell 4 percentage points (while the informal sector rose almost 6 percentage points, the traditional sector diminished by almost 10 points), although this decline was more evident in the dynamic countries (for example, Colombia, Mexico, and Venezuela). To reduce the informal-traditional sector by one-third by the year 2000, an annual GDP growth rate of 7.5 percent would be necessary. Unfortunately, the trend projected on the basis of data for 1950–80 (6.2 percent) indicates that the situation will be stationary in the year 2000, and the serious recession in 1981–84 does not offer grounds for hope that growth will accelerate in the future.[13] In fact, social security coverage has shrunk since 1980 in many countries with the rise of open unemployment and the reversal of growth in the formal-modern sector.

It has recently been suggested that as a means of breaking the vicious circle, social security should be incorporated into an integral policy of de-velopment that would include a change in favor of labor-intensive methods of production to promote full employment and the satisfaction of basic needs.[14] But this approach has been criticized for being unrealistic and for not taking into consideration the heterogeneity of the countries of the region and their diverse degrees of industrialization, agricultural modernization, and demo-graphic transition as well as other development priorities. According to this criticism, universality is possible only in the most advanced countries (Ar-gentina, Chile, Cuba, and Uruguay) and, perhaps in the near future, in coun-tries with an intermediate level of development (Costa Rica and Panama) but not in the rest.[15] Alternatively, it might be possible to expand coverage by replacing the reformed Bismarckian model of social insurance with a social security model that would entail substantial reforms in financing and benefits.

FINANCING

Sources of Financing

Social security in Latin America has been financed basically by means of contributions based on the salary of the insured. The law establishes the wage contribution percentage to be paid by the insured, by the employer, and often by the state (the state acts as a third-party contributor in addition to being an employer). The state also contributes by means of specific taxes, by covering part or all of the system's deficit, or by other subsidies. In the few countries in which the self-employed worker is insured, he or she must pay a contribution (based on estimated income) equal to the sum of the contribution percentages of the salaried insured and the employer. Pensioners must frequently pay contributions on their pensions. The yield of reserve fund investments, especially that of the pensions program offers another source of financing.

According to the first segment of table 4, in fourteen of the twenty countries in Latin America, the contribution percentage assigned to the insured is less than one-third of the total percentage of salary contributions. In five countries the insured's percentage ranges from one-third to one-half of the total. Only in Chile does the insured contribute more than half. In eight of the countries, the insured's contributions cannot exceed a maximum, or ceiling, depending on salary, and in only a few countries do contributions grow progressively larger with increases in salary. The percentage assigned to the state is usually small—less than one-tenth of the total—but this figure does not take into account the other contributions made by the state. Thus, according to the law, the principal source of social security financing is the employer's contribution, which represents more than two-thirds of the total contribution in twelve countries and more than two-fifths in seven others (in Chile it is only one-tenth). The employer's legal contribution expressed as a percentage varies notably from program to program. For workmen's compensation and family allowances the employers cover all costs; in health-maternity care, between 50 percent and 80 percent of the costs; for pensions, between 0 and 66 percent of the costs (in half of the countries less than 50 percent). This is important in relation to the insured's planning horizon and perception of social security contributions. The employer takes a higher share of financing in short-term risks and in those risks that are linked to areas where the employer has direct responsibility, while his share is smaller in long-term risks in areas for which he bears no direct responsibility (for example, pensions; see "The Impact of Social Security on Development," below).

The second segment of table 4 presents the most recently available statistics on the distribution of social security revenues by source for sixteen countries. These statistics corroborate the statements made above even though—as expected—the state's contributions appears much higher than the simple legal percentage would indicate. In practically all countries, the insured contributes less than one-third of revenues (in two of the countries the insured contributes slightly more than one-third but in six countries less than one-fourth), while two-thirds or more is supplied by the employer or the state (with two exceptions). Revenue from investment yield is, with three exceptions, less than one-tenth of the total, and in six of the countries, it does not

TABLE 4

SOCIAL SECURITY FINANCING BY SOURCE IN LATIN AMERICA, CIRCA 1980

	Legal Contribution as % of Salary			% Distribution of Social Security Revenues				
	Insured	Employer	State	Insured	Employer	State	Investment	Other
Argentina	14.0–15.0	21.5	15.3	38.4	49.4	7.4	2.0	2.8
Bolivia	3.5	20.0	1.5	28.7	53.6	6.2	7.9	3.6
Brazil	8.6	14.7	a	**	**	**	**	**
Chile	9.56–27.84	2.85	a	20.5	38.3	34.2	2.0	5.0
Colombia	3.8–5.5	14.67–18.0	a	16. 0	49.8	16.2	6.4	11.6
Costa Rica	8.0	22.6	1.5	27.6	45.9	20.4	5.2	0.9
Cuba	0.0	10.0	a	0.0	——100.0——		0.0	0.0
Dominican Republic	2.5	9.5	2.5	**	**	43.7d	**	**
Ecuador	9.0	9.5	a	37.0	43.0	0.1	19.9	0.0
El Salvador	3.5	8.25	0.5a	23.4	63.0	0.9	11.8	0.9
Guatemala	4.5	10.0	3.0a	31.6	53.1	8.2	6.9	0.2
Haiti	3.5	6.0–9.0	1.2	——26.6c——		69.9	3.5	0
Honduras	4.0–9.0	5.0	3.5	**	**	**	**	**
Mexico	3.75	12.42	1.88	24.0b	50.3	19.7	2.5	3.5
Nicaragua	4.0	11.0	0.5	21.2	58.0	16.2	2.5	2.1
Panama	7.25	15.22	0.8a	28.6	45.1	4.3	9.6	12.4
Paraguay	9.25	16.5	1.5	**	**	**	**	**
Peru	5.0	14.0	2.0a	**	**	**	**	**
Uruguay	12.0–16.0	19.0–29.0	a	25.1	34.0	38.3	1.5	1.1
Venezuela	4.0	7.0–9.0	1.5	26.8	53.5	6.8	12.7	0.2

Sources: Legal contribution based on U.S. Social Security Administration, *Social Security Programs Throughout the World, 1981* (Washington, D.C., 1982) and legislation of the countries. Percentage distribution from ILO, *The Cost of Social Security, 1975–1977* and *1978–1980* except that for Cuba, which was calculated by the author.

a. Taxes, coverage of deficits, and other subsidies.
b. Distribution in 1974.
c. Distribution in 1977.
d. Only reported percentage of state contributions.

**Not available.

surpass 5 percent. Thus it seems—as provided by the law and if we do not take into account actual incidence—that the insured does not defray the bulk of his social security costs, and the situation is more inequitable in the countries with low coverage. In Colombia, for example, total population coverage in 1980 was 12 percent. The insured contributed 16 percent of revenues, while the employer and the state combined contributed 66 percent of revenue. These figures suggest a regressive effect in distribution.

To corroborate this point, it would be necessary to analyze the incidence of social security contributions. Nevertheless, the existing evidence challenges the prevailing juridical assumption, inherited from private insurance, that the insured's payments generate a right to social security and that the "premium" (contribution) and the benefits should correspond closely. This assumption has justified discriminating between the users of social insurance and social welfare and has helped block the expansion of social security coverage in those countries with a small, salaried labor force. To question that juridical assumption paves the way for the replacement of the salary contribution (wage tax) with another type of tax (perhaps an income tax or value-added tax [VAT]) that would make it easier to offer universal coverage and would correct other possible negative economic effects that the wage tax exerts on employment and/or income distribution.

Only a few countries use transfers from the state budget (or from urban enterprises) to cover the rural sector. In Mexico, the state directly contributes to the financing of a health program for marginal rural groups (Coordinación General del Plan Nacional de Zonas Deprimidas y Grupos Marginados: COPLAMAR). Brazil has a social welfare program for health care and pensions that covers the rural sector (salaried, self-employed, and unpaid family workers). This program is financed by taxes on the salary payrolls of urban businesses and on the value of agricultural production. In Costa Rica the state contributes to the welfare program for health and pensions for the rural or urban indigent population that do not qualify under social insurance. Cuba finances health care for all residents totally and directly from the state budget. Finally, in Nicaragua a small group of the population finances health care for the total population through the payroll tax; in this case, health care is no longer an insured's right by virtue of his or her contribution but is given as part of the social welfare system.

In health care, the social security system receives a much greater proportion of resources than the ministry of health, in spite of the fact that the latter is responsible for preventive medicine and in many cases covers the majority of the population in terms of curative medicine. In 1978, for example, the insured population of Bolivia, which was 20 percent of the total, received 64 percent of the health resources. In Colombia 10 percent received 60 percent; in the Dominican Republic 8 percent of the insured received 37 percent; in Ecuador 6 percent received 43 percent of the resources.[16] The social security system extracts a growing percentage of the funds for health care, but in many countries it is reluctant or unable to extend coverage to low-income groups.

Financial Equilibrium

In various countries in the region, social security's financial stability is precarious, and in some, it is in open crisis. The pioneer countries, those with the oldest and most developed systems, confront the greatest disequilibrium. Their expenses are growing because of (1) universalization of coverage; (2) legislation that is too liberal in terms of benefit concessions; (3) a capital-intensive curative medicine system; (4) matured pension programs; (5) greater longevity among pensioners than the original legislation had envisioned; and (6) cost-of-living adjustments in pensions and other benefits.

Conversely, revenues are proportionally less because (1) coverage cannot be further expanded (and if it could, the object would be to incorporate the lowest income groups, which would aggravate the disequilibrium); (2) the number of active contributors is progressively declining in relation to the growing number of passive contributors; (3) evasion and payment delays are prevalent, especially in the countries with high and sustained inflation rates (where a delayed payment implies a reduction in the real contribution); (4) the state, pressured by multiple and urgent necessities, refuses to fulfill its financial obligations, thus accumulating huge debts; (5) social security's tributary burden is already quite heavy, so that it is extremely difficult, politically and economically, to augment contributions or taxes further; (6) inefficient administration of pension funds has resulted in low investment yields or, in countries with high inflation, in negative yields; and (7) the transfer or loan of pension funds to cover deficits in health programs has been impossible to pay back, a problem that has contributed to the decapitalization of funds at a time when reserves are needed for pension payments in matured programs.[17]

Countries in the second group to institute social security (including Mexico and Peru) and all of the late adopters (countries with the least-developed systems) generated financial surpluses in 1980. Nevertheless, the analysis for Mexico and Peru presented in this book indicates that the financial situation deteriorated in these two countries in 1983–84 because a financial deficit was either already present or imminent. The analysis also suggests that there is probably an actuarial deficit in both countries. A more recent study done by the author for the World Bank shows that Ecuador faces a serious threat of financial disequilibrium in the short run as well as an existing actuarial disequilibrium. The situation of the second group is thus mixed and less positive in the mid-1980s than it appeared to be in 1980. Probably the most financially solvent situation is found among the late adopters; the problem in these countries is how to expand coverage beyond one-tenth of the total population.

The grave economic crisis that Latin America has suffered since the beginning of the 1980s has aggravated the financial problems of social security in many countries. The rise of unemployment, a reduction in real salary, and a surge in business bankruptcies have caused social security revenues to decrease. External debt pressures and other urgent domestic necessities have forced many states to reduce or postpone their contributions further. Galloping inflation has accentuated the already existing tendencies toward evasion and delay. Also, in the countries with almost universal coverage, many of the former insured and contributors who are now unemployed receive health care as indigents (hence putting pressure on health care costs) or have chosen early retirement, and the extreme inflation has forced the state to readjust pensions upward to keep them from losing their real value altogether.

Financing Methods

As a result of the financial disequilibrium, many countries in the region, like nations elsewhere, have gradually changed financing methods, slowly abandoning full capitalization and replacing it with methods of partial capitalization. Some of the pioneer countries have adopted the pure assessment (pay-as-you-go) method. There are four basic methods of financing; all of them act to balance the system's revenues and expenditures but in different time periods ranging from one year to infinity, larger reserves being required as the equilibrium period lengthens.[18] The short-term risk program (for example, health-maternity, family allowances, and unemployment) generally use the pure assessment method, in which the equilibrium period is calculated annually and there is a reserve only for contingencies and fluctuations. In some countries, however, this reserve is insufficient to cover the deficit. Initially, almost all of the pension programs (long-term risks) in Latin America adopted the general fixed-premium method with full reserves. This method attempts to maintain equilibrium for an indefinite time (or for a period of several decades) by means of a fixed premium that is actuarially calculated, on the basis of estimates of future obligations (the estimates take into account demographic and economic variables and other factors). But this method precludes increases in benefits without a corresponding adjustment in revenues, requires revenues to be paid punctually and in their entirety, makes it necessary to administer reserve funds efficiently, and creates a need to take periodic actuarial balances.

In practice, political pressures, the lack of administrative controls, inflation, and the unexpected rise in life expectancy have contributed to invalidate all of the prerequisite conditions and have made it necessary to abandon the capitalization method. Some countries therefore adopted the scale-premium method of capitalization with incomplete reserves, in which equilibrium is maintained for a shorter period (for example, a decade), establishing a fixed premium within every time period but normally increasing the premium (scaling it upward) in successive periods. This method defers costs and redistributes them among generations, thereby postponing the problem. It is an essential prerequisite to do periodic actuarial balances and to adjust the premium accordingly for each period. But legal rigidity (several countries fix contributions by law) and political opposition (in response to trade union and business pressures) are strong obstacles to the implementation of such adjustments. In practice, various countries fix only the initial premium, do not determine the duration of the time periods, fail to take actuarial balances, and do not adjust the premium.

Another reason for replacing capitalization methods with pure assessment in the developed countries with universal coverage is the accumulation of an enormous mass of capital. A study by Jean Bourgeois-Pichat in France showed that if the pension fund were capitalized in amount it would approximate the total capital of the nation. In the more-developed Latin American countries with greater coverage, the poor capital market and high inflation rates make efficient management of the funds even more difficult. Several countries eventually replaced the scaled-premium method, either de facto or de jure, with the assessment-of-constituent-capital or the pure assessment methods. But these methods, which use very short periods, demand an even greater flexibility for more frequent increases in revenues (contributions), and this frequency is obviously more difficult to achieve.

Even worse, if the social security systems were incapable of attaining financial equilibrium in the past, when the passive/active ratio was very low, it is even less possible for them to do so now when the ratio has augmented significantly. Thus the transference of the burden to future generations is an evasion in disguise, and the deficit inevitably increases as a consequence. A recent survey of the literature prepared by the Interamerican Development Bank (IDB) concludes: "The persistence of a deficit is the situation generally confronted by the social security systems in Latin America financed by the pure assessment method. This is confirmed by statistics and annual balances of the social security institutions, numerous national and international studies, and the IDB survey's results in the countries of the sample."[19]

Among the pioneer countries, Argentina, Chile (whose old system still encompasses about one-third of the insured), Uruguay, Cuba, and Brazil use formally or actually pure assessment methods with consequent deficit. Having exhausted all the alternative methods of financing that postpone the burdens of the system, some of these countries confront a severe financial disequilibrium aggravated by the global economic crisis of the region. To surmount this crisis, global reform of the social security system is necessary. Already several of the countries analyzed in this book have introduced reforms following drastically different models.

BENEFITS, EXPENDITURES, AND TOTAL COSTS
Benefits and Inequalities

In 1980 the bulk of social security expenditures (72 percent to 95 percent) were committed to benefits. The ILO periodically publishes a valuable distribution of expenditures by program, but problems of comparability limit its usefulness. Not all countries report expenditures in social welfare; in addition, expenditures of the civil servant and the armed forces subsystems enter as a separate category, without distinction between their programs. When percentages in these two categories are very high, they distort the distribution of expenditures of the remaining social security programs.[20] Nevertheless, this information indicates that the pioneer countries devote a higher percentage of their expenditures to pensions (and family allowances), while the countries in which social security appeared at a later date devote a higher percentage of their expenditures to health-maternity programs. (In 1980, in the majority of countries more than half of social security expenditures went for health care, and in six of them, the proportion rose to two-thirds). The reason is, in part, the demographic transition and the maturity of the pension programs. The countries with older pension programs are also the more economically developed and have a significant and growing percentage of the population at retirement age and a greater number of pensioners who live longer. In contrast, the countries with more recent pension programs are the less developed and have a small percentage of their populations at retirement age. Moreover, their pension programs still have not matured, and life expectancy is relatively low. These countries normally use capitalization (mostly partial) methods, and the accumulation of substantial reserves makes it tempting to lend part of them to the health care program. These loans are difficult to amortize, and in the long run they lead to the decapitalization of the pension program, thus creating a disequilibrium when the program begins to mature.

The pioneer countries tend to cover all social risks and to provide a greater number of more generous benefits. Thus Argentina, Brazil, Chile, and Uruguay are the only countries to cover all risks, including unemployment and family allowances. Cuba does not have these programs; it alleges that there is full employment and has given priority to day care centers. A study of five countries (Argentina, Chile, Mexico, Peru, and Uruguay), using information from the beginning of the 1970s, showed that the older the social security system, the greater the number of benefits conceded. The oldest systems have granted exceptional and costly benefits, such as seniority pensions that sometimes permit retirement at age forty-five and old age pensions with low retirement ages set a long time ago when life expectancy was shorter than it is today. In these countries entitlement conditions for health benefits also tend to be more generous. For example, often no qualifying period is necessary or only a few weekly contributions are required; the subsidies paid for health and/or maternity leaves equal salary (or very nearly so); and lavish benefits are sometimes provided, such as orthodontics, contact lenses, and treatment abroad.[21] These countries often have the so-called social benefits, such as subsidized housing, cheap personal loans, stores with subsidized prices, and other recreational and cultural services available to the insured and their dependents.

Stratification of social security in the pioneer countries (at least until the introduction of unification and standardization processes) has typically produced notable inequalities in benefits, with the more powerful groups receiving more and better benefits than the less powerful groups. The five-country study cited above measured the legal differences among five covered occupational groups on the basis of six criteria: legal conditions for entitlement, base salary used to compute benefits, amount of benefit, cost-of-living adjustments in pensions, possibility of collecting various pensions or of combining a pension with paid work, and average time required for processing and receiving benefits. The study also compared the availability of health services (hospital beds and physicians per insured individual) and their quality among groups. The resulting ranking of the groups from best to worst was as follows: (1) armed forces, (2) civil servants, (3) labor aristocracy, (4) private white-collar employees, and (5) blue-collar workers. Nevertheless, according to this study, in the pioneer countries massification of privilege sometimes permitted groups at the base of the pyramid to obtain some benefits previously reserved for groups at the apex.[22] The growing cost of this phenomenon created disequilibrium in the system and eventually made reform necessary, and the elimination or reduction of the most liberal benefits and differences among groups, even though the most powerful (for example, the armed forces) did manage to exclude themselves from the standardization process.

In the countries where social security appeared late, the principal inequality in benefits has resulted from reduced coverage: a minority of the population is protected and accumulates benefits (vertical extension), while the noncovered majority has access solely to public health services and social welfare, both of which generally receive only a small proportion of the available resources.

A common characteristic of the region is the predominance of costly, capital-intensive curative medicine at the expense of less costly and relatively more efficient preventive medicine. The emphasis on the use of high-tech health services is illustrated by the preference for hospitals over ambulatories and health posts, as well as physicians over paramedical personnel, plus the excessive use of medicines and increasingly complex and costly equipment for surgery, laboratory analysis, and cancer and cardiovascular treatment. The enormous cost of the vertical extension of health benefits and services for a minority often makes the horizontal expansion of primary health care for the majority of the population impossible. In 1976, the Brazilian budget appropriated more funds for sophisticated curative medicine, which cared for 10,000 people concentrated in the more developed southern and southeastern regions, than for providing necessary basic services to the 41 million people of the underdeveloped regions of the north and northeast.[23] In Costa Rica the rural health program, with a minimum budget, has done more to reduce mortality and morbidity than the capital-intensive social security services.[24]

Even in the countries with more advanced social security systems, notable inequalities in health facilities and services (and in the levels of health, particularly with regard to problems such as infant mortality) exist among geographic units. Such inequalities are aggravated in countries with less-developed systems. Studies conducted during the 1970s in eight of the region's most-developed countries at various stages of social security evolution (Argentina, Brazil, Chile, Costa Rica, Cuba, Mexico, Peru, and Uruguay) have calculated the following indexes of extreme disparity between the two geographic units (province, state, department, or region) with the best and the worst health service: the index of physicians per 10,000 inhabitants fluctuated between three and eight (in other words, there were three to eight times more doctors per inhabitant in the best unit than in the worst), and the index of hospital beds fluctuated between two and five.[25] We can safely assume that inequality is even greater in the less-developed countries.

Administrative Expenditures

Administrative expenditures for social security are much higher in Latin America than in the developed countries of North America, Europe, and Asia, where they vary between 2 percent and 3 percent of total expenditures. According to ILO, in 1980, Latin American percentages ranged from 4 percent to 6.9 percent in Argentina, Panama, and Costa Rica; 7 percent to 10.9 percent in Chile, Uruguay, and the Dominican Republic; 11 percent to 14.9 percent in Nicaragua, Guatemala, Colombia, El Salvador, and Venezuela (in the 1975–77 ILO report, Mexico and Brazil were in this group; the 1978–80 report does not provide data on them); from 15 percent to 28 percent in Bolivia and Ecuador (no information is provided for Cuba, Honduras, Paraguay, and Peru). With very few exceptions, these percentages increased between 1977 and 1980.[26] Allowance must also be made for the fact that some countries have manipulated their accounting procedures to disguise administrative expenses as other expenditures.[27] In various countries, a law fixed administrative costs as a percentage of total expenditures with the objective of limiting the amount, but the effect has often been the opposite of that intended.

The administrative agencies have frequently become important sources of employment—under political or union influences—and civil service or labor legislation makes it almost impossible to fire employees. It is not difficult to find cases in which the ratio of employees to insured in the region is 13:1,000 or cases in which there are seven employees per hospital bed.[28] In fact, the employees have organized into one more pressure group and have signed collective agreements that grant them higher salaries and better labor conditions and social security benefits than the average insured. (In several countries the employees are exempted from social security contributions or pay at a reduced rate.) Physicians enjoy exceptional labor conditions and, in those countries with nearly universal coverage, constitute a powerful pressure group that has on occasion used strikes to ensure that its demands are met. In 1976, personnel expenditures accounted for 53 percent of health costs in Brazil, and a sample of physicians' salaries in São Paulo showed that they were 50 percent higher than in fourteen developed countries.[29] Doctors exert pressure to ensure that they are employed on many occasions when paramedics could adequately be used at a lower cost.

Last, many countries waste resources by constructing excessively large and luxurious offices and hospitals; frequently the most prominent building in the capital or a city is the social insurance building. Given that 80 percent is an internationally accepted norm for hospital occupancy, many hospitals in the region are underutilized: Brazil, Colombia, Costa Rica, Ecuador, Honduras, the Dominican Republic, and other countries have reported considerably lower occupancy rates.[30] The multiplicity and lack of coordination among medical services often mean duplication of effort and unnecessary cost.

The Growing Costs of Social Security and Its Causes

There are still more reasons why the cost of social security in Latin America is rapidly rising and, in the pioneer countries, has surpassed tolerable limits. According to table 5, total expenditures of social security as a percentage of GDP in 1965–77 grew in twelve countries and declined in five (more detailed information from the six case studies shows that the actual percentages are higher than the table indicates). With respect to these five countries, the only reductions higher than 0.5 percent occurred in Chile and Uruguay, countries that posted record percentages in the late 1960s and early 1970s (in 1971 Chile reached 17 percent), provoking first financial crises and eventually reform in the two systems. Nevertheless, in 1980, Chile had regained its 1965 level. The countries with the oldest programs, highest coverage, and more generous benefits are those with the heaviest burden: 10 percent in Chile and Uruguay; 6 percent to 8 percent in Panama, Argentina, Cuba, Brazil, and Costa Rica; 3 percent to 5 percent in Venezuela, Colombia, Mexico, Bolivia, Ecuador, and Peru; and 1 percent to 2.9 percent in El Salvador, the Dominican Republic, Nicaragua, Guatemala, and Haiti. In 1977, the highest percentages in the region were equal to that of Japan and are also comparable with those of Canada, the United States, the Soviet Union, Spain, Australia, and New Zealand (13 to 14 percent).

The data for 1980 presented in table 5 are available for only twelve countries, but since 1977 social security expenditures have declined as a percentage of GDP: although the percentage increased for three countries (Argentina, Costa Rica, and Chile), in one country the percentage was the same and in eight countries it declined. It should be noted, however, that the method of computing GDP changed significantly between the two ILO surveys (1975–77 and 1978–80): while in the previous survey half of the countries used the old methodology, by the time of the latest survey all countries had adopted the new methodology, and in half of them the shift began in 1978, precisely when the new series began. According to the ILO, there are small differences in the GDP estimates prepared by the old and new methodologies, but such

TABLE 5

SOCIAL SECURITY COSTS IN LATIN AMERICA, 1965, 1977, AND 1980
(PERCENTAGE OF GDP)

| | Revenues | | | Expenditures | | | | | |
| | | | | Total | | | Benefits | | |
	1965	1977	1980	1965	1977	1980	1965	1977	1980
Argentina	3.8	8.0ᶜ	9.7	3.2	7.3ᶜ	9.4	**	7.0ᶜ	8.9
Bolivia	4.3ᵃ	3.5ᶠ	2.7	3.6ᵃ	3.1ᶠ	2.7	3.0ᵃ	2.8ᶠ	2.2
Brazil	4.5	6.2	**	4.3	6.2	**	3.4	5.3	**
Chileʰ	14.1	13.2	12.8	12.2	10.1	10.6	10.0	9.4	9.8
Colombia	1.1	4.5	3.3	1.1	3.7	2.8	1.0	3.3	2.2
Costa Rica	3.8	7.4	8.2	2.3	5.8	7.0	1.9	5.3	6.3
Cuba	8.3	9.2ᵍ	**	**	**	**	8.3	9.2ᵍ	**
Dominican									
Republic	2.9ᶜ	2.6	2.2	2.7ᶜ	2.5	2.0	1.8ᶜ	2.4	1.8
Ecuador	4.1	4.5ᵈ	4.8	2.9	3.0ᵈ	3.0	2.5	2.8ᵈ	2.2
El Salvador	2.4	3.4	2.0	2.2	2.9	1.6	2.1	2.0	1.4
Guatemala	2.0	2.1	1.7	2.0	1.6	1.2	1.8	1.5	1.0
Haiti	**	0.9	**	**	0.8	**	**	0.7	**
Mexico	2.8	3.9ᵈ	**	2.6	3.4ᵈ	**	2.2	2.9ᵈ	**
Nicaragua	2.6	2.8	**	2.1	2.3	**	1.9	2.1	**
Panama	7.3	9.9	8.6	6.0	7.9	6.2	5.6	7.0	5.6
Peru	2.3	**	**	2.9	**	**	**	**	**
Uruguay	10.1ᵇ	11.3	10.4	14.5ᵇ	10.3	8.0	8.7ᵇ	9.1	7.3
Venezuela	3.0	4.5	1.7	3.1	4.1	1.3	3.0	3.8	1.1

Sources: ILO, *El costo de la seguridad social, 1972–1974* and *1975–1977,* with the exception of 1965 in Argentina and Peru, from Mesa-Lago, *Seguridad social y pobreza,* and Cuba from chapter 3 of this book.

a. 1961. b. 1969. c. 1970. d. 1974. e. 1975. f. 1976. g. 1978. h. In 1971 the percentages reached record levels of 19.4, 17.2, and 15.6.

**Not available.

differences do not affect the comparison.[31] There is no way to test the validity of this assertion for Latin America, since the survey does not provide figures for the same year calculated according to both methodologies. In half of the countries reported by the ILO, however, there is a sharp decline in the percentages starting in 1978 (when the new series in the latest survey begins), especially when the figures are compared with data for 1976–77 (available from the previous survey and not reproduced in the latest one). Furthermore, my own estimates of the percentages in 1980 are higher than the ILO percentages for the same year for all Latin American countries except Venezuela, and my 1980 percentages show a persistent increase vis-à-vis the 1977 percentages given by ILO (see table 6, below). Therefore, I conclude that social security costs kept rising at least until 1980.

It is important but difficult to determine the size of the social security burden that is adequate or tolerable for a country. If the percentage of social security expenditures over GDP (SSE/GDP) is the same for two countries but one has twice the income per capita (IPC) of the other, we could conclude that the country with the higher IPC could support the heavier social security burden. Figure 1 depicts the social security burden versus economic capacity for all the Latin American countries in 1980; IPC appears in dollars, on the horizontal axis and SSE/GDP on the vertical axis. Although the curve theoretically represents the statistical norm for toleration of the social security burden, it should not necessarily be regarded as the optimal norm. The countries significantly above the curve presumably have greater difficulty supporting the burden than those significantly below it. Thus, with respect to their economic capacity, Chile, Costa Rica, Uruguay, and Cuba (in that order) shoulder a greater burden than do Venezuela and Mexico. The rest of the countries are relatively near the curve, and it is hard to judge them.

The above comparison does not take into account population coverage. Thus Bolivia and Honduras occupy the same position in figure 1 (they have equal IPCs and SSE/GDPs), but the percentage of population coverage in the first is 3.5 times that in the second. The difference suggests that Bolivia uses the SEE/GDP per insured in a more efficient manner than does Honduras, that Bolivian benefits are lower in quality, or that a combination of the two statements is true. To evaluate the capacity to tolerate the social security burden more adequately it is necessary not only to take coverage into account but also to include other countries in the comparison to broaden the perspective beyond the region.

Health programs account for approximately half of the cost of social security in the region, and the corresponding percentages of health expenditures/GDP in Brazil, Chile, and Colombia (4 percent), Panama (5 percent), and Costa Rica (6 percent) resemble those of the United Kingdom (5 percent), which has one of the most advanced national health systems in the world. Nevertheless, it must be noted that a higher percentage of GDP devoted to health care does not always mean better health conditions, and the levels of health in the United Kingdom certainly surpass those of the above-mentioned Latin American countries.[32] Health expenditures usually increase at a higher rate than income, thus provoking growing deficits. The escalation of health costs, a worldwide phenomenon, is more severe in Latin America because of rapid population growth (in the countries undergoing demographic transition), expansion of social security coverage, excessive administrative costs and inefficiency, and hyperinflation.

The social security financial crisis in several Latin American countries has been met not only by drastic reforms but also with less visible but perverse measures: the fall in the real value of monetary benefits, delays in the processing and granting of pensions (in some cases delays of between two and

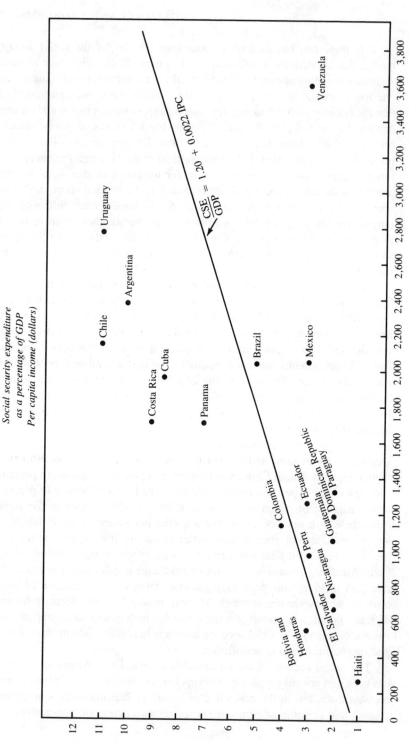

FIGURE 1

SOCIAL SECURITY BURDEN AND ECONOMIC CAPACITY OF THE COUNTRIES IN LATIN AMERICA, 1980

Social security expenditure
as a percentage of GDP
Per capita income (dollars)

$$\frac{CSE}{GDP} = 1.20 + 0.0022 \text{ IPC}$$

SOURCES: Per capita income in dollars from World Bank, World Development Report, 1982 (Washington, D.C., 1982); social security expenditure as a pecentage of GDP from table 6.

three years), and the deterioration of health services. These methods generally have a stronger negative impact among the lower-income insured who depend on social security as their only source of income or health care.

Coverage in the region cannot be expanded (or maintained) under the current level of benefits and administrative structure because the financial burden will become unbearable (as it has in various pioneer countries). Obviously, coverage cannot become universal at the same time that privilege is extended to large groups. As I noted above, a global reform is needed in the area of benefits and should be integrated with reform in the other two areas. I will discuss this subject in chapter 8.

THE IMPACT OF SOCIAL SECURITY ON DEVELOPMENT

Social security, through its health-maternity program, has improved health levels in Latin America; for example, infant mortality has dropped, and life expectancy has increased. Appendix table C shows a positive correlation (P = .05) between social security coverage (for both the total population and the EAP) and life expectancy. Tables in the six case studies also suggest an inverse relationship between social security coverage and infant mortality rates. In addition, social security has significantly contributed to work safety, the assurance of a minimum income after loss of labor capacity, and the security of the worker's dependents to a minimum income after the death of the family head. By making the worker healthier, safer, and more secure, social security has indirectly favored increases in labor productivity.

This section (and the case studies) analyzes the impact of Latin American social security in three aspects of development: savings and investment, income distribution, and employment. I chose these three aspects not because they are most important (for example, vis-à-vis the social security impact on social aspects mentioned above) but because the relationship among them in Latin America has received little serious study. From the outset, it must be said that neither the theory nor the empirical studies are conclusive on these aspects, and their analysis is made even more difficult in Latin America by the absence or unreliability of information on the functional distribution of income between labor and capital, the incidence of social security contributions and taxes, the adequate measurement of benefits (especially health benefits), and the diverse effects on the behavior of employees and workers.[33] Nevertheless, I summarize the current theoretical discussion, the available empirical evidence (almost always obtained outside the region), and several studies of specific countries (and criticism of them) below.

Savings and Investments

The impact of social security on savings and investment depends on the surplus in social security accounts and the reaction that this surplus can stimulate in other sources of domestic savings (private and public sectors) and external savings.[34] The social security surplus/deficit is a result of factors endogenous to the system (for example, types of programs, financing methods, degree of maturity, and administrative costs) as well as exogenous factors (for example, age structure of the population, rate of salary increase, and overall economic situation). As I explained above, short-term risk programs normally use a pure assessment method and are more likely to generate a deficit than a surplus, whereas the long-range programs that use the capitalization methods usually generate large reserves for potential investment. As previously noted, however, there is a general tendency in the region to replace capitalization with pure assessment methods. Also, as we will see later, the region has a poor record of efficiency in the investment of reserve funds. The impact of social security on investment also depends on the sources of financing and the incidence of contributions. The previously cited IDB study concludes that investment rate diminishes more when social security is really financed by the employer than it does when payments are made by the insured or the consumer.[35] The maturity of the pension program depends, among other factors, on its age, the retirement age for pensions, and the age structure of the population. Thus the older the program, the lower the retirement age, the older the population, the larger the passive/active ration, and the lower the surplus—and vice versa. A young population tends to grow rapidly, expanding the labor force, and if the system's coverage grows, its revenues also rise. On the other hand, in an aging population, the potential number of contributors declines and the number of pensioners rises. If real salaries are rising, the contribution base for social security also expands. A severe recession that reduces both employment and real salaries tends to have a negative impact on social security revenues and to lower the surplus.

It has traditionally been argued that social security reduces both individual savings and the demand for private insurance, since the insured expects his contribution to be returned in the form of pensions and, as a result, is not inclined to accumulate a surplus during his active life. On the other hand, earlier retirement lengthens the retirement period and can thus motivate savings during the active period of life. The planning horizon of the insured and his perception of social security contributions (as a simple tax or payment for future benefits guaranteed by a sound actuarial system) influence his savings behavior and his preference for a particular type of social security program (short or long term). In the developed countries, with older populations and more solvent social security systems, the horizon seems further off than in Latin America where—because of the population's relative youth, the financial disequilibrium of social security, and hyperinflation—relatively more importance is given to short-range programs such as health and family allowances.[36] Social security and government compete for the same tributary base, and some scholars assume that there is always a tradeoff among them. But if private savings are insufficient and the state establishes a minimum income level, social security can eliminate state social welfare payments and reduce the public deficit. Social security can raise the cost of exports, making them less competitive (so that countries without social security or with a lighter burden are favored), and can thus reduce potential external savings.

The research and debate on these topics, conducted primarily in the United States and other developed nations, have produced contradictory results: a study of sixteen countries in the Organization for Economic Co-operation and Development (OECD) found no evidence that social security reduces private savings or slows development.[37] If this impact is difficult to evaluate in developed countries, where the statistics are more precise and social security coverage is universal, it is virtually impossible to evaluate in Latin America. Different interpretations exist even within one country; one study done in Chile found that social security had a negative effect on savings, whereas a later study concluded that, after the necessary adjustment, social security had generated a surplus (although a diminishing one) rather than negative savings.[38]

Even though there is controversy about the above mentioned aspects, there is at least a consensus of opinion that the investment of the social security reserve funds in Latin America has been inefficient. In 1977, the ILO reported that in eight out of fourteen counties, the percentage of social security revenues generated by investment yield was lower than 3.5 percent. ILO data for 1980 show that the percentage increased in seven countries, but declined in five (new data were not available for two), and remained below 3.5 percent in five.[39] In almost all of the region, social security agencies are not designed to play the role of financial intermediaries. Their personnel lack experience in investments, and no plans for investments have been developed, or if they have been, they have not been coordinated with national plans. Furthermore, capital markets are poorly developed, and inflation has both devalued reserves and given employers an incentive to retain their contributions and those of their employees, as delaying the payment reduces its real value.[40] The reserves have normally been invested in: (1) bonds and other state obligations, often nonnegotiable, which in practice have been forced loans to cover state budget deficits, thus flooding social security agencies with bonds without value; (2) personal or mortgage loans, generally for insured individuals who, aided by inflation (and the lack of adjustment in the loans), have obtained capital practically free and have thus decapitalized social security; (3) loans to the health programs to cover their deficits, which are laudatory from a social point of view but not economically sound; (4) housing construction, often for the same insured, which generates very little or no revenue because of the freezing of rents, inefficiency of collection, and payments in depreciated money; and (5) in a few cases, investment in agriculture, industry, commerce (for example, stores with state-subsidized prices for the benefit of the insured), and services (for example, cinemas, theaters, and sports) that also have yielded very low returns.[41] In practically the entire region, the return on social security funds is only a fraction of the bank interest, and, in many cases, the real rate of return is negative.

Income Distribution and Employment

Social security's impact on income distribution has also been debated, and very few empirical studies on this issue exist in Latin America. The first noteworthy aspect is the relationship between population coverage and distribution; in general it can be said that the most universal systems are more progressive than those with low coverage. Nevertheless, with very few exceptions, the people below the critical poverty line are not covered by social security. This is the case for the unemployed, self-employed, unpaid family workers, agricultural workers, and domestic servants. A study conducted in the 1970s noted that, while the most-developed countries with a higher degree of coverage were also those with a lower proportion of the poor, the percentage of the EAP not covered in these countries (except in Cuba) exceeded the percentage below the critical poverty level.[42]

Financing can also have regressive effects. In many countries there is a ceiling on the insured's salary contribution such that those with higher salaries pay proportionally less. It has already been noted that the state and the employer pay more than two-thirds of the legal contribution. Even though there is no consensus on the incidence of these contributions, I offer the following summary of the current research and debate.

The state's contribution is often made by means of a specific tax placed on the services or goods produced by the covered group but paid by the entire population. Thus when social security coverage is very low, this tax probably has a regressive effect, as those who are not covered and (who also have lower income) contribute to the system without receiving anything in return. In other cases, the state takes its contribution from general revenues; if the bulk of these come from sales taxes that do not discriminate between essential and luxury consumption, the effect is again regressive when coverage is low. On the other hand, it has been alleged that if there are state subsidies on basic goods and services and/or the bulk of the sales tax is on nonessential or luxury goods, the impact is probably neutral, as the covered group is largely the same group affected by the tax.[43] But even in this case, the noncovered low-income group that does not benefit from social security would contribute to the system in some way (by buying manufactured goods, for example), or the possibility of acquiring the goods and services affected by the tax would become more remote. It must be added that, in stratified social security systems, the state usually assigns a higher contribution (or actually pays its contribution) to the group with relatively higher income while assigning a lower contribution (or making no payment) to the lower-income groups. For example, the state covers the growing deficits of the civil servants and armed forces subsystems, but it is remiss in—or reduces its contributions to—the general subsystem that covers the mass of workers.

Three possibilities exist concerning the incidence of the employer's contributions. The employer may really pay it; it may be transferred "backward," that is, the insured may pay the contribution through a reduction in his real salary; or it may be transferred "forward," that is, the consumer may pay the contribution through higher prices.[44] The theory maintains that, in the long run, enterprises include as production costs not only wages but also fringe benefits (including contributions to social security) and take this total cost into account in terms of marginal productivity. Consider the case in which the employer's social security contribution is introduced or increased. In developed market economies, the supply of labor is assumed to be inelastic (at least in terms of the normal workday and the first family income), and the worker is assumed to negotiate with his employer a "package" of salary compensation that includes fringe benefits such as the contribution to social security, which the worker perceives as part of the salary. If, in addition, social security coverage is practically universal and the employer contribution is standardized (in such a way that the worker cannot avoid incidence by taking a noncovered job or one with a lower contribution), it must be concluded that the worker absorbs the contribution through a reduction in real salary. In the developing economies, on the contrary, the supply of labor is presumed to be elastic because the abundance of manpower and low social security coverage (and/or different contributions in stratified systems) allows the workers to take noncovered jobs or ones with lower contributions. It is also assumed that the worker does not perceive the employer contributions as part of his salary, and thus there is no backward transfer. In this case, the employer has two alternatives: transfer the contribution to the consumer through an increase in prices or reduce employment according to marginal productivity. In any case, the impact is always regressive, whether because of a reduction in employment or because the transfer to the consumer makes individuals who are not covered contribute to the social security of those who are covered.

Empirical evidence regarding transfers is contradictory and almost always reflects the experience of developed nations. A study that took into account contributions by both the employer and the worker found that, in the short run, workers absorbed 75 percent and the employers 25 percent, whereas in the medium and long term, the burden was shared equally between workers and consumers. Another study of 64 countries that took into account only employers' contributions but assumed that the supply of labor was inelastic and that workers regarded the employer's contribution as part of their salaries concluded that the worker absorbed all of the burden. Also, it was adduced that, in the developed countries, the transfer to the consumer could occur in the short run but not in the long run under equilibrium conditions, whereas in Latin America, where there is less competition, what would happen in the long run is unknown. Empirical simulations indicate that absorption by the workers has a less regressive effect than does a transfer to the consumer, although the difference is not significant.[45]

According to the above argument, in the developed countries the insured absorbs the employer contribution through a cut in real salary, and as a result there is a neutral impact on employment and also on distribution (if we assume that the contribution is standardized). In the developing countries, the insured does not absorb the employer's contribution; the employer either absorbs it and reduces the demand for labor, or transfers the cost to the consumer. In this last case, the negative impact on employment would be less, although it would not disappear, as some employers could make the transfer more easily than others (and the noncovered employer would not have to transfer).

The most-developed Latin American countries more closely approximate the first model. In these countries, there is high or almost universal coverage and, according to some scholars, a demand for labor that is inelastic or less than perfectly elastic.[46] But contrary to theory, a backward transfer seems not to occur in the short run (or at least this effect is reduced) because of institutional and economic barriers and different behavioral patterns.[47] First, the intervention of the state through labor and social security legislation is much stronger in these countries than in many developed market economies, and so the law fixes a minimum salary that serves as a lower limit for salary deductions. In addition, in some countries the employer must pay the insured's contribution when his salary is equal to the minimum salary (Mexico) or must pay the difference when the insured's salary is lower than the minimum contribution (Peru); the cost of labor is thus substantially higher for this group. Second, in some of these countries (for example, in Chile at least until the mid-1970s) the price-fixing method most frequently used was average cost plus a profit margin, which facilitates a forward transfer. Third, in countries with protectionist measures for consumer-good industries, price increases are also facilitated. Fourth, workers seem not to perceive the employer's contribution as part of their salaries, as indicated by union pressure on the state to assign a higher contribution to the employer than to the insured and by the fact that collective negotiation does not include the regulation of social security contributions because they are already fixed by law. Fifth, the law and the unions make dismissals for economic reasons very difficult, and the procedure is both lengthy and costly; the employer can, obviously, avoid contracting for additional labor. All of these considerations suggest that the transfer to the consumer—at least in the short run—is the most normal one in these countries (and it is facilitated by oligarchical structures), although before such transfers can be important, the taxed product must have an elasticity of substitution that is close to zero. The impact of the forward transfer on distribution must be regressive as it affects the noncovered, lower-income group, which receives no benefits from the social security system but nonetheless contributes to it. In the few countries that have almost universal coverage, this regressive effect diminishes, if we assume that the contributions are also standardized. In this case, a reversal of the backward transfer could also occur in the medium or long run, an effect similar to that seen in developed economies. Not all employers could transfer the contribution to prices equally, because of differences in competition, elasticity of substitution, and so forth. Nevertheless, there could be an increase in prices sufficiently generalized to feed inflation substantially and to reduce real salaries. Such a price increase may well occur in countries with the most-developed social security systems and very high inflation rates.

Another point of view emphasizes the differences between the formal sector (totally or partly covered by social security) and the informal sector (not covered), differences that are more pronounced in the less-developed countries. In this case it is assumed that the employer's contribution is not transferred (either forward or backward), so that the demand for labor in the formal sector decreases or remains stationary. According to this approach, social security (sometimes combined with a policy of incentives for capital) increases the relative cost of the labor factor versus the capital factor, stimulating a substitution of capital for labor. This distortion unleashes a chain reaction: the formal sector absorbs fewer workers, fewer workers move from the informal to the formal sector, the growing labor surplus has a depressing effect on the salaries of the informal sector, salary differentials expand between both sectors, and as less capital is available to the noncovered sector, its productivity and growth fall in relation to those of the covered sector.[48] A change from wage contributions to a neutral financing system (or to one that does not discriminate between factors, such as the VAT) could correct this problem. In the case studies (especially that of Uruguay), I will analyze the advantages and disadvantages of this reform.

It has been correctly noted that, when the employer's contribution has a regressive effect, that effect cannot be doubled (that is, the employer cannot reduce the demand for labor and also transfer the cost to the consumer)—in other words, both effects cannot operate with equal intensity or simultaneously.[49] But one of the two effects may occur in the short run and the other in the medium or long run, either in the same sector or in different sectors. For example, (1) a reduction in the demand for labor in the covered formal sector could in the long run produce a fall in the real salary in the noncovered informal sector; (2) a transfer to prices could in the long run decrease demand for the products of the covered sector or affect its employment; and (3) a price transfer generalized by almost universal coverage could reduce real salary in the medium or long run.

Although it is impossible to make generalizations when theoretical and empirical bases are so weak, the considerations that I have outlined above suggest that the more economically developed a nation is and the higher its social security coverage, the greater the apparent reduction in real salaries and possibly the less the impact in price transfers. The regressive impact seems to be greater in less-developed countries.

In general terms, benefits seem to have a more progressive impact on distribution than do contributions, but this effect depends largely on the extension of coverage, on legislative standardization, and on the type of program: the more nearly universal and standardized the more progressive the impact should be; in addition, social welfare, health care, and family allowances programs usually have a more progressive impact than pension programs. In practically all countries pensions are calculated as a proportion of the insured's income and thus reproduce the inequalities of the general distribution of income. On the other hand, health benefits are basically equal and are not proportional to income even though, in stratified systems, there are differences in availability and in the quality of services. Furthermore, the poorest groups suffer a higher incidence of diseases (because of inferior nutrition, poorer hygiene, and so forth), and since private medicine is prohibitively expensive for them, the poor use the health program more frequently than the higher-income group. Even though the latter are covered, they normally prefer to use private doctors and clinics and resort to the social security system only in extreme cases. It has nevertheless been argued that health programs appear to be more progressive than they would be if benefits were measured by the amount that the user was willing to pay rather than by their cost.[50] Family allowances also have a more progressive impact than pensions, as they usually are given to low-income families and are equal and not proportional to salary. Furthermore, the poorest families are generally larger than those in middle-income brackets. Finally, social welfare programs are directed at the poorest sectors of the population and thus probably have the most progressive impact on income distribution. As I have already indicated, with the aging of the social security system, a larger percentage of its expenses goes toward pensions, so that the regressive impact increases; nevertheless, the extension of coverage and social welfare programs for those who are not covered compensates for this effect.[51]

Empirical Studies in Latin America on Social Security and Distribution

Empirical studies in Latin America on the impact of social security have examined only a few of the most-developed countries (Argentina, Brazil, Chile, and Costa Rica) and do not always cover all programs. Different methodologies and dates preclude a close comparison of these studies.

The oldest study measured the redistributive impact of the Argentine pension program (1950–60), showing a slightly progressive net effect: 1.7 percent was transferred from the highest income bracket (10 percent) to the rest, which was treated in the aggregate as the lowest income bracket (90 percent). This study could more appropriately have disaggregated the redistributive effect within that 90 percent in order to investigate the magnitude of the transfer between the poorest 30 percent (who were not covered at the time) and the middle-income 60 percent, which had the best protection.[52] A second study compared the average benefits enjoyed by various covered groups in Argentina in 1952–72 and identified an almost perfect positive relationship between the quantity of the benefit and the insolvency of the system: throughout the period, the armed forces paid the highest benefits but suffered the greatest deficit, which was covered by the state.[53]

A study of Brazil conducted in 1973 identified the most progressive impact found for any country among those for which we have information: within the covered urban sector, the poorest group received benefits (health-maternity and pensions) that duplicated their contributions, whereas the highest-income group received back an amount equal to only one-third or one-fifth of its contribution.[54] This study took into account neither the welfare program covering the rural sector, which is partly financed by contributions of the urban sector (financing that must have a markedly progressive effect), nor the armed forces and civil servants (who probably received more than they contributed). Even though the net effect of the general system on distribution is unknown, it was probably progressive.

Two studies have been done in Costa Rica on the redistributive impact of the health-maternity program. The first, on personal income, was conducted in 1973 when there were still contribution ceilings and half of the population was not covered; it showed an almost neutral effect.[55] The second study, on family income, conducted in 1978 (when ceilings had been eliminated and coverage had been notably expanded), indicated a regressive impact on financing but a very progressive impact on benefits and a slightly progressive net effect: a 2 percent transfer from the 20 percent of the population with highest income to the 40 percent of the population with the lowest income.[56]

Chile has been the country most studied in this area, and the majority of studies indicate a regressive effect on income distribution through transfers from the noncovered group to the covered group and, within the latter, through transfers from the lowest income groups to the groups with higher income.[57] The most recent study, conducted in 1969, showed a regressive effect in financing and a progressive effect in benefits, with a slightly progressive net effect; a 0.5 percent transfer from the 20 percent with the highest income to the 30 percent with the lowest income.[58] But this study excluded the non-covered sector, as well as the armed forces and other privileged groups, which means that the total net effect might have been regressive. In the same year, a study limited to the health program detected the only progressive transfer: the lowest income group received average benefits 1.6 times greater than those received by the highest income group.[59]

If studies of the more-developed Latin American countries agree in identifying a neutral or slightly progressive social security impact on income distribution, we might logically suppose that, in the less-developed countries, where coverage is much lower, the impact should be regressive. But it is not possible to prove this hypothesis in the present book.

COUNTRY RANKING BASED ON SOCIAL SECURITY DEVELOPMENT

Table 6 ranks and groups the Latin American countries on the basis of eleven variables that indicate the level of evolution exhibited by the social security systems. Although an effort was made to standardize the data to make them more strictly comparable, there are a few lingering unimportant differences in definition and years of observation.

Methodology of Country Ranking

The eleven variables were standardized, and an unweighted average calculated for each country was used as a score in the ranking in table 6 (see appendix tables A and B). Another six ranking tests assigned different weights to various combinations of variables; these tests yielded slightly different results but all with a ranking correlation coefficient very close to one. The selected ranking score, like the other six, clearly shows three groups of countries that have been categorized as top, middle, and bottom. All of the tests produced highly consistent results in the ranking of the first six countries and the last seven, but various changes occurred in six of the middle countries (Mexico to Ecuador) because their scores were so close that they were very sensitive to any change in weight.

In addition, the scores indicated that Costa Rica and Panama (always ranked in this order) are countries in transition between the middle and top groups, whereas Venezuela and the Dominican Republic (frequently in reverse order) are countries in transition between the bottom and the middle groups. Nevertheless, six of Costa Rica's variables fall within the range typical for the high group, but five variables fall within the typical range of the middle group: the age of the pension program and (related to that variable) the small percentage of expenditures going to pensions, the lack of a deficit, the low passive/active ratio, and the low percentage of the population over sixty-five years. On the other hand, practically all of Panama's variables (except the two demographic ones) fall within the range typical for the middle group. The same is true of Venezuela except in the case of three variables (age of the pension program, percentage of contribution, and age of the population). Finally, nine of the Dominican Republic's variables fall within the range typical for the bottom group (the exceptions being the age of the pension program and the percentage of expenditures going to pensions). For the reasons mentioned above and to simplify the grouping, Costa Rica was put in last place in the high group, Panama in first place in the intermediate group, Venezuela in last place in the intermediate group, and the Dominican Republic in first place in the lower group.

Table 6 seeks to give a global vision of the trajectory of social security evolution in the region, represented by the three groups that classify the twenty countries. While it is true that several variables indicate the excellence of the system (for example, variables 2 and 3, which measure population coverage), others refer to neutral aspects that do not necessarily determine its worth, as in the case of maturity of the pension program or the age of the population (variables 7 and 10). Furthermore, the variables that measure the economic-fiscal burden and financial stability of the system (variables 4–6 and 8–9) are used to identify a problem rather than an advantage. To summarize, while table 6 shows the development of social security systems, it cannot be strictly interpreted as measuring their excellence. For example, the Costa Rican system is younger than that of Argentina, but it has similar population coverage, the financial burden is less, it enjoys a more solvent financial situation, and its tendency toward disequilibrium seems to be less. Thus, if the excellence of both systems was strictly measured, Costa Rica's system would be placed above that of Argentina. In this book, however, I argue that the oldest systems generally indicate the trajectory for social security evolution in the region. It is therefore of interest to see what has occurred in such systems.

Tendencies of the Variables

According to table 6, as a country moves up in the ranking, the variables register the following tendencies: (1) the age of the pension program rises; (2 and 3) the percentages of total population and EAP covered rise; (4) the percentage contribution based on wages rises; (5 and 6) the percentage of social security expenditures rises in relation to GDP and central government expenditures; (7) the percentage of social security costs going to the pension program rises; (8) financial disequilibrium increases; (9) the passive/active ratio increases; (10) the percentage of population sixty-five years and older increases; and (11) life expectancy at birth rises.

These tendencies were examined with a multiple correlation test (see appendix table C). The variables themselves generated positive correlation coefficients that were statistically significant with a confidence level of 95 percent and reflected twenty observations. Of the fifty-five correlations, only three did not have statistically significant results with a 95 percent level of confidence: variables 4 and 8 (legal contribution and deficit/surplus); variables 4 and 11 (legal contribution and life expectancy); and variables 9 and 11 (passive/active ratio and life expectancy). The test results reveal a trajectory for social security such that the advance of one variable tends to mean the advance of the remaining variables.

Other tendencies that do not appear in table 6 but have been discussed

TABLE 6

LATIN AMERICAN COUNTRIES RANKED BY SOCIAL SECURITY DEVELOPMENT, 1980

| | Initial Pension Law[a] (1) | Covered Population[b] | | Legal Contribution[c] (%) (4) | Social Security Expenditures[d] | | | Deficit/ Surplus as % of revenues (8) | Passive/ Active Ratio[f] (9) | Population 65 and older (10) | Life Expectancy at Birth (yrs.) (11) |
		Total (2)	EAP (3)		% of GDP (5)	% of Govt. Exp. (6)	% in Pensions (7)				
Top group											
Uruguay[g]	6	69	81	33	11	39	79	(60)	0.65	10.4	70
Argentina	6	79	69	46	10	38	55	(13)	0.32	8.2	69
Chile	6	67	62	29	11	32	53	17	0.46	5.5	68
Cuba[g]	6	100	93	10	9	13	44	(46)	0.21	7.3	73
Brazil	6	96	96	26	5	38	45	(7)	0.18	4.0	64
Costa Rica	4	78	68	27	9	36	21	0	0.06	3.6	71
Typical range	6	67–100	62–96	26–46	9–11	32–39	44–79	0–(60)	0.18–0.65	4.0–10.4	68–73
Intermediate group											
Panama	4	50	46	21	7	23	34	(11)	0.12	4.4	70
Mexico	4	53	42	18	3	18	21	17	0.08	3.6	64
Peru	5	17	37	21	3	15	35	12	0.09	3.6	58
Colombia[i]	4	12	22	20	4	20	20	(8)	0.05	3.5	62
Bolivia	3	25	18	25	3	14	40	8	0.33	3.2	51
Ecuador	5	8	23	21	3	10	48	36	0.15	3.5	60
Paraguay	4	18	14	20	2	22	31	15	0.07	3.4	64
Venezuela	2	45	50	14	3	15	33	26	0.06	2.8	66
Typical range[h]	3–5	12–53	18–50	18–25	3–7	14–23	20–40	26–(11)	0.05–0.15	3.2–4.4	60–70

Bottom group

Dominican Republic	4	8	14	14	2	16	21	4	**	2.9	60
Guatemala[g]	2	14	33	20	2	14	14	3	0.06	2.9	58
El Salvador	3	6	12	12	2	12	18	23	0.08	3.4	62
Nicaragua	3	9	19	16	2	19	16	34	0.08	2.4	55
Honduras[j]	3	7	13	14	3	12	7	19	0.02	2.7	57
Haiti	2	1	2	12	1	**	10	15	**	3.5	51
Typical range[h]	2–3	1–9	2–19	12–16	1–2	12–16	7–18	3–34	0.02–0.08	2.4–3.4	51–60

Sources: Figures are based on the ECLA questionnaire answered by countries and/or statistical yearbooks and other official publications.

a. Number of decades, before the 1980s, in which the first pension law appeared.
b. Percentage of the total population covered by the health program and that of the EAP covered by the pension program.
c. Total legal percentage over the payroll that the insured, employer, and state must contribute.
d. Social security expenditures include total health expenditures.
e. Deficit or surplus (obtained by subtracting total expenditures from social security revenues) as a percentage of revenues.
f. Quotient of demographic burden, e.g., number of passive insured (pensioners) divided by the number of active insured (contributors).
g. Some figures for Cuba and Uruguay are for 1981; others are for 1980.
h. Calculated by extracting a maximum of one variable out of place (outlier).
i. 1979.
j. 1982.

**Not available.

previously and will be analyzed more profoundly in several of the case studies indicate that as a country's rank increases, its system becomes more stratified (although after a certain point there is a tendency toward unification); the social risks covered and benefits offered increase and the entitlement conditions become more liberal; pure assessment methods increasingly replace full capitalization methods; and the neutral or positive impact on distribution increases, while the generation of savings and investment of the system drops.

A more difficult tendency to prove but one that is also subject to study, has been observed in several pioneer countries (for example, Argentina, Chile, and Uruguay), namely a trend toward the reversal or closing of the cycle in social security development, which is manifested by a reduction in coverage (as a result of unemployment and evasion), by cuts in benefits or hardening of entitlement conditions, and in some cases by privatization of the system.

Stereotypes of the Systems in the Three Groups

In the top group, the stereotype for the social security system is the following: the first pension programs appeared in the 1920s; social security coverage surpasses 60 percent of the total population and the EAP (and is practically universal when care to indigents is included); the total percentage of wage contributions surpasses 26 percent; social security expenditures near or surpass one-tenth of GDP and one-third of central government expenditures; nearly half of these expenditures defray pensions (because of the age of the system, the maturation of the pension program, and the very high life expectancy); and the passive/active ratio is very high, reaching 0.6 (that is a pensioner is maintained by fewer than two contributors for the reasons stated and also because maximum coverage has almost been reached and the population growth rate is low). The system was, or is, stratified, and it tends to exert a negative impact on savings (it operates with a deficit, and the capitalization method is pure assessment) but has a neutral or slightly positive impact on distribution (especially progressive in the health program). The system confronts a serious actuarial and financial disequilibrium and shows a tendency to worsen in the future. Global reform is thus urgent.

In the middle group the stereotyped system fits the following description. The first pension programs appeared between the 1930s and the 1940s; the system covers from 18 percent to 52 percent of the population; the total average wage contribution percentage is 20 percent; social security expenditures average 3 percent of GDP and range from 14 percent to 23 percent of central government expenditures; the majority of these costs are devoted to the health program (because these countries are in the demographic transition and have a high dependency index), whereas only 20 percent to 40 percent is paid in pensions (because of the relative youth of the system and the lower life expectancy); and the passive/active ratio fluctuates from 0.05 percent to 0.15 percent (for the reason stated above and because there is potential for the expansion of coverage plus a high rate of population growth). The system is relatively unified, as some subsystems exist independent of the general system, and its impact tends to be slightly regressive in distribution and moderately positive in the generation of savings (the system generates an accounting surplus and uses the scaled-premium method or the assessment-of-constituent-capital method in the pension program). The system usually suffers from an actual disequilibrium and nears a financial disequilibrium in the medium or long term.

The stereotypical system of the bottom group may be described in the following way. The first pension program appeared in the 1950s and 1960s; population coverage is very limited (less than 10 percent of the total population and 19 percent of the EAP), and it is concentrated in the capital and the most important cities; the wage contribution percentage is very low, from 12 percent to 16 percent; social security expenditures are only 2 percent of GDP and do not surpass 18 percent of central government expenditures; four-fifths of this expenditure is devoted to the health program (because of a high population growth rate), and less than one-fifth goes to the pension program (because of the program's newness and because of very low life expectancy); and the passive/active ratio is extremely low, from 0.02 percent to 0.08 percent (for the reasons stated and because of the high potential to expand coverage and the extremely high rate of population growth). Nevertheless, in some of the countries in this group, the ratio rises because population coverage freezes. The system is basically unified (except in the case of the armed forces) and tends to exert a regressive impact on distribution and a positive one on savings generation (it operates with a substantial surplus and uses the general fixed-premium method or a partial capitalization method in the pension program). At least in the short and medium run, the system does not confront financial disequilibrium, but population coverage must be increased.

The group descriptions presented above suggest that if the actual social security trajectory is not changed, the countries in the middle group (and eventually those in the bottom group) will probably face problems similar to those currently suffered by the top group. Various countries in the top group have experimented with diverse strategies for resolving the crises. To understand the problems, and to analyze said strategies, I chose four countries in different levels of the top group as subjects for case studies: Uruguay, Chile, Cuba, and Costa Rica, plus two countries from the upper part of the intermediate group, Mexico and Peru. These six countries exemplify distinct socioeconomic models and social security strategies that I will analyze in the following chapters. Obviously, a thorough test of the hypothesis of a similar trajectory or evolution of all social security systems in the region would require both a profound analysis of the remaining fourteen countries and the passage of time. This book therefore does not pretend to settle the issue but rather attempts to establish a framework for analysis, to provide empirical evidence from prototyped systems, and to open the matter for debate.

Costa Rica:
A Latecomer Turned Boomer

IN THE LAST two decades, social security advances in Costa Rica have assumed such magnitude that today the country occupies a top position in Latin America. From 1960 to 1982, health coverage of the population grew from 15 percent to 77 percent (87 percent if indigents are included); the infant mortality rate fell from 69 to 18 per 1,000; and life expectancy rose from sixty to more than seventy-one years. Costa Rican social security programs offer protection against all social risks except unemployment, and a program of social welfare provides pension and health care to the lowest income sector of the population. The system is relatively unified, and integration of health care is now under way. A recent study shows that the health program has a net progressive effect on the distribution of income, and even though some geographic inequalities exist in coverage and health services, they have been reduced in the last decade and in the regional context are very small.

Nevertheless, between 1969 and 1980 social security expenditures (especially in health care) multiplied almost five times as a percentage of GDP, with the expansion of coverage, the growing cost of health care, the beginning of maturation of the pension program, the rapid expansion of the bureaucracy and increases in its remuneration, and inefficient administration. Until very recently the state did not fulfill its fiscal obligations as employer, third-party contributor, and entity responsible for social welfare. The resulting substantial state debt in turn created a growing deficit in the health-maternity program and forced it to take out loans and to postpone payments to creditors. The economic crisis of the 1980s has aggravated these problems with the increase in unemployment and the decline in real salaries (reducing revenues), while the number of people protected by social welfare has probably risen and high inflation has elevated costs.

Some of the problems explained above are circumstantial, and some appear to be in the process of being solved. Social security in Costa Rica is not suffering the financial crisis seen in several of the pioneer countries. Nevertheless, in the coming years, Costa Rican social security must face the challenge of maintaining the high levels reached at the beginning of the 1980s and consolidating universal coverage while at the same time reducing costs through increased efficiency so as to avoid regressive effects on income distribution. The Costa Rican authorities are aware of these problems and seem to have reached the conclusion that the old social insurance model has exhausted its possibilities and must be replaced by a new model capable of dealing with the above-mentioned problems successfully.

HISTORICAL EVOLUTION

In the first forty years of this century, Costa Rica, largely because of its political-economic conservatism and lack of industrialization, had limited political participation, few organized pressure groups, and weak unions except in the banana plantations. Social security was limited to *pensiones de gracia* (noncontributory pensions granted since the nineteenth century at the discretion of the government); a half dozen independent pension funds protecting important groups in the public sector (war veterans, teachers, communication workers, the judicial branch, and employees of the public registry and municipalities); and the protection of private white-collar workers against occupational risks. (See table 7). Health care was poor and was provided by state hospitals, the banana companies, and private charity.

In 1941 President Rafael A. Calderón Guardia, wishing to avoid the social instability seen in other countries in the region, procured advice from the ILO and promoted a law creating the Caja Costarricense de Seguro Social (the Costa Rica Social Insurance Fund or CCSS). This agency's two principal programs are health-maternity and pensions. Costa Rica benefited from the lateness with which social security was created; the system came into being in a relatively unified form and provided a fairly comprehensive and standardized structure for the eventual coverage of the entire population.[1] Nonetheless, added later to the existing independent pension funds were funds for presidents; employees of the legislative branch; ministries of the treasury, public works, and transportation; and a state railroad. During its first two decades of operation, CCSS covered a small proportion of the urban labor force, principally civil servants and some private white-collar employees in the capital. But at the beginning of the 1960s, under the influence of the Alliance for Progress and in a favorable domestic climate of political competition, a program of socioeconomic reform was launched that was to change this situation. A constitutional amendment in 1961 mandated universal social security coverage by the end of the decade. The CCSS bureaucracy, backed by this mandate, extended coverage to the majority of industrial, construction,

TABLE 7

SOCIAL SECURITY LEGISLATION IN COSTA RICA,
BY RISK AND GROUPS COVERED, 1886–1983

Year[a]	Risk Protected	Groups Covered
1886, 1958	ODS	Education
1918	ODS	Communications
1923	ODS	Public registry
1924, 1951	OR	All private workers
1935	ODS	Musicians
1939	ODS	Judicial branch
1941	ODS	Municipalities
1941, 1961, 1971	ODS, H/M	General system (CCSS) but limited to the national capital and provincial capitals
1943	ODS	Treasury and legislative branch
1944	ODS	Public works and transportation
1955, 1965	H/M	Expansion of the general system to dependents of the insured
1973, 1978	H/M	Transfer of all public hospital to the CCSS
1974	H/M, ODS	Indigents (through family allowances)
1974, 1976	H/M	Self-employed workers, pensioners, and their dependents

Source: Legislation.

Note: ODS = old age, disability, and survivors' pensions.
    H/M = health-maternity.
    OR = occupational risks.

a. The first date corresponds to the initial law, and subsequent dates correspond to modifications and amplifications.

and commercial workers as well as to their dependents and increased the wage ceilings that had blocked coverage of median- and high-income workers.

The goal of universalization was not attained by the target date, but in the 1970s, the expansion of coverage received a strong new push. Urban blue-collar workers, agricultural workers, the self-employed, domestic servants, and pensioners (in the area of health insurance) as well as their dependents were all added to the system. Furthermore, wage ceilings were completely eliminated, although ceilings were temporarily set on contributions. These were increased gradually and were finally eliminated. In addition, a social welfare program was introduced (with the confusing designation of "family allowances") that allocated resources for pensions and health care to indigents. In 1980, practically the whole population was covered; between two-thirds and three-fifths by social security and the rest by social welfare and public health programs.

Costa Rican social security thus came into being late and evolved slowly (it almost stagnated for two decades), following the trajectory typical of Central American systems, but in 1960–80, coverage within the general system was increased to near universality.

Organizational Structure

The principles of unity and uniformity function relatively well in Costa Rica. The key agency is the CCSS, which operates the two social security programs: pensions (old age, disability, and survivors) and health-maternity. The CCSS also administers two social welfare programs that are financed by public funds: noncontributory pensions (for those who are not covered by social insurance pensions) and health care for welfare pensioners and their dependents as well as for indigents (low-income people not covered by health care under social insurance who lack the means to pay for medical-hospital services). Practically all curative medicine is operated by the CCSS, which also provides some preventive services, such as immunization. The CCSS is an autonomous institution. Until 1970 the insured, the employer, and the state all participated in its administration (the legislative assembly is now considering the reintroduction of this principle).

The Ministerio de Salud (Ministry of Health, or MS) administers various programs: preventive medicine (including programs to control certain contagious diseases), primary health care for low-income people in rural zones (Salud Rural) and for the urban-marginal population (Salud Comunitaria); and infant nutrition. In 1974–78 all MS hospitals were transferred to the CCSS, which then, with the concomitant state financing, assumed the obligation of providing health care for indigents.

The health care system has a pyramidal form; elementary care levels stand at the base, and more complex and specialized forms of health care occur as one moves to the apex. There are five health regions, and the seven provinces are distributed among them. The health-care system belongs to the direct type and is provided through CCSS services throughout the nation. Although the majority of physicians are employed by the CCSS and the MS, private practice is permitted, and physicians constitute an important pressure group.

The Instituto Nacional de Sequros (National Insurance Institute or INS) is a state monopoly responsible for all insurance, including work-related accidents and diseases, even though it relies heavily on the medical-hospital services of CCSS. The family allowance program (FA), part of the Ministry of Labor and Social Security, was initially created with the objective of guaranteeing monetary benefits to low-income workers with minor children, but in practice, it has been converted into a social welfare program that assigns funds to other programs. The two most important of these are welfare pensions (for the elderly, the disabled, and abandoned children not entitled to social insurance pensions), which CCSS administers, and primary health care in rural and marginal urban areas, which MS administers. There are other programs in the areas of unemployment, nutrition, and housing.

Furthermore, as noted above, fourteen independent pension funds (old age; seniority, restricted to some cases; disability; and survivors) cover civil servants. Each of these funds has its own legislation and separate financing. The majority are administered by the Ministry of Labor, while the rest have autonomous administrations. Some of those insured by CCSS can change to the independent funds, the latest being employees of the Ministries of Agriculture and Labor. In 1983, the Legislative Assembly was considering the authorization of another transfer. Finally, a considerable number of pensions (*pensiones de gracia*) are based not on a right but on a bureaucratic decision that takes into account administrative merit.

Even though the Costa Rican social security system is relatively unified and standardized within the Latin American context, there are still inequalities that should be corrected. In 1982, a national presidential commission was created in which all institutions related to social security were to participate. Its goal is to coordinate social security and to integrate the health system completely. CCSS and INS are studying a reciprocal exchange of functions as well as the integration of their services in a new hospital.

In 1983, in consultation with the Ministry of Planning, a health sector was created, presided over by the minister of health, with the power to set all health policies and to implement the integration of the health system. A close personal relationship existed in the first half of the 1980s between the minister of health and the executive president of CCSS. Both were committed to the integration plan and to the search for a more viable and efficient health model that would give greater emphasis to preventive medicine and primary health care.[2] In fact, integration has already been achieved in various zones of four provinces and is being implemented in the capital. Important efforts are being made to define health levels and the referral system better and to decentralize services in order to reduce the concentration in the capital. A standardized map for CCSS and MS is still needed, however; the two still define their regions differently.

On the other hand, unification of the independent pensions funds seems not to be under way, although the Legislative Assembly has for a decade been studying the creation of a national commission that would elaborate laws governing unification. Furthermore, the Ministry of Planning, in the four-year plan 1982–86, strongly criticized the independent funds for having violated the principles of universality and solidarity of social security.[3] At the least, the creation of new pension funds and the transfer of insured groups from CCSS to existing independent funds should be prohibited.

POPULATION COVERAGE

Legal and Statistical Coverage

According to law, CCSS provides compulsory coverage to all salaried workers (including domestic servants) and voluntary coverage to all self-employed workers, in pension programs as well as in health-maternity programs. In the latter, furthermore, it must provide coverage to all pensioners and to the dependents of all insured. The scope of family coverage is generous: it includes the wife or concubine (or disabled husband); minor children (also students until they reach an older age and invalids without age limit); the mother (or father older than sixty-five or disabled); and brothers and sisters (under a certain age limit or disabled). CCSS offers health protection for the group of civil servants covered by independent funds for pensions. Unpaid family workers and the unemployed cannot be insured by CCSS but can receive welfare benefits.

Table 8 shows the population statistics of social security coverage: in health, there was an increase from 15 percent to almost 77 percent in 1960–82, while in pensions, the proportion covered rose from 25 percent to almost 69 percent. (The number of the active insured in independent pension funds is unknown and may amount to 15 percent of total coverage. Health care coverage by the CCSS was therefore used as a proxy for pension coverage, as the former includes the insured in independent funds.) If, on the other hand, the number of welfare indigents and pensioners (177,695) is added to the number of contributory insured, health coverage increases to 84 percent. On the other hand, it must be taken into account that in table 8 dependents of the insured were estimated using the ratio of 1.25, whereas CCSS has occasionally used 0.99; the lower figure would reduce insurance coverage in 1982 to 70.5 percent and the total to 78 percent. The Ministry of Health, for its part, covered 53 percent of the population in 1982 (rural and marginal urban) with preventive services and primary health care, which indicates a duplication in coverage.[4] Workmen's compensation (administered by INS) was limited to 38 percent of the labor force in 1982. Even though the law includes all workers, until recently affiliation with INS was compulsory only for the highest-risk activities, and for the rest, the employer could assume direct responsibility. In practice, many noninsured employers eluded this responsibility, and those injured in work-related accidents and diseases received CCSS care in the end just like cases of nonoccupational risks. A 1982 law has given all employers a four-year period to insure their employees with INS against occupational risks (only the self-employed and unpaid family workers are excluded). INS coverage began to expand in 1983 with commerce and services and will gradually extend to other activities until total coverage is reached in the late 1980s.[5]

DETERMINANT STRUCTURAL FACTORS

The high coverage and rapid expansion of CCSS in the 1970s has been facilitated by several structural factors: the high proportion of salaried workers (75 percent of the labor force); the relatively small proportion of self-employed workers and unpaid family workers (20 percent and 4 percent, respectively);

TABLE 8

SOCIAL SECURITY COVERAGE OF POPULATION IN COSTA RICA, 1960–1982

		Insured Population (thousands)						% of Coverage[c]		Average Annual Growth Rates %				Quotient of Demographic Burden[d]
	Total Population (thousands)	Actives			Passives[a]	Dependents[b]	Total	Total Population	EAP	Total Population	EAP	Actives (Pensions)	Total Insured	
		EAP	Health	Pension[a]										
1960	1,236	372	94	1	1	95	190	15.4	25.3	**	**	**	**	0.542
1965	1,482	430	132	11	2	320	454	30.6	30.7	3.7	2.9	61.5	19.0	0.135
1970	1,732	526	202	125	4	455	661	38.2	38.4	3.2	4.1	62.6	7.8	0.031
1975	1,964	639	327	290	10	736	1,073	54.7	51.2	2.5	4.0	18.3	10.1	0.036
1980	2,279	770	526	378	23	1,184	1,733	76.0	68.3	2.4	3.8	5.4	10.1	0.060
1981	2,342	797	522	376	26	1,175	1,723	73.5	65.5	2.3	3.5	-0.6	-0.6	0.069
1982	2,406	824	558	380[e]	29	1,255	1,842	76.6	67.7	2.3	3.4	1.1	6.9	0.078

Sources: Total population from CELADE, *Boletín Demográfico* 16 (July 1983): 32; EAP 1955–65 from CCSS; 1970–82 from CELADE, *Boletín Demográfico* 15:29 (January 1982). Actives, passives, and dependents from CCSS, *Anuario estadístico, 1965* to *1981*. Percentages, rates, and coefficients calculated by the author.

a. Includes only actives and passives in CCSS; excludes those from independent funds (in 1970 the total number of pensioners was double that which appears in the table, and in 1975 it was 30 percent greater).

b. In 1970–82 the number of dependents was calculated using a ratio of 1.25 for each active insured in health; a later estimate is based on a ratio of 0.99.

c. "Coverage of the total population and the EAP" relates to health; as there is neither a total number of actives in the pension program nor a total of passives, a calculation of EAP coverage based on health was preferred.

d. Number of passives in pensions divided by number of actives (limited to CCSS).

e. Estimated by the author.

**Not available.

the low rates of open unemployment (3.9 percent) and underemployment (9.3 percent); the low proportion of the labor force in agriculture (27 percent); and the small size of the country with its good communication network and high educational and income per capita levels.[6] Yet political commitment was essential in attaining universalization, as is evident from the fact that other countries, with similar structural characteristics, have not been able to achieve this goal.

Differences in Population Coverage

The near universality and unity of the Costa Rican social security system have meant that differences in coverage among geographic areas and economic sectors are much smaller than they are in other countries. Table 9 provides the only available information on total population coverage by province, but it includes only active insured and excludes dependents and passive insured (there is no recent distribution of the EAP by province to make the comparison more exact). For this reason the percentages are lower than they should be. The province with the best coverage is San José (which includes the capital), and the one with the worst coverage is Guanacaste (the most rural province); the degree of coverage in the first is more than twice that in the second. The majority of the insured are in the central region, around San José, where 20 percent of the population and the majority of government activities, industry, and public utilities are concentrated. The majority of the noninsured live in the most remote, underdeveloped, and rural provinces.

Table 10 shows the degree of coverage by economic sector in 1973 and 1979; for the first year self-employed workers are included, but for the second

TABLE 9

POPULATION COVERAGE BY PROVINCE IN COSTA RICA, 1979

Provinces	Population (thousands)	Insured[a] (thousands)	% of Coverage
Alajuela	373	62	16.6
Cartago	235	39	16.7
Guanacaste	206	31	15.2
Heredia	153	32	20.9
Limón	135	36	26.6
Puntarenas	256	41	15.8
San José	798	271	33.9
Total	2,156	512	23.7

Sources: Population from the Dirección General de Estadística y Censos, "Población de la República de Costa Rica por provincias, cantones, y distritos: estimación al 1 de enero de 1979," San José, 1979; CCSS insured from Anuario Estadístico. 1979.

a. Includes salaries anad self-employed workers; excludes dependents of the insured.

TABLE 10
COVERAGE OF EAP BY ECONOMIC SECTORS IN COSTA RICA, 1973 AND 1979

	1973			1979		
Sector	*EAP*	*Active Insured (thous.)*	*% of Coverage*	*EAP*	*Active Insured[a] (thous.)*	*% of Coverage*
Agriculture, cattle, forestry, hunting and fishing	213	49	23.1	207	63	30.4
Manufacturing industries, mines and quarries	71	59	82.3	122	84	68.7
Construction	39	20	51.4	58	26	44.5
Public utilities, transportation, and communications	30	21	68.1	42	30	71.9
Commerce and financial services	81	52	63.3	131	87	66.6
Communal, social, and personal services	119	88	74.4	172	137	79.9
Those doing unspecified jobs and job searching	31	*	*	13	*	*
Total	585	289	49.4	743	427	57.5

Sources: EAP from *Encuesta nacional de hogares, empleo, y desempleo, 1979.* Insured from CCSS, *Anuario Estadístico, 1979.*

a. Includes only salaried workers; as coverage of self-employed did not begin until 1974, the first distribution includes all insured, but the second excludes self-employed.

*Not applicable.

there are figures only for salaried workers. This discrepancy probably explains the differences between the two years that do not result from an expansion of coverage. For example, the reduction in the ratio of coverage between the best and worst covered sector (from 3.6 in 1973 to 2.6 in 1979) and the increase in agricultural coverage (from 23 percent to 30 percent) may in part be due to the expansion of coverage to the countryside but may also be the result of the exclusion (in 1979) of the self-employed, who are concentrated in agriculture and as a group are less fully covered. In any case, the table shows that agriculture is the sector with the worst coverage (although Costa Rica has one of the highest figures for agricultural coverage in the region), while public utilities, transport and communication, industry, and service sectors are the best covered.

Noncovered Population

The sector without health coverage in CCSS comprises four groups. Perhaps the most important are nonsalaried workers with high income (for example, employers, landlords, and self-employed professionals) who are either noninsurable or can voluntarily insure but generally pay for their own health care. The second group is probably that of salaried workers who directly (or through their employer) evade the obligation of affiliation. It was estimated that in 16 percent of salaried workers were not effectively insured in 1979: apparently, many owners of small enterprises do not sign up their employees or hire them for only three months to evade the registration, even though a good number of these employees in practice receive health care through the CCSS as indigents. The third noninsured group are self-employed workers who have decided not to affiliate with the CCSS but who can—if they lack means—receive welfare health care. The last category consists, first, of unpaid family workers who are not directly insurable but can be insured as dependent family members of the insured or as indigents and, second, of the unemployed, who are not insurable but who, in the majority of cases, qualify for welfare health care. In 1982, almost half of the population (in rural and urban marginal areas) received primary health care in facilities of the Ministry of Health. In addition, the noninsured individual with some assets (who does not qualify as an indigent) can receive medical-hospital care and medicines in CCSS facilities by paying a relatively small sum.[7]

Measures to Improve Coverage

The above account makes it obvious that practically all of the country's population is covered, especially in health care. But in the current decade, universal coverage must be insured through measures that are already in the process of implementation: (1) the extension of workmen's compensation to all salaried workers; (2) improved access to health services, especially in the agricultural sector and in the less-developed provinces; (3) extension of pension coverage to the self-employed; and (4) identification of all users of the social security system (CCSS, MS, and INS) so that evasion can be controlled, other irregularities can be corrected, and any low-income group without coverage can be detected.

FINANCING

Sources of Financing

The CCSS is financed by three-part wage contributions plus taxes, state transfers (for welfare programs), the sale of services, investment yields, and foreign aid.

The three-part wage contribution (total) set by law has increased gradually. In 1973–83, it rose from 20 percent to 32 percent, with the largest increase in the employer's contribution (from 9.25 percent to 22.66 percent), followed by that of the insured (from 6.5 percent to 8 percent), while that of the state was reduced (from 4.5 percent to 1.5 percent). In 1983, the employer legally had to pay almost three times as much as the insured (see table 11). If other contributions to related programs are added to the total contributions to CCSS (such as unemployment, savings, and housing) the total wage tax rises to more than 58 percent). In 1983, the Legislative Assembly was discussing various legal projects to create a new insurance or compensation fund for unemployment (and to provide support for social enterprises) that the employer would finance by means of an additional contribution of 8.33 percent.

To the small wage contribution that the state pays to CCSS we must add taxes on domestic production and on the importation of alcoholic and non-alcoholic beverages, the importation of perfumes and luxury goods, the sale of cigarettes, real estate transactions, and payments to the state as well as lottery revenues. In the 1970s the Interamerican Development Bank (IDB) gave a loan of US $30 million to support the expansion of the hospital network and its integration under CCSS.

The investments of the CCSS pension reserve fund have historically generated a very low yield, and if inflation is taken into account, decapitalization of the fund may have occurred. In 1981, loans to the health-maternity program, that delayed its payments of principal and paid very low interest, tied up 42 percent of the fund; another 34 percent was invested in state bonds that paid

TABLE 11

LEGAL CONTRIBUTIONS TO SOCIAL SECURITY BY PROGRAM AND SOURCE
IN COSTA RICA, 1983
(PERCENT OF SALARY OR INCOME)

| Program | Insured | | Employer | State[a] | Total[b] |
	Salaried	Self-employed			
Pensions	2.5	7.25	4.75	0.25	7.5
Health/maternity	5.5	5.0–12.25	9.25	1.25	16.0
Occupational risks	*	*	3.66[c]	*	3.66
Family allowances	*	*	5.0	*	5.0
Total	8.0	12.25–19.5	22.66	1.5	32.16

Source: Legislation.

   a. The state is included not as an employer but as a third-party contributor.
   b. Excludes the contribution of the self-employed insured.
   c. Average premium.

* Not applicable.

half the bank interest rate; and 21 percent had been given out in mortgages at unknown interest rates. The percentage of total CCSS revenues from investment yields rose from 8.5 percent in 1961 to a maximum of 10.6 percent in 1970 and then gradually declined to 2.7 percent in 1982. High inflation in the 1980s probably decapitalized the pension fund: in 1982, 76 percent of this fund was loaned at interest rates of 4 percent to 8 percent, while banks' interest rates fluctuated from 22 percent to 25 percent and inflation reached a record 82 percent. As loans were not adjusted for inflation, amortization was made in devalued money.[8]

In 1980 a law prohibited increasing the number of hospital beds for private users who pay CCSS for services, and included provisions to eliminate private pensioners in these hospitals, in spite of the fact that these hospitals operate at only 73 percent of capacity. Hence, the sale of services to private patients, which generated 3.7 percent of the CCSS total revenue in 1979, declined to 2.1 percent in 1982.[9]

A comparison of the percentage distribution of CCSS revenue by source, between 1970 and 1983, indicates that the revenue from employer payments rose from 36 percent to 44 percent while that of the insured rose from 23 percent to 30 percent, that of the state (including taxes and transfers) fell from 29 percent to 18 percent, and other revenues (investment yields, sale of services and so forth) declined from 12 percent to 8 percent.[10]

In the independent pension funds, the insured's legal contribution is twice the size of that for CCSS, but the state contribution is much greater: twice as much to the education fund and 4.5 times as much to the judicial fund, while in the rest of the funds, the state pays all costs not covered by the insured. Furthermore, in contrast to the CCSS tradition of delinquency and debts, the state is punctual in its payments to the independent pension funds. The Ministry of Health is financed through the state budget and a wage contribution of 5 percent that the employer must pay and is dedicated to helping low-income families, especially children and the elderly. INS is financed by employer-paid rates and yields from investments that are apparently higher that those of CCSS.

Evasion and Payment Delays

A substantial part of the resources the CCSS should receive never materializes, because of the state debt and because of evasion and payment delays on the part of the insured and employers. The accumulated debt of the state in 1977–82 was calculated at 2,011 million colones, an amount equal to the total revenue of CCSS in 1980. This debt encompassed: the wage contribution of the state as an employer, the third-party contribution (including the tax revenues that were collected by the state but were not transferred to the CCSS), and the state transfers to cover the cost of health care to indigents. Also, the family allowance program owed CCSS 9 million colones for health care to welfare pensioners. The figures that I have cited are usually adjusted by audits; for example, the state debt was reduced by one-fourth.[11]

The lack of reliable information about CCSS coverage, as well as the fact that employers and the insured cannot be precisely identified, facilitates evasion, payment delays, and other irregularities. The evasive techniques of small business owners have already been mentioned. When the insured applies for health services, s/he must show a receipt proving that the employer is up-to-date in contributions, but delinquency uncovered by this control instrument does not usually lead to corrective action. The noninsured user either is an indigent or can pay (partly or totally) for health services; the condition of the indigent must be verified, but in practice, CCSS lacks trained personnel, and many users who are able to pay pass as indigents. Furthermore, users with income are given a bill to be paid in installments, but collection control in the CCSS is extremely poor. Apparently, the preestimated billing methods used by the CCSS underestimates the amount of wages and benefits really paid and so becomes another arena for evasion and revenue loss. A study prepared by the World Health Organization and the Pan-American Health Organization (WHO/PAHO) in 1980 showed a serious lack of information and evasion control in CCSS and stated that the collection of payments and debts must become more rapid and efficient. Despite the various measures undertaken at the beginning of the current decade, in 1983 payment delays (principally on the part of employers) rose to 604 million colones, or one-tenth of the CCSS total revenues.[12]

Financial Equilibrium

Until the mid-1970s the CCSS enjoyed financial equilibrium, but after 1979 the situation rapidly deteriorated, largely for the reason already explained but also because of the increase in expenditures. The CCSS usually publishes budget figures for current revenues and expenses, excluding the capital account as well as the payment delays of the state, employers, and the insured. In table 12 the adjustments necessary for comparing actual total revenues and expenditures have been made for 1976–82. The table shows that the pension program normally generates a surplus (although at the end of 1976 it showed a small deficit), whereas the health-maternity program has faced growing deficits since 1980, for a total of 1,700 million colones in 1983 (not shown in the table). In order to cover this deficit (similar to the state's debt to the CCSS), the health-maternity program borrowed 2,032 million colones (approximately half of this sum in loans and interest and the rest in retention of contributions destined for the pension fund) from the pension fund and also incurred a debt of US $22 million to foreign pharmaceutical companies. For the first time, in 1979 the system yielded a net deficit; this was reduced in 1980 and became a small surplus in 1981–82 (equivalent to 0.7 percent or 0.8 percent of revenues), but it is estimated that in 1983 the deficit was 800

TABLE 12

SOCIAL SECURITY BALANCE OF TOTAL ACTUAL REVENUES
AND EXPENDITURES BY PROGRAM IN COSTA RICA, 1976–1982
(MILLIONS OF COLONES AT CURRENT PRICES)

Program	1976	1978	1980	1981	1982
Pension					
Revenues	469	760	924	1,222	2,083
Expenditures	475	740	810	709	1,272
Balance	−6	20	114	513	811
Health/maternity					
Revenues	815	1,686	2,162	2,492	3,852
Expenditures	789	1,654	2,277	2,978	4,202
Balance	26	32	−115	−486	−350
Total					
Revenues	1,284	2,446	3,086	3,714	5,935
Expenditures	1,264	2,394	3,087	3,687	5,474
Balance	20	52	−1	27	461
As percentage of revenue	1.6	2.1	−0.03	0.7	0.8

Source: CCSS, Sección Financiera, July 1983.

Note: Only CCSS; excludes occupational risks, family allowances, Ministry of Health, and independent pension funds.

million colones.[13] The financial situation may become more complicated in the rest of the decade, as 1984 marks the end of the grace period on payments of the US $38 IDB million loan. Furthermore, the pension program will mature, increasing expenditures (see "Benefits, Expenditures, and Costs," below) while the possibility of increasing revenues is limited by the present recession, the near universality of the system, and the low yield on investments.

Financing Methods

Within the CCSS, the health-maternity program uses the pure assessment (pay-as-you-go) method with a contingency fund, while the pension fund in theory uses the general fixed-premium method (also used by the INS). The latter, in practice, has been converted to scaled premium, which means that the premium, rather than remaining fixed for an indefinite time, must be increased at intervals of a certain number of years. An actuarial study conducted in 1980 affirmed that pension payments would be guaranteed at the present contribution level until 1992.[14] This study supposedly took into account demographic tendencies and inflation, but it probably did not predict the deepening of the economic crisis in 1981–83. According to private study, wage contributions will be insufficient for pension payments by 1993 even if the state is assumed to honor all of its obligations.[15]

Measures to Increase Revenues

To deal with the crisis, an emergency plan was introduced in 1982 and was later followed by other measures,[16] some of which related to income: the control of evasion, payment of the state debt, an increase in contributions, an improvement in investment efficiency, and a search for other sources of revenue.

In 1983, the CCSS and the MS completed a study to introduce medical identity cards that classified all users as insured, indigent, or noninsured without means. This project was coordinated with the establishment of a single identification number for fiscal, social security, and other purposes. Assistance from the U.S. Agency for International Development (USAID) could be decisive in reducing evasion and improving the control of payments.

The administration which entered office in 1982, paid the budget obligations of the state (as employer and third-party contributor) for 1981–83, promised to pay in 1984, and negotiated with the CCSS the payment of the accumulated debt (adjusted by audit) up to 1980. Payment of this debt was expected to occur partly through issuing state bonds at 7 percent interest. The state will still owe the difference between its budgetary allocation at the beginning of the fiscal year and actual obligations at the end of the fiscal year that result from wage increases. Since 1983, in order to receive their budgetary allocations, all public agencies have had to show that they do owe nothing to CCSS or that they are negotiating the payment of their contributions. In 1983, USAID approved a loan of US $10 million to the Costa Rican government, which will be responsible for its amortization and will transfer the sum to the CCSS to defray nearly half of the accumulated state debt. In the same year, the CCSS had already paid off half its foreign debt, and it was expected to use the USAID funds to pay the remainder. A law promulgated in 1982 prohibited the health-maternity program of the CCSS from borrowing further from the pension program and from retaining contributions earmarked for other purposes. Since the bulk of the pension fund cannot now be loaned to health-maternity, it is being invested in bank certificates of deposit with higher yield (800 million colones were thus invested in 1982 and between 1,500 and 2,000 million colones in 1983–84). With USAID assistance, the CCSS is receiving investment counseling. The bonds that the state will issue to pay part of its contribution to the health-maternity program will be transferred to the pension program, while the rest of the debt will have to wait for the culmination of negotiations on the payment of the remaining state debt. The CCSS expects to balance the budget in 1984 with the net increase in wage contributions of 4 percentage points that was introduced in 1983; it is assumed both that the accumulated debt of the state from 1980 will be paid and that the USAID loan will materialize.[17]

Even though the above-described measures are generally very positive, more efforts will be required to balance the budget in the long run and to guarantee the actuarial equilibrium of the system. In addition to the urgent need to reduce costs (which I will discuss in the next section), CCSS needs to increase its revenues, and a fresh increase in contributions seems neither economically nor politically feasible.

It might be possible to charge a minimum sum for use of outpatient consulting services and medicines. Not only would this course of action increase revenues, but it would also reduce unnecessary consultation and medicine consumption and would hence curtail costs. Two studies conducted by the CCSS confirmed this hypothesis and indicated that a minimum charge of 10 colones per visit would generate 60 million colones of revenue annually and would reduce the number of consultations by 1 million, or the equivalent of another 70 million colones. A charge of 5 colones for medicines (the lowest income group would be exempted) would reduce unnecessary consumption by 10 percent and would annually generate another 70 million colones of revenue. In the end, the CCSS decided not to introduce these charges, apparently because it feared a negative reaction from the users.[18] Nevertheless, public hospital centers and health posts that take care of the lowest income groups usually solicit a voluntary donation of 5 or 10 colones, a sum that is paid without complaint.

The CCSS should also study the possibility of replacing all or part of the wage contributions with other financing methods (for example, a value-added tax) that would simplify collection and control and would exert a neutral impact on employment. In 1983, a World Bank mission proposed to study this idea and offered to furnish the necessary technical assistance.

Other ways of obtaining revenues should also be studied. The possibilities include the sale of the fund's medical-hospital services to private users, a solution that would take advantage of the fact that more than one-fourth of hospital capacity is not being used. The 1980 law that prohibited this activity would of course need to be repealed.

In accordance with the law, an actuarial revision of the pension program must be done every three years, and one was carried out in 1980; the next was scheduled for 1983 but was not done until 1985. This revision should lead to the formal adoption of the scaled-premium method and should indicate whether charges must be introduced to assure an actuarial balance in the fixed period.[19]

BENEFITS, EXPENDITURES, AND COSTS
Benefits and Entitlement Conditions

The health-maternity and workmen's compensation programs in Costa Rica have both standardized benefits and entitlement conditions, even though there are differences in accessibility and quality (especially in health). Within the CCSS, benefits are uniform in the old-age, disability, and survivors' program, but there are significant differences between the CCSS and the independent pension funds.

In health-maternity, the insured worker is entitled to monetary benefits, such as payments in place of salary, transportation expenses, and prosthesis, as well as health benefits in species or services, such as medical-hospital care, surgery, medicines, dental care (including fillings and orthodontics), and part of the expenses associated with glasses and contact lenses. The insured's dependents are not entitled to monetary benefits but have a right to health benefits except for dental care (extractions alone are covered) and optometry care. The female insured worker is entitled to all benefits in the case of maternity (and also milk for the infant), whereas the wife of an insured worker faces the same limitations as other dependents. In occupational risks, the insured is entitled to similar monetary and health benefits plus pensions for disability (total or partial), while dependents are entitled only to survivor's pensions and funeral aid. Finally, the old age, disability, and survivors' programs conceded pensions to insured workers and/or their dependents (in the case of disability, the worker is also entitled to medical-hospital care).

Within the Latin American context, the legal conditions of the Costa Rican system are fairly strict in health-maternity in terms of the level of monetary benefits and the duration period, but conditions are relatively liberal in terms of the contribution period required for entitlement. On the other hand, health benefits are very generous, and a large number of family members are entitled to them. Entitlement conditions in occupational risks are strict, and benefits are average. Finally, in the old age, disability, and survivors' programs, the CCSS offers liberal entitlement conditions in old age pensions (which can be solicited when the insured is only fifty-seven years old and has thirty-four years of service) and in the number of family members who partake of the survivor's pension (even brothers and sisters are entitled). Yet the conditions are even more liberal in the independent funds. In general, if we take into account that the total wage contribution of the system is one of the highest in the region, benefits of the CCSS (with some exceptions) are not out of line when compared with those in other Latin American countries.

Table 13 shows the advances made in Costa Rica in health services and levels in the last two decades. The expansion of social security coverage must have been a contributing factor, together with other factors such as economic development and programs such as nutrition. It should be noted that the table does not include services, and hence the ratio of hospital beds and doctors per inhabitant must be higher. All of the table indicators except for hospital beds show significant progress. The reduction in infant mortality is impressive, even though the 1960 level was already much lower than the regional average. Mortality rates in 1980 were among the lowest in Latin America, and life expectancy was one of the highest. It should be mentioned that the infant

TABLE 13
HEALTH SERVICES AND LEVELS IN COSTA RICA, 1960–1981

| | Hospital Beds per 1,000 Persons | Physicians per 1,000 Persons | Mortality Rate | | Life Expectancy[a] |
			General	Infant	
1960	4.5	3.7	8.0	68.6	60.2
1965	4.2	4.5	8.1	69.3	63.0
1970	4.0	5.1	6.7	61.5	65.6
1975	3.8	6.7	4.9	37.9	68.1
1980	3.4	8.9	4.1	19.1	71.4
1981	**	10.0[b]	3.9	18.0	71.8

Sources: Luis Asís Beirute et al., "El recurso humano médico en Costa Rica entre 1970–1980," San José, 1981; Ministerio de Salud, Memoria, 1982 (San José: CCSS, 1983); Juan Jaramillo Antillón, Los problemas de la salud en Costa Rica: políticas y estrategias (San José: Litografía Ambar, 1983); and CELADE, Costa Rica: Estimaciones y proyecciones de población, 1950–2025 (Santiago: CELADE, October 1983).

a. Values for five-year periods (e.g. 1955–60 = 60.2) except for 1981.
b. 1982.
**Not available.

mortality rate is a much better indicator of improved health services than general mortality. The extremely low percentage of the latter is due, in part, to low infant mortality and in part to the fact that Costa Rica's population is quite young (as will be seen in table 17).

Inequalities in Benefits

As the CCSS health-maternity program is standardized, inequalities are evident not among occupational groups, but between provinces and possibly also among income levels. In 1979, for example, the province of San José (which includes the capital city) had 6.5 times more doctors (per 10,000 inhabitants) and 5 times more hospital beds (per 1,000 inhabitants) than the province of Guanacaste. Part of the concentration in San José is to be expected; logically speaking, superior medical-hospital services should be available in the capital, where patients from the lower- and median-level services are sent for treatment. But the differences relate in part to other factors. A ranking of the provinces on the basis of the CCSS health services resembles the ranking based on social security coverage (table 9). In addition, a high positive correlation coefficient exists between these rankings and another based on economic development of the provinces (per capita income, percentage of urbanization, and percentage of the labor force in secondary and tertiary activities). Nevertheless, the inhabitants of the most rural and underdeveloped provinces benefit from the MS primary health program, although it has very limited resources in comparison with CCSS. (I will discuss this point later.)[20]

The CCSS and the independent pension funds exhibit significant inequalities in entitlement conditions for the pension program: three funds allow retirement after thirty years of service, regardless of age, and three other funds permit retirement at an age seven years younger than the CCSS and after a period of service between four and ten years of service shorter than does the CCSS. Where the calculation of pensions is concerned, six funds pay 100 percent of the base salary, while CCSS pays 40 percent. In six funds, the base for pension calculations is the last month's or the last year's wage, or an average of the thirty-six highest wages, whereas in the CCSS it is the average of the forty-eight highest wages.[21] Also, as I noted above, the state contributes substantially more to the independent funds than to the CCSS and is paid without delay. Table 14 shows that the average pension in the CCSS is between one-half and one-fourth the average pension of the independent funds. Note that the most influential groups (the Legislative Assembly and the judicial branch) have the highest pensions. If the salaries of these groups corresponded to pensions, and if their contributions and benefits systems were equal to those of the CCSS, social security could be said to reproduce general income inequalities. But in view of the advantages enjoyed by these groups in terms of state payments and the generosity of benefits, one can conclude that the pension program aggravates income inequalities.

The Growing Cost of Social Security and Its Causes

In 1980 social security expenditures in Costa Rica, in relation to GDP and central government expenditures, were the fourth highest in Latin America and approximated those of the pioneer countries. Furthermore, Costa Rican

TABLE 14

DIFFERENCES IN AVERAGE ANNUAL PENSIONS AMONG INSURED
GROUPS IN COSTA RICA, 1982
(COLONES AT CURRENT PRICES)

Insured Group	Average Pension	Ratio[a]
General (CCSS)	33,485	1.0
Public works and transportation	61,494	1.8
Education	74,472	2.2
Communications	87,104	2.6
Judicial	89,433	2.7
Public registry	97,864	2.9
Treasury and Congress	129,322	3.9

Sources: Based on Jorge Montt D., "Pensiones por jubilación en Costa Rica," Instituto de Estudios en Población, Heredia, 1982; and interviews by the author in San José, July 1983, in various independent pension funds.

a. Using CCSS as a base (1.0)

expenditures as a percentage of GDP were higher than in Brazil and as a percentage of central government expenditures were higher than in Chile (see table 6). If the countries are compared using health expenditures alone, Costa Rica leads Latin America with 6.8 percent of GDP. Between 1961 and 1980, Costa Rican social security expenditures in relation to GDP rose almost five times (from 2 percent to 9 percent) and in relation to fiscal expenditures grew almost three times (from 13 percent to 36 percent), without a doubt the most significant increase in the region (see table 15). How can this development be explained, especially if one takes into account the fact that social security in Costa Rica came into being two decades after social security in the pioneer nations and that the population of Costa Rica is much younger than that of pioneer countries? The following sections explain three groups of reasons for this apparent paradox: general factors, factors related to health-maternity, and factors related to pensions.

   General Causes.   Universalization is one of the most important reasons for increases in Costa Rica's social security expenditures: in 1960–82 population coverage in the health-maternity program of the CCSS rose more than 60 percentage points, and if we add the social welfare program, the increase amounts to almost 70 points. Inasmuch as universal coverage has almost been reached, this factor should becomes less important in the future, but because the population growth rate is relatively high (2.4 percent in 1975–80), the demand for health services, and hence expenditures, will continue to grow. Another cause of the increase is the almost complete coverage of all social

TABLE 15
COST OF SOCIAL SECURITY IN COSTA RICA, 1960–1980
(MILLIONS OF COLONES AT CURRENT PRICES)

			Social Security Expenditures[a]		
	GDP	Total Central Govt. Expenditures	Total	GDP	% of Govt. Expenditures
1961	2,929	419	56	1.9	13.4
1965	3,928	649	90	2.3	13.9
1970	6,524	1,192	349	5.3	29.3
1975	16,805	3,544	1,104	6.6	31.2
1979	35,584	8,658	2,764	8.0	31.9
1980	41,405	10,436	3,716	9.0	35.6

Sources: GDP 1961–75 from *Anuario estadístico de Costa Rica, 1977;* 1979–80 from IMF, *International Finance Statistics* (February 1983). Central government expenditures 1961–75 from Banco Central de Costa Rica, *Cifras de cuentas nacionales de Costa Rica, 1957–1977;* 1979–80 from IMF, *Government Finance Statistics Yearbook, 1982.* Social security expenditures 1961–65 from ILO, *The Cost of Social Security;* 1970–75 from CCSS, *Anuario Estadístico, 1970–76,* and Ministerio de Salud, *Memoria, 1982;* and 1979–80 from IMF, *Government Finance Statistics Yearbook, 1982.*

   a. Includes costs of the CCSS and the Ministry of Health; excludes occupational risks expenditures.

risks and the existence of benefits and entitlement conditions that at times surpass the region's average.

Administrative costs of the CCSS in 1977 represented 7 percent of total expenditures, an average for the region but very high for international standards. Furthermore, administrative expenditures apparently rose during the end of the 1970s and continued to do so until 1982. Personnel multiplied almost eight times in 1965–81 (from 1,510 employees to 22,093) as compared with an increase of almost four times in the number of insured (a ratio of 6.2 percent employees per 1,000 insured in 1965 but of 12.6 per 1,000 in 1981). Part of this increase was due to the transfer of hospitals, and of their personnel (between 10,000 and 14,000 employees) to the CCSS in 1973–78, and to the increase in health care to indigents, from a small number to 100,000. But 2,500 additional employees were hired in 1979–82, additional spending that was not justified by a proportional increase in either the number of insured or the number of indigents.[22] In 1970, 58 percent of the operating budget of the CCSS was spent on salaries, and the percentage rose to 67 percent in 1978, although it apparently declined to 57 percent in 1982. Real salaries rose more than three times in 1975–79, and employees received very generous fringe benefits that until recently included a wage contribution exemption for the health-maternity program. Unions constantly push for increases in salary and fringe benefits and block legal dismissals of personnel, while physicians have frequently resorted to strikes to obtain their demands.[23]

Table 16 shows that three-fourths of social security expenditures in Costa Rica are allocated to the health-maternity program. If the expenditures of the MS were included, the proportion would be even larger. But it is noteworthy that the highest proportion was reached in 1970, and the figure then began to decline, while the proportion of expenditures allocated to the pension pro-

TABLE 16

DISTRIBUTION OF SOCIAL SECURITY EXPENDITURES
BY PROGRAM IN COSTA RICA, 1961–1982
(PERCENT)

Expenditure[a]	1961	1965	1970	1975	1982[b]
Old age, disability, survivors	2.7	4.6	6.6	13.3	22.7
Health/maternity	76.7	77.8	78.4	77.4	74.8
Occupational risks	20.6	17.5	15.0	7.3	2.5
Total	100.0	100.0	100.0	100.0	100.0

Source: 1961–1975 from ILO, *The Cost of Social Security, 1975–1977;* 1982 from information from the CCSS, and INS, July 1983.

a. Figures are for the whole system but are limited to benefit expenditures; excludes administration costs and other, nonspecified costs.
b. Distribution of budget expenditures of the CCSS and expenditures of INS.

gram is growing constantly (it multiplied almost eight times in 1961–82) because of the fund's maturation. Within the health-maternity program, a growing percentage of expenditures goes to medical-hospital benefits (from 58 percent in 1960 to 77 percent in 1979), while the percentages allocated to monetary benefits and other expenditures show a tendency to decline. Thus the two most important components with the greatest increases in cost in Costa Rican social security are medical-hospital benefits and pensions, and the latter exhibit the most dynamic trend.

Causes related to the health program. Costa Rica has almost completed the demographic transition period: in 1980, it had the fifth lowest fertility rate in Latin America but also the lowest mortality rates, so that its population growth rate was only slightly lower than the regional average. With the fifth lowest index of demographic dependency in the region (72.4 percent), the Costa Rican population has a disease risk proportionally less than that for the majority of the Latin American countries, and the burden of health costs should also be lower.

One of the principal causes for the rapid increase in the cost of social security is the strong predominance of curative and capital-intensive medicine (operated by the CCSS) over preventive medicine and primary health care (operated by the MS). In 1980 the ratio of expenditures on curative medicine to expenditures on preventive medicine was 4:1 and while the CCSS spent 70 percent of the total health outlays, the MS spent only 17 percent. In 1982, the cost per capita of those covered by the CCSS (insured and welfare recipients) was 2,180 colones (double the amount for 1978), while the cost per capita of those covered by the MS was only 65 colones. An official CCSS document affirms that the primary health care, immunization, and infant nutrition programs of the MS have done more to reduce mortality and morbidity in Costa Rica than the curative programs of the CCSS that treat degenerative and cardiovascular diseases.[24] The director of the best children's hospital in the country proved that the most important factor in reducing infant mortality was the control of infectious diseases, the majority of which are preventable through vaccination and sanitation measures.[25] And the minister of health mentioned the lack of basic equipment and medicines in highly populated rural area as it contrasts with the ultramodern equipment and high technology that abound in the capital to treat a smaller number of patients.[26]

Part of the problem is that in Costa Rica a change in the pathological profile has occurred: the majority of the causes of death are not "diseases of underdevelopment" (such as infectious gastrointestinal diseases) which are relatively easy and inexpensive to eradicate; instead they are the "diseases of development" (such as cancer, heart attacks, and strokes), which are more difficult and expensive to treat. But high costs also result from waste and inefficiency. On the one hand, the new hospitals financed by the IDB in the second half of the 1970s and the beginning of the 1980s were not always built according to functional need criteria but instead had considerable wasted space and expensive decorative detail. On the other hand, several of the old hospitals are in urgent need of repairs and basic equipment.[27] The average national occupancy rate of CCSS hospitals rose from 72 percent to 78 percent in 1976–79, a significant improvement in efficiency, but in the last year, 11 percent of the hospitals had occupancy rates of between 50 percent and 59 percent. The reorganization of infant medical care (for example, decentralization and selective hospitalization), together with preventive methods, made it possible to eliminate a considerable number of beds in pediatric hospitals, but this model has not been applied to adult health care. It is estimated that, for pediatric and gynecological hospitals, the demand for health care in the 1980s will grow much more rapidly than population. Last, 10 percent of health expenditures is in pharmaceutical products, and evidence exists of excess in the prescription and consumption of these products as well as of inadequate control of supplies.[28]

It is noteworthy that part of the costs registered by CCSS are due to the fact that other organizations (the state, the INS, the FA) responsible for financing medical-hospital care by CCSS to the uninsured, do not defray all of the expenses involved in this care. Of the 177,699 uninsured served by the CCSS in 1982, 72 percent were indigents who were the state's responsibility, and the remaining 28 percent were pensioners without means who were the responsibility of the FA. A comparative study of all the health service users in 1980 showed that, in hospital admissions, average number of days of hospital stay, laboratory exams, and medicines, indigents had rates between 1.5 and 12 times higher than the insured. On the other hand, pensioners under the responsibility of the FA had rates from 1.5 to 3 times those of the insured. Also, the two noninsured groups had a higher percentage than the insured of people admitted to the hospital for diseases needing lengthy and complex treatment. Obviously, the noninsured, who have the lowest income, suffer a higher incidence of disease and, as they cannot pay for private care, rely totally on the services of the CCSS. Figures supplied by the fund permit us to calculate that, in 1980, the cost of care per uninsured person was double that per insured, although this difference was somewhat reduced in 1981–82. This calculation does not reveal the entire magnitude of the problem, as the CCSS does not record all of the uninsured whom it serves, does not note the full cost of corresponding services, and apparently underestimates this cost. The state and the FA have not even fulfilled their obligation to cover the cost estimated by the CCSS for care of the uninsured: the accumulated state debt for this concept, in 1977–82, was approximately 1,000 million colones (half the total state debt), and this figure did not include the debt of the FA.[29] A similar problem occurs with the insured of INS who are cared for by contract in facilities of CCSS. It is estimated that 95 percent of the hospitalizations of these insured (involving emergencies and major surgery) are attended by the CCSS, which claims that the real cost of these services exceeds the estimated contract cost. The INS says it is willing to revise the estimate and argues that the problem is due to deficiencies in the CCSS accounting system.[30] Despite its obvious importance, until 1983 no study had been carried out on comparative health costs in CCSS, the MS, INS, and the private sector. INS maintains that visits to doctors and minor surgery in its facilities are less costly than in the CCSS, and this assertion explains the absorption of those services by the INS which, in 1977, were supplied by the CCSS.

Causes related to the pension program. In terms of the pension program cost, Costa Rica has a double advantage over the pioneer countries: it has a newer, less mature program and a younger population. As thirty-four years of contribution are required for retirement at fifty-seven years of age (but twenty years are needed at sixty years of age and ten at sixty-five) and the program began in 1941, there are still not very many pensioners for old age benefits, although there are for disability. As table 17 shows, the proportion of the population over sixty-five was 3 percent in 1960, and this figure had increased only to 3.6 percent in 1980, a lower proportion that in the pioneer nations and comparable to the figure in Mexico and Peru. In terms of revenue, in 1960–80 pension coverage was expanded much more rapidly in Costa Rica than in the pioneer countries, and the elimination of wage ceilings (first those pertaining to incorporation and later those pertaining to contribution) resulted in a significant increase in revenues, which probably compensated for the expansion of coverage to low-income groups. Finally, until the 1980s, Costa Rica had a low unemployment rate, and wages were adjusted to inflation.

But many of the above-mentioned advantages have been gradually disappearing or are balanced, in part, by opposing factors. Table 8 indicates that the quotient of demographic burden (the number of passive insured divided by the number of active insured) rose from 0.031 in 1970 to 0.078 in 1982 and did not rise faster because of the acceleration in coverage. (The quotient of demographic burden is probably greater if independent pension funds— which involve a third of the pensioners—are taken into account, as half of

TABLE 17

DISTRIBUTION OF POPULATION BY AGE GROUP
IN COSTA RICA, 1960–2010
(PERCENT)

Age Group	1960	1970	1980	1990	2000	2010
0–14	47.4	46.1	38.4	36.3	32.5	28.5
15–64	49.6	50.7	58.0	59.6	62.6	65.7
65 and over	3.0	3.2	3.6	4.1	4.9	5.8

Source: Based on CELADE, *Boletín Demográfico* 16:32 (July 1983); calculations by the author.

these funds were created before the CCSS and have more flexible retirement conditions.) But the table shows decreasing rates in the growth of the EAP, while the growth of the active insured in pensions, after accelerating in 1965–80, fell drastically in 1981–82. This drop may be due, in part, to the economic recession that affected employment, but it also represents an expected tendency—that is, the logical decrease of the growth rate of the active insured as the system approaches universal coverage. Also important is the fact that the proportion of the population of productive age in Costa Rica (fifteen to sixty-four years), is smaller than in the pioneer nations.

In the mid-1970s, the pension program began to mature, and table 16 shows that, as the number of pensioners rises, the proportion of social security expenditures destined for pensions also rises; from 2.7 percent in 1961 to 22.7 percent in 1982 (note that the percentage doubled between 1970 and 1975 and almost doubled again between 1975 and 1982). Not only are a greater number of pensioners being maintained by a relatively small number of active contributing insured, but also pensioners live longer. In 1980, it was estimated that 73 percent of males and 82 percent of females reached sixty-five years of age, the second highest proportion in Latin America. In 1950–55, life expectancy for people sixty years of age was fifteen years for men and sixteen years for women, and it must have been even lower when the pension program was established in 1941. In 1975–80, life expectancy for these cohort groups had risen more than two years for men and almost four years for women, and if the group at fifty-five years of age is considered instead (as it is possible to retire at fifty-seven), the respective increases were three years and more than four.[31] These increases surpassed demographers' projections, but it is not known whether they were incorporated into the data used by actuaries. In any case, the quotient of demographic burden in Costa Rica is still very low, and the percentage of expenditures that are dedicated to pensions is much less than in the pioneer nations. But it must be remembered that more than 40 percent of the pension program's reserve funds has been used to subsidize the health-maternity program, and even though these loans are being amortized and now pay interest, the loss resulting from investment of the funds at low or negative rates of return will never be recovered. The decapitalization of the pension fund at the time of the program's maturation suggests that, under the original conditions, the growing obligation to pensions cannot be met.

A final factor of great importance in the increase in pension costs is that these costs have been consistently adjusted for inflation, which is somewhat unusual in Latin America, especially in the last decade. Table 18 shows that, in 1975, 1978, and 1980, real pensions rose in value and, in 1981, had almost doubled their 1970 level. Nevertheless, it must be recalled that the cost of pensions in Costa Rica is a relatively small percentage of social security expenditures, and thus the adjustment of pensions has much less effect on costs than in the pioneer nations.

TABLE 18
REAL VALUE OF ANNUAL PENSIONS IN COSTA RICA, 1970–1981

| | Pensions (thous. of colones) | No. of Pensioners (thous.) | Average Pension per Capita[a] (colones) | Index (1970 = 100) | | |
				Nominal Pension	Inflation[b]	Real Pension
1970	8.4	3.8	2,176	100.0	100.0	100.0
1971	13.7	4.8	2,891	132.8	101.9	130.3
1972	22.6	6.2	3,636	167.0	108.9	153.4
1973	34.1	7.8	4,377	201.1	125.5	160.2
1974	53.9	9.2	5,852	268.9	163.3	164.7
1975	65.3	10.5	6,187	284.3	191.7	148.3
1976	91.3	12.5	7,330	336.8	198.4	169.8
1977	124.3	14.8	8,379	385.0	206.7	186.3
1978	149.8	17.2	8,726	401.0	219.1	183.0
1979	204.3	19.9	10,254	471.2	239.3	196.9
1980	272.4	22.8	11,957	549.4	282.5	194.5
1981	430.6	25.8	16,693	767.0	386.8	198.3

Source: Pensions and number of pensioners from CCSS, Anuario estadístico, 1979–81. Inflation from CEPAL, Estudio económico de América Latina, 1973–81. Average pension and indexes calculated by the author.

Note: The table includes old age, disability, and survivors' pensions in the CCSS and excludes the pensions of independent funds.

a. The calculations of average pensions and pension indexes were made by taking total figures in colones and pensioners.

b. Average annual variation.

The economic crisis of the end of the 1970s, which deepened at the beginning of the present decade, accentuated the financial problems of Costa Rican social security: unemployment rose from 4.1 percent in 1979 to 9.9 percent in 1982, and evasion also rose (these two factors explain the fall in population coverage in 1981, as table 8 shows); payment delays increased, and the state did not fulfill its obligations, at least until 1982; real salaries fell 44 percent between 1979 and 1982, reducing social security revenues; and inflation rose 180 percent in the same period, with a significant impact on costs.[32] All of these developments in turn must have produced an increase in the number of welfare recipients and must thus have increased the costs of the system. Tables 13 and 14 indicate, however, that until 1981 neither stagnation nor deterioration registered in health levels and the real value of benefits, although both may have occurred in 1982–83 (these years saw the strongest deterioration in real salaries).

Measures to Reduce Expenditures

The measures undertaken by the CCSS Emergency Plan to increase revenues have already been summarized; the following focuses on efforts to reduce costs. The plan froze employment, prohibited the substitution of personnel on vacation or with licenses, introduced forced retirement at age sixty, and stimulated voluntary retirement with severance pay, thereby eliminating 1,500 employees. In addition, a study to identify unnecessary or underutilized personnel was undertaken. Nonetheless, until halfway through 1983, there were no massive layoffs of personnel because of the high national rate of unemployment, the certain opposition from unions, and the considerable economic cost of severance pay. The plan also abolished numerous fringe benefits to personnel: exemption wage contribution payments for health-maternity, overtime payments, housing subsidies, free housing for those doing social service, fellowships for foreign study, and extra payments for university degrees; and it also reduced subsidized meals. But a forty-five-day doctors' strike in 1982 led to salary increases that largely offset the above-mentioned savings.[33]

Other measures to reduce costs include: prohibiting hospitals from buying medicine directly in the market, a reduction in the number of medicines on the basic list, development of domestic production of some pharmaceutical products, importation of raw materials to be processed domestically, elimination of extra benefits (such as contact lenses and orthodontics), recycling of disposable articles, prohibition of vehicle purchases, and elimination of the duplication of costly equipment. The closing of several facilities and a freeze on the number of hospital beds have also been considered; a 1981 study of health needs concluded that, if the hospital occupancy rate rose to 95 percent, sufficient hospital beds existed to satisfy demand until 1985. Significant savings in costs should be realized if the emphasis changes from curative and capital-intensive medicine to preventive medicine, primary health care, and the integration of all health services.[34]

USAID is financing a technical assistance program for the CCSS to improve its administrative practices, such as programing purchases, inventory control, cost analysis of industrial production, payment controls, budget elaboration, mechanization of information, and the integration of accounting and the budget. The IDB, in collaboration with the PAHO, is considering a loan for hospital maintenance as well as for other facilities.[35]

A computerized study conducted by the CCSS in 1983 estimated and compared selected indicators to evaluate the cost of services to distinct users (insured, indigents paid for by the state, pensioners paid for by the FA, INS patients, and private users) in order to provide a solid base for readjusting the costs of services provided by the CCSS to other institutions.

Finally, several experiments and studies are being conducted to transfer part of the costs to the private sector and to incorporate this sector for increased efficiency. In 1982–83, the CCSS introduced two agreements with the private sector: (1) private businesses hire a doctor and provide him with the necessary infrastructure (office and nurse) while the CCSS provides support services (laboratory and medicines); and (2) the insured pays for a private doctor's visit and the CCSS provides support services. The INS sells insurance against major medical expense that allows the insured to select a doctor/hospital and then be reimbursed for 60 percent to 80 percent of the expense in accordance with a preestablished tariff.[36] Doctors are considering the creation of cooperatives if more private incentives are introduced by the CCSS. These incentives include reimbursement for part of the costs of private consultation with physicians. This measure would reduce the most serious bottleneck in the CCSS and would provide employment for doctors. Previously, physicians took a negative attitude toward private practice, but the increase in the number of doctors (a surplus of 1,000 physicians is projected for 1987), the economic crises, the freeze on employment in the CCSS, and the fall in doctors' real income have forced them to change their position.[37] Finally, in 1983, the executive director of the CCSS visited the United Kingdom to study experiments in health care, including the payment of doctors in accordance with the number of families registered (rather than the number of visits) and the partial payment of the doctor by the patient.[38]

Other measures that could be introduced to reduce costs might include: (1) the merging of all independent pension funds with the CCSS and subsequent standardization in legal entitlement conditions, so that the costly privileges enjoyed in these funds were eliminated; (2) the elimination of retirement at fifty-seven years of age, with the minimum age fixed at sixty, also fixing of the minimum age at which widows can be eligible for pensions and the elimination of siblings as possible beneficiaries; and (3) the elimination of unnecessary personnel, taking into account that the needs of the insured must take precedence over those of the employees, who could be retrained for other occupations.

THE IMPACT OF SOCIAL SECURITY ON DEVELOPMENT

No studies exist in Costa Rica concerning social security's impact on savings/investment or employment, although there are studies of its impact on the distribution of income.

Savings and Investment

The CCSS pension program, being recent and using the general fixed-premium method (the occupational risks program of INS also) generated a significant surplus. But an important part of this surplus was used to subsidize consumption in the health-maternity program (although it may also have been used for the construction of hospitals). Since the mid-1970s, the pension program's surplus compensated for the deficit in the health-maternity program, basically creating a financial equilibrium—that is to say, no net surplus resulted (see table 12). The relatively heavy burden paid by the insured and the relative solvency of the system (at least until the 1980s) may have reduced the incentive for individual savings. If, as I suggested earlier, the bulk of financing really falls on the employer, the impact on investment must be more negative than if it fell on the insured or the consumer. Finally, until 1982, the pension reserve funds were used to subsidize health expenditures and probably to cover deficits in the state budget (at the beginning of the 1980s, 75 percent of investment was in loans to the health-maternity program and to the state), hence the impact on investment must have been small. Since 1982, however, pension funds have been placed in bank deposits and in the capital market, increasing the impact on investment and yields.

Employment

With respect to the impact on employment, as I have already indicated, legally, two-thirds of the wage contributions are paid by the employer (almost 23 percent over payroll). Because of the advanced labor laws that protect minimum wages and other labor conditions, as well as the militancy of trade unions and other institutional and economic rigidities, the employer could be assumed to pay the greater part of the wage contribution and thus either to lower the demand for labor or to transfer the cost to the consumer. If this interpretation is correct, the increase in unemployment in the 1980s (from 4.1 percent in 1979 to 9.9 percent in 1982) should be a deterrent to further increases in the employer contribution. It would also be counterproductive to create a new employer contribution for the sake of establishing unemployment insurance. In any event these issues require serious study.

Distribution of Income

Social security's impact on the distribution of income appears to be slightly progressive, especially in the wake of the elimination of wage contribution ceilings, the expansion of coverage, and the creation of social welfare programs that provide pensions and health care to the lowest income groups. From the standpoint of financing, the insured's contribution is possibly neutral and that of the state possibly neutral or progressive, as part of it comes from taxes on luxury goods. But if the bulk of the financing comes from the employer and he transfers its costs to the consumer or reduces the demand for labor, the overall impact of financing may be regressive. Benefits, however, probably have a progressive impact because of the system's universality, because care to indigents is free, and because the bulk of expenditures go to the health-maternity program, which usually has a more progressive impact on distribution than the pension program. The net impact of the system is possibly neutral or slightly progressive.

The first study on this subject was carried out in 1973 and measured only the impact of the CCSS health-maternity program on the distribution of personal income. In addition to having serious deficiencies, the study was undertaken prior to the elimination of wage contribution ceilings, the completion of the expansion of coverage, and the introduction of welfare programs. Nonetheless, the study showed that the net impact was slightly progressive. About 2.1 percent of the 2 percent of the population with the highest income, plus 0.2 percent of the next 20 percent of the population were transferred as follows: 1.2 percent to the 20 percent of the population with the lowest income, 0.7 percent to the next 20 percent and the remaining 0.4 percent to the intermediate 20 percent of the population.[39] The second study was conducted in 1978 (when the progressive reforms mentioned above were introduced) and measured the impact of health programs (including not only the CCSS but also the MS and the FA) on family income, so that it is not comparable with the earlier study. The impact of financing was regressive, as families in the lowest income half of the population contributed 3.6 percent more than the half with higher income. On the other hand, the system's total impact was progressive but less so if it was limited to the program of the CCSS: in the total system the poorest 50 percent received 6.3 percent more than in CCSS, while the wealthiest 10 percent received 1.3 percent less in the total system than in CCSS. The net effect of the total system was slightly progressive (but more so than in 1973), with a transfer of 2.3 percent from the wealthiest 30 percent mostly to the poorest 30 percent (see table 19). Nevertheless, if the study had included the pension programs of CCSS and the independent funds, the progressive impact of the system would probably have been reduced.

It has been maintained, rightly, that the transfer of 2.3 percent of family

TABLE 19

IMPACT OF HEALTH PROGRAMS ON THE DISTRIBUTION
OF INCOME IN COSTA RICA, 1978

Decile[a]	Distribution of Family Income (%)		
	Before Health Program	After Health Program	Difference
1	0.7	1.3	0.6
2	2.1	2.7	0.6
3	3.4	3.8	0.4
4	4.6	4.9	0.3
5	5.8	5.9	0.1
6	7.2	7.5	0.3
7	9.1	9.1	0
8	12.1	11.9	−0.2
9	17.2	16.4	−0.8
10	37.8	36.5	−1.3

Sources: Edgar A. Briceño and Eduardo A. Méndez, ''Salud pública y distribución del ingreso en Costa Rica,'' Revista de ciencias económicas, 1:2/2:1–2 (1982): 49–69.

a. In order of increasing income.

income by means of the health program in Costa Rica is, for various reasons, more progressive than table 19 indicates: (1) total health expenditures are too small to have a significant impact on income distribution; (2) if the distribution of income is compared with the distribution of health expenditures, the second is much more progressive than the first; and (3) the health cost per capita in the lowest income deciles is probably much greater than in the highest income deciles.[40] Another, less valid argument states that the referred transfer can practically eliminate, or at least notably reduce, the extreme poverty deficit in the nation (for example, the annual transfer from GDP necessary to eliminate extreme poverty), which was estimated at 2.7 percent in 1980. This argument, however, does not take into account that: (1) the transfer of 2.3 percent from *family income* is substantially less than the estimated transfer of 2.7 percent from GDP; (2) the health program transfers only 0.6 percent of family income to the 20 percent of the population in the lowest income strata (the extreme poverty deficit affects 22 percent of the population); (3) the poverty deficit involves only current transfers and private expenditures and hence excluded investment costs and other components of the health program's expenditures; and (4) the transfer of the health program possibly satisfies needs above the basic ones, which alone are considered in the poverty deficit.[41]

It is impossible to analyze the impact on distribution of the measures introduced by the CCSS in 1982–83 to increase revenues and reduce the expenditures of the system. This topic, like others discussed in this section, demands serious study for more precise evaluation of the repercussions on social security, so that its policies can be programed more efficiently.

3

Cuba:
Socialism and Statization

BY THE END of the 1950s, Cuba, as one of the pioneer countries, had one of the most developed social security systems in the region and was among the top countries in health levels. But the system suffered from extreme stratification, significant inequalities, and severe financial imbalance. Last but not least, it left unprotected the neediest sector of the population.

The advances in Cuban social security in the last quarter century constitute an important achievement of the revolutionary process. The most notable improvements include the creation of a national health system of universal scope that protects the entire resident population; the expansion of coverage in the pension program from 63 percent to 93 percent; the unification and standardization of the pension program, which eliminated its extreme inequalities; the integration of the health system; the reduction in administrative costs and the simplification of the system; and substantial, steady support from the state. In terms of health services and levels, Cuba ranks second in Latin America in the availability of doctors and hospital beds for the population, and first in life expectancy. Together with Costa Rica, it has the lowest infant mortality rate.

Nevertheless, Cuba has two of the problems typical of the pioneer countries: the extremely high cost of social security and its financial disequilibrium. Social security expenditures as a percentage of GDP doubled in 1958–71 (from 6 percent to 12 percent), and although it declined later, in 1980 this percentage was the fourth highest in Latin America. Since the mid-1970s social security has registered a growing deficit that in 1980 equaled almost half of social security revenues (the second highest in the region) and took 1.6 percent of GNP. This financial imbalance has resulted from the universalization of population coverage, from generous benefits and flexible entitlement conditions, from the maturation of the pension program, and from a health care system that—while emphasizing preventive medicine more than most countries in the region—still leans heavily on highly capital-intensive, curative medicine.

Social security is financed by a percentage of the wages paid by enterprises, an amount that is insufficient to keep the system in operation. The possibility of reestablishing equilibrium through an increase in revenues appears remote, and the limited measures undertaken in the last years have aimed to reduce the cost of monetary benefits through temporary postponement of pensions, elimination of benefit payments equivalent to 100 percent of base salary, and erosion of the real value of pensions. These measures have not eliminated the deficit, and therefore study is needed of other, more drastic, measures such as the establishment of stricter entitlement conditions for monetary benefits and a change in the focus of the health system in order to increase efficiency and reduce its high cost.

Paradoxically, even though Cuba has one of the best social security systems in Latin America, statistical information and technical studies of it are extremely scarce. More studies are needed not only for the analysis of a unique model in the region but also for the formulation of effective policies to solve the remaining problems of the system.

HISTORICAL EVOLUTION

The Stratified System

Cuba is one of the region's pioneer countries in social security and, even though it attained a significant level of development prior to the Revolution, the system was stratified and suffered from extreme inequalities and grave financial imbalance.[1] Between 1913 and 1958, fifty-two autonomous pension funds were created: twenty-one covered salaried workers in the private sector (white- and blue-collar), twenty covered professionals, and eleven covered white- and blue-collar workers in the public sector (see table 20). Each fund covered a group of insured from one profession, trade, or sector (for example, lawyers, barbers, and sugar workers), and each had its own legislation, administration, financial source, and benefits. There was no coordination among the funds, much less any transfer of resources among them. Generally the most powerful pressure groups (such as congressional members, governors, and mayors) had the most solvent funds and the most generous benefits, whereas the less powerful groups (such as drivers and barbers) had the poorest funds and the worst benefits. The state, by means of special taxes or general revenue, contributed substantially to the richer funds but contributed only marginally or after long delay or did not contribute at all to the poorer funds. Differences in legal conditions were significant; maximum pensions, for example, fluctuated between 60 and 400 pesos monthly and minimum pensions between 30 and 200 pesos (pensions below the minimum were sometimes paid); some funds permitted retirement at forty-five with fifteen years of employment, while others required sixty years of age and thirty years of employment and a few authorized retirement with thirty years of employment,

TABLE 20
SOCIAL SECURITY LEGISLATION IN CUBA,
BY RISK AND GROUPS COVERED, 1913–1983

Year[a]	Risk Protected	Groups Covered
1913, 1934	ODS	Armed forces
1915	ODS	Communications
1916, 1933	OR	Salaried workers from the public and private sector
1917, 1927	ODS	Judicial branch
1919	ODS	Public employees, public school[b]
1920, 1936	ODS	Police
1921, 1923	ODS	Railroad and telephone workers[b]
1927	ODS	Maritime
1929	ODS	Notaries, recorders of deeds, transportation workers
1934, 1937	M	Salaried workers from the public and private sectors
1935	ODS	Journalists
1938	ODS	Bank employees
1939	ODS	Commercial registrars
1943	ODS	Doctors, sugar workers[b]
1945	ODS	Lawyers, textile workers[b]
1946	ODS	Legal clerks, graphic artists, state workers, barbers and hairdressers, tobacco workers[b]
1947	ODS	Pharmacists[b]
1948	ODS	Customs officials, electricians[b]
1949	ODS	Dentists, veterinarians, architects, commercial workers, flour millers[b]
1950	ODS	Congress members, gastronomists[b]
1951	ODS	Petroleum and radio industry workers[b]
1952	ODS	Insurance and financial workers, nurses[b]
1953	ODS	Brewers
1954	ODS	Civil engineers, stenographers, health sector, construction workers, cattlemen[b]
1955	ODS	Agronomists, schoolteachers (private), educators, comptroller's office workers, agricultural instructors[b]
1956	ODS	Governors, mayors, council members
1957	ODS	Drivers
1959	ODS	Unites institutions of salaried workers in private sector
1960–61	ODS	Unites and regulates public sector institutions
1962	ODS	Unites professional institutions
1963	ODS, TB, H	Unifies entire social security system: regulates and expands monetary benefits to all salaried workers, creates health insurance for entire population, integrates social welfare
1964	ODS, TB	Special system for self-employed workers

(*Continued*)

TABLE 20 (*Continued*)

Year[a]	Risk Protected	Groups Covered
1974	M	New unified maternity system
1976	ODS, TB	Special system for armed forces
1977	OR	Regulates occupational risk prevention and labor hygiene
1979	ODS, TB	New social security system
1983	ODS, TB	Special system for agricultural cooperative members

Source: Legislation.

Note: ODS = old age, disability and survivors' pensions. M = maternity. H = health. TB = temporary benefits. OR = occupational risks.

a. The first date refers to the original law; following dates refer to modifications.
b. Established by separate laws.

regardless of age. It has been estimated that, in 1958, all funds covered between 55 percent and 63 percent of the EAP, the second or third highest percentage in the region, but the neediest groups remained unprotected: the bulk of agricultural workers (only the sectors with strong unions—such as sugar, tobacco, and cattle raising—were covered), the majority of self-employed workers (especially urban marginal groups in services and agriculture), and all domestic servants.

Health insurance (for common illness) did not exist, even though, as in other countries (such as Argentina and Uruguay), an important urban network of mutual-aid-society clinics and nonprofit cooperatives had been developed, supplemented by public hospitals and private clinics. As in the case of pensions, the lowest income strata—especially in rural zones—either received no health care at all or received care of very low quality. Public officials were entitled to one month of sick leave at full salary (plus another month at half pay), whereas workers in the private sector were entitled to only nine days of sick leave, and the legal obligation was not always enforced, especially in the nonunionized agricultural sector. All employed female workers were covered by maternity insurance established in 1934, which provided leave with salary and health benefits, while the wives of the insured were entitled to medical-hospital care. Even though Cuba did not have health insurance early on—as did Chile, Peru, Mexico, and Costa Rica—its general health levels were among the highest in the region (see table 25, below), surpassing those of the countries just named and similar to those of the most advanced countries (such as Argentina and Uruguay). Nevertheless, differences between urban and rural sectors were highly accentuated. Only one rural hospital existed in 1958, and 60 percent of the physicians and hospital beds were located in Havana, the capital city, which housed only 20 percent of the population.

After 1916 the labor force was legally protected against occupational risks through commercial insurance administered by twenty-five private companies, but they charged high commissions and frequently were guilty of abusing injured workers.

Even though the effect of social security on the distribution of income was not measured, it was considered to be regressive: the funds covering the highest income groups had lower contributions for the insured but substantial state contributions, whereas the funds covering the lowest income groups had higher contributions for the insured and received either no state contributions or only meager ones. The noninsured population probably contributed to the coverage of the insured through taxes while receiving nothing from the system in return. Pension reserve funds, especially those of private salaried workers, were invested largely in state bonds—normally used to cover budget deficits—which had little real value and yields. In addition the state did not fulfill many of its financial obligations to the pension funds. About half of these funds had accounting deficits (some of them had to prorate benefit payments), and only 10 percent followed established actuarial practices. In 1957 the general comptroller (Tribunal de Cuentas) predicted that all of the funds, with a few exceptions, would face severe crisis and insolvency in the near future.

Between 1944 and 1957 no fewer than eight studies on social security in Cuba were carried out, and practically all of them recommended reforming the system along the lines of unification. One of these studies, elaborated in 1950 as part of the Word Bank's general report on the Cuban economy, recommended the creation of a single administrative agency, uniform legislation, the elimination of regressive taxes, and the preparation of actuarial studies.[2] Another study, the most comprehensive and technical, which was carried out by an ILO mission, concentrated on the pension programs and recommended unification of the public sector funds and a series of alternative solutions for private sector funds, ranging from total unification—under an autonomous organization—to continuing the funds but with coordination and reform.[3] But the powerful pressure groups systematically opposed reform, and the state was unable to eliminate stratification, inequalities, and financial crisis from the system.

Unification and Standardization of the System

The Revolution reinforced the power of the state and weakened the pressure groups, thus permitting unification and standardization to occur gradually in the system. The state gradually seized all funds and programs: in 1959 the pension funds of private salaried workers; in 1960 the pension funds of the public sector and maternity insurance; and in 1962 the pension funds of professionals and occupational risk insurance. These funds/programs ceased to be autonomous and began to be administered by the Ministry of Labor. The latter standardized contributions and established a general minimum for all pensions (forty pesos in 1960 and sixty pesos in 1969), which represented a substantial increase for the broad low-income stratum of the population. A constitutional reform gave power to the executive to loan the reserve pension funds to national socioeconomic development programs, such as agrarian reform and housing. In the 1960s, all private hospitals, mutual-aid-society clinics, and cooperatives were nationalized and unified under the Ministry of Public Health (MINSAP). The incipient pharmaceutical industry was also nationalized, and from 1965 onward, all doctors had to swear an oath at graduation renouncing private practice in their profession.

The standardization of the social security system and expansion of coverage were brought about through a 1983 law that universalized pension coverage to all the salaried labor force and introduced a national health care program to cover the entire population; established the exclusive responsibility of the state to finance social security; and standardized both entitlement conditions and the method of calculating them. Subsequent laws regulated conditions for pensions and other monetary benefits for special groups: in 1964 professionals, self-employed workers, small businessmen, and the members of fishing and charcoal cooperatives; in 1966 private farmers who, because of old age or disability, had sold their lands to the state; in 1976 the armed forces; and in 1983 members of agricultural production cooperatives. Also, in 1974 and 1977 unified norms for maternity and occupational risks were introduced. Finally, a 1979 law—currently in force—integrated the social security system as a whole and placed it under the administration of the State Committee of Labor and Social Security (CETSS), which replaced the Ministry of Labor (see table 20).[4]

In summary, social security developed early in Cuba, as in other pioneer nations, but in a fragmented manner, responding to pressure groups with diverse powers. The result was a relatively advanced system for the era yet one that was very stratified and unequal and lacked coordination. The Revolution, reinforcing the power of the state, brought about the unification and standardization of the system (with some exceptions) as well as universal coverage.

ORGANIZATIONAL STRUCTURE

The present social security system in Cuba, like that in other centrally planned economies, is run completely by the state, has a high degree of unity and standardization, and is incorporated in national planning. Nevertheless, it is officially reported that there still exist gaps in the planning process that must be filled to create greater rationality and quality in the plans and to permit better evaluation of administrative efficiency.[5] The system integrates social insurance, social welfare, and health care, although these programs are the responsibility of different state agencies.

The principal agency is the CETSS, which is responsible for all aspects of labor and social security such as execution, control, and inspection. The CETSS administers the old age, disability, and survivors' pension program financed by the state social security budget. The CETSS also formulates policy for the social welfare program and controls its execution.

The national health system is administered by the MINSAP and is financed by the state health budget. It relies on an extensive national network of hospitals, polyclinics, and health posts organized in pyramidal form with various levels: the national, the provincial, and the local. The system provides medical-hospital, rehabilitation, and odontological care and medicines for common or occupational accidents and diseases, and maternity. The MINSAP is responsible for curative and preventive medicine (both are well integrated), operates welfare institutions (such as homes for the elderly and disabled), and administers all pharmaceutical enterprises (which satisfy most national demand). Apart from the MINSAP there are rehabilitation centers with their own administration and budget.

Monetary benefits such as subsidies for common illness, maternity, and occupational risks, as well as partial disability and provisional pensions and funeral aid, are administered by state enterprises and are financed by the social security budget.

The Organs of People's Power (OPP), municipal and provincial agencies in which the people participate, administer provisional pensions for the families of retired workers, some partial disability pensions, and funeral aid. These are financed by the state social security budget. The OPPs also confer social welfare monetary benefits as well as some benefits in kind.

The Ministries of the Armed Forces (MINFAR) and of the Interior (MININ) administer all pensions and monetary benefits for these two groups, under their own budgets. These two groups are integrated with the rest of the population in the national health system.

The insured population does not directly participate in the administration of social security except within the OPPs. There are also labor councils that, on the first appeal, resolve claims against state enterprises concerning short-term benefits. However, when the enterprise and the labor council disagree, the council's decision is annulled, and the issue passes to regular courts. Finally, various mass organizations, such as the Committees for the Defense of the Revolution (CDR), the National Association of Small Farmers (ANAP), the Federation of Cuban Women (FMC), and the unions participate in vaccination campaigns, health education, control of contagious diseases, blood donations, and community activities.

The Cuban social security system is the most unified and standardized in Latin America. Nevertheless, there still exist special regulations that favor certain groups over others. I will discuss these differences below.

POPULATION COVERAGE

Legal Coverage

As Cuba does not publish statistics on social security coverage of the population, the analysis in this section must be based exclusively on legal coverage.[6] According to law, the entire population is covered by the health-maternity program for nonmonetary benefits in kind and services. In addition, all salaried workers (in the state and in the cooperative and private sectors) are entitled to monetary benefits—for example, pensions and temporary benefits, such as subsidies in lieu of salary for sickness or accident (common or work-related) and maternity. Finally, the insured's dependents are entitled to survivors' pensions and funeral aid. Family coverage in pensions is generous in scope (but not as generous as in Costa Rica) and includes: widows (although they are entitled to a pension for only two years if they are younger than forty, without children, and capable of working); widowers (if they are older than sixty or disabled); and parents and minor unmarried (or disabled) children. There is neither unemployment insurance (but see "Benefits and Entitlement Conditions" below) nor a program of family allowances.[7]

Members of agricultural-livestock, fishing, and charcoal cooperatives who sell their products to the state have compulsory coverage, and even though they are not salaried workers, they are entitled to the same monetary benefits that salaried workers receive. Members of the armed forces also have compulsory coverage and are entitled to all monetary benefits but under a subsystem that is separate from the general system.

Noncovered Population

Three population groups are entitled to none of the monetary benefits or only part of them. (1) Owners of small farms—the most important private property sector that remains in Cuba—are excluded from all monetary benefits if they are not integrated in agricultural production cooperatives. Nevertheless, elderly, sick, or disabled owners who sell their farms to the state receive, in exchange, a life pension that at the time of death can be transferred to their dependents. (2) Independent workers, such as university or nonuniversity professionals, self-employed workers, and small entrepreneurs in the service sector can choose voluntary coverage in pensions but are excluded from temporary monetary benefits. (3) The unemployed, unpaid family workers, and apparently also domestic servants in the private sector are not entitled to any monetary benefits. Those not covered by insured monetary benefits can, if they are without means, receive social welfare benefits; included in this category are the elderly, the disabled, single mothers with children, and all those whose essential needs are not insured.

The law obviously discriminates against groups that carry out activities which in the state's view should disappear in the future communist society; such groups are partly or fully excluded from compulsory coverage of insured monetary benefits. Although such activities do not conform to the communist ideal in production relationships, they are permitted in the socialist transition stage for practical reasons. The excluded groups are those who appropriate the fruits of their labor as either farm owners or self-employed workers; the state allows them to function temporarily because of their contribution to production. Cooperative members (who represent the intermediate sector between private and state labor) are given full coverage as an incentive to stimulate them to make the transition from private activities to a level considered ideologically higher in production relationships, if not the superior one.

Estimation of Statistical Coverage

Table 21 gives a rough estimate of population coverage, based on the law, the composition of the labor force according to the 1970 and 1981 census, and a 1979 national demographic survey. The total population is assumed to be completely covered for health-maternity, although with differences in access and quality of medical and hospital services, to be discussed below. To calculate pension coverage of the EAP in 1981 (3,617,600), the private farm owners that are not integrated in cooperatives (124,904), the unemployed (121,700), and unpaid family workers (7,025) are subtracted from the group of active insured; the remainder is the population with pension coverage (3,364,000). Also, 46,511 independent workers in 1981 were not covered for temporary monetary benefits and were entitled to voluntary insurance in pensions. EAP coverage must thus be lower than it appears in the table (91.7 percent if none of these workers was insured).[8]

As the rough estimates of table 21 show, Cuba increased health-maternity coverage of the population from 4.2 percent in 1958 (zero if only health coverage is considered) to 100 percent in 1970. This change accounts for the most rapid and universal expansion in the whole region. Coverage of the EAP rose from almost 63 percent in 1958 to 93 percent in 1981, putting Cuba in second place for the region and, if the social welfare program is taken into account, bringing about universal coverage as well. Cuba is one of the few Latin American countries in which the extreme poverty group is covered by the social security system.[9]

Determinant Structural Factors

In the 1960s Cuba replaced the old Bismarckian social insurance model with the social security model. To the extent that the new model is basically

TABLE 21
SOCIAL SECURITY COVERAGE OF POPULATION IN CUBA, 1958–1981

| | Total Population (thous.) | EAP (thous.) | Insured Population (thousands) | | | | % of Coverage[c] | | Average Annual Growth Rates (log) | | | | Quotient of Demographic Burden[d] |
			Actives[a]	Passives	Remaining Insured in Health[b]	Total	Total Population	EAP	Total Population	EAP	Insured Active	Insured Total	
1958	6,824	2,218	1,388	154	*	290[c]	4.2	62.6	**	**	**	**	0.111
1970	8,569	2,633	2,337	363	5,869	8,569	100.0	88.7	1.9	1.4	4.4	32.6	0.155
1979	9,811	3,458	3,100	671[f]	6,040	9,811	100.0	89.6	1.5	3.1	3.2	1.5	0.216
1981	9,724	3,618	3,364	710[f]	5,650	9,724	100.0	93.0	-0.4	2.3	4.2	-0.4	0.211

Source: Total population and EAP: 1958 from Mesa-Lago, *The Economy of Socialist Cuba* (Albuquerque: University of New Mexico Press, 1981); 1970 from population census; 1979 from National Demographic Survey; and 1981 from population census. Actives: 1958 from *Social Security in Cuba* (Coral Gables, Fla: University of Miami Press, 1964); 1970 to 1981 estimates of the author based on Legislation, population census figures, and the 1979 survey. Passives from Mesa-Lago, *The Economy of Socialist Cuba*, p. 171, and estimates based on *24 años de revolución en la seguridad social cubana* (Havana: CETSS, 1983). Percentages, rates, and quotients calculated by the author.

a. Excludes unemployed and unpaid family workers and private farmers not integrated into cooperatives.
b. Coverage according to the law; coverage statistics are not published.
c. "Total population" coverage refers to health (maternity in 1958). EAP coverage means old age, disability, and survivors'pensions.
d. Number of passives divided by active insured.
e. Women employed and covered by maternity insurance.
f. The 1979 survey showed 505,054 retirees and pensioners plus those who received housing payments or welfare assistance from the state whereas the 1981 census showed 607,700. Both figures are much lower than those in the table. The number of pensioners in 1983 rose to 769,800, according to CETSS (figures provided in March 1984).

* Not applicable.

**Not available.

financed by contributions from state enterprises, it could be argued that the barriers to expansion associated with the three-part contribution have been eliminated. But Cuba in fact excludes the nonsalaried sectors from monetary benefits (or makes their inclusion voluntary); these same sectors are typically excluded by countries with a traditional form of financing. Thus, as in the case of Costa Rica, high coverage and its rapid expansion in Cuba were facilitated by a very high percentage of salaried workers (the highest in the region: 92 percent in 1981) and very low percentages of self-employed workers and private farmers (4.4 percent), unpaid family workers (0.2 percent), and unemployed (3.4 percent). In addition, Cuba is a relatively small country with an excellent communication network and a very high degree of urbanization (69 percent). Still, regardless of these favorable structural characteristics, the attainment of universal health coverage in less than a decade is a remarkable achievement.

Differences in Population Coverage

The high degree of universality, unity, and standardization in the Cuban social security system probably makes differences in coverage among occupational sectors and geographic areas small. Unfortunately, this statement cannot be proved as in other countries because coverage statistics for Cuba are lacking. As a proxy, table 22 shows the estimated differences in monetary benefits and health services among Cuba's fifteen provinces in 1982. The table shows that the province City of La Habana (the most developed and urbanized province, where the bulk of industry and services concentrate) receives twice the benefits per capita, has almost six times the number of physicians per 10,000 inhabitants, and has almost three times the number of hospital beds per 1,000 inhabitants than the province of Granma (one of the most rural and underdeveloped provinces). Other rural and agricultural provinces, such as Las Tunas, Holguín, and Guantánamo also have indexes lower than those of La Habana and other more urban and industrial provinces. Nevertheless, in the 1960s, Cuba succeeded in carrying out a program to develop medical and hospital services in rural zones that notably reduced these differences: in 1978 there were fifty-seven rural hospitals and the concentration of beds and doctors in La Habana (21 percent of the population) had been reduced from 60 percent (in 1958) to 39 percent and 36 percent, respectively. Also, as I noted in the case of Costa Rica, a certain concentration of medical-hospital services in the capital and most populated cities is explained by the presence there of higher-level services that legally serve the whole country.

Current inequalities in monetary benefits result from income differences that, although relatively small in Cuba compared with those in the rest of the region, still exist and serve as the basis for calculation of those benefits. When monetary benefits are disaggregated into those of the insured type (for example, pensions) and those of social welfare; it also appears that the most-

TABLE 22

DIFFERENCES IN HEALTH BENEFITS AMONG PROVINCES IN CUBA, 1982

Province	Per Capita Monetary Benefit Expenditures[a] (pesos)	Physicians per 10,000 Persons	Hospital and Welfare Beds per 1,000 Persons
Pinar del Río	66.81	11.8	4.6
La Habana	99.85	14.0	2.6
Ciudad de La Habana	120.48	41.2	11.2
Matanzas	95.47	16.9	5.4
Villa Clara	93.05	11.7	4.2
Cienfuegos	86.09	12.5	4.8
Sancti Spiritus	85.62	10.1	4.5
Ciego de Avila	79.78	11.4	3.5
Camagüey	79.35	13.5	6.3
Las Tunas	65.30	8.9	4.6
Holguín	58.02	8.6	3.9
Granma	50.34	7.2	4.1
Santiago de Chile	58.74	12.8	5.5
Guantánamo	52.83	8.9	5.1
Isla de la Juventud	47.69	16.4	7.2
Total	82.20	17.3	5.9

Source: Estimates of the author based on *Anuario estadístico de Cuba, 1982*, pp. 127, 465, 472–73.

a. Includes monetary benefits (pensions as well as temporary benefits), and social welfare; excludes medical-hospital benefits and administrative costs.

developed provinces receive a very high proportion of the insured type and a very low proportion of the welfare type, whereas, in the less-developed provinces, the opposite occurs. For example, in 1982, the province City of La Habana received the highest per capita pension (98 pesos) and the lowest per capita welfare payment (1.7 pesos), whereas Granma province received the lowest pension (34 pesos) and the highest welfare payment (5.4 pesos).[10] These figures show that, despite the remarkable advances attained, differences in access to (or the quality of) health services and monetary benefits still persist in Cuba. Although these differences have been significantly reduced in the last two decades, their persistence suggests disparities in effective coverage. While the differences in health services between the best- and the worst-endowed provinces are, at times, greater in Cuba than in the other countries studied, there is compensation, as the lower (and higher) levels in Cuba are generally higher than those of the other countries.

Measures to Improve Coverage

Although Cuba has the broadest legal coverage in Latin America and has probably attained effective universality, it is important for figures on statistical coverage to be published. In addition, coverage in monetary benefits should be extended to the small sector that is currently excluded, and efforts to reduce differences among provinces should continue.

FINANCING

Sources of Financing

Prior to the Revolution, a great diversity in wage contributions existed among the fifty-two pension funds. On the one hand, in the salaried workers' funds in the private and public sectors, the insured legally contributed close to half of income, the employer a bit more than one-third, and the state somewhat over one-tenth. On the other hand, within professionals' funds, the insured who enjoyed higher income than salaried workers contributed only one-fourth of income. As the majority were self-employed, the employer contribution was minimal, but the state strongly subsidized this group by contributing three-fifths of income.[11]

In the course of gradual unification of the pension funds, the wage contribution was standardized, so that previous inequities were largely eliminated. In the private salaried workers' funds a wage contribution of 5 percent was fixed for the insured and another 5 percent for the employer (without state contributions); in the public sector salaried workers' funds, the entire contribution (10 percent) was charged to the insured; and in the professionals' funds the insured was also charged the entire contribution (10 percent). Finally, in 1962, the contribution of the salaried workers' funds (for both sectors) was standardized at 10 percent and was paid exclusively by employers.[12]

Table 23 shows the present situation of wage contributions in both the general system and special systems for monetary benefits (there is no information for the armed forces and internal security): (1) the salaried insured (and fishing and charcoal cooperative members) pay nothing, and the 10 percent contribution is paid by enterprises that are all practically state owned;[13] (2) the self-employed pay the entire contribution (10 percent) but on estimated income; (3) agricultural cooperative members pay only 3 percent on average daily income; and (4) the state covers whatever deficit occurs. By means of legal differentiation in placement and quantity of contributions, the social security system establishes incentives for the transfer of independent labor to state labor.

There are no wage contributions for financing medical-hospital benefits, as their total cost is paid for by the state budget assigned to the MINSAP. As the program for occupational risks is not separate from other programs, but instead forms part of the two basic types of benefits, no contribution is involved here either.

According to Marxist theory, value is totally created by labor. From the "total social product" a sum or fund is deducted for accumulation and another

TABLE 23

LEGAL CONTRIBUTIONS TO SOCIAL SECURITY
BY PROGRAM AND SOURCE IN CUBA, 1983
(PERCENTAGE OF SALARY OR INCOME)

	Insured			
Program	Salaried[a]	Self-employed[b]	Cooperative Member[c]	Employer[d]
Monetary benefits[e]	*	10	3	10
Medical-hospital Benefits	*	*	*	*
Total	*	10	3	10

Source: Legislation.

    a. From the private, state, and cooperative sectors.
    b. Upon the conventional monthly salary selected. Voluntary affiliation.
    c. Members of agricultural and livestock (in the fishing and charcoal cooperatives that sell to the state, the same system as for salaried workers is applied). The percentage is on average daily income.
    d. For state as well as private: the latter pays 25 percent for income tax and social security contributions. It is not specified what the contribution of the state-employer is for the armed forces and internal security forces.
    e. Monetary benefits for pensions (old age, disability and survivors'), temporary aid (for disease, maternity, and accident) and social welfare; covers common risks as well as occupational risks.

    *Not applicable.

sum or fund for consumption; part of the latter is used to satisfy collective necessities ("social salary") such as social security and health care. The part of the product that is not returned to the worker is called "surplus product" (surplus value in the capitalist system), and from this comes the social security contribution.[14] In this connection the CETSS states: "Social security is part of the consumption fund disaggregated in salary and social security, and that are extracted from the total social product and included in the annual budget of the nation."[15].

    Apart from the wage contribution (or income contribution), Cuban social security has no funding: there are no reserves and hence no investments; there are no special taxes, lottery revenues, or loans from the exterior directly assigned to the system. Nevertheless, Cuba receives a large amount of economic aid on generous terms from the Soviet Union, and part of this aid may have been used to finance the social security system.[16]

Evasion and Payment Delays

    Although information is scarce, it can be assumed that evasion and delayed payments are of little importance in Cuba for the following reasons. According to the 1981 census, 93 percent of the labor force was employed as salaried workers in the state sector, only 0.7 percent was salaried in the private sector, and 0.9 percent were members of cooperatives. The National Bank of Cuba is responsible for collecting all contributions and for carrying out audits of the system. In addition, periodic fiscal balances and computerized control at the national level should detect irregularities in payments, especially in the state sector. Deficits of the system are automatically covered by the state in the national budget.

The cooperative sector is integrated into the state plan, but contributions are deducted from profits. Although evasion and payment delays in this area also appear difficult, more opportunities and incentives for evasion may exist here than in the state sector. The bulk of the private salaried workers work for small farm owners who are associated with, and supervised by, the ANAP. Nevertheless, in 1982 it was reported that a certain number of these workers operated clandestinely.[17] Evasion is thus possibly greater in this sector.

In any case, the high centralization and strong control, the simplicity of the contribution method, and the single collection agency probably make the Cuban social security system the most efficient in the region in terms of minimizing evasion and payment delays. Finally, according to legislation, evasion and payment delays on the part of an employer do not affect the worker's rights to monetary benefits as long as s/he can prove that s/he is employed.

Financing Method

All social security contributions enter the state budget as one of several sources of income, and in turn, the budget assigns expenditure lines to the CETSS, the MINSAP, the OPPs, the rehabilitation centers, and the state enterprises. The CETSS confirms that "the financing of Cuban social security is based on a method that approximates what we call pure assessment under the state budget."[18] But note that this is a sui generis pure assessment method, as the state absorbs all revenue and covers any deficit in the system, and that the contribution percentage has not been raised in more than two decades. Hence financial equilibrium is established not within the social security system (it has no independent accounting) but within the macroeconomic framework.

Also, as Cuba does not keep individual accounts for the insured, an appropriation in the national budget could be substituted for the enterprise contribution. In accounting terms, this would be simpler and would eliminate collection costs. The sole reason offered for maintaining the enterprise contribution was that given in 1965: the cost of social security should be covered by an increase in labor productivity.[19] But the increase in the cost of social security in the period 1978–82 surpassed the increment in national labor productivity by 3 percent.[20] Furthermore, the connection between the cost of social security and labor productivity in Cuba can be controlled at the macroeconomic level better than at the microeconomic, given that salaries are centrally fixed and that, even though enterprises since the end of the 1970s have had greater flexibility in hiring and firing personnel, their power in this area is much less than in the majority of enterprises in market economies of Latin America. The persistence of the enterprise contribution is thus better explained by symbolic considerations than by practical reasons.

Prior to the 1963 law, the ILO carried out an actuarial study of the system's possible cost. In an official document of 1965, however, it was assured that periodic actuarial balances had no meaning in Cuba as financial instruments; the budget of the following period adjusts for any disequilibrium that occurs.[21] And yet, prior to the social security law of 1979—currently in force—an actuarial study was done to determine the probable cost of the new system.[22] Even though the social security system is not pushed toward equilibrium as conventional systems or pure assessment are, the actuarial balance (which takes into account changes in legal, biometric, and economic conditions) should be important both in determining the future social security burden on the national economy and undertaking the necessary planning measures to adjust this burden in accordance with the country's economic capacity.

Financial Equilibrium

Cuba has sporadically published figures on the partial cost of monetary benefits and health care expenditures, but there is no recent information on the revenue generated by contributions. In the state budgets of 1962–66 the revenues generated by social security contributions were reported, but the budget was then not published for more than ten years, and when publication was resumed in 1978, social security revenue was no longer reported separately. On the expenditure side, while insurance and welfare monetary benefits have always been published in the budget, they have appeared only as part of a large, clustered category that includes cultural and scientific services. Health care expenditures also appears in the budget but are merged with educational expenditures.[23] In several official publications, expenditures of monetary benefits have been separately listed for 1959–82, but the information on health care expenditures is less systematic and detailed.

Table 24 reconstructs the balance of revenues and expenditures for social security monetary benefits. The figures reflect official statistics in the period 1962–74 but only on official expenditures for 1978 to 1982. Income in 1978–82 was estimated by the author at 10 percent of the wage fund (the latter based on official figures). As it was assumed that evasion and payment delays were nonexistent, revenues are probably slightly overestimated. On the other hand, total expenditures must be greater, as the table excludes occupational risk prevention and rehabilitation as well as administrative costs. Finally, it can be assumed that the part of the budget (revenues and expenditures) designated for health care is balanced, hence it does not affect the total balance

TABLE 24
SOCIAL SECURITY BALANCE OF REVENUES AND EXPENDITURES
IN CUBA, 1962–1982
(MILLIONS OF PESOS AT CURRENT PRICES)

	1962	1965	1974	1978	1980	1982
Revenues[a]	322.4	344.5	422.7	459.1	485.1	608.9
Expenditures[b]	151.9	249.8	553.4	648.0	709.3	809.0
Balance	170.5	94.7	−130.7	−188.9	−224.2	−200.1
As a percentage of revenues	52.9	27.5	−30.9	−41.1	−46.2	−32.9

Sources: Revenues for 1962–65 from the national budget published in the *Gaceta oficial;* 1974 from Seminario Latinoamericano de Cuentas Nacionales y Balances de la Economía, *Cuba: Conversión de los principales indicadores macroeconómicos del sistema de balances de la economía nacional (SBEN) al sistema de cuentas nacionales (SCN) 1974* (Havana, March 1982); 1978 to 1982 estimated by author as 10 percent of total wage bill (based on *Anuario 1982*). Expenditures from the same sources as for table 26.

a. Excludes revenues of the health system.
b. Expenditures for pensions, temporary benefits (both excluding the armed forces), and social welfare; excludes administrative expenditures and expenditures for health, prevention, and rehabilitation associated with occupational risks.

of the system. The description presented suggests that the estimated deficit figures are conservative.

Table 24 shows that the social security balance was a decreasing surplus in the first half of the 1960s and a growing deficit in the second half of the 1970s. In 1980 the deficit was almost equivalent to half of revenues: 224 million pesos, representing 1.3 percent of the global social product (GSP) of 17,590 million pesos.[24] Cuba follows the material production system (MPS rather than a system of national accounts SNA). The GSP excludes the value of nonmaterial services ("nonproductive services")—that is, services that are not directly linked to material production, such as social security, health care, education, finance, administration, and defense. In this sense, the GSP should be less than the GDP. On the other hand, the MPS involves a duplication in accounting, as it does not follow the value-added method used by the SNA. In this sense, the GSP should be greater than the GDP.[25] The 1974 GSP was reported at 13,424 million pesos, and a GDP estimate for that year done in Cuba was 9,239 million pesos.[26] The effect of accounting duplication was therefore probably much greater than that of the omission of nonmaterial services, although this discrepancy seems to have been somewhat reduced by the introduction of a change in MPS methodology in 1977. More recently Cuba reported the 1980 GNP at 14,230 million pesos;[27] hence the social security deficit in that year would be 1.6 percent of GNP. As a percentage of income, the deficit was the second highest in Latin America in 1980.

The acceleration of inflation in Cuba in 1980–81 and the erosion of the real value of benefits (which I will discuss below) reduced the 1981 deficit to 29 percent of income, although it rose again, in 1982, to 33 percent. I will discuss this reduction in the rate of cost increase shortly. For the moment it suffices to note that such a reduction is unlikely to be maintained in the future.

Although a Cuban official has roughly estimated that the cost of monetary benefits takes about 20 percent of the wage funds (that is, twice the current 10 percent charged), Cuba's social security administration takes the view that their system shows no deficit. The administrators argue that the state controls the entire economy and guarantees that it will cover any resulting deficit, hence there is no strict dependence on contributions: whatever funds are annually needed are taken from the GSP and are earmarked in the state budget. However, the administrators acknowledge that a limit is imposed by the economic capacity of the country.[28] At this point the discussion may appear to be a matter of semantics, but the crucial facts are, first, that the Cuban system does not have the clear accounting of social security revenues and expenditures that is needed to estimate whether the country can economically afford such a burden and, second, that current expenditures for social security absorb about twice the current contribution of state enterprises.

Measures to Increase Revenue

Within the context of Latin American social security, Cuba in 1980 had not only the second largest deficit and third highest costs (expenditures/GDP) but also the lowest total percentage of wage contribution. Cuban social security has not suffered a financial crisis because the state, since the mid-1970s, has covered its growing deficits. But state support obviously does not solve the problem of the system's heavy burden and financial disequilibrium; the system's revenues must be increased and/or expenditures reduced.

The Cuban government could raise the wage contribution of employers (and independent workers) without encountering the powerful opposition from enterprises and unions that is typical in Latin America. Inasmuch as the state is practically the sole employer and has total control over the economy, basically all that would be needed would be an executive decision. Nonetheless, an increase in wage contributions would be merely an accounting or formal instrument that would balance the social security budget but would not really solve the basic problem.

On the other hand, the establishment of a contribution for the insured salaried workers (and/or an increase in the contribution of independent workers and/or cooperative members) that would reduce real salaries (income) and would thus reduce consumption would possibly eliminate the social security disequilibrium. Another possibility would be to introduce a minimum fee for the use of medical-hospital services and medicines (exempting the lowest income sector of the population); this measure would also have the advantage of controlling excess use of these services. But these methods would have serious political repercussions, would conflict with the carefully preserved image of a system that operates free of charge, and would affect the population's level of consumption.[29] Consequently, attempts to achieve financial equilibrium in the system should attempt to reduce costs.

BENEFITS, EXPENDITURES, AND COSTS
Benefits and Entitlement Conditions

Medical-hospital benefits in Cuba have a uniform system, although there are differences in accessibility and in the quality of services. Within the general system, monetary benefits are standardized, but special systems (including one for the armed forces) exist with different entitlement conditions.

Medical-hospital benefits—to which the total population is entitled except where occupational risks are concerned—include preventive and curative medical care plus odontology, surgery, hospitalization, medicines (only during hospitalization in the case of common accident or disease but at any time for occupational risks, the elderly in nursing homes, and the poor), rehabilitation, orthopedics, and prosthesis (these last three only in cases of occupational risk). Monetary benefits—to which the active insured are entitled except in the case of survivors' pensions received by dependents—include a subsidy in lieu of salary for sickness, maternity, or accident (with a greater percentage of salary if the award relates to occupational risks) and pensions for old age, disability, and survivors. In addition, there is funeral aid, consisting of a casket, transportation, and burial of the insured.

Until the 1980s, there was no monetary benefits for unemployment (although the unemployed are entitled to medical-hospital benefits), as it was adduced that there was full employment in Cuba.[30] According to official figures, open unemployment was reduced from 13.6 percent in 1959 to 1.3 percent in 1970 (one of the most positive achievements of the Revolution), but the rate later rose to 5.4 percent in 1979 and then fell to 3.4 percent in 1981.[31] Even though these rates are very low, unemployment obviously does exist in Cuba. The unemployed, on occasion, have temporarily been maintained on the enterprise payroll or in special funds while they are retrained or find another occupation. With greater unemployment pressure in the 1970s—pressure that was expected to continue throughout the 1980s—the problem has been officially recognized, and some measures have been introduced to deal with the situation; one solution has been to pay 70 percent of the unemployed's salary in certain cases.[32]

Cuban social security does not include a formal program of family allowances in terms of monetary benefits for children. Nevertheless, a national program of day care centers provides food and education to children (from forty-five days to five years old) of working mothers. Originally the program was free; now parents contribute to its financing.[33]

In the Latin American context, Cuban benefits are among the most generous and entitlement conditions among the most flexible. There is no qualification period or time limit on medical-hospital benefits, nor is there a qualification period for receiving sickness subsidy and the qualification period for the maternity subsidy is very low. In addition, the percentage of salary paid as subsidy surpasses the regional average. Although seniority retirement does not exist in Cuba (except in the armed forces), old people retire at ages similar to the legal averages for the region (sixty years for men and fifty-five years for women, both of whom must have completed twenty-five years of employment). These ages appear very low when one recalls that Cuba has the highest life expectancy in Latin America and that women live an average of three years more than men (even more significant in view of the differences in retirement age). Furthermore, Cuba requires five years less employment for retirement than other countries with a similar population age structure and equal retirement ages (Argentina and Uruguay). In addition, in cases of arduous labor, men may retire at fifty-five and women may retire at fifty; again, both must have twenty-five years of employment. Finally, the system establishes a pension minimum that is relatively high in relation to the minimum wage and grants other benefits, such as the exemption of rent payments for housing (normally fixed between 6 percent and 10 percent of family salary or income) to retirees with a monthly family income of less than twenty-five pesos.

Table 25 shows Cuba's progress in health levels and services over the last two decades. As there is no private sector in medicine, the table reports

TABLE 25
HEALTH SERVICES AND LEVELS IN CUBA, 1960–1982

	Hospital Beds per 1,000 Persons	Physicians per 10,000 Persons	Mortality Rate		Life Expectancy[a]
			General	Infant	
1960	4.3	8.9	6.1	35.9	64.0
1965	4.6	7.9	6.4	37.8	65.1
1970	5.0	7.2	6.3	38.7	68.5
1975	4.6	10.0	5.4	27.5	70.9
1980	4.6	15.6	5.7	19.6	72.8
1981	4.5	16.7	6.0	18.5	**
1982	4.5	17.3	5.8	17.3	**

Sources: Boletín estadístico de Cuba and *Anuario estadístico de Cuba*, 1965 to 1982. Life expectancy from ECLA, *Anuario estadístico de América Latina*, 1981.

a. Values for five-year periods (e.g., 1955–60 = 64.0); figures for the last two five-year periods are projections.

** Not available.

all services available in the country. The indicators show notable and systematic progress with three exceptions: (1) a slight relative reduction in hospital beds since 1970 (which is not of great consequence, as the installed capacity is not fully used); (2) a drop in the index of doctors per 10,000 inhabitants in 1960–70, induced by the exodus of one-third of the doctors after the Revolution; and (3) an increase in the infant mortality rate in 1960–70 (less in general mortality) that may have resulted from a decrease in medical personnel and from several infant epidemics, both of which coincided with better statistical coverage. In any case, the indexes that had deteriorated in the first decade of the Revolution were corrected in the second decade and greatly surpassed the prerevolutionary levels. At the beginning of the 1980s, Cuba led the region in life expectancy and had the lowest infant mortality rate (similar to that of Costa Rica). Its numbers of doctors and hospitals per inhabitant were among the highest. But health levels in Cuba at the end of the 1950s were also among the highest in the region. For instance, Cuba's infant mortality rate in 1960 was about half that of Costa Rica. The general mortality index has not been significantly reduced (and will probably increase somewhat in the present decade) because of the gradual aging of the population.[34]

Inequalities in Benefits

Unequal access to and discrepancies in the quality of benefits among the Cuban provinces have already been discussed. The analysis in this section will therefore focus on the legal differences in entitlement conditions for monetary benefits.

The legislation of the general system regulates monetary benefits in a uniform manner but in proportion to salary, in accordance with the socialist principle "to each according to his work." In the 1963 law a fixed ceiling for pensions (250 pesos) was established and, together with the fixed minimum (60 pesos), made pensions fairly equal in amount. The 1979 law—currently in force—replaced pension based on a fixed ceiling with pensions based on 90 percent of salary (with the goal of favoring highly qualified workers). Also it established a scale for the minimum amount, again in accordance with salary (from 60 to 36 pesos and less, according to a decrease in annual salary from 800 to 540 pesos or less).[35] These changes have increased the differences in pension amounts. Thus, while prior to 1979 the ratio between the lowest pension and the highest was 4:1, it can now be as high as 20:1.

The law also establishes differences in benefits and entitlement conditions among groups. Members of the armed forces and internal security have a special system, a difference justified by "service conditions, made unique by constant sacrifice." This system provides conditions superior to those of the general system: (1) seniority pensions, unique in Cuba, which allow retirement with twenty-five years of service regardless of age or at a lower age and with fewer years of service than in the general system; (2) in the calculation of pensions, a larger average base salary and a higher percentage are used; and (3) in the calculation of years of service in certain cases, each year may be counted as two or three years. Disability pensions resulting from "heroic acts in defense of the workplace" or "international missions" are increased 20 percent over the normal percentage calculation.[36] In 1964–74 the "vanguard workers" (that is, those working in enterprises that surpassed production goals, eliminated absenteeism, and reduced pay for extra hours) were entitled to receive 100 percent of their salary in all monetary benefits (this concession was later eliminated for economic reasons). On the other side, independent workers are subject to the special system (under the old law of 1963), in which conditions are inferior to those prescribed by the present law. As the analysis of coverage makes plain, the state estimates differential treatment in order to favor certain key groups and to create disincentives for others.

The Growing Cost of Social Security and Its Causes

As table 26 shows, the cost of social security in Cuba, as a percentage of GDP, doubled between 1958 and 1971 (rising from 6 percent to 12 percent) but declined in the following years, so that in 1980 it was below 9 percent. (Social security expenditures as a percentage of fiscal expenditures are extremely low in Cuba as compared with the rest of Latin America because of the enormous magnitude of Cuban state expenditures, which encompass the entire national economy). In spite of this reduction, Cuba's social security expenditure expressed as a percentage of GDP in 1980 were those of Uruguay, Argentina, and Chile, all of which have older systems. If the costs of preventing occupational risks and rehabilitation, funeral aid, subsidies to the armed forces, and administrative costs were included, the cost of Cuban social security would be greater than it appears in the table. I will analyze the causes of the cost increase below before examining potential measures to reduce it.

General causes. The universalization of population coverage is one of the most significant causes of the cost increase, especially in the health program. In addition the principal risks are covered by more generous benefits and entitlement conditions than those in most countries in the region.

There is a lack of information on administrative expenditures, but Cuba's unified system, its standardization, and the simplicity of collecting contributions and paying benefits as well as processing benefits must reduce bureaucratic costs substantially. According to official figures, the number of employees of the CETSS social security division in 1982 was 173, compared with 5,000 employees in the pension funds in 1958, when the number of insured was much smaller. Although these figures are impressive, it must be remembered that monetary benefits are to a significant extent administered by other institutions, such as the national bank, enterprises, and the OPPs. Also, the health program accounts for the greater part of employment; in 1980

TABLE 26

COST OF SOCIAL SECURITY IN CUBA, 1958–1980

(MILLIONS OF PESOS AT CURRENT PRICES)

	GDP[a]	Total Central Government Expenditures	Social Security Expenditures		
			% of Total[b]	% of GDP	% of Govt. Expenditures
1958	2,629	386	157	6.0	40.7
1962	3,722	1,854	241	6.5	13.0
1965	4,875	2,536	406	8.3	16.0
1971	6,384	c	779	12.2	**
1975	10,173	c	985	9.7	**
1978	12,200	9,168	1,120	9.2	12.2
1980	14,213	9,531	1,229	8.6	12.9

Sources: 1958 GDP from *Revista del Banco Nacional de Cuba* 5:5 (May 1959): 756; 1962–65 estimates by the author; 1971–80 from the Banco Nacional de Cuba, *Informe Económico* (Havana: BNC, August 1982), p. 30. Central government expenditures: 1958 from Grupo Cubano de Investigaciones Económicas, *Un estudio sobre Cuba* (Coral Gables, Fla.: University of Miami Press, 1963), p. 871; other figures from the state budget published in the *Gaceta oficial* and in *Granma*. Social security expenditures: 1958 from *Social Security in Cuba*, pp. 135, 149; the rest from CETSS, *La seguridad social en Cuba* (Havana: CETSS, August 1977), pp. 33, 50, *24 años de revolución en la seguridad social cubana*, pp. 48–49, *Anuario estadístico de Cuba, 1982*, p.126, and health care figures from various sources.

a. In 1962 and 1965 GDP was roughly estimated using the GSP for those years and the relationship GDP/GSP in 1971–81.

b. Includes expenditures for pensions, temporary benefits, health care, and social welfare; in 1958 private sector expenditures are excluded and, in the remainder, expenditures for prevention and rehabilitation for occupational risks, funeral aid, armed forces' subsidies, and administrative costs are excluded.

c. The state budget was not published for these years.

** Not available.

the number of employees in the MINSAP reached 157,933, or 3.6 employees per hospital bed, a proportion much greater than that in Costa Rica but much lower than that in Mexico. Even though Cuban doctors do not constitute a powerful pressure group, as in other countries, they receive one of the highest salaries in the national wage scale. In summary, the administrative costs of the Cuban system are probably very low in comparison with those for the region, but they are not an insignificant cost of social security if all the necessary adjustments are made.

Table 27 shows that the two fundamental components of social security expenditures are pensions and health benefits. Although the former account for a higher percentage than the latter, no clear tendency appears to exist in either, especially in the last decade. (Information received from the CETSS in 1984 indicates, however, that the amount destined for pensions in 1983 was over 50 percent).[37] On the other hand, monetary benefits show a declining tendency, and social welfare appears to be stagnant.

Causes related to the health program. The health budget rose twenty-

TABLE 27
DISTRIBUTION OF SOCIAL SECURITY EXPENDITURES
BY PROGRAM IN CUBA, 1965–1980
(PERCENT)

Expenditure[a]	1965	1971	1975	1980
Pensions[b]	51.4	39.9	45.5	44.4
Health/maternity[c]	38.4	37.7	40.6	42.3
Temporary benefits[d]	10.2	15.9	7.2	7.9
Social welfare and others	**	6.5	6.7	5.3

Sources: See table 26.

    a. Excludes expenditures on occupational risks, prevention and rehabilitation, funeral aid, and administrative costs.
    b. Old age, disability, and survivors' pensions, including those from occupational risks.
    c. Total costs of the national health system, including preventive medicine and administrative costs.
    d. Subsidies for health/maternity and accidents with the exception of those paid to members of the armed forces.

    ** Not available.

five times between 1959 and 1983.[38] But here as elsewhere, the lack of detailed statistical information makes it difficult to evaluate the cost of health care: there are no figures showing how costs are distributed among preventive and curative medicines, costs of salaries, and so forth.

During the revolutionary period, Cuba has devoted substantial attention to preventive medicine and, through massive vaccination campaigns, has succeeded in eradicating certain contagious diseases, such as poliomyelitis and diphtheria, and in substantially reducing the incidence of other diseases, such as tuberculosis, typhoid, and malaria. Conversely, the incidence of diseases not controllable by vaccination, such as hepatitis, diarrhea, syphilis, and blennorrhagia, has increased, apparently because of inadequate hygiene control and a greater freedom in sexual relations.[39] In addition, Cuba has experienced, to an even greater degree than Costa Rica, a change in the pathological profile; in 1982, 70 percent of the causes of death were "diseases of development," such as cardiovascular and cerebrovascular diseases and malignant tumors. In summary, Cuba has eradicated or significantly reduced the diseases most easily controlled and requiring low-cost treatment and now faces the diseases most difficult to eradicate and most costly to treat.

Although Cuba has paid great attention to preventive medicine, its curative medicine is highly capital intensive, emphasizing large hospitals, complex and costly equipment, and abundant medical personnel. Although the per capita consumption of medicine is one of the highest in the region, 81 percent of the medicine consumed nationally is produced domestically and a strict basic list exists, so that costs should be relatively low. At the end of the 1970s, Cuba had one of the highest hospital occupancy rates in Latin America

(81 percent), but even so, one-fifth of the available capacity was not used. On the other hand, the national average for hospital stays was 9.6 days, one of the highest in the region, and the average annual number of doctor's visits was three per inhabitant and rising.[40] In 1982 a new twenty-four-floor hospital was completed in Havana at a cost of 45 million pesos, a sum representing 10 percent of the annual health budget and 0.5 percent of the 1982 national state budget.[41]

Causes related to the pension program. The cost of the pension program in Cuba should tend to grow because of three factors: an aging population, increasing life expectancy, and relatively low retirement ages. Even though the new pension program was introduced in 1963, so that it is one of the most recent in the region, approximately two-thirds of the population had previous coverage, much of it in mature programs with very flexible conditions.

Table 21 shows that the quotient of demographic burden in 1958 was higher for Cuba than for Costa Rica in 1982 and that it has doubled in the last two decades. In 1981 the figure for Cuba was surpassed by that for only three pioneer countries: Uruguay, Chile, and Argentina. The new pension program requires twenty-five years of employment (not contribution), and this employment could have occurred prior to the introduction of the program. In addition, accounting for services rendered is relatively easy.

Table 28 indicates that in the period 1960–80 the percentage of the population over sixty-five years of age rose from 4.8 percent to 7.3 percent, and it will reach 10.9 percent in 2010. These percentages are greater than those for Chile, similar to those for Argentina, and lower than those for Uruguay alone, the highest in Latin America. Furthermore, it was estimated that 76 percent of Cuban men and 82 percent of Cuban women would reach sixty-five in 1980, the highest percentages in the region. Finally, as I have already noted, life expectancy for women is three years more than for men, and women can retire five years earlier. This difference has a notable impact on the cost of the pension program, especially in Cuba, where women have one of the highest rates of participation in the labor force of the region.

TABLE 28
DISTRIBUTION OF POPULATION
BY AGE GROUP IN CUBA, 1960–2010
(PERCENT)

Age Group	1960	1970	1980	1990	2000	2010
0–14	34.4	37.2	31.3	23.5	24.1	21.5
15–64	60.8	56.9	61.4	68.3	67.0	67.6
65 and over	4.8	5.9	7.3	8.2	8.9	10.9

Source: Based on CELADE, *Boletín Demográfico* 16:32 (July 1983). Calculations by the author.

From a positive point of view, as the population age structure of Cuba is similar to that in Chile and Uruguay (older than the Costa Rican population), the proportion of the population at productive age (fifteen to sixty-four years) is very high (61.4 percent), and the dependency index is much lower than in Costa Rica, Mexico, and Peru. These characteristics suggest relatively lower costs in health care for the population of minor age and a greater proportion of adults in the productive age bracket who suffer a lower incidence of disease.

Measures to Reduce Expenditures

As I have previously noted, by cost reduction Cuba can achieve financial equilibrium of the social security system. After salaries, social security monetary benefits constitute the principal source of income for the population. With the enactment of the 1963 and 1979 laws, it was affirmed that the level of these benefits should be adequate for the economic situation of the country and its level of development.[42] Three methods of achieving this objective have been tried.

At the beginning of the Revolution, retirement was facilitated for political reasons, and for the sake of administrative changes and enterprise nationalization. The result was a wave of 56,000 new pensions in the period 1959–61. A second wave of pensioners (85,000) occurred in 1963–65, when those covered by the 1963 law and the owners of farms affected by the agrarian reform law of 1963 began to receive pensions. The number of pension applications rose from 20,000 in 1959 to 110,000 in 1964. For this reason, as table 27 shows, the greatest proportion of expenditures for pensions—more than 51 percent—occurred in 1965. Partly to reduce this cost and also to deal with a labor deficit in key sectors of the economy, in 1965–67 a national campaign to postpone retirement was launched. As a result, 60,000 insured who had applied for pensions in 1964 canceled their requests and returned to work. In 1971, the proportion of social security expenditures going to pensions declined to less than 40 percent. Later, in 1970s, because of unemployment pressure, the previous policy was reversed, and 200,000 people retired.[43] Consequently, social security pension expenditures rose in the second half of the 1970s (see table 27).

Cuba has traditionally been a country with low inflation. In the revolutionary period, inflation has been strongly controlled, at least until the 1980s. Although no official statistics on inflation existed at the time of concluding this book, table 29 shows an inflation index, calculated by the author, on the basis of official data of economic growth at constant and current prices. This index permits us to calculate the real value of pensions in the period 1962–81. In the period 1962–68, real pensions declined but then rose somewhat in 1970 because of the 1969 increase in the minimum pension. Since then, the real pension has gradually fallen and in 1981 it was approximately half the 1962 level. The greatest fall in the real value of pensions occurred in

TABLE 29
REAL VALUE OF ANNUAL PENSIONS IN CUBA, 1962–1981

	Pensions (millions of pesos)	No. of Pensioners (thous.)	Average Pension per Capita (pesos)	Index (1970 = 100)		
				Nominal Pension	Inflation	Real Pension
1962	152	213	713	90.2	79.2	114.0
1965	208	298	699	88.4	93.4	94.6
1970	286	363	790	100.0	100.0	100.0
1971	311	394	790	100.0	106.1	94.3
1972	344	432	796	100.7	112.5	89.5
1973	383	470	816	103.2	119.4	86.4
1974	417	507	823	104.1	126.6	82.3
1975	448	544	824	104.3	134.3	77.7
1976	473	581	814	103.1	133.7	77.1
1977	492	629	781	98.8	129.3	76.4
1978	508	652	778	98.5	134.2	73.4
1979	523	671[a]	779	98.6	142.3	69.3
1980	542	690	785	99.4	148.1	67.1
1981	553	710[a]	779	98.6	160.7	61.4

Sources: Pensions and numbers of pensioners from CETSS, La seguridad social en Cuba, pp. 33, 50, and 24 años de revolución en la seguridad social cubana, pp. 48–49, 66; and Anuario estadístico de Cuba, 1982, p. 126. Inflation index based on Carmelo Mesa-Lago, "Cuba's Centrally Planned Economy: An Equity Tradeoff for Growth," Vanderbilt University, 1983; and Anuario estadístico de Cuba, 1984, pp.84, 88. Average pension and indexes calculated by the author.

Note: Old age, disability, and survivors' pensions.

a. Interpolations by the author.

1981 when, because of an increase in wholesale and consumer prices, an inflation rate of 8.5 percent was registered, one of the highest of the revolutionary period. At the end of 1981 the minimum pension was to be increased from sixty to sixty-four pesos monthly, to at least compensate for the higher cost of living, but there is no statistical information on the average pension to use for the 1982 calculations.[44] In any case, one method of controlling pension costs has apparently been to avoid adjusting pensions fully to the cost of living, especially in the last decade.

Costs for temporary monetary benefits rose from 10 percent of social security expenditures in 1965 to almost 16 percent in 1971. In part the reason was the concession of benefits equivalent to 100 percent of salary to vanguard workers, but in 1974 it was decided that this cost was excessive and inflationary, and it was suppressed. The percentage of these monetary benefits therefore declined in 1975.

The last two methods described above contributed to reducing the cost of social security as a percentage of GDP in the second half of the 1970s (see table 26) but could not prevent the increase in the deficit, at least until 1982 (see table 24). Moreover, these methods have limits (especially the lack of adjustment in pensions), and other pressures discussed in this chapter will probably increase social security costs in the current decade. Hence Cuba must apply other techniques to cut expenditures.

In reducing costs a key area is benefits with too flexible entitlement conditions. For example, the retirement age for women could be increased from fifty-five to sixty years, so that it equaled that of men, as in Nicaragua and the Dominican Republic, countries with a much lower life expectancy than Cuba. A more drastic measure would be to increase both retirement ages to sixty-five years of age, as in Mexico, or to sixty for women and sixty-five for men, as in Brazil—again, countries with lower life expectancies than Cuba. These measures would be difficult to implement in the 1980s because of unemployment pressure but would be more feasible in the 1990s, when unemployment is predicted to lose importance once the labor market has entirely absorbed the baby boom of 1960–66. Certain benefits that in addition to being costly involve differential treatment, such as seniority pensions for the armed forces, could be eliminated.

Inasmuch as Cuba has very low administrative costs, it is difficult to make cuts in this area. Nevertheless, there appears to be room for increased efficiency. For example, the number of hospital beds could be kept at present levels in order to increase utilized capacity, the length of hospital stays could be reduced, and the excessive consumption of medicines restricted. Health personnel may currently be underutilized, and there is apparently an excessive use of doctors for functions that could be carried out at a lower cost by paramedics. Finally, Cuba has possibly the largest hospital facilities in the region, which are more than sufficient to cover its health needs. Even though much has been done, a greater emphasis could be placed on the development of rural clinics and other lesser institutions that would improve access to medical services in the most isolated areas of the country.

THE IMPACT OF SOCIAL SECURITY ON DEVELOPMENT

The information published in Cuba on employment and savings/investment is deficient, and official figures on the distribution of income have never been published. To this weak base must be added other problems such as the sui generis nature of Cuban social security and the lack of specialized studies on the subject. Such problems make serious analysis very difficult. This section is thus only reflective and poses more questions than it answers.

Savings and Investment

As we have seen, Cuban social security follows a financing method that resembles pure assessment but with equilibrium at a macroeconomic level and without even a contingency reserve. There are no individual accounts for the insured, and the system has ended in a deficit in recent years. The pension program enjoys the solid state guarantees, and the insured can be safely assumed to have a large measure of confidence in it. It must be added that there are very minor incentives for individual savings in Cuba; payment of 2 percent interest on savings accounts was only recently introduced. The conclusion here appears to be that social security, at the least, does not contribute to savings and investment and may have a negative impact on both.

Employment

In centrally planned economies, the wage contribution, although paid by the employer, should have a neutral impact on employment or at least a smaller one than in market economies. The slight increase in unemployment in Cuba in the second half of the 1970s reflects factors apparently exogenous to social security. In other words, the increase in the labor supply (as children born during the baby boom of 1960–66 entered the labor market) combined with an economic slowdown and a greater emphasis on labor productivity have affected employment.

In Cuban price formation three components are included: the cost of production, taxes, and profits. The different taxes include those on circulation, profits, and social security. Thus the cost of social security should be charged to prices.[45] But the monopolistic character of state enterprises and the scarce or nonexistent competition among them, as well as the crucial role played by the state in price fixing, capital allocation, and employment regulation, mean that the diverse combination of production factors should affect neither enterprise profits nor the demand for labor.

Nevertheless, since the middle of the 1970s a new system of economic direction and planning (SDPE) has been introduced. This system gives greater powers of decision making to enterprise managers in the areas of hiring personnel and investment, and also stimulating competition among enterprises. Although SDPE is not yet fully operational, it might be supposed that when it is the administrators would have incentives to cut their production costs, thus reducing the amount of the social security wage contribution by substituting capital for labor. But the probability of this happening appears small, given that the state will still control the bulk of capital allocations for investment (a development or investment fund for enterprises under the SDPE was initially considered but was later discarded) and will still maintain full employment as a high priority.

Income Distribution

Rough estimates of income distribution in Cuba under the Revolution indicate a large reduction in income inequality,[46] and in such an egalitarian economy, the impact of social security must be marginal. The new social security system is obviously much more progressive than the prerevolutionary one, but it is not clear that the present system (especially since 1979) redistributes from the high-income groups to the low ones. Legally, the insured does not pay the wage contribution, and monetary benefits are related to salary or income. Since 1979, differences among pensions have been expanded by eliminating fixed ceilings and floors and by relating both to salaries. Medical and hospital benefits are standard, although there are differences in the accessibility and quality of the services, and the least-developed provinces are those with the fewest services. Finally, some benefits are clearly redistributive, such as the exemption of rent payments for housing for low-income retirees and the free provision of medicines (outside hospitals) and other social welfare benefits to the lowest income groups. In summary, social security probably has a neutral impact on income distribution, but in the final analysis this is not as important in Cuba, where the distribution of income (before social security payments) is probably the most egalitarian in the region.

4

Chile:
Pioneer in Adoption and Privatization

CHILE IS the pioneer nation in social security in the Western Hemisphere. At the beginning of the 1970s, its system occupied one of the top positions in Latin America. It covered all social risks plus more than 70 percent of the population (it was practically universal when health care and welfare pensions were taken into account), it provided one of the most generous benefit packages as well as the most liberal entitlement conditions, and it stood out in terms of health levels and services.

But social security in Chile (even more than that in Cuba and Uruguay) developed in a fragmented manner. Through state concessions to pressure groups that flourished in the long period of pluralistic democracy, one of the most stratified systems in the region was forged, with significant inequalities among the different groups covered. The maturity, universality, and generosity of the system, as well as the aging and high life expectancy of the population (with low retirement ages), and the massification of privilege brought increasing costs in the system, in 1971 reaching 17 percent of the GDP, a historic record that has not been equaled since. In spite of its heavy burden, the system was in a state of financial equilibrium. This phenomenon was explained in large part by the very high wage contributions, which reached a maximum of 65 percent, the highest in the region together with the figure for Uruguay. The state substantially contributed to the system, but it is debatable whether it did so as a third party—promoting equilibrium—or in connection with its obligations as employer and provider of social welfare. In any case the general fixed-premium method eventually had to be replaced by the pay-as-you-go method, and the declining surplus was transferred to the insured through subsidized housing and loan programs. Various reform projects of the system (among them the most comprehensive produced in Latin America) could not be implemented in spite of the efforts of successive administrations with diverse ideological inclinations.

105

The interruption of democracy, the destabilization of pressure groups, political parties, and unions, and the concentration of political power permitted the military government to carry out a reform in the second half of the 1970s that included standardizing crucial aspects of the system, eliminating its most blatant inequalities, increasing the efficiency of the administration of health care, and initiating a process of unification. However, unification has not equaled the level reached by Cuba, Peru, and Uruguay because Chile's pension funds have not been merged, separate administrative groups continue, and differences among the subsystems remain. At the beginning of the 1980s, a new pension program was established on the basis of mandatory private savings and the full capitalization method, to be administered by lucrative private insurance companies that compete among themselves. These corporations have captured two-thirds of the insured, who must pay a commission for the insurers' services. In addition, part of the health system has been privatized.

The erosion of the real value of pensions and the reduction of public health expenditures until the mid-1970s were principally responsible for the decrease in the cost of social security to 9 percent of GDP just at the time the reform began. Although these cuts generated substantial savings, they were balanced by a one-third decrease in the total wage contribution, which in turn resulted in the elimination of the employer's contribution and the reduction of the insured contribution in the new pension program. Thereafter, the cost of social security again increased and in 1980 reached 11 percent of GDP, the highest in the region together with that of Uruguay.

The cost of Chile's social security is difficult to reduce or control—especially in the old pension program—because of past generosity and irreversible demographic factors; furthermore, most possible methods of saving have already been tried. The old pension program has been left with the oldest insured and those closest to retirement and with a growing financial deficit. Conversely, the new pension program covers the youngest insured, receives their contributions as well as state transfers (for the value of the accumulated contributions in the old program), and has generated reserves equivalent to 30 percent of the total deposits in the financial system.

Although Chile has fewer ways of reducing costs than other countries, several more measures could still be tried in the old pension program: complete its unification, reduce inequalities in pensions, complete individual accounts, and unify the collection of contributions so as to permit greater control of evasion and payment delays. In the long run, the most important factor in the reduction (or at least the control) of the system's expenditures will be the success or failure of the new pension program. If the private insurance companies were to become truly competitive, reduce their operating costs, decrease the commission charged to the insured, maintain a high investment yield (through diversification of portfolio and the development of a capital market), and pay adequate pensions, the new system would consolidate and would survive the disappearance of the old system, and thus would become a feasible alternative for the region.

HISTORICAL EVOLUTION

The Stratified System

Chile is the pioneer country in social security in the Western Hemisphere, as it was the first to introduce social insurance. But, even more than its counterparts in Cuba and Uruguay, Chile's system evolved during the first seventy years of the twentieth century in a gradual and stratified manner through state concessions to the powerful pressure groups that flourished in the climate of pluralistic democracy. At the beginning of the 1970s, the system granted protection against all social risks (old age, disability, death, occupational risks, common illness, unemployment, and family allowances) and covered more than two-thirds of the population. This was the second highest coverage in the region. Because of the long democratic period, strong unions, and political mobilization, a peculiar phenomenon occurred: the massification of privilege. As the lower social strata acquired power, they exercised pressure on the state to offer them some of the generous conditions enjoyed by the privileged groups.[1]

After the end of the nineteenth century and through the first quarter of the twentieth, only three pension programs appeared in Chile: one for the armed forces (which also received health protection), one for civil servants, and one for railroad workers. There was also a workmen's compensation program for blue-collar workers. In the period 1924–25, under the presidency of Alessandri Palma, the two most important pension programs were founded: the Social Insurance Service (SSS) covering blue-collar workers (who also received health-maternity protection) and the Social Insurance Fund for Private (White-Collar) Employees (EMPART). In addition, the Civil Servants' and Journalists' Fund (CANAEMPU) was created and extended benefits to this group. In the following fifty years, independent pension programs were established for various occupational groups, such as the merchant marine (two programs), police, racetrack employees (six programs), bank employees (five programs), municipal workers (three programs), and last, although only partly, the self-employed. The health-maternity program for blue-collar workers evolved and became the national health service (SNS), which integrated various services and also protected indigents. Health care perpetuated the separation of blue- and white-collar workers with the creation of a separate program, the Employee's National Medical Service (SERMENA). In addition to private and public employees, SERMENA covered other groups. To these two principal health programs and that of the armed forces were later added separate programs for the police, bank employees, and other groups. In addition, various independent programs emerged for each group on occupational risks, family allowances, and unemployment (see table 30).

At the beginning of the 1970s, the "system" was a legislative and bureaucratic labyrinth with hundreds of institutions and programs: thirty-one for

TABLE 30

SOCIAL SECURITY LEGISLATION IN CHILE,
BY RISK AND GROUPS COVERED, 1855–1983

Year[a]	Risk Protected	Groups Covered
1855, 1915	ODS, H	Armed forces
1888	ODS	Civil servants
1911, 1916–18	ODS	Railway workers
1916, 1924	OR	Blue-collar workers
1924, 1952	ODS, HM	Blue-collar workers
1924, 1937	ODS	Private white-collar workers
1925	ODS	Civil servants, journalists
1925, 1937, 1952	ODS	Merchant marine (two groups)
1925–27	ODS	Police
1936, 1941	ODS	Various groups in racetracks
1937	FA, U	Private white-collar workers
1940	U	Railway workers
1943, 1952	U, ODS	Municipal workers
1946	ODS, OR, HM	Bank workers
1952	FA	Civil servants, armed forces, police
1952	HM	Indigents
1953	FA, U	Blue-collar workers
1953, 1968	HM	Civil servants, private white-collar workers, merchant marine, municipal workers
1954	H, OR	Police
1954	U	Armed forces
1957	ODS	State bank workers
1968	OR	All (except the armed forces)
1968	ODS, OR, H	Armed forces
1972	ODS, H	Small merchants, artisans, and other self-employed workers
1974–79	ODS, HM, FA, U	Various unification measures and/or total or partial uniformity of the old system
1981	ODS, HM	Introduction of new system with AFPs and ISAPRE that privatize these programs

Sources: Carmelo Mesa-Lago, *Social Security in Latin America* (Pittsburgh, Pa.: University of Pittsburgh Press, 1978), and subsequent legislation

Note: ODS = old age, disability, and survivors' pensions. H = health. M = maternity. OR = occupational risks. U = unemployment. FA = family allowances. AFP = administrators of pension funds. ISAPRE = Health Insurance Institutes.

a. The first date corresponds to the initial law and subsequent dates to modifications and amplifications.

old age pensions, thirty for seniority pensions, thirty for disability pensions, thirty-five for health-maternity, fifty-five for social welfare, and dozens more for family allowances and unemployment. Each institution had its own legislation, administration, financing, and benefits, with notable differences among them. At least half a dozen public agencies had supervisory functions over the system, but there was no effective central coordination. The principles of unity, uniformity, and solidarity did not operate, but as a result of the pluralistic democracy, there was, at least in private sector institutions, three-party representation in the administration of the system.

In the same period, the high cost of Chilean social security set a record surpassed only by that of the most developed countries of Europe. It was alleged that the high cost had a negative impact on employment (see below), but that the system had a slightly progressive impact on income distribution. (However, as we shall see, there is contradictory evidence about the latter.) The system was also criticized for requiring a large state subsidy, but this was also debatable.

Various studies on social security reform were conducted in Chile from the mid-1950s to the beginning of the 1970s. They described the inequalities of the system and recommended its legal, administrative, and financial unification; uniformity of entitlement conditions for benefits; elimination of privileges; and universalization of coverage. The most important study was undertaken in the early 1960s by the Prat Commission. Three years in the making, at twenty-five volumes and more than 1,500 pages, it became the most comprehensive report on social security ever produced in Latin America.[2] New attempts at reform failed under the presidencies of Frei and Allende; no government had sufficient power over both the pressure groups and the political opposition to implement the needed reform.

Reforms and Privatization of the System

The extraordinary powers assumed by the military junta and the elimination or destabilization of pressure groups, political parties, and trade unions allowed this government both to take control of the social security institutions and to introduce a series of reforms in 1974–79. These reforms partly reduced the existing multiplicity and eliminated the most notable and costly privileges: (1) In unemployment, a universal and uniform benefit system was introduced. (2) In family allowances, payments were made uniform and a common fund was created. (3) In pensions, a minimum uniform benefit was established, equal retirement ages were fixed for the whole system, seniority pensions were eliminated and *pensiones perseguidoras* (whose amount was adjusted with the retiree's salary prior to retirement), cost-of-living adjustments were made uniform, and welfare pensions were expanded. (4) In health, the two principal programs (for blue- and white-collar workers) were coordinated under the Ministry of Health, and entitlement conditions were made uniform, although in practice differences between the two groups remain. (5) Severance-pay loans and other benefits were eliminated. (6) Employer contributions to the pension program were discontinued, and it was planned that by 1986 employer contributions to the family allowance and unemployment programs would also be eliminated. The reforms excluded the armed forces and the police and did not touch the occupational risks programs.[3]

In line with the reformed old system, the 1981 new pension and health systems were established, administered by lucrative private companies that compete for the insured, who are charged a commission for services: the administrators of the pension funds (AFPs) and the Health Insurance Institutes (ISAPREs). This reform reflects the ideology of the Chilean model of the "social market economy" in which the state plays a subordinate role, thus transferring part of the social security system to the private sector.

The new pension system is actually a compulsory private savings program: an individual account is opened, and into it are deposited the contributions of the insured, which are then invested in the capital market and yield revenues. The insured in the old system had a five-year period (which expired in 1986) to decide whether to remain in this system or change to the new one, but having once left the old system, the insured could not return to it. (Nevertheless, in 1983 a new law authorized some 600 insured to return to the old system; they had almost completed their requirements for retirement but, lured by the alleged advantages of the new system, had transferred to it.) Since 1983 all salaried workers and wage earners who enter the labor market are automatically affiliated with the new system, while self-employed workers can join voluntarily. One is free to select any AFP and can change at will. Originally, a change could be made every 30 days, but now 180 days are required. The old system is expected to disappear in the long run and to be replaced by the AFPs.

The new private health system is of less importance than that of pensions because its presumed objective is not to replace the old system but to complement it and develop private medicine. Only the insured of the AFPs can join the ISAPREs, which offer various health plans with diverse benefits— and costs—but never lower than those existing in the old system. The insured can freely change ISAPREs and can return to the old system if they wish.

In summary, the Chilean social security system, as the pioneer in Latin America, developed before any other and, through the interaction of the state and pressure groups, reached universal coverage for social risks and almost universal population coverage, but at a high cost and with serious problems of stratification and inequality. The extraordinary powers assumed by the military government permitted it to reform the old system by standardizing some benefits and entitlement conditions, but it failed to complete the process of unification and uniformity. In addition, new systems were created in pensions and health that basically functioned as private insurance.

ORGANIZATIONAL STRUCTURE

The current Chilean social security system is probably the least unified and uniform of any in the six country cases; it is actually one of the most stratified in Latin America. The reform of the old system promoted the process of unification and uniformity but without reaching the levels achieved by Cuba, Peru, and even Uruguay.

It is interesting to explore why, despite the increased power of the state over pressure groups and their social insurance agencies, the unification of the old pension system has not been completed. One explanation is that the original idea was not to merge the institutions but only to standardize them in basic respects.[4] An opposing viewpoint is that full unification was planned initially, but this project was blocked by the opposition of insured groups who wanted to keep their privileges.[5] A third interpretation is that the goal of full unification encountered serious administrative problems, such as the difficulty of merging enormous bankrupt institutions with smaller solvent ones, the need for individual accounts to have been completed earlier, and the difficulty of achieving still more economies of scale.[6] Some government officials do not reject the possibility of future unification, and it has been noted that a law was drafted in 1983 with this objective in mind. In any case, the old system has a projected life of forty to fifty years.[7] The old pension system has achieved neither a merging of the various funds nor legislative uniformity among diverse institutions, but three groups have been formed with joint administration that collects contributions and processes and pays benefits: (1) blue-collar workers, private white-collar workers, and railroads, (2) municipal and racetrack workers, and (3) the merchant marine. The remaining institutions continue with independent administrations: civil service, bank employees, armed forces, and police (the last two groups have remained practically untouched by the reform and depend, as before, on the Ministries of Defense and the Interior).[8] All of the old pension programs, except the two cited above, are under the sole jurisdiction of the Ministry of Labor and Social Insurance, which appoints their directors (hence the three-part administration no longer exists) and exercise supervision through two subsidiary agencies. The Superintendency of Social Security, which existed before the reform, continues to perform audits but has lost the other functions that it previously exercised. The Institute of Social Insurance Standardization, created in 1980, proposes methods to reform the system, manages the individual accounts, and administers a special fund. The latter is financed by state contributions, the sale of institutional assets, and investment yields; its objectives are to cover deficits of the old system and to finance the transfer to the new system of the accumulated contributions in the old system.[9]

The new pension system currently has twelve AFPs, but two of these cover half of all those affiliated. The system is controlled by the Superintendency of the AFPs, which authorizes its operations, sets its regulations, handles the registry, publishes statistics, and supervises the accounting, reserves, investments, and benefit payments. The AFPs have a separate pension fund into which the contributions of the affiliated insured are deposited. This fund is invested and, according to yield, pays a dividend to the insured, each of whom has a separate account.

The old health system (SNS and SERMENA) has been unified under the Ministry of Health and is administered by the National Health Fund (FONASA). The old medical-hospital facilities have been integrated into the National System of Health Services (SNSS), although they have been reorganized into twenty-seven regional health services with their own administrations. Although FONASA centralizes the public health budget (and finances the SNSS health services), it does not have its own facilities but instead contracts with private doctors, hospitals, clinics, and other services. Indigents and blue-collar workers (under a certain salary level) are entitled to free care in the SNSS health services. White-collar employees (as a remnant of the old system) are entitled to free choice; three levels are now available with increasing rates. FONASA finances an equal amount for the three levels, hence subsidizing between 25 percent and 50 percent of health care. The insured buy a voucher in FONASA (which includes the subsidy) for any of the three levels (paying the difference out of their own pockets) and use this voucher to pay for services; the providers of services, in turn, redeem the voucher in FONASA. Theoretically, blue-collar workers are also entitled to free choice, but few exercise the right because of the cost of the services. On the other hand, white-collar workers may use the health services of SNSS (paying the minimum level), but in practice they do not do so as they prefer private services. Independent health services are still maintained for institutions such as the armed forces, the police, and railroads. In 1984 there was under study a law that would integrate these independent services under FONASA, perhaps with the exception of the armed forces and the police.[10]

In the new health system there are, at present, fifteen ISAPREs, but the biggest two cover 56 percent of the affiliated insured. Only the largest ISAPRE has its own hospital and services. The others lack their own services and hence contract with private doctors, hospitals, and other services. The Ministry of Health supervises the system and enforces the existing regulations.

The workmen's compensation program continues to be operated by the old social security institutions as well as by three employers' mutual aid societies and one public agency. Family allowances have been equalized and unified under the administration of a single fund. Finally there is a uniform system of unemployment compensation, but its administration is the responsibility of the old social security institutions. All of these programs are supervised by the Ministry of Labor and Social Insurance.

Although the Chilean state plays a secondary role, subordinate to the market, and an important part of the pension and health programs has been privatized, the state still plays a crucial role in social security. The pension program is now under greater control from the Ministry of Labor and Social Insurance than ever before. The three-part administration has been eliminated, and the state subsidizes the growing deficits. The health program is under the Ministry of Health, and even though there is greater decentralization and, supposedly, privatization of services, FONASA controls the entire public budget. The new pension system is private but compulsory and is tightly regulated by the state; in addition, the majority of investments are in state bonds and the state recognition of contributions in the old system involves a transfer of public funds. Still, the Chilean system shows the greatest participation by the private sector of any country in the six case studies.

The project of making the old system more unified and uniform should be completed through merging pension funds, fully unifying the administration, and standardizing conditions not yet affected by the reform. The health system should integrate the few remaining independent programs. A single mechanism should be created for collecting contributions as well as for gathering, consolidating, and publishing statistics of the system.

POPULATION COVERAGE

Legal and Statistical Coverage

Chilean social security legislation—like that in Cuba and Uruguay—has the broadest coverage in Latin America. It incorporates all salaried workers and wage earners (including those in agriculture and domestic service) as well as self-employed workers (who have mandatory coverage in the old system but voluntary in the new). Both the noninsured and the insured who do not meet the entitlement requirements are entitled to welfare pensions if they lack resources (if they are indigents) and can receive free health care and a special family allowance. The unemployed who are not entitled to unemployment compensation (even if they are enrolled in a public employment welfare plan) also qualify for welfare pensions, free health care (for three months after they have become unemployed), and family allowances. Since 1983, those insured in the AFPs who lose their jobs need not pay commissions during the first year of unemployment. The insured's dependents, including spouse and children, as well as pensioners and their dependents, are entitled to nonmonetary benefits for health-maternity.

Table 31 shows social security statistical coverage but excludes welfare pensions and free health care; hence the table underestimates coverage. The table includes data up to 1980 and thus refers to the old system, since the new system had not yet been created. The multiplicity of institutions may have meant an overestimation of coverage because the same insured may be covered by more than one institution. The figures of active insured are based

TABLE 31
SOCIAL SECURITY COVERAGE OF POPULATION IN CHILE, 1960–1980
(THOUSANDS)

	Total Population	Insured Population					% of Coverage[b]		Annual Average Growth Rates (log)				Quotient of Demographic Burden[c]
		EAP	Active	Passive	Dependents[a]	Total	Total Population	EAP	Total Population	EAP	Actives	Total Insured	
1960	7,585	2,389	1,691	269	2,590	4,550	60.0	70.8	**	**	**	**	0.159
1965	8,510	2,660[d]	1,964	441	3,064	5,469	64.3	73.8	2.3	2.2	3.0	3.7	0.225
1970	9,368	2,932	2,217	614	3,523	6,354	67.8	75.6	1.9	2.0	2.5	3.0	0.277
1973	9,861	3,156[d]	2,404	713	3,911	7,028	71.2	75.9	1.7	2.6	2.7	3.4	0.297
1975	10,196	3,322	2,425	810	4,025	7,260	71.2	73.0	1.7	2.6	0.4	1.6	0.334
1980	11,104	3,788	2,337[e]	1,071	4,070	7,478	67.3	61.7	1.7	2.6	-0.7	0.6	0.458

Source: Total population from CELADE, *Boletín demográfico* 16:32 (July 1983). EAP 1960 from census and 1970, 1975, and 1980 from CELADE, *Boletín demográfico* 15:29 (January 1982). Insured population from SSS, *Seguridad social: Estadísticas, 1965 a 1980,* and INED, *Compendio estadístico, 1982.* Percentages, rates, and coefficients calculated by the author.

a. Based on the number of family dependents or estimated using the trend of the dependent/active insured ratio (between 1.53 in 1960 and 1.74 in 1980).
b. Total population coverage refers to health and EAP coverage to old age, disability, and survivors' pensions.
c. Number of passives divided by number of active insured.
d. Extrapolation of the author.
e. Adjusted by adding the insured in the armed forces and police in 1979 to the rest of the insured in 1980.

**Not available.

on affiliates, not necessarily on contributors. Although the distinction is important in terms of evasion, it is not so important where benefit rights (especially health benefits) are concerned, as the affiliate could receive health care for several months after the last contribution had been made. The percentage of total population coverage rose from 60 percent in 1960 to 71 percent in 1973; it then stagnated and later fell to 67 percent in 1980. The percentage of EAP coverage in pensions rose from 71 percent in 1960 to 76 percent in 1973, later declining to 62 percent in 1980. Of total covered insured, approximately 69 percent were in the blue-collar fund (SSS), 12 percent in the private white-collar fund (EMPART), 10 percent in the fund for civil servants (CANAEMPU), and only 9 percent in the rest.[11] There is a lack of coverage data for occupational risk, unemployment, and family allowances, but coverage in these programs must be similar to that in the pension program.

The decline in the percentage of population coverage in the period 1975–80 may be a result of the high unemployment in this period, the increase in evasion, and the correction of double counting in the major insurance funds after partial unification had taken place. Because of the shrinkage in population coverage in the Chilean system and the advances of other countries, in 1980 Chile had fallen to sixth place in Latin America with regard to coverage and ranked last among the countries of the highest group. But it must be remembered that as insurance coverage fell, an increase in welfare coverage must have occurred. Both the level and the quality of welfare coverage are lower, however. (For example, the amount of the welfare pension is one-third of the regular minimum pension.)

There are no statistics after 1980 consolidating coverage in the old and new systems. The AFPs' data indicate that the number of affiliates rose from 501,693 in May 1981 (when the system began) to 1,741,000 in December 1982 and 1,804,035 in April 1983. (In the last year 96 percent were salaried workers and 4 percent were self-employed workers.) Since April 1983 the same figure has been repeated, and although it is acknowledged to be an underestimate in need of revision, by mid-1984 a revised figure still had not been given.[12] Statistics of the old system have not been published, but the superintendency of social security estimates that the number of affiliates (excluding the armed forces and police) had fallen to 1,033,556 in 1981 and to 648,263 in 1982.[13] If the number covered in the armed forces and police in 1979 (110,546) is added to the latter figure, the total for the old system in 1982 should have been about 760,000. Adding the figures of the old and new systems in 1982 gives a total of about 2,500,000, equal to 63 percent of an EAP estimated at 3,976,000.[14] If these calculations are accurate, coverage in 1982 was slightly higher to that of 1980, with about 70 percent of the insured in the new system and 30 percent in the old.

The above calculations, however, are affected by duplication. A significant number of those who shifted to the new system did not notify the old system of their action, and the AFPs did not check to see whether people were new affiliates or had shifted from the old system, so it was possible for individuals to be counted in both. An insured who changes institutions can be registered in various AFPs, especially in the agricultural sector, with a frequent change of employer and registration under different names. In EMPART one-third of those registered do not have identification cards with a single verified code number, and the situation is worse in the SSS.[15] An official estimate that takes these problems into account puts the number of AFP affiliates in 1983 at 1,400,000 and that of the old system at 870,000, for a total of 2,270,000 insured, or 57 percent of the EAP.[16] These numbers relate to affiliates, but the number of active contributors is less, as we will see.

Concerning the health-maternity program, a recent study estimated that 40 percent of the population was covered by the SNSS; another 40 percent by FONASA and independent institutions (within this group, in 1983, 49 percent were treated in the first level, 41 percent in the second, and 10 percent in the third; 10 percent by ISAPREs and private insurance companies; and the remaining 10 percent by private medical-hospital services).[17] It was originally predicted that, at the end of 1983, there would be 100 ISAPREs, with 300,000 contracts and 1,000,000 affiliates, but the actual figures were much lower: 15 ISAPREs, 108,000 contracts, and some 400,000 affiliates, or 3.4 percent of the total population.[18]

Determinant Structural Factors

Social security's rapid expansion and high degree of coverage in Chile has been aided—as in Costa Rica, Cuba, and Uruguay—by various structural factors: the high proportion of salaried workers and wage earners (67 percent of the labor force); the relatively small proportion of self-employed workers (25 percent) and unpaid family workers (4 percent); the small proportion of the labor force in agriculture (23 percent); the very high degree of urbanization (81 percent); and a good communication network. Adding the percentages of the EAP in the formal sector (54 percent) and the modern sector (14 percent) yielded a total of 68 percent in 1980. If the percentage of domestic servants (6 percent) covered in Chile is added to this figure, the percentage increases to 74 percent—equal to the percentage of EAP coverage in the mid-1970s.

On the other hand, although Chile in 1980 had a fairly low underemployment rate (9.7 percent), the rate of open unemployment was the second highest in the region (9 percent), and it doubled by 1982 (19 percent). Furthermore, even though the census figures for 1982 are not available, a comparison of the distributions of the EAP by occupational category in 1970 and 1978 indicates a reduction in the percentage of salaried workers combined with an increase in the percentage of self-employed workers and unpaid family workers.[19] This increase could explain, in part, the decline in insurance coverage of the EAP in the past decade.

Differences in Population Coverage

While we do not know how the total insured population is distributed by region, table 32 shows the differences among regions in terms of EAP coverage. In Chile, unlike other countries, the highest coverage is found not in the metropolitan region, where the capital city is, but instead in four other regions: Magallanes-Antarctica (12), Tarapaca (1), Antofagasta (2), and Atacama (3). The reason is that these four regions have the highest GDP per capita in Chile plus urbanization percentages similar to that for the metropolitan region. In addition, regions 1, 2, and 3 hold the concentrated wealth of the country's mineral deposits and have been the cradle of the trade union movement. Region 12 is a petroleum center and contains one of the most important military bases in the country. These four regions, in addition to their wealth and strategic importance, have the smallest populations (with one exception) and are the most highly concentrated in Chile. On the other end of the spectrum, the two regions with the lowest percentage of coverage (Los Lagos and Araucania) are also those with the lowest per capita GDP and, with relatively large and dispersed populations, are the least urbanized and have the lowest per capita GDP.[20] A statistical analysis using figures from 1960, although not strictly comparable (as it was done among the provinces), showed that the provinces with the worst and best coverage were the same

TABLE 32
EAP COVERAGE BY REGION IN CHILE, 1980

Region	EAP (thousands)	Active Insured (thousands)	% of Coverage
Metropolitan (Santiago)	1,491.9	915.1	61.3
1. Tarapacá	80.6	73.3	90.9
2. Antofagasta	96.6	86.2	89.2
3. Atacama	59.5	42.5	71.4
4. Coquimbo	114.9	72.2	62.8
5. Valparaíso	386.9	217.8	56.3
6. B. O'Higgins	179.7	125.5	69.8
7. Maule	223.3	133.2	59.6
8. Bío-Bío	454.1	286.9	63.2
9. La Araucania	208.7	82.0	39.3
10. Los Lagos	270.7	136.5	50.4
11. Aysén	23.9	13.7	57.3
12. Magallanes-Antárctica	44.0	41.8	95.0
Total	3,635.5	2,226.9	61.2

Sources: EAP from INE, Compendio estadístico, 1982. Insured from SSS, Seguridad social: Estadísticas, 1980.

a. Excludes the armed forces and police, which are concentrated principally in the metropolitan region.

as those in the 1980 regions, with the sole exception of Magallanes, where, because of the exploitation of oil, coverage almost doubled.[21]

Table 33 notes the differences in the degree of social security coverage among economic branches in 1970 and 1980. The estimates suffer from defects related to changes in the definitions of branches and the high percentage of insured in unspecified activities in 1980. Although these shortcomings preclude an accurate comparison between the figures for the two years, the table at least indicates that the sectors with the best coverage (several are over-covered because of statistical defects or double counting) are mining, public utilities, manufacturing, and construction industries, while the lowest coverage is in agriculture. (Even though the distributions are not strictly comparable, they indicate an increase in coverage for agriculture and a decline

TABLE 33
EAP COVERAGE BY ECONOMIC SECTOR IN CHILE, 1979 AND 1980

Sector	1970			1980		
	EAP (thous.)	Active Insured[a] (thous.)	% of Coverage	EAP[b] (thous.)	Active Insured[a] (thous.)	% of Coverage
Agriculture, cattle, forestry, and fishing	570.2	476.0	83.5	529.7	310.5	58.6
Mines and quarries	81.2	100.1	123.3	71.8	116.3	162.0
Manufacturing	446.5	456.7	102.3	524.1	471.1	89.9
Construction	175.2	149.6	85.4	151.4	160.2	105.8
Electricity, gas and water	20.0	28.1	140.5	24.5	26.8	109.4
Transport, storage, and communications	165.6	121.1	73.1	211.1	149.8	71.0
Commerce, restaurants, and hotels	302.0	217.4	72.0	589.4	299.7	50.8
Financial services, insurance services, etc.	45.1	571.2	78.0	101.0	528.9	46.0
Communal, social, personal, and other services	687.2			1,056.8		
Unspecified	240.5	97.1	40.6	6.5	163.5	c
Total	2,733.5	2,217.3	64.0	3,256.3	2,226.9	68.4

Sources: EAP from INE, *Chile series estadísticas, 1981,* and *Compendio estadístico 1982.* Insured from SSS, *Seguridad social: Estadísticas, 1971/72* and *1980.*

a. The original distribution relates to the two principal funds (SSS for blue-collar and EMPART for white-collar workers), to which the insured in other funds have tentatively been added.
b. Employed EAP.
c. The large number of insured in "other activities" distorts the distribution.

for services—probably personnel—and commerce.) Of the case studies for which this type of information exists, Chile has the highest percentage of coverage in agriculture. In part the reason is the relatively high proportion of salaried and unionized workers in this sector in Chile as compared with other countries.

Noncovered Population

The previous analysis has identified various groups without any social security coverage or with very little. With respect to self-employed workers, in 1982 it was estimated that there were approximately 76,000 insured in the old system and 79,653 in the new; the total of 155,653 insured is 21 percent of the employed workers in this category (737,000).[22] (The number of self-employed workers insured by the AFP fell from 171,645 in January 1982 to 73,624 in April of the same year. The official reason was a cleaning out of the files, but it could also have been in part a result of the economic crisis.) Also in 1982, there were 679,100 unemployed with either no insurance coverage or with coverage for a short period only, and to this figure must be added those in employment welfare plans. Finally, some 116,000 unpaid family workers also lacked insurance coverage.[23] The total of noninsured in these three groups was 1,376,000, equivalent to 39 percent of the EAP in 1982. Table 31 shows that, in 1980, 38 percent of the EAP was not covered. It is presumed that the insured in agriculture are wage earners and that the noninsured are small proprietors, self-employed workers, unpaid family workers, and the unemployed, so that the bulk of the noninsured are already included in the above calculation. But some of the wage earners in agriculture (and possibly in personal services and commerce) are probably uninsured because of evasion. Nonetheless, it must be remembered that the noninsured sectors are protected by social welfare programs even though these are of lower quality than the insurance programs.

Measures to Improve Coverage

To determine with certainty which individuals are insured and which are not, it is necessary to correct the figures for the old and new systems. An identity card with a unique, verifiable code and individual accounts in both systems (to eliminate duplication) are needed to achieve this goal. It was announced that consolidated figures for coverage in both systems would be published at the end of 1983, but the figures had not materialized by mid-1984.

Coverage of the self-employed in the new system should be made mandatory. Also, the effort to improve coverage in the less-developed regions and in the most poorly covered economic sectors, such as agriculture, must continue. The exemption in the payment of commissions to the AFP during the first year of unemployment has been a positive step.

FINANCING

Sources of Financing

Before wage contributions were partly standardized, large differences in percentage contributions existed among insured groups. At the end of the 1960s, the total wage contribution ranged from 14 percent to 66 percent (one of the region's two highest); the employer was expected to pay the largest part, from 2 percent to 52 percent, and the insured the smallest, from 2 percent to 19 percent. The state contribution was fixed as a percentage of wages in a few cases and was small (5.5 percent) but in most cases consisted of special taxes (for example, on government payments, entertainment tickets, legal documents, imports and exports, transportation, bank deposits, and bets) or subsidies to cover deficits. The distribution of income by source in the entire system showed that four-fifths came from employers plus the state and less than one-fifth from the insured. The ratio of the employer contribution plus that of the state to the insured contribution was 6 in the armed forces, 3.6 in the institutions covering blue-collar workers, 2.5 in those covering private white-collar employees, and 1.2 in those covering civil servants.[24]

The reforms of the last ten years notably reduced the percentage of total contribution but with important differences among institutions. In all institutions of the old and new systems, the employer contribution was eliminated except in the case of occupational risks. For unemployment compensation and family allowances, a gradually declining tax was fixed, and it is projected to disappear in 1986, but the tax goes to the treasury, not to the social security institutions (see table 34). The state no longer pays a contribution over wages and has apparently eliminated special taxes. The value of the contributions of those in the old system who moved to the new system is honored, however, by means of a "recognition bond" in the name of the insured. The bond must be cashed at the time that the insured qualifies for the pension, while in the old system the payment would have been distributed throughout the life of the pensioner. This bond represents half the capital of those who will retire in the next two decades. It is adjusted for inflation and pays an annual interest. In addition the state must finance the growing deficits of the old system and pay welfare pensions and health care as well as unemployment subsidies and family allowances in both systems.

The insured's contribution is higher in the old system than in the new. The old system's contribution ranges from 24.8 percent to 29.9 percent among the three principal groups (although there are higher and lower contributions in other institutions), whereas in the new system it is 19.7 percent. In the new pension program there is a minimum contribution percentage (it is the same for salaried and self-employed workers) that is tax-exempted; voluntary additional contributions can be made at a rate that fluctuates, depending on the AFPs. Those who transferred to the new system benefited from a reduction in the contribution percentage (from 5 to 10 percentage points), thus increasing their net income. This reduction is not enjoyed by those who remain in the old system (see table 34). The transfer incentive has been justified by the argument that the reduction was possible because of the greater efficiency of the new system as compared with the old. But the real explanation appears to relate to the savings resulting from the reforms of 1974–79 that applied to both systems but benefit only the new one.[25]

The collection of contributions is not unified. The AFP collects contributions only for the pension program; the others are collected by the old institutions. The contribution for health-maternity, which increased from 4 percent to 6 percent in 1981–84, is transferred to FONASA or to the ISAPRE, depending on the affiliation of the insured.

In addition to contributions, the affiliates of the new system must pay the AFP a commission for services (a fixed sum and a percentage over their

TABLE 34
LEGAL CONTRIBUTIONS TO SOCIAL SECURITY
BY PROGRAM AND SOURCE IN CHILE, 1984
(PERCENTAGE OF SALARY OR INCOME)

	Old System					New System		
	Insured							
Program	Blue-Collar Workers	Private White-Collar Workers	Civil Servants	Employer	State[a]	Insured	Employer	State
Pensions	18.89	19.94	18.81	*	Subsidy	10.00[b] 3.70[c]	*	Bond of recognition
Health/maternity	5.74	6.55	5.59	*	Subsidy	6.00	*	*
Occupational risks	*	*	*	0.85[d]	*	*	0.85	*
Unemployment	*	*	*	e	All	*	e	All
Family allowances	*	*	*	e	All	*	e	All
Other[f]	0.21	1.35	5.51	*	Subsidy	*	*	*
Total	24.84	27.84	29.91	0.85		19.70	0.85	

Source: Legislation and information from the SSS and AFP, June 1984.

   a. Covers the deficit of the institutions and funds welfare pensions and health care.
   b. Contribution for old age pension.
   c. Average contribution for disability and survivors' pensions, which fluctuated between 3.5 percent and 3.9 percent.
   d. Not paid in civil service, as the state assumes the responsibility. The 0.85 percent premium is the base and, according to risk, an additional premium up to 3.4 percent is paid.
   e. When the employer's contribution was discarded, a tax of 3 percent was set. It was later reduced to 2 percent and was expected to disappear in 1986. But the money goes to the treasury, not to the social security institutions.
   f. Funeral aid and severance pay; the latter is not available for blue-collar workers.

   * Not applicable.

contributions). The commission varies, depending on the AFP, and should, in the long run, be reduced to a minimum because of the competition among AFPs. Despite signs of greater competition, the same original twelve AFPs are functioning, and the possibility of new AFPs entering the market is very limited because of the large investment required. In 1981, when the program began, 63 percent of all affiliates were concentrated in two of the AFPs and 81 percent of them in four. Although a deconcentration process has occurred, in 1983 the two major AFPs still had 49 percent of the affiliates and four of them had 67 percent. It is argued, however, that the 1983 percentages are lower than the concentration percentages in Chilean industries.[26] In 1981–83 the average fixed commission doubled (a 30 percent real increase), but the average percentage commission was reduced by 10 percent, so that it is difficult to calculate whether there has been a significant overall net change. Nonetheless, the increments affected the contributors with the lowest salary, and it has been estimated that the cost of the commission for the insured during an average of forty-five years will be between 37 percent and 47 percent of the capital of their individual account.[27]

The old system is based on the pay-as-you-go method and, for that reason, has no investments. The new system (AFP) is based on full capitalization (as in private insurance) and in May 1984 had accumulated 121,000 million pesos (approximately $1,100 million at the free exchange rate), equivalent to 30 percent of all deposits in the financial system. At the beginning of 1984, 50 percent of the investment was in letters of credit, 44 percent in state bonds, and the remaining 6 percent in long-term deposits and debentures of private and public enterprises. Approximately 72 percent of investment was in state bonds or in deposits or mortgages in either state banks or banks rescued by the state.[28] The investment had very high yield in the first two years of the system: an average annual real rate of 22 percent over contributions and a rate over the individual account that ranged from 10 percent to 21 percent, in accordance with the income of the contributors.[29]

Evasion and Payment Delays

As I have already stated, the number of affiliates in the old system as well as in the new (see table 31) is much higher than the number of contributors. The superintendency of the AFPs regularly publishes the percentage distribution of contributors but not the absolute figures. The extent of payment delays and evasion in the new system therefore cannot be known with certainty. The superintendency of social security has estimated, unofficially, that in the 1970s the overestimation of affiliates above contributors was 30 percent. A large number of the SSS insured (especially agricultural and domestic service workers) joined the program to receive health care but made very few contributions. In SERMENA the insured received health care for several months after their last contribution and, when they owed a great deal, obtained a new identity card saying that they had just begun to work.[30]

As previously noted, the number of affiliates in the AFPs, after duplication has been eliminated, is an estimated 1.4 million. Of these, only 900,000 paid regular contributions in 1983; hence evasion and payment delays amounted to about 36 percent. As in the old system, affiliates in the new system pay their contributions only sporadically, in order to ensure that they receive health care.[31] Because of the high interest rates, in 1981–82 many employers retained their contributions and placed them at short term in the financial market, as the high yield permitted them to pay the fine later and make a profit; this problem was later corrected by the superintendency.[32]

To control evasion, it is imperative that the single identification number and individual accounts be completed. Several problems relative to identification have already been mentioned. It is reported that, in the SSS the establishment of individual accounts is under way, aided by centralized information; there was a single code and archive. This processing appears relatively easy in CANAEMPU as well; the state and public agencies kept good records. But the situation in EMPART is more complicated, as the information is dispersed in innumerable contribution forms. In 1983 it was predicted that completion of the individual account would take from four to six months in the SSS, from eight to ten months in CANAEMPU, and from one to two years in EMPART, but a year later, it was announced that the latter would take some five years.[33] In the new system the AFPs must keep the individual account up-to-date and must periodically inform the insured of their balance. Nevertheless, as I have noted, duplication is a serious problem, and statistics on the actual number of contributors have still not been published. Finally, control of evasion and payment delays is complicated by the diversity of collection agencies, for example, AFPs and various institutions in the old system, several of which have contracted with banks for this work.

Financial Equilibrium

Table 35 presents the balance of revenues and expenditures in the old Chilean social security system for 1968–80. All programs appear to generate a surplus (except for a deficit in both family allowances in 1978 and 1980 and unemployment in 1978), and the general balance also shows a surplus that grew from 7.5 percent of revenues in 1968 to 17 percent in 1980. The current official viewpoint is that this surplus was due to the substantial contributions that the state made as a third party, which rose from 28.6 percent of expenditures in 1978 to 41.4 percent in 1980, the highest percentage in Latin America. Without the state contribution, the 1980 deficit would have risen to 26 percent of revenues, and thus it is concluded that the old system was saved from bankruptcy only by the growing state subsidy.[34]

An opposing viewpoint is that the state contribution was made partly

TABLE 35
SOCIAL SECURITY BALANCE OF REVENUES AND EXPENDITURES
BY PROGRAM IN CHILE, 1968–1980

	1968	1970	1975	1978	1980
Pensions					
Revenues	3,592	8,396	2,533	33,931	79,313
Expenditures	3,120	6,862	2,034	24,874	62,842
Balance	472	1,534	499	9,057	16,471
Health/maternity					
Revenues	852	2,606	1,040	13,884	33,989
Expenditures	960	2,588	948	13,184	25,736
Balance	− 108	18	92	700	8,253
Occupational risks					
Revenues	146	409	134	1,510	3,850
Expenditures	132	297	87	1,297	3,165
Balance	14	112	47	231	685
Family allowances					
Revenues	1,970	4,769	2,140	10,031	14,564
Expenditures	1,872	4,545	1,816	10,562	17,166
Balance	98	224	324	− 531	− 2,602
Unemployment					
Revenues	48	131	59	1,142	3,139
Expenditures	36	64	40	1,147	2,731
Balance	12	67	19	− 5	408
Total[a]					
Revenues	7,294	17,019	6,194	63,727	143,238
Expenditures	6,746	14,968	5,165	53,727	118,834
Balance	548	2,051	1,029	10,000	24,404
As percentage of revenue	7.5	12.0	16.6	15.7	17.0

Source: SSS, *Seguridad social: Estadisticas, 1966, 1970, 1971–72, 1975–76, 1977–79,* and *1980.*

Note: The figures in the table are millions of escudos for 1968–70 and millions of pesos for 1975–80, both at current prices.

a. Includes other benefits not specified above: severance pay, contribution refunds, life insurance, funeral aid, etc.

because the state did not directly fulfill its obligations as employer (the percentage of wage contribution paid was lower than that paid by the private sector) and hence was doing so indirectly through the subsidy. In 1980, 53 percent of the state contribution went to the pension program for civil servants, who received pensions far greater than those of blue-collar workers and private white-collar workers, as we will see below. Another substantial part of the state contribution (44 percent in 1980) applied to the health-maternity and pension programs of blue-collar workers. This sum was to finance health care and pensions for those with the lowest income and so was really a state welfare program. It is interesting to note that four-fifths of the civil servants have remained in the old system because of its advantages over the new. Thus the state will have to continue subsidizing this group just as it did prior to the reform.[35] Besides, the cost of welfare pensions and health care has risen because of the increase in the number of indigents receiving these services.

Since 1980 no official figures of the old system's accounting balance have been published, but the 1974–79 reforms and the creation of the new system have obviously provoked a sharp disequilibrium in the old system. The elimination of the employer contribution and the transfer of two-thirds of the insured (especially the relatively younger ones) substantially reduced income. On the other hand, costs have gradually risen because those insured who are relatively close to retirement have remained in the old system. Furthermore, since 1982 the economic crisis—with its resulting high unemployment, fall in real salaries, and increases in evasion and payment delays—further reduced income, while the adjustment in pensions for inflation further increased expenditures.

Recently figures on contribution income in the old system (which now constitutes almost all income) as well as figures on expenditures have been reported: in 1981 the deficit rose to 47,975 million pesos and in 1983 more than doubled: 110,012 million pesos (approximately $1.2 billion at the unofficial exchange rate).[36] This growing deficit is basically covered by the state through subsidies of the Institute of Social Insurance Standardization.

As previously noted, in three years of operation the new system accumulated a reserve of $1,000 million (similar to the old system's deficit in 1983). The contribution reduction notwithstanding, this reserve is a logical outcome in a newly created program with a large group of insured who cannot retire during the first five years of the program's operation. In addition, the investment yield has been very high.

The economic crisis seriously affected the AFP but did not affect the pension funds, as these have accounts separate from the other operations of the AFPs. In addition, the state has established a series of guarantees for the funds: diversification of the investment portfolio, minimum yield, and minimum reserve capital to guarantee that yield. In fact, the funds benefited from the high yield during the years of crisis, although a significant fall in the yield is expected in the future. On the other hand, the AFPs have suffered huge losses (2,787 million pesos in 1981–83, or about $30 million at the unofficial exchange rate). These losses, however, were almost eliminated in 1983, when several AFPs began to generate profits (the losses or gains of the AFPs affect its investors but not its affiliates, at least theoretically). Apparently it was predicted that the AFPs would incur losses in the first two or three years because of the high costs of putting them in operation.[37]

But the AFPs overcame the crisis only with the help of the state, which, by intervening in banks facing imminent bankruptcy, assumed the majority of the shares of the four largest AFPs. One AFP on the verge of bankruptcy, however, was taken over by the creditor banks. According to the law, if an AFP fails, it is dissolved, and its pension fund is administered by the super-intendency until another AFP takes charge of it.[38] Without the intervention of the state, a general bankruptcy could have occurred, endangering the financial stability of the system. Also, as I have already noted, 72 percent of the pension fund investments are in state bonds or in state banks or in banks in which the state has intervened. Finally, the future stability of the system depends not only on contributions and investment yield, but also on the recognition bonds that the state must deliver to account for the contributions paid by the insured to the old system. In mid-1983 only 7 percent of the insured had received the recognition bond, but issuance of all remaining bonds by 1985 was planned.[39] In summary, the financial stability and solvency of the new system depend strongly on the state.

In the health sector, approximately 3 percent of the affiliates of the AFP—those with higher income—have transferred to ISAPREs. The result has been a deficit fluctuating at between 7 percent and 9 percent of the resources that FONASA receives to finance health care of AFP affiliates.[40] This deficit could partly explain the increases in contributions from 4 to 6 percent for health-maternity. The ISAPREs must maintain a minimal capital plus a deposit of guarantee and must assure benefits through contracts with a minimum duration of one year. The average monthly contribution to the ISAPREs at the end of 1983 was 3,419 pesos, relatively high for the income level in Chile. Because of the economic crisis in that year, the number of terminated contracts was 37 percent greater than the number of contracts subscribed.[41]

Financing Methods

The pension program in the old system was originally based on the general fixed-premium method but gradually evolved until 1952, when it changed to the pure assessment method. This program faces a growing disequilibrium that requires increasing state subsidies. It is not known whether a recent actuarial study of this program has been done.

The pension program of the new system is based on full capitalization, as in private insurance. Theoretically, the basic premium in this program is uniform and should guarantee all future obligations, if the reserves are adequately invested. But the equilibrium of this program has been partly assured by maintaining the oldest insured in the old system and by state support through the bond of recognition and the financial bailout of the AFPs during the crisis. The program is expected to reach a point of stability in some twenty-five years, when income from contributions and investment equals expenditures. Nevertheless, this period could be shortened if the investment policy were modified (see below) or if the state were not to endorse the bulk of investment, which is in state bonds and state banks or in banks in which the state has intervened.

The rest of the social security programs probably use the pure assessment (pay-as-you-go) method and require state transfers.

Measures to Increase Revenue

In both systems tighter control of evasion and payment delays is required. To that effect it is necessary to complete the national identification system and individual accounts as well as to unify collections. The contribution percentage paid by the insured in Chile (even in the new system) is probably the highest in Latin America: it is 1.5 times greater than that of Uruguay, 3 times that of Costa Rica, and 5 times those in Mexico and Peru. Also, in the health-maternity program, the insured (except for indigents and blue-collar workers) not only pay a relatively high wage contribution percentage but must also pay directly for a substantial part of the services. For this reason and because of the nation's difficult economic situation, it is not advisable to increase the tax burden upon the insured. As we will see in chapter 7, the employer contribution was reduced in Uruguay, but a value-added tax (VAT) replaced the lost income (either partly or totally). In Chile, it is not known whether the income lost with the elimination of the employer contribution has been replaced by part of the income from the VAT introduced in 1975. In any case, the state has fulfilled its obligations through the required transfers to balance the old system. But before we can recommend other sources of financing, we must appraise the combined impact on employment of both the VAT and the elimination of the employer's contribution.

Benefits, Expenditures, and Costs

Benefits and Entitlement Conditions

It is difficult to summarize the benefits and entitlement conditions in Chile and to compare them with those of other countries because of the differences between the old and new systems. This is especially true of the pension program but also of the options within the health program. In any case, Chile is one of a half dozen Latin American countries that cover all social risks.

In the health-maternity program the insured is currently entitled to monetary benefits, such as payments in lieu of salary for sickness or maternity. Those covered by the SNSS directly receive benefits in cash as well as services such as periodic examinations, medical-hospital care, surgery, medicines, and dental care. Those covered by FONASA receive from 25 percent to 50 percent of the cost, depending on the level of services, while those covered by the ISAPREs have a greater variety of service levels. Dependents entitled to nonmonetary health benefits usually include the spouse, children, and parents. In cases of occupational risks, the insured individuals are entitled to better monetary benefits than for nonoccupational risk and similar health benefits plus prosthesis and rehabilitation. In the old pension program, the insured or their dependents are entitled to old age, disability, and survivors' pensions (in the case of disability, the worker is also entitled to medical-hospital care) as well as funeral aid. Before the reform, the institutions that covered white-collar employees also provided seniority and unemployment pensions. In the new system, the old age pension program gives the insured the option of either purchasing a lifetime income through commercial insurance (based on the accumulated capital in the individual account) or agreeing with the AFP on monthly payments of such capital. Coverage for disability and survivors' pensions requires an additional contribution. The unemployment program pays a monetary subsidy equivalent to three to twelve monthly wages and during this period assures the continuation of coverage on family allowances and nonmonetary health benefits. The family allowances program pays a uniform monthly sum for dependents, including spouse, children, grandchildren, and parents. Finally, for those who lack income, there are welfare programs for pensions (for those over sixty-five and for those over eighteen who are disabled), health care, unemployment, and family allowances.

Within the Latin American context, the present legal conditions of the Chilean system are very generous in health benefits, both monetary (with very few exceptions) and in-kind benefits or services for the insured and his dependents. (But it must be remembered that, except for those covered by the SNSS, the insured must defray at least half of the nonmonetary benefits.) Conditions for old age retirement (after the 1970s reforms) are the strictest in Latin America after those of Mexico and Guatemala: sixty-five years of age for men and sixty for women with fifteen years of contribution in both cases. But before the reform it was possible to retire for old age in some institutions at fifty years of age (for example, in banking) and in others with only fifteen or twenty-five years of service at any age (for example, in the congress, the armed forces, the banks, and journalism)—that is to say, to retire when younger than forty. Conditions for disability and survivors' pensions are currently average within the region or are slightly stricter than the regional average. Current conditions are adequate when compared with those in other countries when one takes into account that the global wage contribution percentage in the old system is one of the three highest in the region and is average in the new system. The problem is the high cost of existing pension obligations and acquired rights under the old system, plus high cost-of-living adjustments and the existence of family allowances, unemployment compensation, and social welfare programs, which are available in only a few countries.

Table 36 shows Chile's advances in health levels and services in the last two decades; all services available in the country are included. All indicators in the table show progressive improvement except hospital beds per inhabitant

TABLE 36
HEALTH SERVICES AND LEVELS IN CHILE, 1960–1981

	Hospital Beds per 1,000 Persons	Physicians per 10,000 Persons	Mortality Rate		Life Expectancy[a]
			General	Infant	
1960	4.0	7.3	12.3	120.3	56.2
1965	4.2	7.1	10.8	97.3	58.0
1970	3.8	7.5	8.9	82.2	60.6
1975	3.8	8.3	7.3	57.6	63.8
1980	3.4	9.4	6.7	33.0	67.6
1981	3.3	9.7	6.2	27.0	68.0

Sources: Banco Central de Chile, Indicadores económicos y sociales, 1960–1982; INE, Compendio estadístico 1981, 1983, and Demografía, 1981; CEPAL, Anuario estadístico de América Latina, 1981; and CELADE, Boletín estadístico 17:33 (January 1984), and projections for 1980–85.

a. Values for five-year periods (e.g., 1955 − 60 = 56.2); with the exception of the 1981 figure, which is an estimate for the year based on the 1980–85 projections.

after 1965. In 1980, Chile occupied fourth place among the six case studies in terms of health-service indicators (the same relative position it occupied twenty years earlier), third place in terms of mortality rates, and fourth place in life expectancy (showing in these two indicators an advance from the country's relative position in 1960). Chile's reduction in the infant mortality rate is one of the most notable in Latin America—especially since 1975. In terms of closing the gap, Chile leads the six case studies with a decrease of 78 percent in 1960–81. The Ministry of Health reports a new reduction of infant mortality in 1983 with 21 per 1,000, which puts Chile just after Cuba and Costa Rica. Some of the factors that have contributed to the decline in infant mortality are: the reduction in regional differences, the decrease in the birth rate, the increase in real expenditures for health (targeted to health care for mothers and infants as well as to lactation programs), and the greater availability of potable water and sewers.[42]

Inequalities in Benefits

Benefits and entitlement conditions, as we have seen, are uniform in the family allowances, unemployment, and occupational risks programs. In the pension program some conditions have been standardized in both systems (for example, in retirement for old age). The new system is completely uniform, but differences still exist within the old system. In the health-maternity program, entitlement conditions have been standardized with some exceptions. It is alleged that the technical level of curative medical care in the SNSS and the three levels of FONASA is uniform and that differences exist only in terms of waiting time, the variety of specialists, and the hospital environment, but this aspect has not been properly studied.[43]

The differences in population coverage among regions correlate with the medical-hospital services available in them. In 1980, the number of doctors per inhabitant in Magallanes-Antarctica was 2.4 times greater than in La Araucania, while the number of hospital beds per inhabitant was 1.5 times greater. In general, the most-developed regions (Magallanes, Antofagasta, Santiago, and Valparaiso) had health services superior to those of the less-developed regions (La Araucania, Los Lagos, and Aysen). In 1980 the infant mortality rate in Santiago and Magallanes was half that of La Araucania and Los Lagos. Nevertheless, regional differences have been considerably reduced in the last two decades, and in 1980 they were among the lowest in Latin America.[44]

Table 37 shows the differences, within the old system, in average pensions among insured groups in both 1972 and 1980. The armed forces and the police received an average pension that was from six to seven times greater than that of blue-collar workers in 1972 and from seven to eight times greater in 1980. Banking employees and civil servants also enjoyed pensions superior to those of blue-collar workers. The differences in the ratio of pensions had risen by 1980. It should be remembered that these differences not only re- flected inequalities in income but also resulted from strong state subsidies to civil servants (who received 53 percent of the total state contribution in 1980)

TABLE 37

DIFFERENCES IN AVERAGE MONTHLY PENSIONS AMONG INSURED
GROUPS IN CHILE, 1972 AND 1980

	1972		1980	
Insured Group	*Average Pension*[a]	*Ratio*[b]	*Average Pension*[a]	*Ratio*[b]
General Average	**22,328**	**2.0**	**54,266**	**2.0**
Blue-collar workers' fund (SSS)	11,705	1.0	27,701	1.0
Private white-collar workers' fund (EMPART)	18,753	1.6	46,184	1.7
Civil servants' fund (CONAEMPU)	40,926	3.5	89,077	3.2
Banking fund[c]	57,418	4.9	157,014	5.7
Police fund	69,843	6.0	190,863	6.9
Armed forces' fund	79,873	6.8	221,259	8.0

Source: Author's calculations based on SSS, *Seguridad social: Estadísticas, 1971–72* and *1980.*

Note: Figures are given in escudos and pesos at current prices. The monetary system was changed in 1975: 1,000 escudos = 1 peso.

  a. Arithmetic average of all existing pensions.
  b. Taking the SSS as base (1.0)
  c. Weighted average of the four banking funds.

and to the armed forces and the police. It is not possible to compare the average pension in the old system and the new in 1983, as the AFPs still have not granted old age pensions and there are no disaggregated figures for the armed forces and the police. It is possible, however, to make a comparison limited to disability and survivors' pensions grouping the armed forces and the police with the other pensions. In this context, the comparison of 1983 with 1980 shows that differences among civil servants and private white-collar and blue-collar workers were similar; the average of "other pensions" (including the armed forces, police, banking, merchant marine, and so forth) was 4.5 times higher than that of blue-collar workers; and the average pension in the AFPs was 3.8 times higher than that of blue-collar workers but inferior to that of "other pensions" in the old system.[45] Differences among pensions in Chile in 1980 were much greater than those in Costa Rica (see table 14) and Uruguay (see table 71) and were probably similar to those of Mexico (see table 49); no data on this subject are available from Cuba and Peru.

The Growing Cost of Social Security and Its Causes

Table 38 shows the evolution of the cost of social security in Chile in the period 1963–80. Social security expenditures as a percentage of GDP rose in 1963–71 from 10 percent to 17 percent, establishing, in this last year, a historic record that has not been equaled since. After 1971, with the economic deterioration, the percentage fell to 9.3 percent in 1975, but later, with the economic recuperation, it rose again, reaching 11 percent in 1980, still the

TABLE 38
COST OF SOCIAL SECURITY IN CHILE, 1963–1980
(MILLIONS OF PESOS AT CURRENT PRICES)[a]

	GDP	Total Central Govt. Expenditures	Social Security Expenditures		
			Total	% of GDP	% of Govt. Expenditures
1963	9	2	1	10.0	50.0
1965	19	4	2	12.1	53.5
1971	129	38	22	17.2	59.0
1973	1,246	326	119	9.6	36.5
1975	42,091	12,465	3,900	9.3	31.3
1980	1,075,269	367,104	118,833	11.0	32.4

Sources: GDP 1963–77 from El costo de la seguridad social, 1972–74 and 1975–77; 1978–80 from the Banco Central de Chile, Indicadores económicos y sociales, 1960–1982. Central government expenditures 1963–72 from Indicadores económicos y sociales, 1960–1982; 1973–80 from IMF, Government Finance Statistics Yearbook, 1982. Social security expenditures for 1963–77 from ILO, El costo de la seguridad social; 1978–80 from SSS, Seguridad social: estadísticas 1977–79 and 1980.

a. The 1963–73 figures were converted from escudos to pesos (1 peso = 1,000 escudos).

highest in Latin America together with Uruguay. As a percentage of total central government expenditures, social security expenditures reached 59 percent in 1971, falling to 32 percent by 1980. Even though there is no information on total social security expenditures after 1980, figures on health care expenditures show a rise in 1981 and a deterioration in 1982–83 because of the economic crisis.[46]

General causes. As in the cases of Costa Rica and Cuba, the universalization of population coverage is an important cause of the Chilean increase in social security outlays. In addition, Chile is one of the few countries of the region to cover all social risks. Prior to the reform, it had a very generous benefit package with excessively liberal entitlement conditions.

Administrative costs in the old system took 7.7 percent of expenditures in 1980, an average figure in the region. Information is not available on the number of employees in social security institutions and the cost of their wages, but because of the still-existing multiplicity of institutions, employment must be very high. Partial unification has reportedly resulted, between 1981 and the beginning of 1982, in the elimination of 300 administrative offices and a 40 percent reduction in personnel (two-thirds of the managerial positions). Still, in mid-1983, there was a personnel surplus of 25 percent, people who continued to receive salary although they were working for other institutions.[47] In the health sector the cost of personnel was proportionally reduced partly because of the fall in real salaries but also because of a greater increase in the use of paramedic and auxiliary personnel in place of physicians.[48]

Theoretically, the competition among AFPs should reduce administrative costs to a minimum, but in practice, the AFPs have recruited insured through very expensive publicity campaigns ($22.5 million in the first year of operations) and more than 80,000 salesmen, who work on commission. The insured appear to choose the AFP not on the basis of its performance (for example, lower commissions and contributions and higher yields) but as a function of the image created by the communication media.[49] A 1982 survey found that 75 percent of the AFP affiliates did not know what they paid, and 23 percent said that they knew but were actually mistaken.[50] The superintendency of the AFPs and some of the AFP directors have acknowledged that a significant reduction in costs has not occurred and that competition in the system should focus on reducing commissions and increasing yields.[51]

Table 39 shows that the fundamental and growing component of social security outlays is pension expenditures (53 percent in 1980), followed by expenditures on health-maternity (22 percent). In third place are family allowance expenditures, which have exhibited a declining tendency since the mid-1970s (14.5 percent in 1980) because of the standardization of the program and the decrease in the amount of the highest allowances. The occupational risks and unemployment programs combined have a small but increasing proportion (5 percent) due, in the second case, to rising unem-

TABLE 39
DISTRIBUTION OF SOCIAL SECURITY EXPENDITURES
BY PROGRAM IN CHILE, 1965–1980
(PERCENT)

Expenditure[a]	1965	1968	1970	1975	1978	1980
Pensions	44.4	44.4	43.7	48.1	46.3	52.8
Health/maternity	14.2	15.1	13.7	16.9	24.5	21.7
Occupational risks	**	1.5	1.1	1.4	2.4	2.7
Family allowances	29.5	28.3	30.8	25.3	19.7	14.5
Unemployment	0.7	0.7	0.6	1.0	2.1	2.3
Other[b]	11.2	10.0	10.1	7.2	5.0	6.0

Source: SSS, Costo de la seguridad social chilena, año 1980 (Santiago,1982).

a. Excludes certain health costs (e.g., prevention), administrative costs, and surpluses going to the reserve fund. In distribution this table does not correspond with table 35 except for the years 1978 and 1980.

b. Severance pay, contribution refund, life insurance, funeral aid, etc.

**Not available.

ployment. The remaining benefits (severance pay, life insurance, and so forth) exhibit a declining tendency (6 percent in 1980) because several of them have been eliminated. The analysis below focuses on the cost of the pension and health programs.

Causes related to the pension program. In 1980 the percentage of Chilean social security expenditures in pension programs was the third highest in the region, greatly surpassed by Uruguay and only slightly so by Argentina. The causes of such a high and growing percentage are the following: the oldest pension legislation in Latin America (even though the new system began in 1981, practically all of the insured were already covered in the old system, and the time accumulated in it was credited); universality of coverage, generous pensions, and very liberal entitlement conditions (in the majority of the institutions of the old system except the SSS); the fourth oldest population in the region; and the sixth highest life expectancy. (See table 54, below). On the other hand, the real value of pensions has notably deteriorated, even though there was a partial readjustment in 1977–80.

According to table 31, the quotient of demographic burden (not including welfare pensions) rose from 0.159 in 1960 to 0.458 in 1980, the highest in Latin America after that of Uruguay, twice that of Cuba, and eight times greater than that of Costa Rica. The 1983 quotient can be calculated as 0.553 or 0.638, depending on whether the number of active insured in 1983 was 2.27 or 1.97 million (see above) and using the figure of 1.26 million passives, including both systems and welfare pensions.[52] The quotient of demographic burden varies significantly among the three principal sectors of insured in the old system: in 1980 it was 0.869 among civil servants, 0.379 among blue-collar workers, and 0.273 among private white-collar employees.[53] The rate of growth of the EAP leveled out at 2.6 percent in the 1970s, while that of active insured (affiliates, not necessarily contributors) fell from 2.7 percent to minus 0.7 percent in part because of the universalization of coverage but also because of the economic crisis.

From 1960 to 1980, the percentage of the population older than sixty-five in Chile rose from 4.3 percent to 5.5 percent (the fourth highest in the region), and it is predicted to reach 8 percent in the year 2010. (See table 40). Life expectancy in 1980 was 67.6 years, the sixth highest in Latin America, and women had a life expectancy six years higher than men. In the old system old age retirement for most insured (white- and blue-collar workers and civil servants) came at sixty-five years for men and fifty-five for women. Private white-collar employees, however, could retire with twenty-five to thirty years of service at any age, and civil servants could retire with twenty to twenty-five years of service; the other groups had even lower retirement ages and years of service. A woman in the public sector could retire at forty-three with a life expectancy of thirty-three years and a man at forty-eight with a life expectancy of twenty-five.

A study conducted in 1970 estimated that the elimination of seniority pensions and the increase in the retirement age to sixty-five for men and sixty for women would permit a reduction in the global wage contribution (to pay pensions equivalent to 85 percent of the average salary) of 15 or 37 percentage points, depending on whether the population was stable or stationary.[54] The reforms of the 1970s, which introduced some of these recommendations, permitted the percentage of the global contribution for the old system to be reduced by 19 percent that of the new system by 38 percent. The impact of the change in the cost of the system has recently been estimated as a savings of 60 percent of the actual value of the pensions for each worker and 40 percent of the total cost of pensions in the EMPART.[55] Also, since the new system will not grant old age pensions until 1986 (although it will make awards for disability and survivors) and the insured population is young (in 1983, 70 percent of those insured by AFPs were under forty years of age),

TABLE 40

DISTRIBUTION OF POPULATION BY AGE GROUP IN CHILE, 1960–2010
(PERCENT)

Age Group	1960	1970	1980	1990	2000	2010
0–14	39.2	38.1	32.5	30.6	28.0	25.4
15–64	56.5	57.1	62.0	63.5	65.3	66.6
65 and over	4.3	4.8	5.5	5.9	6.7	8.0

Source: Based on CELADE, *Boletín Demográfico* 16:32 (July 1983); author's calculations.

this program costs much less than the old system (which has been left with the double burden of pension currently being paid and the oldest insured, who are close to retirement).

Table 41 shows that in 1964–71 the real value of pensions doubled, and since pensions accounted for 44 percent of social security outlays, such an increase largely explains the jump in the proportion of social security expenditures over GDP from 10 percent to 17 percent in this period. (See table 38). Conversely, in 1971–75, the real value of pensions diminished to 40 percent so that social security costs could be reduced to 9.3 percent of GDP. From 1976 to 1980 the real value of pensions rose (as did social security costs), but in 1980 pensions stood at 60 percent of the 1971 level. Even so, the proportion of social security expenditures in pensions reached the record figure of 53 percent in 1980 (see table 39). After a possible increase in 1981, the real value of pensions probably decreased in 1982–83.[56] In this period the average pension has deteriorated more than average salaries, and family allowances have also fallen in real value.

TABLE 41
REAL VALUE OF ANNUAL PENSIONS IN CHILE, 1964–1980

| | Pensions (millions of pesos) | No. of Pensioners (thous.) | Average per Capita Pension (pesos) | Index (1970 = 100) | | |
				Nominal Pension	Inflation	Real Pension
1964	0.5	380	1.4	16	24	66.7
1965	0.8	436	1.9	23	31	74.2
1966	1.2	484	2.5	30	38	78.9
1967	1.6	514	3.2	39	45	86.7
1968	2.3	545	4.2	51	51	89.5
1969	3.1	591	5.3	64	74	86.5
1970	5.1	614	8.3	100	100	100.0
1971	9.3	643	14.5	175	127	138.0
1972	15.4	689	23.3	281	264	106.6
1973	51.0	713	71.6	864	1,428	60.5
1974	345.0	750	459.3	5,537	8,535	64.8
1975	1,526.0	810	1,885.0	22,725	40,899	55.5
1976	5,816.0	862	6,747.6	81,345	136,111	59.8
1977	14,459.0	916	15,791.7	190,376	291,006	65.4
1978	24,085.0	975	24,690.9	297,659	436,509	68.2
1979	38,962.0	1,023	38,094.3	459,244	595,398	77.1
1980	58,100.0	1,070	54,265.6	654,197	794,261	82.4

Sources: Pensions and number of pensioners from SSS, Seguridad social: Estadísticas, 1967–69 to 1980; inflation from ECLA, Estudio económico de América Latina, 1966, 1969, and 1980; average pension and indexes calculated by the author.

Note: Figures represent the average annual variation in 1964–70; corrected in 1971–80. The figures prior to 1975 have been converted from escudos to pesos; includes all pensions, even welfare pensions.

Causes related to the health program.   Chile, like Cuba, Uruguay, and Argentina, has already undergone the demographic transition: its fertility rate is the fourth lowest in Latin America, its mortality rate is the sixth lowest, its rate of population growth is the fourth lowest, and its rate of demographic dependency is the third lowest. In 1980, the proportion of the population at productive age—a group with relatively low health risks—was 62 percent, near the proportion of Uruguay and higher than that of the other four case studies.

But as in the other more-developed countries in the region, Chile has also changed its pathological profile. In 1982, 57 percent of the principal causes of death were circulatory, malign tumors, and accidents, while only 31 percent were digestive tract and respiratory diseases.[57] Like Costa Rica, Cuba, and Uruguay, Chile is now coping with the diseases that are most difficult to eradicate and with very high treatment costs.

The two contradictory health tendencies noted above and the heavy pension burden explain why a very low but growing percentage of Chilean social security expenditures is dedicated to health (see table 39). Nevertheless, in the last decade, a series of measures to control public expenditures on health have not hindered health care to rise despite the fact that the availability of hospital beds has not varied in any significant degree. Emphasis was put on primary care, with preference going to mothers and infants, nutrition, and sanitation, thereby reducing infant mortality noticeably. Priority was also given to the readaptation and maintenance of the hospital infrastructure and to the construction of rural clinics, medical posts, and health stations, thus reducing regional differences in health services. Paramedical and auxiliary personnel were increased—at a lower cost—in place of medical personnel, real salaries were reduced, in the SNSS the percentage of utilized hospital capacity was increased (it reached 76 percent in 1980), and the annual average number of days of hospital stay was decreased (from 11.6 in 1970 to 8.8 in 1982).[58] Nevertheless Costa Rica has a better record than Chile in both indicators, while that of utilized hospital capacity is higher in Cuba and that of hospital stay is shorter in Mexico. In addition, there has been, in Chile, a notable increase in the rate of several contagious diseases, such as typhoid fever and hepatitis. The reason appears to be a reduction in the Ministry of Health's inspections of establishments that process or serve food.[59] In 1983 a publicity campaign was launched to combat typhoid fever, but the cost of the vaccination was very high and free vaccination of the poorest segment of the population had little impact.

Estimates of total health expenditures, in real terms, indicate a fall in 1970–74, followed by an increase; in 1978 the 1970 level had been recovered and, in 1980, expenditures had risen to 15 percent above that level. Other estimates of public health expenditures, also deflated, successively show a decline, a recovery, and a new decline, with the level in 1983 still below that in 1974. There is a consensus that the private sector has increased its percentage of the value added in health, but discrepancies exist as to the magnitude of such increase. For example, from 51 percent to 66 percent in 1974–80 and from 60 percent to 63 percent in 1972–80.[60] In any case, this tendency is partly explained by the changes already discussed: FONASA's use of private services, payment by the insured of 50 percent to 75 percent of their health costs, and the creation of the ISAPREs.

Measures to Reduce Expenditures

Part of the high cost of Chilean social security is explained by historical factors (the excessive generosity of the past) and demographic factors (the aging of the population) that are either irreversible or very difficult to change in the short or medium term. Furthermore, in the last ten years a package of drastic measures was introduced to reduce expenditures. These included: (1) eliminating excessively generous benefits (for example, seniority pensions, the *pensión perseguidora*) and the increase in the minimum age for old age pensions (the real value of pensions has deteriorated); (2) unifying and partially standardizing of the old system; (3) reducing personnel and real salaries as well as the emphasis on using paramedical and auxiliary personnel rather than physicians; (4) giving priority to primary care, mothers and children, nutrition, sanitation, and reducing regional differences; and (5) transferring part of the cost of health to the insured.

Even though Chile has less room to reduce expenditures than other countries, several measures could still be adopted: (1) to complete the unification and standardization of the old system; (2) to eliminate remaining unnecessary personnel; (3) to reduce the very high pensions of the most powerful groups in the old system and to make the retirement ages for men and women equal in both systems; (4) to maximize the use of hospital capacity; (5) to institute universal free immunization for those contagious diseases that show an increase and to tighten the control of the sanitary conditions that are responsible for such diseases; and (6) to reduce the operating costs of the AFPs, focusing competition among them on minimizing commissions and increasing investment yields.

THE IMPACT OF SOCIAL SECURITY ON DEVELOPMENT

Chile is the only one of the six country cases to have studies on the impact of social security on savings/investment, employment, and the distribution of income.

Savings and Investment

A recent study on this subject compares the impact in the old and new systems.[61] It is suggested that the state contribution to the pension program of the old system represented not a dissaving but instead a partial payment of the state obligations as employer and a mechanism of state redistribution (see above). After the state contribution has been deducted, it is calculated that the program generated a net surplus of 20 percent over revenues in the 1940s and the beginning of the 1950s but that the surplus fell to less than 10 percent in the 1960s (as previously stated, the program changed from a pure assessment method to the pay-as-you-go method). The surplus would have been higher had it not been for the fact that a significant part of the revenues was transferred to the first generation of pensioners, who received pensions over and above what they had contributed during their active lives (with a system of full capitalization they would have received only between one-half and two-thirds of what they actually received). The reserves of the fund were invested in loans and housing programs for the insured, but as some of these were not adjusted for inflation, in practice they also became transfers. It may be concluded that the old system did not generate added savings but helped to redistribute income between generations without substantially reducing government savings and investment.

Theoretically the new pension program should promote more savings and develop a capital market. The study mentioned above estimates that the capital accumulated by the AFPs could reach 10 percent of GNP (of 1981) in 1986 and 20 percent in 1991. (In mid-1984 that capital was equivalent to 30 percent of the total deposits in the financial system, and it was predicted in the near future to account for between 70 percent and 90 percent of national savings.)[62] The study further argues that, because the state subsidizes the growing deficit of the old system, and pays the bond of recognition to the new, the privatization of both the system and the contribution involves an enormous transfer of resources from the public to the private sector. To increase the net aggregate investment, greater external savings and/or lower government expenditures or higher taxes are required. Before the effects of these measures may be measured adequately, they must be separated from the system itself. Furthermore, the study maintains that the system has had less impact on the growth of the capital stock than on its control and distribution, through the transfer of the indicated resources and the control of the AFPs by a small number of financial conglomerates. Capital markets in Latin America—argues the study—are generally small and segmented and in several countries are controlled by a few financial conglomerates. Under these circumstances the accumulation of huge funds involves a high risk of instability as well as a concentration of wealth. Also the hypothetical advantage in administrative efficiency is doubtful, given the high cost of sales and publicity typical of the insurance industry. Finally, the study predicts that, in the near future, the system will reduce its rate of capitalization and/or the state will control the pension funds.

A commentary on the cited study suggests that the new Chilean system was modeled on private pension funds in the United States but failed to take into account the fact that a large enough capital market did not exist in Chile and overestimated the capacity of the private sector to absorb the substantial increase in financial resources, a deficiency aggravated by the current economic crisis.[63]

I have noted that, at the end of 1983, 46 percent of the AFP funds invested were in state bonds, 11 percent was deposited in or was in mortgages issued by the state bank, and close to 15 percent was deposited in, or was in letters of credit issued by, commercial banks in which the state had intervened. In total, 72 percent of the AFPs' investment funds were directly or indirectly controlled by the state. Furthermore, 100 percent of the investment was in debt instruments that encouraged the exaggerated indebtedness of the economy and, in the long run, could cause most of the national savings to be invested in loans.[64] Finally it is argued that current investment rules allow investments in big but risky businesses or banks and inhibit investment in smaller businesses with lower risk.[65]

The AFP Investment Commission believed that the situation described above involved a serious risk, as the state did not invest the majority of its resources productively.[66] In turn, the superintendency of the AFPs warned that it was necessary to diversify investment, especially toward the private sector; that the AFP should be transformed from collector agencies to efficient investment agencies; and that this transformation was necessary because, as the old system's debt grew, the state would increasingly be tempted to use the new system's funds.[67] A more cautious position, although favorable to diversification and privatization, argued that, with a small and poorly competitive capital market, priority should be given at the start to investment security.[68]

To cope with this situation, at the end of 1983, the government began to prepare a legal draft to modify the AFP investment rules. It still had not been approved by mid-1984. The draft authorizes the investment of the pension funds in private companies, beginning with those of the state (up to 50 percent) and, within two years, including private ones (up to 30 percent). Investment in real estate, direct housing loans, and other similar instruments is excluded, either because of difficulties in their administration or because of the risk involved. The investment in companies controlled by the state would be in enterprises with high stability and profitability (water and electricity are given as examples), while the investment in private stock companies would be subject to various requirements; for example, one stockholder could not control more than 20 percent of the companies' stocks, and the pension fund could not invest more than 5 percent of its resources in one single company. The draft also speaks of establishing a risks classification commission, which would determine a company's level of risk by voluntary petition of the same.[69]

Even if the draft is approved, the bulk of investment would continue to be channeled through state instruments, although the debt instruments could be reduced. But the possibility of real diversification in the long run depends on the eventual development of the capital market and solid and competitive stocks, objectives whose achievement was still not in sight after three years of AFP operations.

Employment

In the first half of the 1970s, three studies were done in Chile on the impact of social security wage contributions on employment. All three presume that this type of financing increases labor costs, thus reducing the demand for labor. A shift toward taxes that do not discriminate among the factors of production would avoid the negative effect on employment (for a detailed study of this theme, see chapter 7). The increase in employment that would be generated by this change is measured by the elasticity of the demand for labor in relation to its cost. The three studies used explicit estimates of that elasticity as well as different implicit assumptions, hence the results, although positive, were all different.[70]

The three studies were conducted prior to the introduction of the new system and the elimination of the employer contribution. But another study, completed in 1980, tried to evaluate the impact on employment of two measures of the reform with opposite effects: (1) the increase in the old age retirement age and the elimination of the seniority pension, which by postponing retirement of white-collar employees (workers under the SSS did not enjoy seniority pensions) should increase the supply of labor or decrease labor demand for new contracts; and (2) the reduction of the rate at which the employer contributes, which should reduce the cost of labor and increase employment opportunities. With respect to the first effect, it is unknown what proportion of those with seniority pensions continue to work after retirement. The study analyzes two possibilities: that no one continues to work, in which case a 1–2 percent increase in unemployment is estimated once the transition period has ended, and that half of the pensioners continue to work (or that all work half time), in which case unemployment would increase between 0.5 percent and 1 percent. The net effect on employment (if we take both possibilities into account) is that, if all retirees continued to work, employment would diminish, whereas if only half continued to work (a more realistic hypothesis), employment could diminish or increase, according to the elasticity of the demand for labor.[71]

It should be noted that this last study took into account only a reduction in the employer contribution, not its elimination, and thus the net positive effect should be greater. The open unemployment rate in Chile fell from 7.4 percent in 1980 to 6.7 percent in 1981 but rose to 11.9 percent in 1982 and to 15.7 percent in 1984. This behavior, however, was probably more a cumulative effect of the neoliberal policies and circumstantial factors than it was associated with the social security reform. Therefore a new study is needed to measure the impact of this reform on employment.

Distribution of Income

Various studies were conducted to determine the impact of the old social security system on the distribution of income. One, done in 1965, measured the net transfers among insured groups and found that, in absolute terms, blue-collar workers (70 percent of the insured, with the lowest income) received a net transfer somewhat greater than that of the other groups (with higher income). In per capita terms, however, blue-collar workers received half of what private white-collar employees received and one-fifth of what civil servants and military got.[72] Another study, limited to pensions, showed more regressive results, since, in absolute terms, the blue-collar workers received half of that obtained by private white-collar workers and one-fourteenth of that received by civil servants and the military, while the differences were much greater in per capita terms.[73] Also, in 1959, 1965, and 1971, reports from the Prat Commission, the superintendency of social security, and the National Planning Office (ODEPLAN) calculated that the uninsured paid a growing share of the insured's social security: 41 percent, 44 percent, and 50 percent.[74]

The most recent study of the old system encompassed only the three major groups (SSS, EMPART, and CANAEMPU) and was based on 1969 figures. This study discovered that social security had a regressive effect on financing, a progressive effect on benefits, and a slightly progressive net effect on the distribution of family income: an income transfer of 1 percent from the 9 percent with the highest income to the 61 percent with the lowest income, whereas 38 percent, with an average income, stayed the same.[75] The study, however, excluded the sector without coverage as well as the armed forces and other groups of the labor aristocracy; the incorporation of these groups in the calculations should probably have accentuated the regressive effect of the system. Another study, also carried out with 1969 figures, was limited to the health sector and registered a notable progressive transfer: the average benefit received by the lowest income strata was 1.6 times greater than that of the highest strata.[76]

There is still no study measuring the impact of social security on the distribution of income after the reform.[77] Certain aspects of this reform probably have a progressive effect on distribution: (1) standardizing the old age retirement age and the elimination of the seniority pension and *pensiones perseguidoras* negatively affected middle-income groups (white-collar employees) but very few, if any, of the low-income groups (blue-collar workers); (2) equalizing family allowances, the unemployment subsidy, and the minimum pension, as well as the expansion of welfare pensions and family allowances, and the standardization in the adjustment of pensions to the cost of living relatively favored the lowest income group; (3) eliminating the employer contribution, so that the insured became principally responsible for financing, eliminated the possible tax incidence on the consumer or the negative impact on employment, both of which were generally regressive; and (4) reducing the differences in health services among regions favored the least-developed regions.

On the other hand, some aspects of the old system persist, combined with characteristics of the new system that probably have a regressive effect: (1) the decline in population coverage that probably affected the lowest income groups (these could receive social welfare benefits but with lower levels/quality than those of insurance); (2) the preservation, in the old system, of different entitlement conditions and notable inequalities in pensions that are not merely justified by income; (3) the establishment of a strict correspondence between premium and benefit in the new system that eliminates any possible redistributive function, and the commissions of the AFP that tax the low-income groups proportionally more; and (4) the accentuation of discriminatory levels in health care, corresponding to income.

The official position is that the AFPs and the ISAPRE do not have (and should not have) a redistributive function—that is the province of social welfare measures.[78] A global study is badly needed to determine the net effect of the new social security system on the distribution of income.

5

Mexico:
The Challenge of Universalization

THE GENERAL Mexican social security system was created in 1943, at the time of the Beveridge plan, but it was preceded by various programs that covered several pressure groups. Today the system is only relatively unified, as three independent subsystems and other groups with special regulations within the general system have impeded the elimination of inequalities. Population coverage grew slowly in the first two decades and was limited to salaried workers in the most populated urban areas, but later coverage expanded more rapidly, penetrating the rural and marginal-urban zones with innovative programs. In 1960–83 health coverage rose from 12 percent to 60 percent (including the welfare programs or social solidarity programs in the general system), while pension coverage rose from 16 percent to 42 percent, so that Mexico stood just behind the pioneer countries.

In the last twenty years Mexico has also advanced in terms of health services and levels, but it still ranks fifth among the case studies, and given its level of development and abundant resources, greater progress should have been achieved. In addition, the social solidarity programs are too recent to have had a significant impact on health levels, although with continued expansion, their effects will be tangible in the current decade. In spite of some positive action, the distribution of health expenditures still greatly favors the institutions of social security and curative medicine over those of social welfare and preventive medicine.

Given that Mexican social security covers half of the population, it is surprising that its cost has only risen from 2 percent to only 3 percent of GDP, one-third of the percentage spent by the pioneer countries. Although these figures may somewhat understate the case, they can be explained to a great degree by the relative unification, a fairly recent pension program, and a less liberal benefit package than that of the pioneer countries. These expenditure-limiting factors, together with the youthfulness of the population, the progressive incorporation of contributors, and the fulfillment of the financial obligations of the state, also explain why the total wage contribution, the

143

eighth lowest in the region, has increased only from 14 percent to 18 percent in the forty years of the general system's existence.

The general system generated a net surplus, at least until 1983, but the health and maternity program (which absorbs more than two-thirds of the outlays) yielded a systematic deficit. This was covered by loans and investments from the pension program, which gradually caused its decapitalization. The economic crisis has precipitated the financial imbalance, but Mexico has more time, space, and resources to confront this problem than other countries.

Taking advantage of these opportunities, Mexico should shore up the finances of social security in the current decade, and reach universal coverage. The expansion of social security, the incorporation of two independent subsystems into the general system, and the promulgation of the general health law are all positive steps taken in the last few years. But it is necessary to introduce a national health system, to cover the lowest income sector, to complete the unification of the system, to eliminate inequalities among insured groups and geographic regions, and to increase the administrative efficiency of the system. To achieve these goals it is crucial for Mexico to take the definitive step that will transform social insurance into social security, establishing a model that will both satisfy the basic needs of the population and be financially viable in the long run.

HISTORICAL EVOLUTION

In the first century after independence (1821–1924), an old age and survivors' pension program (*montepío*) for civil servants was the only program introduced in Mexico.[1] No significant changes in this area were generated by the revolution, although the constitution of 1917, in a pioneer article of labor law for the region, broke the long tradition of liberal philosophy and established that the state could intervene to regulate working conditions. But this article only timidly made the employer responsible for occupational risks.

In the following twenty years, five powerful pressure groups successively obtained social security programs in pensions and occupational risks from the state. Three of these groups also received health and maternity protection. These groups were civil servants from the federal government (who improved their old program of *montepío*); the military (who retained political power in these years); federal teachers (organized in a strong union that frequently resorted to strikes and participated in politics); and the workers in three strategic sectors of the economy: petroleum, railroads, and electricity. These three groups of the labor aristocracy were also very active in trade unions and politics and achieved their programs through collective agreements with the federal government (see table 42). In all this time, the only program that benefited the laboring masses was that for occupational risks, introduced in 1931, almost fifteen years after the constitutional mandate. In the adminis-

TABLE 42

SOCIAL SECURITY LEGISLATION IN MEXICO,
BY RISK AND GROUPS COVERED: 1925–1983

Year[a]	Risk Protected	Groups Covered
1925, 1959, 1983	ODS, H/M, OR	Federal civil servants
1926, 1946	ODS, OR	Armed forces
1928	ODS, H/M, OR	Public teachers
1931	OR	Public white-collar and blue-collar workers
1935, 1966–1970	ODS, OR	Petroleum workers
1936–38, 1948, 1966–70	ODS, H/M, OR	Railroad workers
1941, 1966–70	ODS, H/M, OR	Electricity workers
1943	ODS, H/M, OR	Private white-collar and blue-collar workers[b]
1954–1955	ODS, H/M, OR	Permanent rural workers, members of *ejidos*, members of cooperatives, and small farmers
1960	ODS, H/M, OR	Seasonal rural workers and temporary urban workers
1963	ODS, H/M, OR	Sugar workers
1970	ODS, H/M, OR	All salaried workers or wage earners
1971–73	ODS, H/M, OR	Tobacco and sisal workers
1973	ODS, H/M, OR	Domestic servants,[b] self-employed, employers[b]
1974	ODS, H/M, OR	Coffee and palm workers
1962, 1973	day care centers	All those under IMSS
1973–74	H/M	Marginal groups (social solidarity)
1979–83	H/M	Rural population (IMSS-COPLAMAR)

Source: Mesa-Lago, *Social Security in Latin America* (Pittsburgh, Pa.: University of Pittsburgh Press, 1978), and later legislation.

Note: ODS = old age, disability, and survivors' pensions. H/M = health and maternity. OR = occupational risks.

a. The first date corresponds to the initial legislation and subsequent dates to modifications and amplifications.
b. The date of incorporation has been postponed.

trations of Madero, Obregón, and Cárdenas, various legal projects for social security were elaborated, but none was successful.

In 1943, under the presidency of Avila Camacho, a conservative administration, the law was enacted that ordered the creation of social insurances for old age, disability and death, health-maternity, and occupational risks, theoretically covering all white- and blue-collar workers. In order to implement this legal mandate, the Mexican Institute of Social Insurance (IMSS) was created. This institute would eventually develop the general system for the entire country.[2] IMSS population coverage was very limited for almost two decades and was concentrated in the Federal District (DF) and in some important cities. But if the horizontal expansion of coverage was slow, the same could not be said for the vertical expansion of benefits to the groups already covered: the armed forces, and railroad and electrical workers. In

1959 federal civil servants enlarged their benefits and created a new administrative entity: the Institute for Social Security and Services of State Workers (ISSSTE), which eventually incorporated teachers and the federal police. The employees of IMSS were favored with a collective agreement that offered them more advantageous benefits than those insured by that institution.

In the mid-1950s, the slow expansion of IMSS coverage to rural sectors began, covering permanent salaried workers, members of *ejidos* integrated into cooperatives and societies, small farmers, seasonal salaried workers, and workers on important plantations such as sugarcane, sisal, tobacco, and coffee. (Interestingly, this process was preceded and accompanied by a growing agricultural union organization, outbreaks of rebellion in the countryside, and the establishment of politically active national organizations.) But in spite of these legal advances, coverage of the agricultural population at the end of the 1960s did not reach 7 percent of the EAP. Yet the insured of IMSS—which should have covered all salaried workers since 1970—received additional benefits, including a program of "social benefits" that was initiated in the mid-1950s and rapidly expanded.

With the presidency of Echeverría, a basis was created for the more rapid expansion of IMSS coverage for rural and marginal-urban groups, especially in the health-maternity program. In his inaugural address, the new president established the end of the 1970s as the term for extending coverage beyond the salaried sector, with the goal of covering at least 50 percent of the population. To this effect a new law was promulgated in 1973 stating that social security should not be the "prerogative of a minority" but instead should include marginal groups and the neediest sectors. It also stated that such expansion could not be further delayed, as added delay would not only be "imprudent" but would also "deepen the differences among the inhabitants of the country," perpetuating a "dual society with a few privileged members and a majority [without protection]." The law called for "social solidarity" to undertake the task of transforming social insurance into social security but warned that this transformation could not occur quickly "in a country that is just barely beginning the process of development," and it should not endanger the financial stability of the IMSS.[3]

The indicated conflict was reflected both in the text of the law and in its implementation. Those already insured received new benefits (for example, day care centers, pension adjustments, and expansion of coverage age for children) but, although the law established that self-employed workers (urban and rural), domestic servants, small businessmen, and the rest of the *ejido* members should have compulsory coverage in the IMSS, the incorporation date of these groups was postponed. It was, however, conceded that they should have the option of voluntary insurance. To offer health services to the marginal sectors, the IMSS wage contribution ceiling was increased, and the federal government gave financial support to establish a program of "social

solidarity.'' Medical-hospital care began in 1974 with the adaptation of buildings and the construction of new clinics and hospitals. In 1977, under the
presidency of López Portillo, the COPLAMAR program was created (General
Coordination of the National Plan for Deprived Zones and Marginal Groups),
and in 1979 IMSS and COPLAMAR signed an agreement to offer medical-
hospital care (in coordination with the secretary of health and welfare) to 10
million inhabitants in marginal rural zones. This new program, financed by
the federal government, provided the impulse for the construction of new
clinics and hospitals and notably increased the number of users. With the
administration of Miguel de la Madrid, the COPLAMAR disappeared as such,
but the program continued, operated by the IMSS.[4] In 1983, if we include
the figures for IMSS-COPLAMAR coverage, the social security system of
Mexico had a statistical coverage of almost 60 percent of the total population.

Several steps have also been taken in the 1980s to unify and integrate
social security in Mexico. In 1980 the independent electricity subsystem was
incorporated into the IMSS (although with special funding and regulations),
and the same occurred with railroad workers in 1982. Thus in 1984, only
three important groups remained outside IMSS: federal civil servants, the
armed forces, and petroleum. Although various administrations have suggested unifying these three groups within the IMSS, they are so powerful that
they have managed to remain independent. Also in 1983, a general health
law passed that promotes the coordination of all administrative entities in this
field and the eventual creation of a national health system.

In summary, the general social security system of Mexico appeared late
and was preceded by the creation of a small number of independent subsystems
protecting pressure groups. Coverage in the general system expanded slowly
in the first two decades but later—especially in the health-maternity program—grew more rapidly. In the 1980s several steps were taken to integrate
some of the independent groups into the general system. Still, three independent groups persist, and for this reason the Mexican system must be classified as only relatively unified and uniform.[5]

ORGANIZATIONAL STRUCTURE

The principal autonomous agency is the IMSS, which gives all salaried
workers (basically in the private sector) compulsory coverage while offering
self-employed and other groups voluntary coverage. IMSS administers five
programs: pensions, health-maternity, occupational risks, daycare centers, and
''social benefits.'' It also administers various special programs (or has ad hoc
regulations) for diverse groups: social solidarity and IMSS-COPLAMAR (for
marginal and rural and urban groups), employees of IMSS, electrical and
railroad workers, workers in the sugar, sisal, coffee and cotton industries,
and so forth. The medical-hospital network of IMSS is the most extensive in

the country. There is three-party participation in the IMSS administration: by the insured, the employers, and the state, although the latter plays the dominant role.

The ISSSTE, an autonomous organization, offers compulsory insurance for all employees of the federal government. The programs administered by ISSSTE include pensions, health-maternity (through ISSSTE's own services and contracted ones), occupational risks, life insurance, day care centers, and social benefits. ISSSTE also covers, by contract, employees of the states and municipalities, although many of these are covered by independent funds and by state and municipal hospitals. Finally, several autonomous organizations, such as the Bank of Mexico, have their own programs.

The Mexican State Oil Enterprise (Pemex) has its own independent programs in pensions, health (with their own and contracted services), occupational risks, and other types of benefits.

The armed forces also have independent programs. The army and the air force are covered by the secretary of defense, which operates its own medical-hospital services and programs for occupational risks, life insurance, funeral aid, housing, and subsidized stores. The navy receives equivalent services through the secretary of the navy. In addition, both groups have a pension program, administered by a common independent fund, and personal and housing loan programs through a special bank. The secretary of the interior covers the federal district police for pensions and life insurance (this group is covered for health-maternity by the ISSSTE).

The secretary of sanitation and welfare (SSA) manages preventive medicine and sanitation, operates the national network of federal hospitals, coordinates—with state and municipal governments—the corresponding hospitals, supervises the health services of the social security agencies, and administers a social welfare program for homeless children, the elderly, and the disabled. The Federal District also has significant medical-hospital resources. The National System for Family Integral Development (SNDIF) is concerned with unprotected groups, both urban and rural. It focuses especially on the population of infants and pregnant women and therefore offers some health services.

The health care provided by all of the cited agencies takes the typical pyramidal form, with diverse levels of care that increase in complexity and specialization. Although efforts have been made since the 1960s to coordinate all of Mexico's medical-hospital services of the country, considerable duplication and many gaps still exist. Some of the new programs are better coordinated. The IMSS-COPLAMAR, for example, has its own services for the first and seconds, but its members use the facilities of the SSA at the third level. The IMSS relies principally on its own services for the insured population (it had 49 percent of the hospital beds in 1982), but contracts with the SSA (which has 30 percent of hospital beds), the ISSSTE (11 percent of hospital beds), and state or private hospitals in zones where it does not have its own facilities. The ISSSTE relies much more heavily on contracted services. The armed forces (5 percent of hospital beds) and Pemex (2 percent) rely on their hospitals in the Federal District and some important urban centers, contracting services in other areas. The general health law enacted in 1984 distributes jurisdiction and the user population among the various administrative agencies. It also entrusts the coordination of the effort to create the national health system to the SSA (assisted by a Council of General Health). The two major tasks are to elaborate the rules of collaboration and territorial jurisdiction among all health services in the country and to integrate preventive and curative medicine.

As I have already noted, several steps have been taken in the 1980s in favor of the unification of the general system and the improved coordination of the health system, but this process must be furthered and consolidated. The subsystem of Pemex should be incorporated into IMSS, as was done previously with the electricity and railroad subsystems. Also, ISSSTE should incorporate all of the state, municipal, and autonomous agencies' programs. Once this goal is achieved, the unification of IMSS, ISSSTE, and the armed forces programs should be attempted. The standardization process will be more difficult, as there are significant differences among covered groups even within the IMSS. The consolidation of the national health system would be a significant step in the planning and rationalization of the sector and essential to achieve universal coverage.

POPULATION COVERAGE

Legal and Statistical Coverage

In accordance with the law,[6] the IMSS is required to cover all salaried workers who are not under other subsystems, including members of cooperatives and *ejido* members who are organized in societies. Although the law also establishes the obligation to cover other groups, at the moment these groups are entitled only to voluntary incorporation: self-employed workers (including professionals, small merchants, and craftsmen), family industry workers, domestic servants, nonassociated members of *ejidos,* small landowners, and entrepreneurs and employers. The ISSSTE is obliged to cover employees of the federal government, the Federal District, federal schools and police, and some public agencies, such as certain universities. It also voluntarily covers senators and representatives. Workers in state, municipal, and autonomous agencies are covered by the ISSSTE, the IMSS and their own services (the armed forces and Pemex are in the latter category). The general system, and practically all of the subsystems, provides a health-maternity program to pensioners and to the following dependent members of the family of the insured and pensioner: spouse (or companion), minor children

TABLE 43   SOCIAL SECURITY COVERAGE OF

					Insured[a]		
						Total	
	Total				*Rural COPLA-MAR*[c]	*Without COPLA-MAR*	*With COPLA-MAR*
	Population	*EAP*	*Active*	*Passive*	*Dependents*			
1960	37,073	9,721	1,521	72	2,969	*	4,562	*
1965	43,500	11,564	2,706	148	5,953	*	8,807	*
1970	51,176	13,679	3,845	287	8,201	*	12,333	*
1975	60,153	16,332	5,681	417	15,329	*	21,427	*
1980	69,393	19,423	8,158	634	22,028	6,236	30,820	37,050
1981	71,284	20,109	9,036	686	24,350	8,614	34,072	42,686
1982	73,188	20,807	8,912	752	24,079	9,653	33,743	43,396
1983	75,107	21,511	8,977	799	24,248	10,782	34,024	44,806

Source: Total population and EAP from CELADE, *Boletín demográfico* (July 1983), and *Mexico: Estimaciones y proyecciones de población, 1950–2000* (September 1982). Insured population from Mesa-Lago, *Social Security in Latin America* (Pittsburgh, Pa.: University of Pittsburgh Press, 1978); IMSS, *Memoria estadísticas 1981,* and *Informe mensual de la población derechohabiente, diciembre 1983;* ISSSTE, *Anuario estadístico, 1970 a 1982;* SPP, *Manual de estadísticas básicas sociodemográficas: Salud y seguridad social, 1978;* and *Agenda estadística, 1971–1983,* and IMSS, "Ambito geográfico del Programa IMSS-COPLAMAR," November 4, 1983. Percentages, rates, and quotients calculated by the author.

(and older if they are students or disabled), and parents. Dependents are also entitled to funeral aid, survivors pensions, and some social benefits.

Table 43 shows the expansion of social security statistical coverage in Mexico between 1960 and 1983; it includes all groups except for state, municipal, and public agency employees with their own services (many of these, however, have health agreements with the IMSS and the ISSSTE and thus appear within the total insured population). Although there should not be significant duplication in the insured EAP, an important overestimation is reported in the total population, because if both spouses work and are insured, they generally register each other and their children as dependents. A similar effect occurs with parents who are reported by various insured children.[7] Coverage figures for the IMSS-COPLAMAR in table 43 are the most recent estimated by this program, and they represent substantial reductions over prior statistics that inflated coverage between 75 percent and 120 percent; for example, the original figures reported were 13.8 million in 1980 and 18.7 million in 1983, respectively, compared with 6.2 million and 10.8 million on the table.[8]

As previously stated, social security population coverage in Mexico expanded very slowly at first. This slow start is reflected in table 43 which shows that only 12 percent of the EAP were covered in 1960 (pensions) and less than 16 percent of the total population (health). In the 1960s, with the gradual expansion of the IMSS (an expansion that occurred geographically

POPULATION IN MEXICO, 1960–1983   (THOUSANDS)

| % of Coverage[b] | | | Annual Average Rate of Growth (log) | | | | |
| Total Population | | | | | Insured | | Quotient of Demographic Burden[d] |
Without COPLA- MAR	With COPLA- MAR	EAP	Total Population	EAP	Without COPLA- MAR	With COPLA- MAR	
12.3	*	15.6	**	**	**	**	0.047
20.2	—	23.4	3.2	3.5	12.2	14.1	0.055
24.1	—	28.1	3.3	3.4	7.3	7.0	0.075
35.6	—	34.8	3.3	3.6	8.1	11.7	0.073
44.4	53.4	42.0	2.9	3.5	7.5	7.5	0.078
47.8	59.9	44.9	2.7	3.5	10.8	10.5	0.076
46.1	59.2	42.8	2.7	3.5	−1.4	−1.0	0.084
45.3	59.7	41.7	2.6	3.4	0.7	0.8	0.089

a. Includes IMSS, ISSSTE, and official or estimated figures for PEMEX, railways, electricity, and secretaries of defense and the navy.

b. Total population coverage refers to health and EAP coverage to old age, disability, and survivors' pensions.

c. Adjusted estimates of health coverage of the rural population by IMSS-COPLAMAR.

d. Numbers of passives divided by number of actives.

*Not applicable.

**Not available.

as much as within the rural salaried sector), the previous percentages were almost doubled, although in 1971, 78 percent of the municipalities of the country were still not covered by IMSS. Another leap in coverage occurred in the 1970s, especially after the 1973 law. Table 43 begins to report the IMSS-COPLAMAR coverage in the 1980s (although it actually began in the mid-1970s), and it shows the acceleration of coverage in the health program, increasing 350 percent between 1980 and 1983. The difference in total population coverage when the IMSS-COPLAMAR population is included gradually rose from 9 to 14 percentage points in 1980–83. This upward trend represents the increase in population coverage in marginal rural groups. Coverage of the EAP grew less (2.4 times) between 1970 and 1981. Note that, because of the economic crisis, the percentage of EAP coverage and that of the total population (especially when IMSS-COPLAMAR is excluded) decreased in 1982–83. In the last year almost 60 percent of the total population and almost 42 percent of the EAP were covered. According to 1980 coverage (if the IMSS-COPLAMAR is included), Mexico ranked seventh or eighth in Latin America, heading the group of countries at the middle level (see table 6, below).

Since the beginning of the 1960s, the IMSS has covered a growing proportion of the country's insured. In 1982 the percentage distribution of insured per institution was as follows: 84 percent in the IMSS (of which one-fourth were in the IMSS-COPLAMAR), 13 percent in the ISSSTE, 2 percent in

Pemex, and 1 percent in the armed forces.[9] Within the general compulsory system of the IMSS, 55 percent of the active insured are permanent workers, and 45 percent are temporary. The statistical health coverage for the SSA is unknown, as is the national coverage for occupational risks.

Determinant Structural Factors

Mexico has managed to expand coverage to a level surpassed only by the pioneer countries and Costa Rica, and approximated by Panama. EAP coverage in 1980 (42 percent) just barely surpassed the percentage of the EAP in the urban formal sector (40 percent), and, if to this is added the modern rural sector (19 percent), coverage fell below the sum of the two and obviously did not extend to the informal-traditional sector (40 percent) (see table 3, below). There are no recent figures on the composition of the labor force by occupational categories, but according to the 1970 census, only 42 percent were blue- or white-collar workers (salaried), while 21 percent were day laborers or rural peons, 19 percent were self-employed, and 18 percent were members of *ejidos,* unpaid family workers, or employers.[10] If all the salaried workers are summed together, the resulting percentage (63 percent) is lower than the figure for all the countries with higher social security coverage than Mexico (except for Venezuela) and almost equals that of Panama, which has similar coverage. The general results of the 1981 census still have not been published, but it will probably report a slight increase in the percentage of salaried EAP. Mexico, with its large territory that includes extensive deserts, mountains, and jungle, and a dispersed and isolated population, faces various natural obstacles to the expansion of coverage.

Open unemployment in Mexico has traditionally been reported as low for regional levels (about 4 percent in 1960–80) but with a tendency to grow, whereas the rate of underemployment in equivalent unemployment is also relatively low (13 percent in 1980) but with a tendency to decrease. These have been positive factors in the expansion of coverage, but the increase in open unemployment in the 1980s (12.5 percent in 1983) and possibly an increase in underemployment, could have been influential in the decrease in EAP coverage in 1982–83, especially among temporary workers.[11]

Mexico has gone beyond the expansion limits of the Bismarckian social insurance model because of social solidarity and the IMSS-COPLAMAR programs, which have notably expanded the health coverage of the total population.

Differences in Population Coverage

Table 44 presents the differences among the states of Mexico in the degree of health coverage for the entire population. It should be noted that coverage in the more rural states is overestimated, as the table's figures include the inflated coverage of the IMSS-COPLAMAR in 1980. The Federal District

TABLE 44

COVERAGE OF TOTAL POPULATION BY STATES IN MEXICO, 1980

State	Total Population (thous.)	Total Insured[a] (thous.)	% of Coverage
Distrito Federal	9,640	9,682	100.4
Aguas Calientes	521	261	50.1
Baja California	1,262	743	58.9
Baja California Sur	228	141	61.8
Campeche	382	162	42.4
Coahuila	1,607	1,143	71.1
Colima	350	180	51.4
Chiapas	2,158	429	19.9
Chihuahua	1,991	974	48.9
Durango	1,193	510	42.7
Guanajuato	3,135	962	30.7
Guerrero	2,236	523	23.4
Hidalgo	1,559	372	23.9
Jalisco	4,419	1,837	41.6
México[b]	7,768	420	5.4
Michoacán	3,137	621	19.8
Norelos	960	394	41.0
Nayarit	750	287	38.2
Nueva León	2,536	1,872	73.8
Oaxaca	2,586	444	17.2
Puebla	3,378	947	28.0
Queretaro	753	373	49.5
Quintana Roo	217	142	65.4
San Luis Potosí	1,719	499	29.0
Sinaloa	1,938	916	47.3
Sonora	1,541	1,027	66.6
Tabasco	1,183	418	35.3
Tamaulipas	1,978	1,020	51.6
Tlaxcala	564	39	6.9
Veracruz	5,415	2,107	38.9
Yucatán	1,063	576	54.2
Zacatecas	1,178	214	18.2
Total	69,347	30,243[c]	43.6

Source: Total population and insured from SPP, Instituto Nacional de Estadística e Informática, *Información estadística: Sector salud y seguridad social* (México City: INEI, 1984). Percentages calculated by author.

a. Includes IMSS (including IMSS-COPLAMAR), ISSSTE, Pemex, and armed forces.
b. Excludes the Federal District.
c. Includes 5,460 insured abroad.

appears to have total coverage (probably due to the duplication that has already been explained, accentuated in the capital), and coverage in Nuevo Leon and Coahuila is greater than 70 percent. Meanwhile, the states of Oaxaca, Zacatecas, Chiapas, and Michoacan have coverage between 17 percent and 20 percent, and the states of Tlaxcala and Mexico have the lowest coverage: 5 percent to 7 percent. The difference in coverage between the Federal District and Tlaxcala was 14.5:1. In general, the most developed states (as measured by GDP per capita, the degree of urbanization, and the index of marginality) have the highest social security coverage, while the least-developed states have the lowest coverage.[12] A comparison between EAP coverage (the IMSS plus the ISSSTE) by states in 1969 and 1980 indicated that, while the percentage of coverage had increased in all the states, the ratios between the Federal District and the six worst-covered states remained almost unaltered, with the sole exception of Tabasco, which because of the petroleum boom increased its coverage five times between 1969 and 1980.[13]

Table 45 shows the differences in the degree of EAP coverage by economic sectors in 1970 and 1980. The calculations suffer from various defects: (1) changes in the definitions of economic sectors; (2) difficulties in assigning insured groups to each sector, especially those of the ISSSTE; and (3) the impossibility of counting and assigning the insured in *health* of the IMSS-COPLAMAR to the agricultural sector, as the available figures are aggregates of the total insured population. In spite of these problems, the table gives an idea of the inequalities in pension coverage. The government sector is over-covered, and the public utilities and petroleum sector approach total coverage. The industrial and transportation sectors greatly surpass the national average, and the agricultural and construction sectors remain way below the national average.

Uncovered Population

In 1983, according to table 43, 40 percent of the total population and 60 percent of the EAP were not covered by social security. The previous sections have identified the groups in Mexico that are either not covered or have extremely low coverage: (1) unemployed who are not entitled to coverage and who, in 1982, represented 12 percent of the EAP; (2) independent workers, unpaid family workers, domestic servants, unassociated *ejido* members, and small landowners and employers who are currently entitled only to voluntary coverage; and (3) salaried rural workers, especially temporary ones, who, although entitled to compulsory coverage, are not always insured, whether because of faulty execution of the law or because of evasion.

Nevertheless, part of these sectors, especially the marginal-urban and marginal-rural, can obtain health coverage in the IMSS-COPLAMAR program and the services of the SSA, the SNDIF, and the Federal District. In Mexico there are no welfare pension programs, and the welfare services of the SSA

TABLE 45
EAP COVERAGE BY ECONOMIC SECTORS IN MEXICO, 1970 AND 1980

	1970			1980		
Sectors	EAP (thous.)	Active Insured[a] (thous.)	% of Coverage	EAP (thous.)	Active Insured[a] (thous.)	% of Coverage
Agriculture, cattle, forestry, hunting, and fishing	5,103	74[b]	1.4	6,384	364[b]	5.7
Mines and quarries	95	7	7.4	150	32	21.3
Manufacturing industries	2,169	1,257	58.4	3,691	2,066	56.0
Construction	571	48	8.4	997	49	4.9
Public utilities, petroleum	138	132[c]	95.6	349	335[c]	96.0
Transport, storage, and communications	369	250[d]	67.7	698	316	45.2
Commerce	1,197	529	44.2	1,995	752	37.7
Services	2,158	339	15.7	3,791	1,416	37.3
Government	407	421[e]	103.4	998	1,435[e]	143.8
Unspecified	747	0	0.0	898	164	18.2
Total	12,955	3,066[f]	23.7	19,951	6,840[f]	34.2

Sources: 1970 from Carmelo Mesa-Lago, Social Security in Latin America (Pittsburgh, Pa.: University of Pittsburgh Press, 1978); 1980 EAP from X Censo de población y vivienda, 1980, preliminary data; insured from IMSS, Memoria estadística, 1981, ISSSTE, Anuario estadístico, 1981, and SPP, Agenda estadística, 1983.

a. Permanent insured population in the IMSS (excludes occasional, temporary, and self-employed workers) plus insured in other funds as specified. Figures for 1970 correspond to those for 1969.

b. If, in 1970 the ejido members, small farmers and other agricultural workers are included, the insured population increases to 336,000 (6.6 percent). If, in 1980, IMSS-COPLAMAR was included, the active population insured for health should have risen significantly.

c. Includes insured in Pemex and electricity; in 1980 this figure was adjusted to include an estimate of insured in mines and quarries who worked in petroleum and gas extraction.

d. Includes insured in railways.

e. Includes ISSSTE, part of whose insured belong to the service sector.

f. Excludes the armed forces and other small groups (and IMSS-COPLAMAR in 1980).

are insufficient to satisfy the needs of the population. Even though the health sector has advanced somewhat in the last decade, the lowest income group (including the critical poverty group) either is not covered or has the worst coverage. Table 43 shows, in addition, that those without coverage are concentrated in the least developed states of the country.

Taking into account both the absolute deficit of medical-hospital services and that prompted by the geographic and institutional concentration, a study of COPLAMAR estimated that in 1978 real health coverage, if all existing services were counted, was only 54.7 percent: social security was responsible for 24 percent, social welfare for 18.4 percent, and private services for 12.3

percent. The study concluded that 45.3 percent of the total population lacked real coverage.[14]

Measures to Improve Coverage

The most effective program to expand health coverage in recent years has been that of the IMSS-COPLAMAR, which is based on a decentralized system in three levels: first, rural-medical units (3,000 in 1983, located in areas with fewer than 5,000 inhabitants); second, rural hospitals (61 in 1983, located in rural areas with fewer than 10,000 inhabitants); and, third, a specialized level that uses the infrastructure of SSA. The target is to increase coverage from 10.9 million to 15.7 million, although a goal of 18.7 million was initially mentioned. In addition, coverage of the insured of the general system of IMSS is to be increased by 3.5 million, while SSA is expected to attend the majority of the noncovered population, especially infants and pregnant or nursing women.

To confront the significant increase in open unemployment, coverage to the unemployed has been expanded so that it extends from two to six months after dismissal. A project for the mid-1980s is to incorporate all independent workers, who until now have only had voluntary coverage, into compulsory coverage in the IMSS. Other groups that, since the 1973 law, should have had compulsory insurance, such as domestic servants, unassociated *ejidos* members, and small landowners, must also be incorporated in the short run.[15]

The projection of nominal coverage of the social security institutions prepared in the mid-1970s indicated that, by the year 2000, more than 60 percent of the total population of the country would be covered, a goal that was apparently realized in 1983. But the above-cited study of COPLAMAR on *real* capacity argues that, if the present model is followed, the increase of coverage in 2000 will be quite small. To attain universal coverage in the year 2000, this study proposes a modification, on a national scale, of the health model to make it resemble the three-level structure of the IMSS-COPLAMAR; this modification would, from the very beginning, give high priority to the first level; concentrate in 1990–2000 on the expansion of the second level; and brake growth at the third level.[16]

FINANCING

Sources of Financing

IMSS is financed by three-part wage contributions plus federal government transfers for welfare programs and investment yields. The total wage contribution has increased from 13.63 percent in 1943 to 18.04 percent in 1983 and is still one of the lowest in the region (see table 6). The contribution percentage for the pension program has not increased in forty years, the percentage for the health-maternity program has increased from 6 percent to

9 percent, and that for occupational risks from 1.63 percent to 2.04 percent. In addition, 1 percent has been added for day care centers. The total wage contribution in force (18.04 percent) is distributed in the following manner: 3.75 percent from the insured (salaried), 12.415 percent from the employer, and 1.875 percent from the federal government (as third-party contributor). The self-employed/voluntarily insured must pay 13.125 percent, which equals the sum of the contribution percentages of the salaried worker and the employer (excluding the contribution to occupational risks). Pensioners and their dependents make no contribution for health benefits (see table 46).

Note that the contribution percentage of the salaried worker is less than one-third of the contribution percentage of the employer and less than one-fifth of the total percentage contribution. The insured are classified in nine salary groups, but all pay an equal percentage; a maximum ceiling for contributions exists that is equal to ten times the minimum salary in the Federal District. The employer must pay the insured's contribution when he receives a minimum salary. The contribution of the federal government is equivalent to 20 percent of the employer contribution and is increased to 50 percent in the case of cooperatives and similar associations. In addition, the federal government finances 65 percent of the social solidarity program and all of

TABLE 46
LEGAL CONTRIBUTIONS TO SOCIAL SECURITY (IMSS AND ISSSTE)
BY PROGRAM AND SOURCE IN MEXICO, 1983
(PERCENTAGE OF SALARY OR INCOME)

| Program | IMSS | | | | | ISSTE | | |
| | Insured | | | | | | | |
	Salaried	Independent	Employer	State[a]	Total[b]	Insured	State[c]	Total
Pensions	1.50	5.250	3.750	0.750	6.00	6.0[f]	6.00[f]	12.00
Health-maternity	2.25	7.875	5.625	1.125	9.00	2.0	6.00	8.00
Occupational risks	*	*	2.04[d]	*	2.04	*	0.75	0.75
Other	*	*	1.00[e]	*	1.00	*	5.00[g]	5.00
Total	3.75	13.125	12.415	1.875	18.04	8.0	17.75	27.75

Source: Current legislation.

a. These figures represent the state only as third-party contributor, not as employer.
b. Excludes the independent insured's contribution.
c. State as employer.
d. Average premium: the premium fluctuates between 0.263 and 6.533, depending on risk.
e. Day care centers.
f. Part of the contribution goes to social benefits.
g. Contribution for housing programs.

*Not applicable.

the IMSS-COPLAMAR program. Although the users of the IMSS-COPLA-MAR program do not have to make payments, they must contribute with community work for sanitation, prevention, vaccination, and detection activities.

In 1982, the employers contributed 61 percent of the income of the IMSS, the insured 20 percent, and the federal government 11 percent. The remaining 8 percent was generated by investment (this percentage shifted back and forth between 3.5 and 7.9 in 1950–82). The IMSS was required by law to invest up to 85 percent of its reserves in buildings and equipment (for the health services, daycare centers, administrative offices, and social benefits), up to 10 percent in public bonds, and the remaining 5 percent in mortgage loans. The law also has determined that the average investment yield cannot be lower than the interest rate that serves as a base for actuarial calculations (5 percent). This figure is not only very low in relation to the current bank rate (50 percent) but also is calculated on assets that have not been reappraised.[17] Although up to 85 percent of the reserves are invested in buildings and equipment, the amount of the investment in this area reached only 35 percent in 1977 and had fallen to 17 percent in 1981. These figures reflect the fact that these assets have not been reappraised.[18] The actuarial study of 1982 projected lower investment yields in 1984–85. The health-maternity program has absorbed a substantial part of the pension program's reserves, paying an interest of 5 percent of the initial value (therefore without readjustment of the loans for inflation), and as a result the pension fund has been partly decapitalized.[19]

The ISSSTE is financed by wage contributions from the insured (8 percent) and the federal government (17.75 percent) for a total of 25.75 percent, an amount substantially greater than the total IMSS wage contribution, which is 18 percent (see table 46). The percentage wage contribution paid by an individual insured by the ISSSTE is more than twice that paid by an individual insured by the IMSS, but it is also true that the percentage contribution paid by the federal government is much higher than the combined percentages paid to the IMSS by the employers and the federal government. In 1982, 51 percent of ISSSTE revenue came form the federal government, 31 percent from the insured, and 18 percent from investment yields.[20]

Social security for the armed forces and the employees of Pemex is entirely financed by the federal government, and the insured pay nothing. Such was also the case for electrical and railroad workers, but it is unknown whether this special treatment has been retained since their incorporation into IMSS.[21] Also, the federal government almost completely finances SSA and finances 95 percent of SNDIF.

Evasion and Payment Delays

There is no information regarding evasion and payment delays by the IMSS, although the great number of employers and insured and the high inflation rates of the last years must have fueled both in the private sector. The actuarial study of 1982 recommended among other things the strict fulfillment of the contributors' payment obligations. Unlike other countries, the state in Mexico has fulfilled its obligations to the IMSS as well as to the ISSSTE and the other subsystems.

Financial Equilibrium

Table 47 presents the combined balance of revenues and expenditures of the IMSS and the ISSSTE in 1972–81. The pension program accumulated the larger surplus, while the health-maternity program yielded a systematic

TABLE 47
BALANCE OF REVENUES AND EXPENDITURES IN IMSS AND ISSTE
BY PROGRAM IN MEXICO, 1972–1981
(MILLIONS OF PESOS AT CURRENT PRICES)

Program	1972	1975	1978	1981
Pensions				
Revenues	7,103	16,126	33,934	87,468
Expenditures	2,925	6,403	12,390	32,239
Balance	4,178	9,723	21,544	55,229
Health-Maternity				
Revenues	7,656	16,436	34,227	89,696
Expenditures	8,911	18,853	41,314	98,864
Balance	− 1,255	− 2,417	− 7,087	− 9,168
Occupational Risks				
Revenues	1,481	3,067	6,303	19,550
Expenditures	1,178	2,697	6,000	15,584
Balance	303	370	303	3,966
Day Care Centers				
Revenues	*	850	2,587	6,777
Expenditures	*	222	661	2,397
Balance	*	628	1,926	4,380
Total				
Revenues	16,240	36,479	77,051	203,501
Expenditures[a]	14,560	32,536	71,224	168,389
Balance	1,680	3,943	5,827	35,112
As percentage of revenue	10.3	10.8	7.6	17.2

Sources: IMSS, *Memoria estadística, 1981;* ISSSTE data from Sub Direcctión de Actuaria y Estadística, March 1984.

a. Includes other ISSSTE expenditures, such as loans, stores, and warehouses, housing, funerals, and other services.

*Not applicable.

deficit, and the total balance resulted in a surplus which, in 1981, equaled 17 percent of income. A separate listing of the balance of the IMSS and ISSSTE—not shown in the table—suggests that the first has a more solid financial situation than the second. For all years shown in the table, the total balance of the IMSS resulted in a surplus that fluctuated between 9.3 percent and 15.4 percent of income. On the other hand, the ISSSTE produced a surplus in 1972 and 1975 but generated deficits in 1978 and 1981. The highest deficit was that of 1978, at 14 percent of income. In both institutions the health-maternity program was the debtor and principal cause of the total deficit.[22] Information is not available for the rest of the subsystems.

Nevertheless, the financial solidity of the IMSS is more apparent than real. The 1982 actuarial study concluded that the surplus would diminish and, if the necessary corrective measures were not undertaken, a very reduced margin would be left for carrying out the provisions of the actuarial reserves. Furthermore, the allocation of sufficient resources for investment in 1983–85 would be very difficult.[23] I will discuss this and other financial problems.

Financing Methods

In addition to being the general system, the IMSS is also the only institution for which detailed information can be obtained. According to the law, an actuarial study must be done every three years, but because of economic instability in the current decade, the study has been done annually with a three-year projection. The latest available actuarial study is that finished at the end of 1982; a new study was carried out at the end of 1983, but its results were not available at the time of this writing.[24]

The pension program theoretically uses the general fixed-premium method, but in practice, the scaled-premium method has been applied since 1973. Although the latter is based on six-year periods, the premium (percentage of total wage contributions) has not been increased since the program was created in 1943. The 1982 actuarial study projected that all current premiums (including those for pensions) could be maintained in 1983–85. The study also recommended continuing with a plan for the reconstitution and investment of reserves. The study reported an increase of 96 percent in reserves in 1982 and projected a similar increase for 1983. But because the inflation rate was practically equal to the increase of the reserves in 1982–83, the latter—in real terms—stagnated at best. Nevertheless, a preliminary estimation indicated that, at the end of 1983, the effective reserves were only one-third of the projected amount, and even if this target was attained, the reserve would equal 8 percent of the cost of pensions in 1984, a small percentage even for a contingency fund. Thus the pension program is virtually functioning on a pure assessment method (pay-as-you-go) unless its premises are modified.[25]

The health-maternity program uses the pure assessment method. Even though the premium has increased from 6 percent to 9 percent since the inception of the program, the current premium is insufficient to finance expenditures; in forty years of operation, it has shown a deficit in thirty-seven. In all these years the program has been financed by transfer (in the form of loans or investments) from the pension fund (and also from the occupational risks fund) and has thus decapitalized it. (In 1977 it was estimated that the pension fund premium would have to be increased from 6 percent to almost 10 percent to balance this program until the end of the century, assuming that the draining of its funds by the health-maternity program would be stopped. As this development has not in fact occurred, the premium for the pension program today would have to be much greater.) It is calculated that the health-maternity program would need a premium of 13 percent to begin the amortization of its debt to the pension program, but paying an interest of only 5 percent on the *real* value of its physical plant.

The occupational risk program follows the method of assessment of constituent capital. A transfer of the reserves of this program to the health-maternity program has also occurred. The 1982 actuarial study recommended increasing the reserve to balance the program actuarily, but the projected reserve for 1983 (in the event that it was reached) in real terms would equal 65 percent of the reserves existing in 1981.[26]

Finally, the programs of social benefits and day care centers use pure assessment. These programs have benefited from investment in equipment by the pension fund, although less than health-maternity, and have possibly contributed (especially social benefits) to its decapitalization.

Although a precise evaluation must be postponed until the results of the 1983 actuarial study are available, the above discussion indicates that, in the short run, IMSS must undertake several steps to balance its system, including a possible change in the financing method and an increase in revenues and/ or a decrease in expenditures.

Measures to Increase Revenues

It is suggested that the first step to increase revenue should be the elimination of the wage contribution ceiling in the IMSS. This measure would not only improve the equilibrium but also would have a progressive effect on distribution. For the same reasons, the insured of the independent subsystems (armed forces and Pemex) or recently incorporated subsystems (electrical and railroad industries), as well as the employees of the IMSS, should pay a contribution proportional to that of the general system and the package of exceptional benefits that they enjoy. The premium of the IMSS health-maternity program should be required to cover its expenditures, without relying on transfers from other programs. The IMSS pension program premium should be increased so that it either balances the scaled-premium method or builds an adequate contingency reserve. Although the total wage contribution percentage of IMSS (and especially that of the insured) is one of the lowest in the region, the present economic crisis in the country would make it difficult to increase. However, a strong economic recovery, combined with Mexico's energy resources, could rapidly improve the situation. Legal investment regulations of the IMSS would also have to be modified to promote greater investment efficiency and yields. Finally, future actuarial studies of the IMSS could be done, using a more realistic base (for example, in terms of inflation) and also taking into account the observations of this chapter. A reform of the Mexican social security system should give attention to other changes, such as alternative sources of financing and a reduction in its costs.

BENEFITS, EXPENDITURES, AND COSTS

Benefits and Entitlement Conditions

In addition to the general system, there are various subsystems in Mexico with diverse benefits and entitlement conditions. Their diversity complicates an analysis of them and any comparison with other countries. This section describes the programs of the general system of IMSS, which has the strictest entitlement conditions in the country.

In health-maternity, the insured worker is entitled to a subsidy in lieu of salary as well as health benefits in kind and services, such as medical-hospital care, surgery, and medicines. The insured's and pensioner's dependents are entitled to the same nonmonetary health benefits. The female insured worker, in the event of pregnancy, is entitled to maternity subsidy, obstetric care, subsidies for milk and for the infant's basket, and day care services. In occupational risks, insured individuals are entitled to a subsidy in place of salary, as well as prosthesis, orthopedics and rehabilitation, and disability pensions; dependents are entitled to survivors' pensions and funeral aid. The pension program concedes pensions for old age, disability, unemployment, and death in addition to funeral aid. Family allowances are limited to pensioners, as are assistance in covering marriage expenditures and day care centers. The social benefits program includes educational, cultural, athletic, recreational, housing, vacation, and funeral services. The voluntary insured are entitled to all of the above benefits less those for occupational risks and social benefits. The social solidarity program offers nonmonetary health benefits as well as preventive, educational, and detection health services. There is no unemployment program.

Within the Latin American context, the legal conditions of IMSS in health-maternity are average or more flexible than the average, with few exceptions. On the other hand, entitlement conditions for old age pensions are the strictest in Latin America (together with Guatemala), as they require the insured (male or female) to be sixty-five years old and to have contributed for ten years; nevertheless, only a few countries in the region concede unemployment pensions, and the entitlement conditions for other pensions are average. In addition, the social benefits conceded exist in very few countries. Thus the benefit package of IMSS is average in the region or slightly more generous than the average, with some exceptions (the subsystems have better conditions; see below). Still, only seven countries in the region have a total percentage contribution below that of Mexico, and of these, six have much more limited population coverage and benefits.

Table 48 shows Mexico's progress in health services and levels in 1960–80; the table includes all medical services available in the country. A recent study done in Mexico evaluated vital statistics and reached the conclusion that some indicators are underestimated, especially the infant mortality rate; for example, the figure for 1970 has been adjusted from 68.5 to 100 per 1,000.[27] The majority of the indicators of the table show progressive improvement except for hospital beds per inhabitant, which has deteriorated since 1965, and the infant mortality rate, which rose in 1966–70 but later declined rapidly. In 1980, Mexico ranked fifth among the case studies in terms of health indicators, without experiencing any significant change in its position relative to these countries in 1960. In view of the vigorous economic development that occurred in this period, the health levels might have been expected to improve more.[28] The delay in the extension of coverage to the countryside and the prevalent health model partly explain this phenomenon.

Inequalities in Benefits

There are notable inequalities in health benefits both among geographic units and among groups covered. In 1979, the Federal District had approximately six times as many hospital beds per inhabitant and four times as many

TABLE 48
HEALTH SERVICES AND LEVELS IN MEXICO, 1960–1980

	Hospital Beds per 1,000 Persons	Physicians per 10,000 Persons	Mortality Rate		Life Expectancy[a]
			General	Infant	
1960	1.7	5.6	11.5	74.2	56.3
1965	2.0	5.2	9.8	61.0	59.2
1970	1.4	6.8	10.1	68.5	60.8
1975	1.3[b]	7.8[b]	7.2	49.0	62.7
1980	1.2	9.3	6.4	38.8	64.4

Sources: Dirección General de Estadísticas, Compendio estadístico, 1960 to 1976; SPP, Anuario estadístico de los Estados Unidos Mexicanos, 1977 to 1981; SPP, Agenda estadística, 1983; and CEPAL, Anuario estadístico, 1981.

a. Values for five-year periods (e.g., 1955–60 = 56.3); the last two five-year periods are projections.
b. 1974.

doctors per inhabitant as the states of Chiapas and Oaxaca. A ranking of the states according to their health services and levels would resemble the ranking based on social security coverage. The Federal District and the most-developed states have the best health services and the highest health levels, while the least developed states have the worst services and lowest health levels. Nevertheless, a comparison among the states based on the number of beds per inhabitant in 1969 and 1978 indicated a reduction in the extreme inequalities.[29]

With respect to groups covered, the subsystems have more generous benefits and more flexible entitlement conditions than the IMSS. For example, the ISSSTE offers—in addition to the benefits available under IMSS—seniority pensions, life insurance, compensation when the individual is not entitled to a pension, and broader programs for housing, loans, and subsidized stores. Those insured by the ISSSTE receive retirement pensions at an age ten years earlier than that required by the IMSS, and if the insured has thirty years of service, s/he can retire at any age. Thus the ISSSTE insured may retire twenty years younger than the IMSS insured. A study that compared the IMSS and the subsystems in the 1970s in terms of benefit generosity resulted in the following ranking: (1) armed forces; (2) ISSSTE, Pemex, electrical, railroad, and IMSS employees; and (3) the IMSS itself.[30]

Table 49 compares the benefits of the diverse groups in 1971 and 1980. The general system (IMSS) is last in all the indicators except for the uninsured, who are not entitled to pensions and whose medical services are the worst. In 1980 the armed forces had 3.4 times more physicians per insured than the IMSS, and Pemex had twice the number of doctors as the IMSS and almost four times more than the uninsured. In 1971–80 there was no significant decrease in the differences among the institutions with the best and the worst health services, except that the armed forces and Pemex appeared to have broadened their advantages, while the railroads and ISSSTE seemed to have lost ground. But the ISSSTE health services' figures are underestimated in both years, as they do not include the significant services obtained under contract.

The Growing Cost of Social Security and Its Causes

Table 50 does not include all social security costs, as it excludes all of the subsystems except the ISSSTE; furthermore, health expenditures appear to be underestimated. The National Institute of Statistics has reported that, in 1980, expenditures on health alone were equal to 3.9 percent of GDP.[31] According to the table, the cost of social security (including health) rose from 2 percent of GDP in 1960 to 4.7 percent in 1975 and fell to 3 percent in 1980. Until the petroleum boom in the second half of the 1970s, social security expenditures—in each five-year period—rose at almost twice the rate of GDP growth, but after the boom, GDP rose 1.6 times more than social security expenditures. In 1980, social security expenditure as a percentage of GDP in

TABLE 49
DIFFERENCES IN PENSIONS AND MEDICAL SERVICES
AMONG INSURED GROUPS IN MEXICO, 1971 AND 1980

	1971			1980		
Insured Group	Average Pension	Hospital Beds per 1,000 Persons	Physicians per 10,000 Persons	Average Pension[a]	Hospital Beds per 1,000 Persons	Physicians per 10,000 Persons
General (IMSS)	1.0	1.8	12.3	1.0	1.2	11.8
Federal government (ISSSTE)[b]	6.4	1.9	27.1	3.8	1.3	15.9
Petroleum	**	1.9[c]	17.6[c]	**	1.4	24.9
Railway	6.4	4.2	14.8	**	3.2	14.8
Armed forces[d]	5.5	3.6	17.7	**	4.1	23.8
Uninsured[e]	*	1.2	4.4	*	1.1	6.7

Sources: Author's calculations based on the *Anuario estadístico compendiado 1970* and *1972;* SPP, *Agenda estadística, 1983;* IMSS, *Memoria estadística, 1981,* and ISSSTE, *Anuario estadístico, 1981.*

a. Using IMSS as base (1.0).
b. Includes only direct services of ISSSTE and not those contracted with other institutions.
c. 1970.
d. Secretaries of defense and the navy.
e. Services of the secretary of health and welfare, the Department of the Federal District, private institutions, and others.

*Not applicable.
**Not available.

Mexico was similar to that in Peru and was one-third of the comparable percentage in four other case studies. Within the regional context, Mexico occupied an intermediate position: eight countries had a higher percentage, five had a similar percentage, and six had a lower one. But the Mexican percentage was probably actually somewhat higher, as I have already noted. The causes of the moderate increase in costs are discussed below.

General causes. Although Mexico has expanded population coverage, it has done so much less than Costa Rica, Cuba, Chile, and Uruguay. In addition, benefits and entitlement conditions in Mexico are more restricted than in these countries. Largely for this reason, social security costs in Mexico are average (or slightly lower than average), and such costs grow at a relatively slow rate.

An important factor in the cost of social security is administrative expenditures; Mexico has the highest in the case studies and one of the highest in the region. In 1982, administrative expenditures of the IMSS took 18 percent of total revenues and reached 19.5 percent in 1983. The ratio of IMSS employees per 1,000 insured rose gradually from 6.8 to 7.5 in 1975–82, while in the ISSSTE it rose from 9 to 10.4 in 1980–82. Information on employees

TABLE 50

COST OF SOCIAL SECURITY IN MEXICO, 1961–1980

(MILLIONS OF PESOS AT CURRENT PRICES)

			Social Security Expenditures		
	GDP	Total Central Govt. Expenditures	Total	% of GDP	% of Central Govt. Expenditures
1961	163.8	20.4[b]	3.2	2.0	15.7
1965	252.0	36.7[b]	6.5	2.6	17.7
1970	418.7	52.7[b]	12.7	3.0	24.1
1975	998.3	161.6	46.7[a]	4.7	28.9
1980	4,276.5	750.2	137.6[a]	3.2	18.2

Sources: 1961–70 from Carmelo Mesa-Lago, *Social Security in Latin America* (Pittsburgh, Pa.: University of Pittsburgh Press, 1978); ILO, *El costo de la seguridad social: Novena encuesta internacional, 1972–1974;* and Mexico's Dirección General de Estadísticas de México, *Anuario estadístico compendiado, 1962* to *1972.* 1975 and 1980 from IMF, *Government Finance Statistics Yearbook, 1982;* SSP, *Anuario estadístico de los Estados Mexicanos, 1977* to *1981;* and SSP, *Agenda Estadística, 1982* and *1983.*

a. Includes IMSS, ISSSTE, and health expenditures of the central government.

b. According to the federal government budget and excluding expenditures of decentralized agencies and state enterprises.

in the health sector indicate higher ratios in Pemex and the armed forces.[32] The special pension fund of IMSS employees is largely financed by that institution, as personnel contributions are insufficient. The 1982 actuarial study warned that the increase in benefits to personnel should be controlled, as it could affect the financial stability of the IMSS.[33]

Table 51 shows that in 1965–81 the health-maternity program took more

TABLE 51

PERCENTAGE DISTRIBUTION OF SOCIAL SECURITY EXPENDITURES

BY PROGRAM IN MEXICO, 1965–1981

Expenditure[a]	1965	1970	1974	1981[b]
Pensions	16.7	19.1	19.1	20.9
Health/maternity	73.3	71.8	70.9	64.9
Occupational risks	10.0	9.1	10.0	12.8[c]
Day care centers	**	**	**	1.4
Total	100.0	100.0	100.0	100.0

Sources: 1965–74 from ILO, *El costo de la seguridad social, 1971–74;* 1981 from IMSS, *Memoria estadística, 1981.*

a. Only for benefits in 1961–74.

b. Includes only IMSS.

c. Goes in part to pensions.

**Not available.

than two-thirds of social security expenditures, although with a declining tendency, while the pension program took one-fifth and showed a slightly increasing trend. These are the two principal components of expenditures, given that the day care centers absorb only one-tenth of total expenditures and occupational risks take an insignificant percentage. There is very little financial information on social benefits; although their share of expenditures is probably small, this program is nonessential, and it should not have been introduced before universal coverage had been reached in the two fundamental programs, health-maternity and pensions.

Causes related to the health program. Mexico is still in a period of demographic transition: in 1980 its fertility rate was higher than the regional average and its mortality rate much lower, hence its population growth rate (3.3 percent) was high and above the Latin American average. Among the six case studies, Mexico has the highest percentage of population under fourteen years of age, and its percentage of the population sixty-five and older is equal to that of Costa Rica (see table 52). The Mexican percentage of demographic dependency (100.8 percent in 1970 and 93.4 percent in 1980) surpassed that of the other case studies and is the fourth highest in the region.

The change in the pathological profile in Mexico has not advanced as much as in the other case studies (except in Peru), which suggests that a high proportion of the diseases can be eradicated at a relatively low cost. In 1980 the three principal causes of death in Mexico were infectious intestinal diseases, pneumonia, and postnatal complications (for a combined percentage of 27 percent), while cerebrovascular, cardiac, and degenerative diseases were much less important (8 percent). Among children under one year of age, the first three diseases cited caused 67 percent of deaths.[34] In the IMSS-COPLAMAR program, 44 percent of reported deaths are caused by the ''diseases of underdevelopment,'' and a high percentage of infant mortality is caused by malnutrition.[35]

But a very small proportion of health expenditures are dedicated to combating these diseases. In 1981, social security institutions, which covered 60 percent of the population, accounted for 85 percent of health expenditures,

TABLE 52

DISTRIBUTION OF POPULATION BY AGE GROUP IN MEXICO, 1960–2010

(PERCENT)

Age Group	1960	1970	1980	1990	2000	2010
0–14	45.6	46.7	44.7	39.1	34.1	29.4
15–64	51.0	49.8	51.7	57.2	61.7	65.6
65 and over	3.4	3.5	3.6	3.7	4.2	5.0

Source: Based on CELADE, *Boletín demográfico* 16:32 (July 1983); calculations by the author.

while social welfare institutions, which should protect the remaining 40 percent of the population, accounted for only 15 percent. It should be noted that in social security coverage the welfare sector of IMSS has been included (social solidarity and the IMSS-COPLAMAR), which in 1981 protected 12 percent of the total population and 24 percent of those covered by IMSS, but received only 3 to 4 percent of its budget.[36] At the beginning of the 1980s, curative medicine absorbed 90 percent of health expenditures and preventive medicine the remaining 10 percent.[37] A change in health care priorities in favor of preventive medicine, sanitation, and other types of primary health care oriented toward the rural population (which suffers a high risk of disease but receives a small share of health resources) could considerably reduce morbidity and general and infant mortality caused by diseases of underdevelopment.

Mexican social security has hospital facilities that are among the best in Latin America, but they are often wasteful of space and have many unnecessary decorative details. It is difficult to evaluate the efficiency of these facilities because administrative statistics are scarce. For example, the 1981 *IMSS Statistical Yearbook* did not publish the percentage of hospital beds occupied. It is known, however, that in 1982 the figure was 67 percent in the IMSS-COPLAMAR program and 70 percent in the ISSSTE, both very low in comparison with the other case studies, except for Peru. Information on the average days of hospital stay is better: in 1982 it was 4.6 days in the IMSS (4 in the IMSS-COPLAMAR), 5.7 in the ISSSTE, and 9.5 in the armed forces. Except in the last case, the figure for average days of hospital stay in Mexico is lower than those in the other five case studies. But the excessive number of employees is, without doubt, an important cause of high health costs. At the beginning of the 1980s, IMSS had between 1.5 and 2.5 times more employees per hospital bed than the other five countries, and the hospital employee/bed ratio was even higher for Pemex and the armed forces.[38]

Finally, the lack of coordination in the health system induces excess capacity (and duplication) in some geographic areas and for certain groups and deficits in health care elsewhere.

Causes related to the pension program.   The figure for pension expenditures as a percentage of social security expenditures in Mexico is similar to that for Costa Rica; it is lower than that of only six countries in the region (see table 53) and grew very little in the 1970s (see table 51). This phenomenon has causes similar to those in Costa Rica. The pension program is much more recent than that of the pioneer countries, two years younger even than Costa Rica's, and its first payments did not begin until the 1950s. In addition, as coverage was not significantly expanded until the last two decades, a relatively small number of people qualified for entitlement in the first twenty years of the program. The percentage of the population over sixty-five years of age was 3.6 percent in 1980, equal to that of Costa Rica and Peru and far below that of the pioneer countries. The percentage projected for the year 2000 in Mexico (5 percent) is the lowest for the six case studies (see table 52). Life expectancy in 1980 (sixty-four years) was the second lowest in the six case studies. Retirement age for old age pensions in the IMSS (sixty-five years) is the highest in Latin America and is the same for both sexes; the retirement ages for the subsystems are much lower, but the proportion of insured in these is only 16 percent of the total.

Because of these factors and the relatively rapid expansion of coverage in the last two decades, the quotient of demographic burden rose from 0.047 in 1960 to only 0.089 in 1983 and is the lowest in the six case studies except for that of Costa Rica. Although both total population and EAP growth rates have fallen since the mid-1970s, the active insured growth rate is still from two to four times the size of the other two rates, except in 1982–83, because of the intense economic crisis (see table 43). The IMSS has estimated that a stationary situation in the pension program (that is, when the growth rates of active and passive are equal) will not occur until after 2022.

Possibly the factor with the most weight in the increase of pension costs is the adjustment of pensions for inflation. To make this adjustment, the IMSS uses the average annual salary of the last five years as a base. It has been estimated that, if salaries increase by 60 percent because of inflation, the base for pension adjustments will be 38.5 percent (with constant salary). Therefore, if there is a high rate of inflation (Mexico's rate in 1982 and 1983 was about 100 percent), the initial sum of the pension will already be devalued. In 1981, the average old age pension was equivalent to 37.6 percent of the average insured salary, which, because of the contribution ceiling, was way below the national average salary.[39] Until 1973 pensions were readjusted by executive decision. It was decided to adjust them every five years from 1973 until 1982, and since 1982 they have been adjusted annually. The nominal minimums for pensions were increased five times in 1976–83 but failed to achieve any real increase.[40] Table 53 shows that the average real per capita pension almost tripled in 1960–75, but the original base was very low and the real pension started to decline in 1976.

Although the costs of pensions will grow in the long run and will become a preponderant factor in social security expenditures, Mexico has enough time to deal with this situation. As we have already seen, the fundamental issue has been the decapitalization of the pension fund by the health-maternity program. Therefore the most serious short-run problem is how to balance this program.

Measures to Reduce Expenditures

The cost of social security in Mexico is moderate for regional levels and is probably adequate for the country's level of development. More advisable

TABLE 53

REAL VALUE OF ANNUAL PENSIONS (IMSS) IN MEXICO, 1960–1981

	Pensions (millions of pesos)	No. of Pensioners (thous.)	Average per Capita (pesos)	Index (1970 = 100)		
Year				Nominal Pension	Inflation[a]	Real Pension
1960	66	49	1,347	47.5	80.0	59.4
1961	85	58	1,466	51.7	80.7	64.1
1962	112	70	1,600	56.4	82.2	68.6
1963	144	77	1,870	66.0	82.6	79.9
1964	180	92	1,956	69.0	86.1	80.1
1965	211	105	2,009	70.9	87.8	80.8
1966	257	121	2,124	74.9	88.9	84.2
1967	315	143	2,203	77.7	91.5	84.9
1968	397	163	2,436	85.9	93.3	92.1
1969	507	184	2,755	97.2	95.4	101.9
1970	618	218	2,835	100.0	100.0	100.0
1971	778	234	3,325	117.3	105.5	111.2
1972	915	253	3,617	127.6	110.8	115.2
1973	1,195	265	4,509	159.0	124.2	128.0
1974	1,613	300	5,377	189.6	153.6	123.4
1975	2,492	327	7,621	268.8	176.6	152.2
1976	3,184	364	8,747	308.5	204.6	150.8
1977	4,444	402	11,055	389.9	264.1	147.6
1978	5,447	443	12,296	433.7	310.3	139.8
1979	7,108	489	14,536	512.7	366.8	139.8
1980	9,994	536	18,646	657.7	463.2	142.0
1981	13,781	584	23,598	832.3	592.5	140.5

Sources: Pensions and number of pensioners from IMSS, *Memoria de labores de 1967*, and *Memoria estadística, 1971* and *1981*. Inflation rate from ECLA, *Estudio económico de América Latina, 1967*, to *1982*. Averages and indexes calculated by the author.

Note: Figures include old age, disability, survivors', and occupational risks pensions.

a. Annual variation average consumer prices in 1970–81, January to December wholesale prices in 1960–69.

than a decrease in costs is better use of the system, with different priorities and increased efficiency.

I mentioned the project to develop a new health model in Mexico that will allegedly make it possible to reach universal coverage at a relatively low cost.[41] The new law for the creation of a national health system provides the opportunity to study the viability of this project and its implementation carefully, with the necessary adjustments. In any case, the national health system should integrate all of the existing services in the public sector, eliminate duplications, and improve the use of existing capacity.

This section has suggested other measures to reduce expenditures and increase efficiency: (1) allocate a much higher percentage of health expenditures to preventive medicine and primary health care and decrease the emphasis on curative, capital-intensive medicine; (2) reduce the size of administrative and health personnel; (3) make the benefits of the subsystems (both inside and outside the IMSS) equal those of the general system; (4) eliminate seniority pensions and raise the age for old age pensions in the subsystems; and (5) eliminate or reduce social benefits and shift these resources to the expansion of coverage in priority programs such as primary health care.

THE IMPACT OF SOCIAL SECURITY ON DEVELOPMENT

There are no published studies of the effect of Mexico's social security system on savings/investment and income distribution, although there is one study of its impact on employment.

Savings and Investment

The pension program of the IMSS, because it is fairly new and because it initially used the general fixed premium and later the scaled premium, has generated a substantial surplus. A large part of this surplus has been used to subsidize health-maternity and social benefits programs, through investment in buildings and equipment. Until 1983, surpluses in the pension program compensated for deficits in the health-maternity program, but the mid-1980s saw the danger of a net disequilibrium of the system for the first time. Because of the progressive decapitalization of the pension fund, the program really uses a pure assessment method. Social security may have had a positive impact on investment, but this situation may change in the future. The relatively small contribution that the insured pays must not have been a strong disincentive to individual saving, especially among the medium- and high-income strata that benefit from the contribution ceiling. If the bulk of the financing is really paid by the employer, this fact should have a more negative impact on investment than it would if it were paid by either the insured or the consumer.

Employment

Mexico has an abundant work force, and the labor supply should be elastic. The employer must pay two-thirds of the total wage contribution, although this percentage is very low compared with that of Costa Rica and Uruguay. The transfer of this contribution to the insured appears to be limited by labor and social security legislation. Thus the employer legally must pay not only his contribution but also that of the insured when the latter receives a minimum salary. According to the Confederation of Chambers of Industry, this obligation increased the cost of the minimum salary by more than 14 percent in 1976.[42] As only 42 percent of the EAP has coverage and there are subsystems in which the insured either pays no contribution or pays a much lower percentage than that of the general system, it is possible to evade the wage contribution.

If the employer's contribution cannot be transferred to the consumer (for example, because of control of certain prices), we would expect a decrease in the demand for labor and the substitution of capital for labor. This viewpoint is taken by a recent study of the impact of social security on employment in Mexico. The study calculates the effect on employment if the value-added tax were substituted for the wage contribution. (Chapter 7 analyzes this notion in more detail.) To this effect, the study applied two methods (which I discussed in the Chilean case) to the manufacturing industry in Mexico in 1978. The result of the calculations was positive: an increase in employment that varied from 1.7 percent to 9.6 percent, depending on the method used, or the equivalent of 48,000 to 362,000 new jobs.[43] One critic of this study agrees with its results at the aggregate level, but not at the level of the industrial sectors and charges that the methodology applied to the Mexican case overestimates the impact on employment by assuming a single elasticity of substitution for all sectors.[44]

Distribution of Income

The most progressive aspects of the Mexican social security system are the IMSS expansion of population coverage to low-income groups, the IMSS welfare health programs, and the exemption of the wage contribution by IMSS insured who receive only the minimum salary. Conversely, there are various regressive elements in this system: (1) 58 percent of the EAP lack pension coverage, 40 percent of the total population lack health coverage, and those excluded from the system are, in general, the lowest income groups; (2) the ceiling on the wage contribution allows the insured with the highest income to contribute proportionally less than those with medium or low income (except of course those who receive only the minimum salary); (3) the state either totally finances or strongly subsidizes subsystems that cover groups with higher income than the uninsured; (4) among the states there is a positive relationship between higher income and better social security coverage and health services (and vice versa); and (5) the welfare health services receive a much lower proportional allocation of resources than those of social insurance, and there are no welfare pensions in Mexico.

In 1984, the IMSS began to design a study on the impact of its programs on income distribution. This study is expected to measure the incidence of financing and expenditures, and the net transfers among different income, work-risk, and age groups as well as among sectors.[45]

A recently published study suggests that the present strategy for the short- and long-run satisfaction of basic needs (including social security) in Mexico suffers from its close interdependence on the distribution of income, the demand profile, and the productive structure. To satisfy the total population's basic needs in the year 2000 with the current strategy, it would be necessary to increase investment in hospitals by an average annual rate of 10 percent in 1981–2000. As this course of action is impossible, the study proposes various ways to modify the distribution of income, in order to achieve a more "progressive" (egalitarian) distribution.[46]

Peru:
A Midstreamer's Premature Crisis

PROGRESS IN Peruvian social security has been moderate in the last two decades, and many of the system's characteristics place it at the midpoint for the region. Important advances were made at the end of the past decade with the transformation of the relatively stratified system into one that is relatively unified and uniform, although inequalities still persist. But total population coverage rose only from 9 percent to 19 percent in the period 1961–83, while that of the EAP rose from 25 percent to 38 percent. For its population coverage, Peru is located in exactly the middle of the ranks of Latin American countries.

Over the last two decades there has been a significant improvement in Peruvian health standards, but they were still among the lowest in the region in 1980: the infant mortality rate was one of the highest and life expectancy one of the shortest. The low-income sector is excluded from social security, and the least-developed geographic areas have the poorest coverage and the worst health services. In 1980, the Ministry of Health, which theoretically assists 66 percent of the population, received only half of the resources allocated to the Peruvian Social Security Institute (IPSS), which covered 17 percent of the population.

Because of the low coverage, a benefit system that is average, and a relatively recent pension program, social security costs in Peru rose slowly, from 2 percent of GDP in 1961 to 3.4 percent in 1982. At the beginning of the 1980s, the financial burden of Peruvian social security (measured as a percentage of GDP) was equal to the regional average. The lack of IPSS statistics and accounting balances for almost ten years (1973–80) makes it difficult to analyze the system's financial equilibrium precisely. Nevertheless, the available figures show a total surplus until 1982, although the amount as a percentage of revenues decreased. Furthermore, the health-maternity program ran a deficit that was covered by transfers from the pension and occupational risks programs. Since 1983 the system has yielded a total deficit principally due to the state's delay in its payments and to evasion and payment

174

delays on the part of private employers. The debt for both concepts in 1983 was similar to somewhat less than half of IPSS total revenues in 1982. Other causes of the disequilibrium have been the freezing of the wage contribution percentage, the very low or negative yield on investments, and administrative irregularities and high costs. The deepening economic crisis at the beginning of the decade acted as a catalyst, with its negative effect on employment, real salaries, and fiscal expenditures.

The 1980–85 government prepared an ambitious social security program aimed at expanding coverage and putting the system on a sound basis, but administrative problems combined with the economic crisis prevented it from reaching such goals. Nevertheless, several positive steps were taken in the financial area: the state began to pay its debts, strong pressure was placed on employers to fulfill their obligations, technical aid was requested from international agencies to improve administrative efficiency and the actuarial system, and some expenditures were reduced. The financial problems confronting the system appear to be principally the legacy of a decade of poor administration. Once these problems are overcome, the country must dedicate itself to expanding coverage through a system of basic benefits that is economically viable in the long run.

HISTORICAL EVOLUTION

The Stratified System

Social security in Peru evolved in a more stratified manner than in Costa Rica and Mexico but less so than in Cuba and Chile and hence occupies an intermediate position (see table 54). Following the regional pattern, Peruvian pressure groups were able to obtain separate programs, and at times treatment of an individual group even took into account its various components. During the brief democratic interim in the 1960s, the two principal pension programs were established that covered the largest groups of blue- and white-collar workers (a separation—as in the Chilean case—that reflects the different treatment of the two groups by the labor legislation), along with other funds for small blue-collar groups. At the end of the 1960s, social security was truly a labyrinth, with more than 2,000 legal decrees and dozens of funds each with their own legislation, financing, and benefits.[1] Some of these funds were completely independent or were administered by other funds either through separate accounts or special regulations. There was no coordination even between the two principal programs. Worse yet, in Peru stratification was not accompanied by the high population coverage typical of the pioneer countries. Although coverage rose somewhat in the 1960s, at the end of the decade only about one-tenth of the total population and one-third of the EAP had social security coverage.

The armed forces were the first group to obtain coverage through ad hoc

TABLE 54
SOCIAL SECURITY LEGISLATION IN PERU,
BY RISK AND GROUPS COVERED, 1850–1963

Year[a]	Risk Covered	Group Covered
1850, 1910, 1923	ODS, U	Armed forces
1850, 1936, 1941	ODS, U	Civil servants
1950, 1960		
1911, 1935	OR	Blue-collar workers
1934	ODS	Callao stevedores
1936	H/M	Blue-collar workers
1946	S	White-collar workers
1947	ODS	Jockeys
1948	H/M	Civil servants and white-collar workers
1950	H/M	Armed forces
1961	ODS	Blue-collar workers
1961–62	ODS	Civil servants and white-collar workers (newly hired)
1965	ODS	Congress, judiciary, public registers, state and university teachers
1965,1978	U, H/M	Fishermen
1966–68	ODS	Independent chauffeurs (taxi owners)
1970	ODS	Domestic servants
1972	ODS	Fishermen
1972	ODS	Armed forces system standardized
1973–74	ODS	The system for white- and blue-collar workers and civil servants, and other groups, unified and standardized
1979	H/M	The system for blue- and white-collar workers and civil servants, standardized and unified
1980	ALL	New unified and standardized system (IPSS), excluding only the armed forces

Source: Mesa-Lago, *Social Security in Latin America* (Pittsburgh, Pa.: University of Pittsburgh Press, 1978); and subsequent legislation.

Note: ODS = old age, disability, and survivors' pension. H/M = health/maternity. OR = occupational risks. U = unemployment pension or compensation. S = seniority pension.

a. The first date corresponds to the initial law and subsequent dates to modifications and amplifications.

pension programs and hospitals for each of the four branches: army, navy, air force, and police.

Civil servants were the second group to obtain coverage with a pension program and, together with private white-collar employees, a health-maternity program. The initial pension program for this group covered all those hired prior to 1962 in the central government, in more than 100 autonomous institutions, and in all the departments and municipalities. Those hired after

1962 joined the general pension program for white-collar employees created in 1961–62. In addition, there were several independent pension funds for powerful groups such as the executive, legislative, and judicial branches (which separated elected officials from bureaucrats), diplomats, autonomous institutions (such as the central bank and private pension funds), and the educational sector (with notable differences among its various subgroups). Finally, there were numerous compulsory funds for life insurance, retirement lump-sum programs, and so forth.

Private white-collar workers had two general programs: health-maternity and pensions. There was also a seniority pension program for employees of large enterprises. Employers were responsible for insuring their employees against occupational risks through private insurance companies.

Blue-collar workers also had two separate general programs: health-maternity (one of the first such programs established in Latin America) and pensions (created at almost the same time as the program for private white-collar workers). The blue-collar workers' general system administered various subsystems. Some of the latter had separate funds (taxi drivers and stevedores) and others only special regulations (domestic servants, newspaper sellers, hairdressers, and the voluntarily insured). Finally, there were four blue-collar funds independent of the general blue-collar system: fishermen (with separate funds for pensions, health-maternity, and unemployment); the stevedores of the Callao Port (health-maternity); and jockeys (pensions and health-maternity). Occupational risks were covered through contracts with private insurance companies.

In the first half of the 1960s, various studies of the social security system were carried out with the assistance of the ILO and the Iberoamerican Social Security Organization (OISS). These studies focused on the general pension and health-maternity programs for white- and blue-collar workers.[2] Toward the end of the decade, the system faced financial problems, as the state owed it a substantial sum. Several measures undertaken to achieve a certain degree of coordination and standardization were both tardily introduced and weak; the state lacked the power to carry out a comprehensive reform of the system.

Unification and Standardization of the System

The military government reinforced the power of the state and controlled or coopted the majority of the pressure groups. Although in the first years this government contributed to the complexity of the system, it eventually made the system unified and uniform by means of the following measures: (1) in 1968–70 the designation of reorganization commissions to manage and integrate the general programs of white- and blue-collar workers; (2) in 1970 the incorporation of social security and health care into the first five-year plan (1971–75); (3) in 1971 the incorporation of the occupational risks program

into the general blue-collar system; (4) in 1972 the standardization of the
armed forces pension programs; (5) in 1973 the creation of a standardized
pension program that integrated the general blue- and white-collar programs
and some of the subsystems but excluded the armed forces, civil servants
under the old system, and the three independent blue-collar pension funds;
(6) in the 1970s, gradual integration of the white- and blue-collar workers'
hospitals, which culminated, in 1979, in standardized legislation for the
health-maternity program; and (7) in 1980, a few days before the end of
military rule, creation of the Peruvian Social Security Institute, the sole ad-
ministrator of the general pension and health-maternity programs.[3]

The reform of the 1970s greatly improved unification and standardization
but did not significantly expand population coverage (the reform only incorporated domestic servants and made optional insurance available to independent workers). Furthermore, the process of unification and standardization
has been criticized recently for its lack of planning and effective control,
frequent changes and accelerated rates, improvisations, and inefficiency. Although the social security bureaucracy boomed in 1974–80, accounting balances were not published, a registry of employers and insured was not created,
inventories were not made, statistical series were not carried out, and actuarial
studies were not prepared. Furthermore, because of state control of information, "problems remained hidden" and "the protests or criticisms concerning the deficiencies of the system were not exposed to public opinion."[4]
Finally, the state stopped fulfilling its financial obligations to social security,
thus accumulating a massive debt.

The IPSS was born on the eve of the return to democracy but was too
weak to overcome the fatal legacy of statistical and accounting ignorance,
administrative chaos, and financial difficulties of social security. The new
government put the IPSS into operation under provisional regulations and
with ambitious goals, including universalization of coverage and financial
stability.[5] Although several important steps were taken, the serious economic
crisis compounded with political conflicts prevented most goals from being
achieved. Worse yet, the first board of directors of IPSS had to be removed
because a scandal was uncovered by an exhaustive bicameral investigation
that initially targeted the military administration but eventually extended its
inquiry into the new government.[6] (Although such an investigation weakened
the IPSS, it was a credit to the new democratic government, which—possibly
for the first time in the region—permitted a thorough scrutiny and revelation
of grave administrative irregularities that probably exist in other countries but
are covered up). Finally, the basic juridical instrument of IPSS—its organic
law—has been delayed more than three years in Congress, and even though
it was approved by the Senate in 1983, it still required the approval of the
House of Representatives in March 1984.

In summary, Peruvian social security evolved in a stratified manner but without reaching the high degree of population coverage attained by the pioneer countries. The unification and standardization of the system were inefficiently achieved in the 1970s and were not accompanied by a significant expansion of coverage. The new democratic government, inheriting these problems (which had worsened with more than ten years of neglect) and confronting serious economic and political crisis, worked to shore up finances but was not able to expand coverage.

ORGANIZATIONAL STRUCTURE

Currently, the Peruvian social security system is unified and standardized with some exceptions.[7] The IPSS is the principal institution and operates three programs: health-maternity, pensions, and occupational risks. The IPSS is an autonomous agency with legal but practically weak three-party participation in its administration by the insured, the employers, and the state.[8]

The health-maternity program of IPSS is the most unified and standardized in the country; it encompasses all of the insured with the exception of three groups that have separate services (their own or contracted): the armed forces, fishermen, and jockeys.

The IPSS pension program covers three groups: (1) private white-collar employees except for a small group that used to have a separate fund now administered by IPSS; (2) civil servants except for the following three groups, which have independent funds: (a) civil servants hired prior to 1962, who remain in the old fund; (b) white-collar workers of autonomous agencies hired prior to 1962, each of which has a separate fund; and (c) magistrates of the judicial branch, legislators, diplomats, state teachers, and university professors, hired prior to 1973, who also have their own fund; (3) blue-collar workers, including two groups with special regulations (domestic servants and the optional insured) plus two groups with separate funds administered by the IPSS (taxi owners and stevedores) but excluding two groups with independent pension funds (fishermen and jockeys). The armed forces also have an independent pension fund with uniform regulations for their four branches.

The IPSS occupational risk program covers only blue-collar workers; employers can make agreements for complementary insurance with private insurance companies. White-collar workers are covered by life insurance for which their employers contract with insurance companies supervised by the Ministry of Labor.

The Bank of the Nation collects all wage contributions destined for the IPSS from employers who, in turn, collect wage contributions from their employees. The bank also records revenues and expenditures, pays interest on the deposits, and pays all monetary benefits.

The health system needs greater integration. The IPSS has its own curative services, but it also contracts with other health providers in geographic areas where it lacks its own services or where these are insufficient. Insured white-collar workers theoretically maintain the old privilege of "free choice" (something blue-collar workers have never had), which enables them to select medical-hospital services from private or public carriers, pay for these out of pocket, and later be reimbursed by the IPSS according to a tariff. In practice, free choice has eroded because of the low reimbursement paid by IPSS. The health system of the IPSS takes on a pyramidal form, with three types of facilities: rural health posts, polyclinics, and hospitals organized in three levels (zones, regions, and centers). Hospitals and polyclinics, where white- and blue-collar workers previously received separate care, have now eliminated this discriminatory treatment except for the hospitals of Lima and Arequipa, even though their doctors are integrated. The Ministry of Health also has its own facilities (and is responsible for the programs of sanitation and vaccination), as do enterprises in isolated places (for example, mines and oil wells), charitable societies, and the private sector. The armed forces have hospitals for each branch: army, navy, air force, and interior (police); civil servants in the armed forces are covered by the IPSS but have free choice. Fishermen and jockeys do not have their own facilities and use contracted services.

Although notable advances in social security unification and standardization have occurred in the last few years, several anachronisms still remain and should disappear. These include the independent pension and health-maternity funds for fishermen and jockeys as well as the funds that are separate, although within the IPSS, for taxi owners and stevedores. All these programs should be completely integrated within the IPSS. The independent funds of civil servants and the armed forces pose a more complex problem. The civil servants' independent funds (for those hired prior to 1962 and 1973, depending on the case) are justified on the principle of acquired rights; since these funds are in the red, their integration into the IPSS would be problematical legally and also financially. As these funds are now closed (new entries are not allowed), their populations will gradually shrink until they disappear. But such is not the case with the armed forces, whose system is open. It is revealing that the military, which accomplished the unification of the Peruvian social security system, excluded only themselves from such a process. This arrangement is not confined to Peru, since the armed forces in all of Latin America have separate systems, with the sole exception of Costa Rica, which has no armed force.

The Acción Popular government did not consider any of the above-mentioned steps, but its social security plan proposed the establishment of a national health system that would coordinate IPSS and MSS services, emphasize preventive medicine, decentralize services, and improve the hospital and polyclinic network. Although important progress was made in these last two areas,[9] nothing was really done to integrate the health services. The democratic transition of power to the Alianza Popular Revolucionaria Americana party (APRA) in 1985 opens new possibilities and challenges for social security reform in Peru.

POPULATION COVERAGE
Legal and Statistical Coverage

According to law, the IPSS covers all salaried workers, whether they are civil servants, private white-collar workers, or blue-collar workers (also covered are members of "social property" and cooperative enterprises) except for groups with their own funds. Health-maternity coverage is more extensive than pension coverage, as fewer groups have independent health funds, and pensioners and dependents are covered together with the actively insured. However, dependent coverage is more limited in Peru than in other Latin American countries: the insured's spouse is entitled to maternity benefits, but not health, while children under one year are entitled to health benefits. Voluntary insurance ("optional") is available for self-employed workers and also for those who once had compulsory insurance but have lost it and are not eligible for pensions. The occupational risks program of the IPSS covers all salaried workers in the private and public sectors (in the latter only if the employee did not have previous coverage), including those in agriculture, mining (in isolated places miners are covered by private enterprises), fishermen, domestic servants, and members of cooperatives. White-collar workers are excluded, but they do have life insurance and can be covered by IPSS monetary or health benefits in case of occupational risks.

Table 55 shows gross estimates of the statistical coverage of the population. The IPSS has neither a unique registry nor individual accounts for the insured, and because of the multiplicity of programs and their diverse coverage, an insured may be registered in one IPSS program but not in another. For example, a state civil servant hired before 1962 appears as an IPSS insured in health-maternity but not in pensions or occupational risks, but if the civil servant was hired after 1962, he also appears in pensions. In 1973 a decree ordered the creation of a unique registry, and in 1978 a system was designed for the purpose—with the assistance of the Organization of American States—but was not implemented. Coverage figures were not recorded in the 1970s, and a census of the insured conducted in 1981 had serious defects and has not been published.[10] The number of active insured in pension funds independent of IPSS is not known (civil servants of the state and autonomous agencies hired before 1962 and those of the legislative and judicial branches, diplomats, and state and university teachers hired before 1973). Since these groups are insured in the IPSS health-maternity program, table 55 relies on health coverage as a substitute for pension coverage. In addition, the table includes an estimate of the insured in the armed forces and fishing funds, excluding only the small group of jockeys.[11]

According to table 55 estimates, total population coverage in health doubled in the 1961–83 period, going from less than 9 percent to about 18 percent. Such low coverage results from the strict limitation on the number of dependents entitled to health benefits. EAP pension coverage grew from almost 25 percent in 1961 to 38 percent in 1983, a very slow expansion, especially after the mid-1960s. Occupational risks coverage (not shown in the table) was 20 percent of the EAP in 1980–82, much lower than pension coverage because white-collar workers were excluded.[12] In terms of population coverage, Peru was at the midpoint of the region in 1980, although in age both its health program and the initial pension program for civil servants are surpassed only by the five pioneer countries.

Determinant Structural Factors

Unlike Costa Rica, Cuba, and Chile, where universalization of coverage was facilitated by the high percentage of salaried workers, Peru's low percentage of salaried labor has impeded the expansion of coverage. In 1982 only 45 percent of the EAP was salaried in Peru; self-employed workers constituted 49 percent of the labor force, and unpaid family workers made up almost 6 percent. The 37 percent of the EAP covered by social security in 1980 barely exceeded the 35 percent of the EAP in the formal sector (see table 3, above). Furthermore, a good part of Peru's extensive territory consists of mountains and jungles; expansion of health services in these vast, isolated zones is extremely difficult. Widespread poverty and the diversity of languages and cultures pose additional problems to universalization.

Differences in Population Coverage

Table 56 shows the different degrees of population health coverage among the twenty-five departments of Peru. The department with the best coverage is Lima (with coverage almost twice the national average), followed by the adjacent Callao, where the principal port is located; 58 percent of the country's insured are in these two areas. The departments of Ica, Tacna, and Arequipa also have much higher coverage than the national average. These five coastal departments have the highest index of urbanization (between 78 and 99 percent) and per capita GDP and are where most government, industrial, commercial, transportation, and financial activities are located. The departments with the lowest degree of coverage (between 3 percent and 4 percent) are located in the sierra or highlands region: they are Apurimac, Ayacucho, Cajamarca, Huancavelica, Puno, and Amazonas. (Although a large part of the latter's territory is located in the jungle region, its population is concentrated

TABLE 55

SOCIAL SECURITY COVERAGE OF POPULATION IN PERU, 1961–1983

(THOUSANDS)

	Total Population		Insured Population				% of Coverage[d]		Annual Average Growth Rates (log)				Quotient of Demographic Burden[e]
	Population	EAP	Active[a]	Passive[b]	Dependents[c]	Total	Total Population	EAP	Total Population	EAP	Actives	Total Insured	
1961	10,218	3,260	808	13	61	882	8.6	24.8	*	*	*	*	*
1965	11,467	3,655	1,156	23	86	1,265	11.0	31.6	2.9	2.9	9.4	9.4	0.016
1969	12,829	4,146	1,474	40	111	1,625	12.7	35.6	2.8	3.2	6.3	6.5	0.020
1975	15,161	4,922	1,656	146[f]	507	2,309	15.2	33.6	2.8	2.9	2.0	6.0	0.027
1980	17,295	5,719	2,142	211	663	3,016	17.4	37.4	2.7	3.0	5.3	5.5	0.088
1981	17,755	5,910	2,225	230	698	3,153	17.8	37.6	2.7	3.3	3.9	4.5	0.098
1982	18,226	6,102	2,311	243	730	3,284	18.0	37.9	2.7	3.2	3.9	4.2	0.103
1983	18,707	6,293	2,400	256	807	3,463	18.5	38.1	2.6	3.1	3.9	5.4	0.107

Sources: Total population from INE, Perú: Compendio estadístico, 1982 (Lima: INE 1983). EAP 1961–69 from Oficina Nacional de Estadística y Censos, Anuario estadístico del Perú 1969; 1975–83 from Boletín demográfico 15:29 (January 1982). Insured population 1961–69 from Mesa-Lago, Social Security in Latin America (Pittsburgh, Pa.: University of Pittsburgh Press, 1978); 1975–83 from IPSS figures provided in 1983 and 1984. Percentages, rates, and quotients calculated by the author.

a. For 1961–69 the figures refer to pension coverage and excludes fishermen and jockeys. From 1975 on, the figure for insured pensioners excludes civil servants and white-collar workers of autonomous agencies (hired before 1962) as well as workers in the legislative and judicial branches, diplomats, and state and university teachers (hired before 1973). As these groups have IPSS health coverage, health coverage in 1975–82 was used, and to it was added an estimate for the armed forces and fishermen. Only jockeys have been excluded.

b. Includes old age, disability, and survivors' pensioners from (Compulsory Social Insurance) SSO and SSE in 1961–68 plus those of FEJEP in 1969. From 1975 on, this figure includes pensioners from the standardized system plus those for occupational risks; excludes the armed forces, fishermen, and jockeys.

c. Includes only the wives (entitled to maternity benefits) of those active insured in SSE in 1961–69. From 1975 on, this figure includes wives (entitled to maternity benefits) and children under one year of age (entitled to health benefits) of the active and passive insured of IPSS.

d. "Total population" coverage means health and/or maternity; EAP coverage means old age, disability, or survivors' pensions (but using health coverage as a subrogate).

e. Number of passives divided by the number of active insured.

f. Author's interpolation.

*Not applicable.

TABLE 56

POPULATION COVERAGE BY DEPARTMENT IN PERU, 1981

(THOUSANDS)

Department	Total Population[a]	Insured[b]	% of Coverage
Amazonas	255	8	3.1
Ancash	818	80	9.8
Apurimac	323	8	2.5
Arequipa	706	123	17.4
Ayacucho	503	14	2.8
Cajamarca	1,046	28	2.7
Callao	443	109	24.6
Cuzco	832	39	4.7
Huancavelica	347	13	3.7
Huánuco	485	23	4.7
Ica	434	89	20.5
Junín	852	81	9.5
La Libertad	963	116	12.0
Lambayeque	674	101	15.0
Lima	4,746	1,265	26.7
Loreto	445	38	8.5
Madre de Dios	33	2	6.1
Moquegua	101	14	13.9
Pasco	213	28	13.1
Piura	1,126	94	8.3
Puno	890	33	3.7
San Martín	320	16	5.0
Tacna	143	28	19.6
Tumbes	104	9	8.6
Ucayali	201	15	7.5
Total	17,005	2,374	14.0

Source: INE, *Perú: Compendio estadístico 1982* (Lima: INE, 1983).

a. Census of the population, excluding omitted population, particularly in the jungle; if figures for these were included, the total number would be 17,762,231.

b. Population with health benefit coverage; excludes the armed forces.

in the sierra.) These departments have the lowest urbanization index (between 21 and 36 percent) and the lowest per capita GDP. Also, the bulk of the indigenous population is concentrated in this area, and its principal economic activity (with one exception) is agriculture and livestock.[13] Lima's degree of coverage is eleven times that of Apurimac. A similar comparison done with 1961 figures indicates that over a twenty-year period, geographical inequalities remained about the same.[14] Although there are no statistics on the distribution of the insured by economic sector,[15] it can be guessed that those with the best coverage are workers in the civil service, finance, industry, fishing, and transportation, while those with the worst are agricultural laborers.

Noncovered Population

Although as in other countries there is not enough information to identify the uncovered sector with precision, its general outlines can be determined on the basis of the law, the above discussion, and additional information. In 1981, there were more than 2 million self-employed workers in Peru and only about 50,000 optionally insured, the bulk of whom were self-employed. In other words, 98 percent of the self-employed, concentrated in agriculture and personal services, were not insured. In addition, there were 442,774 unpaid family workers and 355,700 unemployed urban workers; neither they nor their family dependents were covered.[16] Finally, an unknown percentage of salaried workers who had directly evaded the obligation were also not covered. It can be presumed that these groups encompass the lowest income strata of the population, including the critical poverty sector. The only service that these groups receive are health services from MS and charitable societies, but these are insufficient to help this large mass of the population (see above). Peru, unlike other countries, has no welfare pensions, although there are charitable societies, homes for the elderly, and other welfare institutions; however, these again are insufficient to cover the basic necessities.

Measures to Improve Coverage

IPSS was planning to expand coverage in mid-1984, beginning with the dependents of the present insured: children up to six years of age (with preventive medicine and basic curative care) and spouses (with full health protection).[17] Since 1980 the wage contribution that the state must pay to IPSS has been used to extend coverage to the rural sector. As of 1984, an organic law draft of IPSS, under discussion, prescribed the expansion of health coverage (beginning with preventive medicine and basic medical care) to the self-employed, to agricultural workers, and to small merchants as well as to minor children and dependent spouses. Implementation of this plan would require the integration, or at least the coordination, of all the existing health services (IPSS, MSS, and charitable societies), as well as the expansion of services at the first level, especially in the rural zones.

The organic law draft reiterated the need for a unique registry of insured as well as for a national identification system to be maintained in computerized form.[18] This instrument, initially ordered more than ten years ago, would have to be preceded by a national census of insured, to be conducted with international technical assistance.

FINANCING

Financing Sources

IPSS is financed mainly by three-party wage contributions. Prior to the unification process, the three major insured groups had diverse contributions:

those for pensions were standardized in 1973, and those for health-maternity in 1979. In 1983 the total contribution was 21 percent; only six countries had higher contributions, and only two were equal to that of Peru (see table 6). The total contribution was distributed as follows: 5 percent by the insured, 14 percent by the employer, and 2 percent by the state (see table 57). As is typical of the region, the employer's legal contribution was almost three times that of the insured, or twice if the occupational risks program was excluded. Since 1980, the state contribution has been earmarked for the expansion of health benefits to the low-income population, but the state has traditionally not fulfilled its obligations. It is unknown whether the previously mentioned contribution was paid and, if so, whether it reached its agreed-upon destination. Self-employed workers and other optionally insured persons pay a contribution of 7.5 percent, equivalent to the sum of the percentages paid by the salaried insured and the employer. Increases in wage contributions can be instituted only by law.

Contributions are calculated on the total remuneration of the insured, but a ceiling is fixed in relation to the minimum salary of Lima. This ceiling increased in the period 1980–83: from 5 to 10 times the minimum salary for the insured's contribution and from 5 to 7.5 times the minimum salary for the employer's contribution. Sums exceeding the ceiling pay only 50 percent, up to a maximum equal to the ceiling. Part of the revenues resulting from the ceiling increase have been used to finance minimum pensions for those insured who did not contribute enough to gain entitlement. On the other hand, the contribution has a floor equal to the minimum salary earned in the area where the insured works (one-third of this minimum is the floor for domestic

TABLE 57

LEGAL CONTRIBUTIONS TO SOCIAL SECURITY BY PROGRAM
AND SOURCE IN PERU, 1983

(PERCENTAGE OF SALARY OR INCOME)

| | Insured | | | | |
| | Salaried[a] | Independent | Employer | State | Total[b] |
Program					
Pensions	2.5	7.5	5	1	8.5
Health/maternity	2.5	7.5	5	1	8.5
Occupational risks	*	*	4[c]	*	4.0
Total	5.0	15.0	14	2	21.0

Source: Legislation.

a. Contributions have both minimum and maximum limits.
b. Excludes the contribution of the independently insured.
c. National average. Contributions vary between 1 percent and 12.5 percent, according to risk.

*Not applicable.

servants); if the insured receives less than the minimum, the employer pays the difference in the contribution. Adjustments of the minimum salary have stayed far below inflation; for example, in 1983, salaries were increased by only 20 percent, while inflation rose 111 percent; hence the real contribution has been reduced. There were plans to increase the ceilings until they could be eliminated.[19]

In addition to the wage contribution, the IPSS receives other, lesser revenues from fines and donations as well as from yields on investment. In 1981 the latter generated 6 percent of revenues, mostly from interest and dividends. By law, the IPSS must hold its deposits in the Bank of the Nation, which pays interest on these long-term deposits; the bank charges a commission for its services to the IPSS: revenue collection, accounting, and payment of monetary benefits. Officials of the bank allege that it pays an effective interest rate only 2 percent lower than that of the financial market and that the services it provides to the IPSS greatly exceed its commission. Thus, according to these officials, the lower interest rate they pay compensates for the low charge for services.[20] But the bicameral investigation of 1983 concluded that the bank did not report, in a regular and reliable manner, the amounts collected, that payments to the IPSS account were at times six months delinquent, that occasionally the bank had charged excess commissions that it took up to fourteen months to return (these last two irregularities inflicted large losses on the IPSS because of inflation), and that the IPSS deposits in the bank yielded a much lower interest rate than that of the financial market (an irregularity that is against the law) and that, after inflation had been taken into account, the interest rate was sometimes negative.[21]

In 1981 the financial investments of the IPSS (93,836 million soles) were distributed as follows: 67 percent in long-term deposits, 14 percent in bank certificates, 17 percent in housing or personal loans, and 2 percent in state bonds. Capital investments (72,153 million soles) were distributed as follows: 72 percent in construction projects (mostly facilities for the health-maternity program), 23 percent in equipment, and the remaining 4 percent, other.[22] According to the bicameral investigation of 1983, no studies exist on the profitability of IPSS investments, but they are estimated to have a negative rate of return and thus have resulted in large losses. Investments in rental properties produced a negative real yield because of delinquent payments (many of the buildings were occupied by squatters), very low rents (not adjusted for inflation), and poor efficiency in collection. Although 23 percent of the capital investment in 1981 was principally in this instrument, it generated only 0.08 percent of revenues. Amortization and debt service of loans was also very inefficient because of delinquency and the fact that payment were made in money devalued by inflation.[23]

Outside the IPSS—that is, in the independent pension programs of the state and armed forces—the insured contributes 6 percent and the employer (the state) another 6 percent. But in the armed forces, all of the costs of current pensions and those that correspond to personnel active before 1974 are totally paid by the state. Contributions to health-maternity are the same as those of civil servants covered by IPSS. Nevertheless, the health system of the armed forces is entirely financed by the state.[24]

Evasion and Payment Delays

The most serious financial problems that the IPSS faces are evasion and payment delays. The causes are: ignorance of the number of insured and employers because there is no registry; lack of balances from 1973 to 1980 and, hence, of records of what is owed; the bad example of the state, which is the principal debtor; the stimulus of inflation to delay contribution payments; the very poor inspection system, made worse by a tradition of fraudulent agreements with debtors; and the chaotic judicial proceedings to collect debts, which are also riddled by corruption. In 1980 a Peruvian legal scholar affirmed that only certain private enterprises and their insured were charged; this, he argued, in addition to being discriminatory, had impeded the expansion of coverage.[25]

The state debt (including the central government, departments, provinces, autonomous agencies, and public enterprises) was officially estimated by the bicameral investigation at 126,000 million soles for 1980–82, and it was considered impossible to calculate the 1969–79 debt.[26] IPSS officials have given diverse figures for the amount of the state debt: 123,000 million in 1977–81, 128,930 in mid-1982, and 141,403 in mid-1983 (these last two figures included no specified period for the debt).[27] In 1983, the state paid 80 percent of its annual obligations (contributions as employer and retention of the insured); in addition it recognized 80,000 million soles as the 1977–81 debt, giving in payment bonds yielding the banking interest rate. Finally, the total debt of 1975–76 is being estimated, and payment with medical equipment is expected.

Employer evasion before the economic crisis fluctuated from 15 percent to 20 percent and, in the early 1980s, from 35 percent to 40 percent. So many enterprises owe money to IPSS, it is said, that all of the lawyers in the country will not be enough to file all of the judicial demands for collection. The private sector debt, which has already been estimated (in a very rough manner, as there are no trustworthy figures) at 36,000 million soles in mid-1982, rose from 60,000 million to 203,989 million between the beginning and end of 1983 (thus the debt increased 51 percent in real terms in one year). From 1975 to 1983 debt payment facilities were offered six times to those delinquent, but as there was no control on compliance, these were not effective. In 1984 a new moratorium on fines and interest was decreed, permitting payment agreements of up to twenty-four months in industry and sixty months in agriculture; this has been combined with a multimedia campaign financed with money owed to IPSS. Furthermore, in March 1984, health care was suspended to insured persons whose employers were behind in social security payments. As a result employers were obliged to negotiate payment agreements with IPSS. In addition, a single registry system of payments with computerized receipts was introduced that, it is hoped, will both simplify collection and make it more effective.[28]

In 1983 the combined debt of the private and state sectors fluctuated from 159,000 to 344,000 million soles, according to diverse estimates, or from $70 million to $150 million.

Financial Equilibrium

According to the bicameral investigation, estimates of 1973–80 accounting balances of IPSS are unreliable because of incomplete and inconsistent documentation and inadequate accounting procedures. In 1980 an accounting consulting firm was hired to reconstruct the balances for these years, to design an accounting system, and to incorporate it into the data processing system, but in 1981 in spite of the fact that the term of the contract had expired, the firm had not fulfilled its obligation.[29] In view of such problems, the figures in table 58 must be taken with extreme caution. Although the table shows a deficit beginning only in 1982 in the health-maternity program, other information from IPSS indicates that this deficit started in the early 1970s. On the other hand, the table shows a surplus in both the pension program and the total balance, although this surplus exhibits a decreasing tendency in relation to total revenues.

The economic crisis of the 1980s had a negative impact on IPSS real revenue because real salaries fell in 1973–83, unemployment worsened, and evasion and payment delays rose. In 1983, it was estimated unofficially, the IPSS deficit was 168,000 million soles, 37 percent of that year's revenue of 450,000 million soles. In 1984 the deficit of the health-maternity program was projected officially to be 108,000 million.[30]

The deficit in the health-maternity program has traditionally been covered by loans from the pension program, and the former has paid neither amortization of capital nor adequate interest. In 1973–82 these loans rose to almost 26,000 million soles, and the health-maternity program took an additional 13,600 million soles from other creditors. In this period the IPSS is estimated to have lost 10,000 million soles in interest. It is also reported that 50 percent of the money collected by the IPSS for the occupational risks program has been transferred to the health-maternity program. Nevertheless, since 1983, the pension fund has stopped making loans to the health-maternity program.[31]

If the accounting information available for IPSS is deficient, the situation is even worse for the rest of the system. But everything appears to indicate that practically all of the independent funds (for example, taxi owners and civil servants outside IPSS) suffer from financial disequilibrium.

TABLE 58
SOCIAL SECURITY BALANCE OF REVENUES AND EXPENDITURES BY
PROGRAM IN PERU, 1975/76–1982

Program	1975/76	1980	1981[a]	1982
Pensions				
Revenues	**	**	97.9	177.8
Expenditures	**	**	68.3	105.2
Balance	**	**	29.6	72.6
Health/maternity				
Revenues	**	**	114.9	154.4
Expenditures	**	**	104.4	215.6
Balance	**	**	10.5	−61.2
Occupational risks				
Revenues	**	**	19.3	25.0
Expenditures	**	**	**	**
Balance	**	**	**	**
Total				
Revenues	38.2	144.9	271.7	397.0
Expenditures	31.1	128.2	233.2	380.0
Balance	7.1	16.7	38.5	17.0
As percentage of revenue	18.6	11.5	14.2	4.3[b]

Sources: Total from IPSS, Dirección de Contabilidad Presupuestal, 1984. 1981 disaggregation from IPSS, Dirección General de Planificación y Presupuesto, 1983; and 1982 from Javier Slodky, "Seguridad social y participación de los asegurados," Lima, Fundación Friedrich Ebert, 1984.

a. Details based on the original budget, not on the implementation.
b. Another source indicates a deficit equivalent to 7.9 percent.

**Not available.

Financing Methods

The IPSS health-maternity program uses the method of pure assessment with a security reserve. Since the beginning of the 1970s, this program has run a deficit, and contributions to it should have been raised in 1979 but were not (because of political-economic difficulties). It is calculated that the contribution to this program must be increased by 1.5 percent every five years. In order to achieve equilibrium, not only would contributions have to be raised by 3 percent, but also the security reserve would have to be reconstituted.

The pension program uses the scaled-premium method with five-year periods. There is a consensus that this program has an actuarial deficit, given that contributions should have been raised in 1979 and were not. If the percentage contribution were increased by 3 percent, this program could reach equilibrium, but given the transfer of funds to the health-maternity program, such a goal would be feasible only if the investment were recovered. As recovery does not appear possible, the increase in the contribution would have to be much higher. IPSS officials are therefore considering modification of the financing method of the pension program to assessment of constituent capitals.

The occupational risks program uses the method of assessing constituent capitals. As there have been transfers of the reserves of this program to the health-maternity program, it probably has a deficit, but an actuarial evaluation is needed to assess the real situation.

By law, actuarial studies of the IPSS must be done every five years. The latest study was done in 1981 but was not put into practice and could not take into account the inflationary spiral of 1982–83. In 1983, a permanent actuarial office was created at IPSS, and an actuarial study was to be finished in 1984.[32]

Measures to Increase Revenues

In 1980, the IPSS introduced a series of policies to increase revenues, explained above. In addition the bicameral investigation and the organic social security law, under discussion in 1984, recommended the following measures: (1) creation of an up-to-date single registry of employers and insured, purging the registry of pensioners, updating the individual accounts, and enforcing nationally the single payment form, all with the goal of reducing fraud and evasion; (2) subscription of a detailed contract of obligations between the Bank of the Nation and the IPSS so that the latter can verify contribution payments, ascertain the rapid payment of collections, fix a reasonable commission, improve the accounting system, and place deposits at an interest level at least equal to that of the financial market; (3) complete the agreement between the state and IPSS for the recognition of the state debt and its form of repayment; (4) start requiring government officials, at all levels, to specify in their budgets the contribution to be paid to the IPSS (violation of this obligation should be considered embezzlement of funds and should result in the automatic dismissal of the official); (5) obligation of the bicameral budget commission to consign the corresponding amounts for the payment of both the state debt and the state current contributions annually; (6) conduct audits of all debt records, sue debtor employers, impose a surcharge for payment delays not inferior to the banking long-term interest rate plus an additional 50 percent, and institute control of delinquent payments; (7) undertake an inventory and evaluation of IPSS assets, readjust rental contracts for housing, and introduce an effective collection method; (8) expand coverage (and hence contributors), increase contribution rates to achieve actuarial equilibrium, and eliminate the maximum contribution ceilings; (9) invest reserves at the maximum yield available in the financial market and prohibit loans between IPSS programs; and (10) modify the financing methods in view of the real possibilities of equilibrium, carry out actuarial studies every five years, and execute their recommendations.[33]

BENEFITS, EXPENDITURES, AND COSTS
Benefits and Entitlement Conditions

Within IPSS there is uniformity in benefits and entitlement conditions, but outside this organization there are three independent health-maternity programs and six pension programs. There are also differences in the accessibility and quality of the health services offered by the IPSS.

In the IPSS health-maternity program, the insured is entitled to one type of monetary benefit, the subsidy for illness in lieu of salary (women are also entitled to subsidies for maternity and lactation), as well as benefits in services and kind, such as medical-hospital and dental care, surgery, medicines (limited to an official list), rehabilitation, and prosthesis and orthopedic apparatus. (A very costly benefit involves paying for the treatment of the insured in foreign countries if the treatment is not available domestically.) The insured's wife is entitled only to maternity care, and children under one year are entitled to health benefits in services and kind, including vaccination and preventive control. The insured white-collar worker (a leftover from the old system) retains the right to free choice. In occupational risks, the insured are entitled to similar monetary and health benefits plus disability pensions, and dependents are entitled to survivors' pensions. The pension program includes pensions for old age, disability, survivors, and unemployment (early retirement in case of dismissal). Dependent family members are also entitled to funeral benefits (provided by IPSS services or by contract or by the payment of an equivalent sum) and, if they are not entitled to a survivors' pension, receive a lump sum when the insured dies. There is neither unemployment compensation (except for the unemployment/early retirement pension) nor family allowances.

Within the Latin American context, the legal conditions of the Peruvian system are strict in the health-maternity program in terms of the qualification period for receiving monetary benefits, but conditions are relatively liberal concerning the percentage paid over salary as subsidy and the duration of the period in which benefits are provided. On the other hand, the qualification period for receiving health benefits in service or in kind is one of the two longest in the region, and the number of dependents entitled to these benefits is one of the most restricted. Benefits are average (except for payment of services abroad). In terms of pensions, the retirement age for old age pensions is relatively low, compared with the regional average; the IPSS requires sixty years for men and fifty-five for women with fifteen and thirteen years of contribution, respectively. (In case of unemployment, the insured is permitted to retire five years earlier.) Conditions for disability pensions and the number of relatives entitled to survivors' pensions are average. Once we take into account that in Peru the total wage contribution ranks in the upper half of that of all countries in the region, benefits are adequate with very few exceptions.

Table 59 traces the evolution of health services and standards in Peru in 1960–82. Although the indicators are the lowest of any in the six case studies examined in this book, all have shown continual improvement except for hospital beds per 1,000 inhabitants. Regardless of this improvement, 1982 levels in Peru were among the lowest in the region, and according to oral information, some of these indicators have deteriorated in recent years.

Inequalities in Benefits

The IPSS health-maternity program is the most standardized in the country and excludes only three groups, the only important one of these being the armed forces. Table 60 offers a rough comparison among the services available to IPSS insured and to other groups in the population. The nonpublic sector has the highest ratios and with some exceptions cares for the highest income sector. The armed forces have the second highest ratio of physicians per inhabitant but an average ratio of hospital beds; the covered population for this group is probably overestimated in the table, however, thus understating the ratios. The two-thirds of the population who have access only to MS and charitable services have the lowest ratios: one-third of the physician ratio and

TABLE 59

HEALTH SERVICES AND LEVELS IN PERU, 1960–1982

	Hospital Beds per 1,000 Persons	Physicians per 10,000 Persons	Mortality Rate		Life Expectancy
			General	Infant	
1960	2.4	4.5	18.4	140.9	48.0
1965	2.4	4.7	16.5	130.6	50.4
1970	2.1	4.8	14.0	116.2	54.0
1975	1.9	6.1	12.2	106.6	56.3
1980	1.7	7.2	11.3	101.5	57.8
1981	**	7.6	11.1	100.2	58.2
1982[a]	1.6	8.1	10.9	98.6	58.6

Sources: Hospital beds and physicians (1960–70) from CEPAL, Anuario estadístico de América Latina, 1981. The rest from Anuario estadístico del Perú, 1969, Perú: Compendio estadístico, 1981 and 1982, figures from INE, 1984, and Ministerio de Salud, Proyecciones de población por regiones de salud y utilización de indicadores del sector; 1980–1985 (Lima: MS, 1983).

a. The Ministry of Health's indicators are more favorable than those of the INE in 1982: 1.8, 8.4, 10.1, 87.6, and 58.6. INE officials assured me, however, that since the mid-1970s health levels in the country have deteriorated.

**Not available.

TABLE 60
DIFFERENCES IN MEDICAL SERVICES AMONG POPULATION
GROUPS IN PERU, 1980

Group	Population Cared for (1982) (thous.)	Hospital Beds (1980)		Physicians (1981)	
		Total	Per 1,000 Persons	Total	Per 10,000 Persons
Social Security (IPSS)	2,370	4,512	1.9	3.000	12.6
Armed forces and police	1,280[a]	2,098	1.6	1,860	14.5
Ministry of Health and others[b]	12.030	16,108	1.3	4,698	3.9
Nonpublic sector[c]	2,550	5,596	2.2	3,984	15.6
Total	18,230	28,708	1.6	13,542	7.4

Sources: Figures for population cared for are based on a percentage distribution of the Ministerio de Salud, *Proyecciones de poblacion.* Hospital beds and physicians from the Ministerio de Salud, *Información básica sobre infraestructura sanitaria, 1983* (Lima: MS, 1983), and additional information, Lima, 1984. Ratios calculated by the author.

  a. Apparent overestimation.
  b. The Ministry of Health has 96 percent of all hospital beds and 79 percent of the physicians; the rest are in charitable societies, state enterprises, local governments, and other public agencies.
  c. Private, profit-seeking institutions, philanthropic institutions, enterprises, agroindustrial cooperatives, agricultural societies of social interest, and other nonpublic institutions.

about two-thirds of the hospital-bed ratio of the IPSS insured. To a large degree, these figures explain the low national health levels in Peru registered in table 59.

There are also notable inequalities in health levels among the departments of Peru. In 1981 the department of Lima had sixty-three times more doctors per inhabitant and five times more hospital beds per inhabitant than the department of Apurimac. A ranking of the departments by health levels greatly resembles their ranking by social security coverage (table 56). The most developed departments have the best coverage (Lima, Callao, Arequipa, Tacna, and Ica) and the highest ratios of doctors and hospital-bed per inhabitant, whereas the least-developed departments have the lowest social security coverage (Apurimac, Cajamarca, Amazonas, Ayacucho, and Puno) and the lowest levels of health services.[34] In the pension program there are significant inequalities between IPSS and the independent funds. For example, members of the armed forces and civil servants (hired before 1962) are entitled to seniority pensions after a minimum of 15 years of service for men and 12.5 for women, regardless of age. Also in the armed forces, if the insured has accumulated thirty years or more of service, his/her pension is equivalent to the full salary currently paid to the position held by the insured prior to retirement; furthermore, if the insured has thirty-five years of service, the pension is equivalent to the salary currently paid for the next higher position.[35]

TABLE 61

COST OF SOCIAL SECURITY IN PERU, 1961–1982

(BILLIONS OF SOLES AT CURRENT PRICES)

	GDP	Total Central Govt. Expenditures	Social Security Expenditures		
			Total	% of GDP	% of Central Govt. Expenditures
1961	73.3	9.9	1.7	2.3	17.2
1965	131.4	22.9	3.3	2.5	16.6
1970	267.1	47.9	**	**	**
1975	627.4	131.4	19.4ᵃ	3.1	14.8
1980	5,598.6	1,370.1	179.3	3.2	13.1
1981	9,495.6	2,273.1	337.9	3.6	14.9
1982	15,312.8	3,560.0	521.9	3.4	14.7

Sources: GDP from INE, Cuentas nacionales del Perú, 1950–1982 (Lima: INE, 1983). Government expenditures from the Banco Central de la Reserva del Perú, Cuentas Fiscales 1960–1980, and Memoria, 1980 and 1981. Social security expenditures, 1961–65, from Carmelo Mesa-Lago, Social Security in Latin America (Pittsburgh, Pa.: University of Pittsburgh Press, 1978); the rest from Perú: Compendio estadístico, 1981, and IPSS, Gerencia Financiera, 1984.

a. Estimated by the author, disaggregating the expenditures of the two-year period 1975–76.

**Not available.

The Growing Cost of Social Security and Its Causes

As table 61 shows, the cost of Peruvian Social Security rose from 2.3 percent of GDP in 1961 to 3.4 percent in 1982. As a percentage of government expenditures it saw a reduction in the second half of the 1970s—because of the readjustment in those years—with a slight recuperation in 1981–82. The cost of social security in Peru, as a percentage of GDP, is similar to that of Mexico and, within the regional context, is considered moderate: eight countries have a higher percentage, five have an equal percentage, and six a lower one. I will discuss the causes of this moderate increase in cost below.

General causes. Unlike Cuba, Costa Rica, and Chile, Peru is far from attaining universality in population coverage: in fact, coverage has risen only some 4 or 5 percentage points in the last fifteen years. In addition, Peru's risk coverage is below that of these countries, and its benefits and entitlement conditions are more restricted. This restricted coverage largely explains the relatively low cost of social security in Peru and the slow growth of this cost.

Yet administrative expenditures appear to be very high (although the information available is imprecise): in 1981 the combined expenditures for "central administration" and "inscription, disbursement, and collection" accounted for almost 10 percent of outlays. In addition, a rather vague budget category of "financial administration" absorbed another 20 percent.[36] In 1968–83 the number of IPSS employees almost tripled, from 13,000 to 32,000 (these figures should be taken as approximations), while the total number of insured only doubled. In 1983 there were 9 employees for every 1,000 insured in IPSS, compared with almost 13 per 1,000 in Costa Rica but 7.5 per 1,000 in Mexico. A good number of employees reportedly collect their salaries without working, and the personnel skills are said to be low and personnel control and supervision inefficient. The IPSS also confronts labor discipline problems, and unions interfere in the hiring of personnel.[37] The remuneration of personnel as a percentage of total social security expenditures rose from 21.6 percent in 1975–76 to 27.3 percent in 1981 (three times the percentage reported as administrative expenditures for the same year).[38] Physicians' salaries account for the majority of salary expenditures. By means of a powerful association and the frequent use of strikes, physicians have been the occupational group least affected by the decline in real salaries in recent years.[39] In 1976–80 medical personnel in the Hospital Rebagliati, one of the principal hospitals of Peru, rose 50 percent, while outside consultations declined by 30 percent and hospital admissions by 20 percent.[40]

According to the bicameral commission report, part of the IPSS outlays have been lost in the past because of administrative irregularities such as the purchase of equipment overpriced by as much as 25 percent, the construction of hospitals and the acquisition of equipment, goods, and services without public bids, and the embezzlement of funds.[41] A change in the management of the IPSS in 1983 appears to have corrected most of these irregularities.

Table 62 shows that the health-maternity program took approximately two-

TABLE 62

DISTRIBUTION OF SOCIAL SECURITY EXPENDITURES BY
PROGRAM IN PERU, 1975/76–1983
(PERCENT)

Expenditure	1975–76	1980	1981	1982	1983[a]
Pensions	43.3	34.8	32.6	33.1	32.3
Health/maternity[b]	56.7	65.2	67.4	66.9	63.1
Occupational risks[b]	**	**	**	**	2.0
Other[c]	**	**	**	**	2.6

Sources: 1975/76–1982 based on the balances of the implemented budget, IPSS, Gerencia Financiera, 1984; and 1983 from the Dirección General de Planificación y Presupuesto, 1983.

a. To June 30, 1983.
b. Includes monetary and medical-hospital benefits.
c. Subsidies for lactation and funeral aid.

**Not available.

thirds of social security expenditures in 1980–82, although the percentage began to fall in 1982. Pension expenditures were approximately one-third of outlays in 1980–83, and the percentage appears to be stable. The proportion of expenditures for occupational risks and other services is very small.

Causes related to the health program.   Peru has not completely entered the demographic transition phase, as its fertility and mortality indexes are much higher than the corresponding averages in Latin America. As a result, Peru's population growth rate and dependency index are, respectively, somewhat above and somewhat below the regional averages. Among the six case studies, Peru has the second highest demographic dependency index, 11 percentage points above the Costa Rican index, which is the closest. Thus the percentage of the Peruvian population with a high health risk (mostly children under fourteen years of age) is very high, although it is lower than that of Mexico. This fact could explain the high proportion of social security expenditures in health, but two-thirds are spent in Peru on care for the active insured of productive age (who have a lower health risk), since health insurance protects only dependent children under one year of age. In addition, preventive medicine is seriously neglected in Peru.

In Peru the change in the pathological profile has not advanced as in Chile, Costa Rica, Cuba, and Uruguay. In 1982, 53 percent of deaths were still due to infectious and parasitic diseases, and only 18 percent were caused by degenerative diseases. Within the group of contagious diseases, 44 percent were caused by deficient environmental sanitation and 10 percent could have been prevented by immunization. In 1982 the MS covered 65 percent of the population but received half of the health resources assigned to IPSS, which covered only 18 percent of the population (see tables 55 and 60). In the same year, immunizations against diphtheria, polio, whooping cough, measles, and tetanus (done by MS in 95 percent of the cases) did not reach more than 25 percent of the children under one year of age, and 15 percent of the population lacked potable water, while 64 percent lacked sewerage.[42] With greater immunization, improved sanitary conditions (for example, through a program of portable latrines), and an increase in health education, the indexes for infant mortality and contagious disease morbidity could be reduced at a relatively low cost.

The health system needs greater coordination and comparative evaluation of costs. One of the problems is that the insured receive double attention: from the IPSS and from the private clinics under contract. Services from the latter are excessively costly, because of tariffs that are arbitrarily fixed, as there are no reliable estimates of the average cost of attention in IPSS on which to base them. In addition, tariffs are indexed to inflation, and as the health-maternity program of IPSS has not raised contributions, the debt with these clinics under contract is growing rapidly. The agreements expired in

1984, and IPSS did not renew many of them. To cope with the increased demand, IPSS has constructed new polyclinics, which were expected to save 24,000 million soles in the second half of 1984 alone. Also a national identification system and a single clinical history are being considered as means to eliminate the duplication of health care.[43]

Currently free choice does not involve a high cost to IPSS. The insured absorbs the major part of the cost of the service because the reimbursement tariff has not been adjusted since 1980. Furthermore, as there is also a considerable delay between the request for reimbursement and the payment, inflation devalues its real value even more. Nevertheless, instead of taking advantage of the erosion of free choice to eliminate this discriminatory treatment between white- and blue-collar workers, in 1984 the IPSS was planning to revitalize this system. Revitalization would include inscription of doctors, clinics, and pharmacies, the adjustment of tariffs with an actuarial base, and changes in the reimbursement procedure to expedite it.[44]

Other important social security costs are medicines and health subsidies. Until 1983 a basic list of medicines did not exist, but after 1983 one was introduced in both IPSS and the clinics under contract as well as for free choice services. This list is expected to net savings of 18,000 million soles annually. The health subsidy was very costly, as IPSS was obliged to pay it to the insured even when the employer did not fulfill his financial obligations. Starting in April 1984, the delinquent employer is forced to pay the insured's subsidy directly, a measure that is expected to cut expenditures by 6,000 million soles.[45]

Last but not least, the inefficiency of the health service administration is an important cause of the relatively high costs. Control of hospital stays is very poor: in 1983 the national average of days for hospital stays was 9.8, much higher than the averages for Chile, Costa Rica, and Cuba, which are themselves high. In spite of the large number of doctors, six-month delays in obtaining appointments, failure to maintain schedules, and the assignment of too many patients to one doctor have been reported.[46]

Causes related to the pension program. The first pension program for civil servants in Peru is one of the oldest in the region and thus one of the most mature and most costly. Furthermore, when the new pension program was established in 1962, the old program remained closed, and so the number of active insured under it must be small and will eventually disappear. Unfortunately, figures for this program are not available.

The two major pension programs (blue- and white-collar) were created in 1961–62, so that they are the most recent among the six country cases. In addition, all civil servants in state and autonomous agencies, hired prior to the creation of the program, were maintained in the old program, and another group of civil servants did not enter the new program until 1973. Peru has another advantage in that its population is young and the percentage over sixty-five years of age is the lowest among the six case studies except for Costa Rica (see table 63). Life expectancy in Peru is not only the lowest in the six case studies but also the fourth lowest in the region, while the retirement age is only slightly lower than the Latin American average and the entitlement conditions for other pensions are average. Finally, pensions have not been adjusted to the cost of living—as in Costa Rica and Mexico—but have been devalued rapidly, even more than in Costa Rica, Cuba, and Uruguay (see table 64). For all of these reasons, the cost of pensions in Peru has not increased as in the pioneer countries, and it is relatively stagnant.

On the other hand, the increase in population coverage has been very slow; in fact, growth rates for both active insured and total insured are declining. The quotient of demographic burden rose from 0.027 in 1975 to 0.107 in 1983, in part because of the slow growth of the active insured and also because of the maturation process of the pension program (see table 55). In any event, the Peruvian figure in 1980 was not only lower than that of the pioneer countries but also lower than that of the majority of Latin American countries.

A cause of cost increases is the low retirement age for women (fifty-five years), five years less than that for men in spite of the fact that women in Peru have a life expectancy 3.5 years longer than men. When life expectancy at time of retirement is compared for both sexes in 1980, women have an average of six years more than men. Also, women can retire with two years less service. Another cause of the cost of pensions is the lack of an up-to-date registry of pensioners and of effective inspection. This deficiency has permitted such irregularities as the continuation of pension payments after the holder has died.[47]

Measures to Reduce Expenditures

I will discuss several types of measures in this section, including some in the process of implementation or officially recommended (as of 1984) and some that derive from the previous analysis.

IPSS has obtained a loan from the World Bank to develop a computer system that will be used for affiliation, control of contributions and payments,

TABLE 63

DISTRIBUTION OF POPULATION BY AGE GROUP IN PERU, 1960–2010
(PERCENT)

Age Group	1960	1970	1980	1990	2000	2010
0–14	43.3	44.0	41.8	39.2	35.6	30.7
15–64	53.3	52.5	54.6	57.1	60.1	64.1
65 and over	3.4	3.5	3.6	3.7	4.3	5.2

Source: Based on CELADE, Boletín demográfico 16:32 (July 1983). Calculations by the author.

TABLE 64
REAL VALUE OF ANNUAL PENSIONS IN PERU, 1972–1982

	Pension (billions of soles)	No. of Pensioners[a] (thous.)	Average per Capita Pension (soles)	Index Nominal Pension	Inflation[a]	Real Pension
1972	1,649	52	31,950	100.0	100.0	100.0
1973	2,060	57	36,081	112.9	109.5	103.1
1974	**	60	**	**	128.0	**
1975	3,750[b]	63	59,904	187.5	159.2	118.5
1976	5,927[b]	70	84,804	165.5	211.2	125.7
1977	**	79	**	**	291.7	**
1978	**	95	**	**	460.3	**
1979	**	104	**	**	771.9	**
1980	35,277	119	294,930	923.1	1,228.8	75.1
1981	60,788	136	444,257	1,290.5	2,155.3	64.5
1982	102,785	148	692,622	2,167.8	3,545.5	61.1

Sources: Number of pensioners and pension values from IPSS, Gerencia Financiera, 1984. Inflation from CEPAL, *Estudio Económico de América Latina, 1976* to *1982*. Averages and indexes calculated by the author.

Note: Pensions include old age, disability, and survivors' pensions plus occupational risks in IPSS; excludes the public sector outside of IPSS, the armed forces, fishermen, and jockeys are excluded.

a. Average annual variation.
b. The original figures are from the two-year period 1975–76 and were disaggregated by the author.

**Not available.

registries of insured and pensioners, accounting, and budgets. The IPSS has also requested technical help from the ILO to carry out an actuarial revision of the system, and techniques of the private sector are being used to improve efficiency.[48]

From an organizational point of view it is advisable to: (1) unify and standardize the independent subsystems and integrate the health system; (2) carry out a study of unnecessary and underutilized personnel and create a plan to cope with the surplus and increase the qualifications of personnel; and (3) avoid the creation of new programs (such as family allowance and unemployment) until universality has been reached in already existing programs.

In the health area, greater resources must be assigned to MS to extend its preventive services of immunization and sanitation as well as primary health care. It is important to improve hospital efficiency, reduce the average length of hospital stays, and control doctors' schedules. The free choice system and the payment of medical-hospital care abroad should be eliminated, and the gradual reduction in contracted services should be continued. The number of medicines on the basic list could also be reduced and the expansion of domestic pharmaceutical production promoted.

In the pension program, the registry of pensioners should be updated and the retirement age for women should be made equal to that of men. The deterioration of real pensions (in 1982 their value was half that in 1976) has helped reduce costs, but the majority of the pensions are insufficient to cover basic necessities. The organic law draft stipulates a periodic adjustment of pensions in accordance with the cost of living, preceded by an actuarial study, and giving preference to the lowest pensions.

Finally, one way to cut expenditures would be to transfer them in part to the private sector. The Peruvian constitution permits the coexistence of complementary insurance entities (public and private) that could improve the benefits of the general system. The IPSS itself can arrange complementary benefits with additional contributions. Such involvement of the private sector should absolutely not become a back door through which the stratified system can be reintroduced. For example, one possibility that has been considered is exempting the contribution to the IPSS for those public or private institutions that offer better health benefits than the IPSS. Such method would run counter to the solidarity of the system by reducing revenues that could be partly used in the expansion of coverage to low-income groups.

THE IMPACT OF SOCIAL SECURITY ON DEVELOPMENT

There are no studies, of any type, concerning the effect of Peruvian social security on savings/investment, employment, and distribution. The available information is so deficient that only a speculative treatment of these themes is possible here.

Savings and Investment

The IPSS pension program uses the scaled-premium method and must have contributed to national savings, but the transfers to the health-maternity program and the very low or negative investment yields must have decapitalized the system and will probably be replaced by the assessment-of-constituent-capital method. The other pension programs, as well as the health-maternity program, not only lack reserves but also are running deficits.

Employment

In Peru there is abundant labor, and in 1983 the unemployment rate rose to almost 9 percent (in Lima), which indicates an elastic supply of labor. The employer must legally pay almost two-thirds of the total wage contribution to IPSS. The transfer of this contribution to the insured worker appears to be limited by strong union pressure and labor legislation. For example, the law even orders the employer to pay the difference between the insured contribution and the legal minimum contribution when the former is lower. In addition, as only 38 percent of the EAP is covered, the insured has ample space to evade the wage contribution; in fact, an increase in the informal sector has been reported partly to evade paying such contributions. The employer's opportunity to transfer his contribution to prices has been limited by the acute recession and price controls, although the liberalization of prices in recent years reopens the possibility of this transfer.[49] If indeed a transfer to the consumer had occurred, then the probable negative effect on employment would have been reduced. On the other hand, those without social security coverage (the large majority of the population) would contribute, through prices, to the system that protects a minority of the population, which probably has higher income than the majority of the sector without coverage.

Distribution of Income

Evidence of a very general nature indicates that the Peruvian social security system plays a regressive role in income distribution: (1) the low percentage of population coverage and the exclusion of the lowest income sector; (2) the wage contribution ceilings to IPSS that allow the insured with higher income to contribute less, proportionally, than those with medium or low incomes (except those who are below the contribution minimum); (3) the existence of groups with independent programs receiving strong state subsidies (for example, certain civil servants, the armed forces); (4) the absence of welfare pensions; (5) the positive relationship, in the departments, between higher income and better social security coverage and health services (and vice versa); and (6) the extremely small amount of resources assigned to the MS, which covers two-thirds of the population, compared with the assignment to IPSS.

Uruguay:
The Troubled Welfare State

URUGUAY IS one of the principal pioneers of social security on the continent and the prototype of the social welfare state. With both pressure from interest groups and competition among political parties, all aided by a climate of pluralistic democracy, Uruguayan social security was fully developed by the beginning of the 1960s and stood at the forefront of Latin American systems. It covered universal health coverage, if the population protected by mutual aid societies was included. It offered one of the most generous benefit packages in the region with the most flexible entitlement conditions and stood out for its medical and hospital services and health levels.

The other side of Uruguayan social security was it accentuated stratification and the notable inequalities among both occupational groups and geographic areas. Furthermore, the cost of the system reached almost 15 percent of GDP and 62 percent of fiscal expenditures, while the total wage contribution rose to 65 percent, all establishing historic records in the region along with Chile. In part the high cost was due to the universality of coverage, the maturity of the pension program, and the aging of the population and its high life expectancy. But it was also due to the excessive generosity of benefits, the massification of privilege, and the overinflated bureaucracy and administrative inefficiency. In spite of the heavy burden on the payroll and a labyrinth of taxes, the system was in financial disequilibrium and hence required huge state transfers.

Since the end of the 1960s, a process of social security unification and standardization has occurred in Uruguay, first through the reinforcement of executive powers and later through the greater centralization of political power, the destabilization of democracy, and the demobilization of several pressure groups. But by 1984, that process had not succeeded to the same degree as its counterparts in Cuba and Peru; independent funds and significant differences among subsystems still persisted, and even with the relatively unified system, some inequalities were also preserved. The social security expenditure/GDP ratio was gradually reduced to 8 percent in 1980, but since then, it has again risen. In 1980 an increase in the value-added tax (VAT) replaced part of social security wage contributions and taxes. The objectives of this shift were to eliminate the previous distortion in factor costs, to reduce production costs, to promote employment, to increase real salaries, and to promote the competitiveness of exports. It is not clear whether these objectives were achieved in 1980 and part of 1981. In any event, the economic crisis and deterioration in the ensuing years have made it difficult to evaluate the effectiveness of the VAT. In 1980–82, with the reduction in the wage contribution and an upward readjustment of pensions, the deficit of the system worsened, reaching 80 percent of revenues. This deficit was covered with transfers from the state, but it is unknown whether revenues from the VAT have been sufficient to finance such transfers.

Special demographic characteristics and a long tradition of generous benefits have confronted Uruguay with more difficulties than other countries in balancing its system (in 1982 its quotient of demographic burden reached a continental record of 0.8). Although important measures have been introduced, such as administrative rationalization, partial unification and standardization, and the application of the VAT, more drastic measures are needed to complete the standardization of the system, to balance it financially, to eliminate the existing inequalities, and to maintain the levels attained in eight decades of social security development. The return of democracy in Uruguay provided both an opportunity to tackle these problems and a challenge.

HISTORICAL EVOLUTION

The Stratified System

As one of the pioneer countries in social security in the region, Uruguay's system (like those of Cuba and Chile) appeared early but developed in a gradual and fragmented manner in the first seventy years of the twentieth century and became very stratified. With a few minor exceptions, the system began early in the century with the initiative of President José Batlle and under the influence of the progressive wing of the Colorado party. But as in other countries with pluralistic democracies, pressure groups played a crucial role in its evolution after the beginning of the 1920s. As a result there emerged diverse programs for economic sectors (for example, industry and commerce), occupations (for example, stevedores, textile workers, and domestic servants) and specific activities (such as refrigeration, wool, and leather industries). In addition, the competition between the two traditional political parties (Blanco and Colorado) in Uruguay contributed to the stratification of the system through extensive legislation that provided concessions to various groups in return for electoral support.[1]

On the other hand, the Uruguayan system attained one of the highest levels of population and risk coverage in Latin America. In the mid-1960s the system covered all social risks (old age, disability, death, occupational risks, maternity, nonoccupational accident and disease, unemployment, and family allowances). In addition, it had universal pension coverage of the EAP, and two-thirds of the population had health coverage. In the early years Uruguay, like Cuba and Argentina, developed a complex system of mutual aid societies and cooperatives for health care that preceded (and later complemented) the various programs of health insurance that did not appear until the 1960s.

Following regional patterns of social security development, the Uruguayan armed forces were the first group to receive protection in all of the programs, except for family allowances, in which they were the second. Next came civil servants, the first to obtain protection in two programs and the second in two others. In Uruguay the division of private sector workers into two large groups (white-and blue-collar) did not occur as it did in Chile and Peru. But there was a division between occupational groups and economic sectors with varying power. The labor aristocracy (for example, civil servants, banking, and the wool, leather, and meat industries) were the first to receive protection, whereas the last were the groups with less power (rural workers and domestic servants). It is remarkable, however, that Uruguay in 1919 became the first country to establish a pension program for indigents (see table 65).

In 1967 there were more than fifty social security institutions: ten pension funds (the six principal ones were grouped into three pairs in the 1930s); sixteen family allowance funds coordinated by a Central Board of Family Allowances (CCAF) (plus an additional number of family compensation funds); sixteen health insurance funds (plus a goodly number of additional health programs); six unemployment programs; an indeterminate number of maternity programs; and a single occupational risks program administered by a state agency. Each of these programs had its own legislation, administration, financing, and benefits, and there was no central coordinating agency. Differences and inequalities among the programs—especially pensions—were considerable; those protecting the more powerful groups provided better benefits and received greater state support by means of specific taxes.

In the 1960s several studies concerned with the reform of the social security system (in particular the pension program) recommended its partial unification,[2] but as in other countries, the power of the pressure groups, a problem complicated by the weakness of the regime of the collegiate government, kept this reform from being carried out.

Unification and Standardization of the System

The 1967 constitution reinstated the presidential regime, with strong executive power and recentralization of the decision-making power. This centralization helped in the initiation of the unification process; the three principal pension funds (civil service–education, industry-commerce, and rural–domestic service) were grouped under the administration of a new agency: the

TABLE 65
SOCIAL SECURITY LEGISLATION IN URUGUAY
FOR RISKS PROTECTED AND GROUPS COVERED, 1835–1982

Year[a]	Risk Protected	Group Covered
1835, 1907, 1941	ODS	Armed forces
1838, 1904, 1920, 1940	ODS,[b] OR	Civil servants
1896	ODS	Public teachers
1914, 1920	OR	White-and blue-collar workers
1919	ODS	Indigents
1919	ODS[b]	Public utilities workers
1920	ODS[b]	Stevedores
1923, 1948	ODS[b]	Jockey clubs
1925–26	ODS[b]	Bank and stock market workers, longshoremen
1928–29	ODS[b]	White-and blue-collar workers in corporations and other groups
1934, 1941[c]	OR	All
1934–38	ODS[b]	Remaining blue-and white-collar workers, employers
1942–43	ODS[b]	Domestic servants and rural workers
1943	FA	Blue and white-collar workers
1944–45	U	Meat, wool, and leather workers
1948	H/M	Congress members, state bank workers
1950, 1960	FA	Civil servants, armed forces
1954	ODS	Professionals
1954	FA	Rural workers
1958	U	Industrial and commercial workers
1958	M	All workers
1958, 1960	FA	Unemployed, pensioners
1961	U	Tobacco and glass workers
1960–66	H	Transportation and construction workers, wool, leather, wood, metal, textile workers, bank and industrial workers, graphic artists, designers, sailors[d]
1965–66	U	Longshoremen, rural workers
1971–72	H	Civil servants, beverage workers, glass, leather, and restaurant workers
1967–82	ODS, U, FA, H	Gradual unification and standardization process of these programs, with some exceptions

Source: Carmelo Mesa-Lago, *Social Security in Latin America* (Pittsburgh, Pa.: University of Pittsburgh Press, 1978), and legislation.

Note: ODS = old age, disability, and survivors' pensions. H = health. M = maternity. OR = occupational risks. U = unemployment. FA = family allowances.

a. The first date corresponds to the initial law and the subsequent dates to modifications and amplifications.
b. Includes unemployment pensions.
c. Effective application of the law.
d. Established by separate laws.

Social Insurance Bank (BPS). The increase in the power of the armed forces, the control of trade unions, the closing of the parliament, and the eventual establishment of the military government reinforced the political power of the state and promoted the demobilization and elimination of many pressure groups. A series of decrees enacted in 1973–82 ordered the gradual integration, under the state, of the bulk of the Uruguayan social security system.

In 1973 the state intervened in the CCAF; in 1978 it reduced to five the sixteen family allowance funds; and in 1979 practically all of the family allowance funds were merged and, with the maternity program, placed under a new General Directorate of Social Security office (DGSS) created in the Ministry of Labor and Social Security. In 1975–76 a single health insurance system was established for the private sector, and in 1979, almost all of the independent health insurance programs were merged under DGSS. In 1975, the administration of various unemployment insurance agencies was unified; in 1979 these programs were transferred to DGSS; and in 1981 all of the remaining programs, save one, were incorporated into DGSS. In 1979, the BPS was eliminated, and the major pension funds were transferred to DGSS. The standardization of wage contributions within DGSS took place in 1968–84 (see above).

In spite of the unification process, various social security programs still remain independent of DGSS: seven pension funds, the occupational risks program, two health funds (as well as numerous health programs in the public sector), and one unemployment program. Within DGSS, all of the programs have been standardized except for the three pension programs, which continue to operate with separate administrations and funds as well as different benefits and financing (wage contributions in industry-commerce and rural–domestic service have been standardized but not in civil service–education). The unification and standardization process in Uruguay has not reached the levels attained in Peru and Cuba, although stratification has been reduced to a much larger extent than in Chile.

In summary, as in other pioneer countries, the Uruguayan social security system arose early and, thanks to pressure groups and political parties, attained universal coverage of social risks and population but with acute stratification and inequalities. The strengthening of state power and the weakening of the pressure groups culminated, under the military government, in a process of standardization and unification of the system—under the state—albeit not to the extent seen in other countries.

ORGANIZATIONAL STRUCTURE

The central Uruguayan social security agency, which has taken over and combined the majority of the programs of the old stratified system, is the Dirección General de Seguridad Social (DGSS), located in the Ministry of

Labor and Social Security.[3] The DGSS has six offices: (1) three pension offices, which administer, separately, the civil service–education fund (for civil servants of the state, autonomous agencies, and other public agencies, plus the educational subsystem), the industry-commerce fund (which also includes transportation, construction, and nonstate services), and the rural–domestic service fund (which also administers welfare pensions); (2) the office of family allowances, which includes the maternity program; (3) the office of health insurance; and (4) the office of unemployment insurance. In 1982 a law ordered the offices of health, unemployment, and family allowances to be combined, but it has not been implemented.

Occupational risks are administered by the State Insurance Bank (BSE), which has a monopoly on all insurance in the country and, although it is a state agency, operates for profit as a commercial insurance company.

Outside DGSS there are seven independent pension funds: for bank employees, public notaries, and university professionals (these three funds are theoretically autonomous but are strongly controlled by the executive); permanent and temporary racetrack workers (two autonomous funds); and military and police (these two funds are administered by the Ministries of Defense and the Interior). The only unemployment program independent of DGSS is that for stevedores. There are no independent family allowance programs in the private sector, but an indeterminate number of these exist in the public sector.

In the health area there is very little coordination among the two hundred–odd administrative agencies. The Ministry of Public Health (MSP) has the major national network of hospitals and clinics (with 65 percent of the hospital beds), followed by the private sector (17 percent of the beds) and mutualities and cooperatives (11 percent). The armed forces and the police have their own hospitals and health services (3 percent of hospital beds). The State Insurance Bank (BSE), the university hospital, and the maternity program of the DGSS family allowances program operate the remaining services.[4] The DGSS health office does not have its own facilities but functions as a reinsurance agent; the insured receive services from a mutualistic society. In addition, there are a number of important private insurance companies and health funds, also without their own services. BSE contracts with other institutions in the countryside.[5]

The state intervenes more in Uruguay's system than in any other of the six case studies except for Cuba. The DGSS depends directly on the state, as do the BSE, the armed forces' programs, and the MSP. In addition, three of the pension funds are controlled by the executive. Three-party participation does not exist in Uruguay, as representation of the insured and employers in the administration was eliminated in the 1970s.

The process of unification and standardization of Uruguayan social security should be completed by integrating the independent programs, merging the three DGSS pension funds, and enacting legislation to standardize benefits and entitlement conditions. In addition, the multiple health programs should be integrated or at least coordinated.

POPULATION COVERAGE

Legal and Statistical Coverage

Uruguay's social security legislation—together with that of Cuba and Chile—has the broadest population coverage in Latin America.[6] Compulsory pension coverage is provided by DGSS to all salaried and self-employed workers not covered by the seven independent funds. According to law, all agricultural workers and domestic servants must be covered by the corresponding office of DGSS. Compulsory pension coverage of the self-employed (a category that includes small farmers and merchants) is unique among the six case studies. In Chile such coverage is compulsory in the old system but voluntary in the new, while in Costa Rica and Peru this coverage is voluntary, and in Cuba and Mexico it does not exist. The majority of the self-employed workers covered by the DGSS are included in industry-commerce (for example, business owners and salesmen) and in rural–domestic service (for example, small farmers and domestic servants); other groups of self-employed workers are insured in the university professionals' and notaries' independent funds. Finally, there is a program of welfare pensions (noncontributive) for indigents—that is, for those over sixty years of age or for the disabled (regardless of age) who lack resources. (Chile, Costa Rica, and Cuba have similar programs.)

All employers must provide coverage for occupational risks through BSE. Family allowances and maternity coverage are universal but provided by various agencies, as the private sector must be covered by DGSS, while the public sector is protected by a variety of programs. Unemployment coverage is the least extensive, as it includes only a limited number of occupational groups.

In legal terms, health coverage is the most difficult to analyze. The health insurance office of the DGSS must protect all those in the private sector who do not have other protection, but it excludes all rural workers and domestic servants. The public sector probably has universal coverage through diverse legal formulas: direct provision of services, contracts with other institutions, and reimbursement of mutual aid fees and medicine costs. It must be kept in mind that the system of mutual aid societies and cooperatives covers a wide sector of the population. Finally, the hospitals of MSP and the university must provide free care to those without resources. To do so, MSP issues a health card with different categories based on income: 72 percent of the users have no income and pay nothing; the tariff then rises from 20 percent to 100 percent of the cost of service, according to income.[7]

Table 66 shows gross statistical estimates of social security population coverage. Such data are incomplete, partial, and at times doubtful and thus require clarifications of various sorts. (1) The figures for active insured in pensions are estimates made by the author based on official figures from the independent funds for all years (except the armed forces, which provided figures only for 1975, 1979, and 1983) and from DGSS for 1983 (the insured from DGSS in 1975–82 were estimated by subtracting other insured, unemployed, unpaid family workers and evasion from the EAP). (2) The official figures for passives include all pensioners (from the DGSS and independent funds) except the military and police since 1975, so that there has been underestimation from that date on although probably not very much. (3) The figures for dependents are based on the recipients of family allowances covered by DGSS but exclude beneficiaries of the public sector and thus entail substantial underestimation. The calculation of total population with health coverage (by summing actives, passives, and dependents) is simply an approximation; as in Uruguay these insured are not covered by a single central health program as in Costa Rica and Peru. Also, because of the underestimation explained above, plus the exclusion of coverage by mutual aid and cooperative societies and of services contracted by MSP, the total population coverage in health estimated in table 66 must be much lower than the real coverage.

Another distortion, although in the other direction, is the overestimation of coverage, especially in pensions, which is clearly visible in 1960 and 1965. The cause of this distortion is double coverage—that is, cases in which the same person is covered by more than one fund. For example, civil servants work half a day and may hold another job in the private sector; self-employed workers can offer their services in various occupations or sectors covered by different funds; and because the registry is not up-to-date, a person who changes occupation (and insuring institution) may appear in the table more than once.[8] With the unification program initiated in 1967 and strengthened in the 1970s, this problem has been gradually eliminated. According to the DGSS, all duplication among the insured has been eliminated, and the only possibility of double counting that remains relates to overlap between the insured of the DGSS and the independent funds. In 1983, 87 percent of those with pension coverage were in the DGSS, 8 percent in the armed forces, and 5 percent in the other categories. Thus, if duplication exists, it must be very small.

If we take into account the above warnings, table 66 shows a consistent fall in the percentage of pension coverage from 117 percent in 1965 to 72 percent in 1983. Up until 1975, the main explication for the decrease was the elimination of double counting; the decline in 1982–83 is fundamentally due to the increase in unemployment and evasion. In 1980, EAP coverage in Uruguay was the third highest in Latin America, and this position was probably

TABLE 66
SOCIAL SECURITY COVERAGE OF POPULATION IN URUGUAY, 1960–1983
(THOUSANDS)

	Total Population	EAP	Insured Population				% of Coverage[d]		Annual Average Growth Rate (log)				Quotient of Demographic Burden[c]
			Active[a]	Passive[b]	Dependents[c]	Total	Total Population	EAP	Total Population	EAP	Actives	Total Insured	
1960	2,538	987	1,077	276	251	1,604	63.2	109.1g	**	**	**	**	0.256
1965	2,693	1,049	1,230	358	275	1,863	69.2	117.3g	1.2	1.2	2.7	3.0	0.291
1969	2,791	1,067f	1,035	451	340	1,826	65.4	97.0	0.9	0.4	-4.2	-0.5	0.436
1975	2,828	1,094	906	494	390f	1,790	63.3	82.8	0.2	0.4	-2.2	-0.3	0.545
1980	2,908	1,123	912	596	485	1,993	68.5	81.2	0.6	0.5	0.1	2.2	0.654
1981	2,927	1,129	927	616	494	2,037	69.6	82.1	0.6	0.5	1.6	2.2	0.664
1982	2,947	1,137	868	634	481	1,983	67.3	76.3	0.7	0.7	-6.4	-2.7	0.730
1983	2,968	1,143	827	680	483	1,990	67.0	72.4	0.7	0.5	-4.7	0.4	0.822

Sources: Total population from the Dirección General de Estadística and Census, *Uruguay, 1983: Anuario estadístico*. EAP 1960–65 from ECLA, *Statistical Yearbook of Latin America*; 1970–85 from DGSS, November 1983. Insured 1960–69 from Carmelo Mesa-Lago, *Social Security in Latin America* (Pittsburgh, Pa.: University of Pittsburgh Press, 1978); 1975–83 estimated by the author on the basis of *Uruguay, 1983: Anuario estadístico* and DGSS, *Memoria, 1982, Boletín estadístico* (March 1983), and information from November 1983 and May 1984. Percentages, rates, and quotients calculated by the author.

a. Active contributors in the pension program; includes the funds integrated into DGSS and the independent funds.
b. Retirees and Pensioners for old age, disability, and survivors' insurance; excludes the military and the police since 1975.
c. Beneficiaries of family allowances in DGSS.
d. "Total population" coverage means health and/or maternity; EAP coverage is pension coverage.
e. Number of passives divided by number of actives.
f. Author's interpolation.
g. Overcoverage because some of the insured have more than one affiliation.

**Not available.

maintained in 1983, in spite of the decrease in coverage. It must also be noted that, with welfare pensions, coverage must be universal. As I mentioned above, total population coverage is significantly underestimated; the table shows in this sense little variation, with approximately two-thirds of the population covered. In 1982, a family health survey found that only 20 percent of the population lacked entitlement to insurance or mutual aid agencies, but this 20 percent was sheltered under the MSP,[9] and so coverage was practically universal (see above). In pension and health coverage, therefore, Uruguay can be compared with Chile, Costa Rica, and Cuba. Figures for occupational risks coverage do not exist.

Determining Structural Factors

Universal coverage in Uruguay (at least in pensions) has been facilitated by the same structural factors that characterize Chile, Costa Rica, and Cuba: (1) a high proportion of salaried workers (69 percent of the labor force in 1975); (2) a relatively low proportion of self-employed and unpaid family workers (24 percent and 2 percent, respectively) as well as agricultural workers (16 percent); (3) a small informal-traditional sector (27 percent in 1980, the second lowest in Latin America); and (4) the small size of the country, its good communication network, cultural homogeneity, educational level, and an extremely high degree of urbanization (83 percent). On the other hand, the open unemployment rate has been relatively high (fluctuating between 7 percent and 15 percent in 1968–83, with rates above 10 percent in 1976–78 and 1982–83), but the rate of equivalent underemployment has been the lowest in Latin America (4 percent in 1970 and 7 percent in 1980).[10] As in Chile, Cuba, and Costa Rica, there has also been a political commitment in Uruguay to universalizing the system, in large part a result of the competition among political parties until the beginning of the 1970s.

Differences in Population Coverage

On the one hand, as pension coverage is practically universal, there should be no differences in the degree of coverage among the departments of Uruguay. On the other hand, an analysis of health coverage differences among departments is impossible because of the lack of statistics. Table 67 attempts to fill this void with information on the percentage distribution of health coverage by different institutions among the departments and also shows the percentage of the total population without coverage. The latter is very small (fluctuating between 0 and 3 percent), thus offering fresh confirmation that health coverage is practically universal. With few exceptions, the most-developed departments (measured by GDP, income per capita, and degree of urbanization)[11] have higher coverage by mutual aid societies and cooperatives (for example, Montevideo, Maldonado, Canelones, Florida, Colonia, and

TABLE 67
DISTRIBUTION OF HEALTH COVERAGE BY INSTITUTIONS
AND DEPARTMENTS IN URUGUAY, 1981
(PERCENT)

Department	MSP	Mutual Aid Societies and Cooperatives	Private	Other[a]	Without Coverage
Montevideo	11.2	77.8	1.6	7.1	2.3
Artigas	43.1	21.5	28.7	6.7	*
Canelones	23.1	59.2	7.2	7.4	3.1
Cerro Largo	42.8	31.8	18.9	5.4	1.1
Colonia	15.9	45.9	23.8	13.1	1.3
Durazno	35.7	35.3	13.1	15.3	0.6
Flores	41.0	26.9	20.0	12.1	*
Florida	30.8	55.1	6.1	7.2	0.8
Lavalleja	28.4	53.1	14.8	3.7	*
Maldonado	15.0	63.6	19.5	1.9	*
Paysandú	35.5	46.0	12.9	4.5	1.1
Río Negro	37.3	47.0	3.2	10.5	2.0
Rivera	45.3	24.9	23.2	6.1	0.5
Rocha	33.6	42.7	17.8	5.9	*
Salto	29.9	51.6	15.9	2.6	*
San José	32.7	43.9	15.6	7.8	*
Soriano	36.1	34.5	19.8	7.9	1.7
Tucuarembo	30.2	25.6	41.3	2.8	0.1
Treinta y Tres	46.9	39.2	9.4	4.4	0.1

Source: Based on Uruguay, 1983: Anuario estadístico.

Note: Institutions are in the capitals of the departments and throughout the Department of Montevideo.

a. Includes care in the workplace.

*Not applicable.

Paysandú), whereas the least-developed departments have higher coverage by the MSP (for example, Rivera, Cerro Largo, and Flores).

The quality of medical-hospital care offered by the mutual aid societies is higher than that of the MSP, but the cost of affiliation in the former is becoming prohibitive. As a result the societies are gradually losing members and MSP coverage is increasing. The family health survey of 1982 showed that the higher the income of health care users, the greater the coverage by mutual aid societies and military health institutions (and probably by private ones also), while the lower the income, the greater the coverage by the MSP (the lowest income users are not entitled to coverage but receive welfare coverage).[12]

Another way of evaluating the geographic differences in coverage is to compare the services in the capital with those in the rest of the country. In

1980, Montevideo had 44 percent of the total population yet had 80 percent of all doctors and 67 percent of hospital beds, and in 1982 it received 69 percent of total unemployment benefits and 65 percent of health benefits. On the other hand, in 1980 the interior had 56 percent of the population but only 20 percent of the doctors and 33 percent of the hospital beds, and in 1982 received 31 percent of unemployment benefits and 35 percent of health benefits.[13]

Noncovered Population

Although pension coverage, and apparently health coverage, are universal in Uruguay, it has already been shown that there are geographic differences in the availability of health services. According to law, rural workers and domestic servants are not entitled to health coverage in DGSS and thus have access only to welfare services from the MSP. The unemployed are not covered either (except those included in the corresponding insurance), nor are unpaid family workers. The unemployed group grew noticeably in 1982–83. Although rural workers have pension coverage, most specialists believe that they are the group with the worst coverage, as labor and social security legislation are poorly implemented in the rural areas, unions are very weak, seasonal work is common, and employment opportunities scarce. The heavy rural-urban migration (especially to Montevideo) is evidence of the important differences in income and social services, within which social security stands out. It has also been mentioned that indigents are entitled to a welfare pension, but its amount is considerably lower than the average of the other pensions, and it is insufficient to cover basic necessities.[14]

Measures to Improve Coverage

Although Uruguay has one of the highest degrees of population coverage in the region, statistics on pension and health coverage should be published in order to eliminate the underestimation and duplication noted here, and to define the sector lacking coverage. In addition, statistics should be compiled on occupational risks coverage. The development of a single up-to-date registry and national identification system would be appropriate means to this end. It would also be advisable to incorporate rural workers and domestic servants into the health insurance of DGSS, to reduce the inequalities in health services among departments, and to decentralize such services from Montevideo toward the interior. Unemployed workers should also be granted coverage for six months after dismissal.

FINANCING

Financing Sources

Before unification and standardization came about, there was a great diversity in legal wage contributions (both total and disaggregated) among the three major funds that were later incorporated into DGSS (see table 68). In 1969, the total percentage fluctuated between 15 percent and 65 percent; the insured paid between 5 and 21.5 percent, and the employer between 10 and 43.5 percent. State contributions (not included in the table) differed among the three groups and were made through subsidies and multiple taxes on imports and exports, sales of products (agricultural and livestock, alcoholic beverages, and tobacco), real estate rents and so forth.

From 1969 to 1984, wage contributions were gradually standardized, with varying effects for the three groups. In 1984, the insured in the three pension funds paid the same contribution percentage (13 percent). This signified a decrease for civil service–education and an even greater one for industry-commerce, but an increase for rural and more so for domestic service, the two lowest income groups. The employers' pension contribution was standardized in 1984 and was set at 10 percent for industry-commerce, and rural–domestic service (reducing the first and increasing the second) but stayed the same for civil service–education. The health contribution appears uniform in the table, but in reality, it is applied only to industry-commerce as rural–domestic service is excluded from this program and civil service–education has independent programs with varying contributions. In 1969, the wage contribution for family allowances was applied only to industry-commerce;

TABLE 68

LEGAL CONTRIBUTIONS TO SOCIAL SECURITY IN URUGUAY, 1969 AND 1984
(PERCENTAGE OF SALARY)

Program	1969			1984		
	Insured	Employer	Total	Insured	Employer	Total
Pensions[a]	**5–8**	**5–20**	**10–37**	**13**	**10–20**	**23–33**
Civil service–education	15	15–20	30–35	13	15–20	28–33
Industry–commerce	17–18	19	36–37	13	10	23
Rural–domestic service	5	5	10	13	10	23
Health[b]	3	5	8	3	4	7
Family allowances[b]	0.5	14.5	15	*	*	*
Occupational risks[c]	*	5	5	*	5	5
Total	5–21.5	10–43.5	15–65[d]	13–16	15–25	28–41

Sources: 1969 from Carmelo Mesa-Lago, Social Security in Latin America (Pittsburgh, Pa.: University of Pittsburgh Press, 1978), pp. 96–97. 1984 from DGSS (information provided November 23, 1983).

Note: Only for the three groups integrated into DGSS in 1979. The contribution of the state is not included as it is not fixed as a percentage of salary.

a. Pension percentages in 1984 include family allowances and unemployment.
b. Applied only to industry-commerce; in civil service–education, this was paid for entirely by the employer in 1969.
c. Average national premium.
d. Excludes contributions to the two unemployment funds.

*Not applicable.

this contribution was entirely paid for by the state in civil service–education; in the rural category, it was fixed in accordance with the extension and value of cultivated land, and it was not paid in domestic service. In 1984, the contribution for family allowances had been standardized (calculated within the pension contribution) for two groups, the exception being civil service–education, for which the state continued to pay. In 1984, the maximum total contribution percentage had declined (from 65 percent to 41 percent), while the minimum percentage had increased (from 15 percent to 28 percent). The net effect of this change has been a reduction in real social security income because the increase in contributions has been applied to the lowest income group, while the decrease in contributions has benefited the two higher income groups, which, combined, hold the majority of the insured. To compensate for the decrease in revenues, a VAT was introduced in 1980. I will discuss this tax shortly (also see chapter 4).

Table 68 does not include the contributions of independent groups (except racetrack workers); these contributions have not been affected by the process of standardization. In 1969, the funds for university professionals and notaries were financed by a contribution from the insured, similar to that in industry-commerce, plus taxes on the services provided by these professionals or on the sale of articles either related or not related to their professions. In the military fund, the insured paid a contribution similar to that in civil service–education; the state paid for some programs completely and covered the deficit in others. In 1982, more than 86 percent of the health expenditures of the military fund were subsidized and 89 percent of the subsidy came from the state budget. In the banking fund, the insured's contribution was similar to that in industry-commerce, but the employer's contribution was double.[15] Wage contribution of the two racetrack funds for pensions has been standardized, so that in contribution they are equivalent to industry-commerce and rural–domestic service.

State subsidies for health financing favor higher income groups. In 1982 state subsidies to the insured of autonomous agencies and the military were, respectively, 100 percent and 50 percent greater than the state subsidy to those covered by the MSP. Of the latter, 54 percent fell in the lowest quintile of family income and only 12 percent in the highest quintile, whereas only 12 percent of the insured in autonomous agencies and the military fell in the lowest quintile of family income, but 40 percent fell in the highest quintile.[16]

Although information concerning investments is scarce and highly aggregated, investment yields apparently constitute an insignificant source of social security financing. In the DGSS, the 1982 reserves were equal to 2 percent of total assets, and investments generated only 0.4 percent of revenues.[17] The independent funds of the private sector (professionals, public notaries, and racetrack workers) had proportionally higher reserves, and investments probably generated a higher percentage of revenues (in 1969 an average of about

4 percent),[18] but this added amount is of very little importance in the general system.

Evasion and Payment Delays

Historically, the high wage contribution and inflation rates in Uruguay have constituted a strong stimulus to evasion and payment delays among employers, who frequently acted in concert with the insured. This phenomenon is most common in small enterprises where the employer declares fewer employees and lower salaries, especially where seasonal and temporary employment predominates. Because of high inflation, the penalties for delinquency (payment delays) have been less than the gains obtained by delaying payment. Furthermore, the moratoria, by granting long periods for repayment without adjusting debts, have substantially reduced the real debt. Also, the state has traditionally avoided its obligations, and as a result special taxes have proliferated in Uruguay. In the past, the state has delayed its payments in the same manner as private employers, to reduce its real contributions substantially.[19]

The unification of the major funds within DGSS has established the basis for centralization of information and control of evasion and payment delays (through the Center for Data Processing and the Collection and Supervision Section), yet although there is information on the measures taken, statistics on their results have not been published. In 1982, the files began to be consolidated as an individualized registry of contributors began to be instituted. Nevertheless, at the end of 1983, DGSS publications had still not reported the number of active insured contributors. The substitution of the VAT for part of the employer's contribution and specific taxes has simplified the tax payment system. In 1982 a standardized system of declaration and payment of all social security taxes began throughout the country, and enterprises and collection began to be controlled by computer.[20] Finally, the significant reduction in the inflation rate in 1981 and 1982 eliminated incentives to delay payment, but the tripling of the inflation rate in 1983 reestablished them. My own gross estimates indicate that evasion rose from 6 percent in 1981 to 8 percent in 1982 and 9 percent in 1983.

Financial Equilibrium

Table 69 presents the balance of revenues and expenditures of the Uruguayan social security system; in the first year it is limited to the three major funds, later incorporated to the DGSS; in subsequent years it covers the entire system with the exception of the military and the police. On average, the revenues/expenditures of the DGSS programs represent 90 percent of the total system, without including the armed forces. The surplus in 1976 became a deficit in 1978, which grew to be 81 percent of revenues in 1982. There are two fundamental causes for the enormous financial disequilibrium. First, real revenues gradually decreased because of the cut in the total wage contribution percentage; in 1982, these revenues were equivalent to 63 percent of the 1976 level. Second, real expenditures remained stable in 1976–78, fell in 1979, began to increase in 1980, and grew rapidly in 1981–82; in the last period they had decreased to 36 percent above the 1976 level.

Table 69 shows that the principal reason for the financial disequilibrium has been the growing deficit of the pension program, which, in 1982, was responsible for 79 percent of the total deficit; the increase in the pension deficit in 1980–82 was due mainly to the readjustment of pensions to the cost of living (see chapter 5). The deficits in family allowances and unemployment

TABLE 69
SOCIAL SECURITY BALANCE OF REVENUES AND EXPENDITURES BY
PROGRAM IN URUGUAY, 1976–1982
(MILLIONS OF NEW PESOS AT CURRENT PRICES)

Program	1976	1978	1980	1982
Pensions				
Revenues	998	2,138	5,073	7,416
Expenditures	938	2,232	6,000	13,331
Balance	60	−94	−927	−5,915
Health				
Revenues	65	190	600	793
Expenditures	50	155	407	718
Balance	15	35	193	75
Family Allowances[a]				
Revenues	168	398	506	691
Expenditures	148	402	908	1,302
Balance	20	−4	−402	−611
Unemployment				
Revenues	12	63	112	5
Expenditures	12	58	129	559
Balance	0	5	−17	−554
Total[b]				
Revenues	1,243	2,789	6,290	9,284
Expenditures	1,148	2,847	7,444	16,804
Balance	95	−58	−1,154	−7,520
As percentage of revenues	7.6	−2.1	−18.3	−81.0

Source: 1976 from DGSS, *Boletín estadístico* 1:1 (1980); 1978–82 from *Uruguay, 1983: Anuario estadístico.*

Note: The 1976 figures are limited to the three principal funds; subsequent figures encompass all of the system except for the military and police.

a. Includes maternity.
b. Includes other revenues/expenditures.

(the increase of the deficit in the latter in 1982 resulted from unemployment doubling) represented 15 percent of the total deficit in 1982. Paradoxically, the health program generated a surplus (although a declining one in 1982), but this program covers only one-fourth of the active population and functions as a reinsurance.

In 1978–82 the most solvent funds were those of university professionals, public notaries, and bank employees, which almost invariably generated a surplus. Within the DGSS, the three major funds yielded deficits in 1982; the smallest deficit was in industry-commerce (42 percent of revenues), followed by the civil service-education deficit (106 percent of revenues); the largest deficit was in rural-domestic service (1,010 percent of revenues).[21] There is no official information on the armed forces' funds, but it is reported that, in 1982, the military fund had a deficit equivalent to 150 percent of its revenues, while the police fund's deficit rose to 173 percent of revenues; both deficits were covered by the state.[22]

Since 1980, at least, the deficit of DGSS has been covered by transfers from the central government, using revenues generated by the VAT introduced that year to compensate for the cutbacks in wage contributions. A study published by the Institute for the Integration of Latin America (INTAL) affirms that, in 1980, the deficit of the system was entirely covered by transfers from the central government using the VAT revenues earmarked for social security; these transfers were equivalent to 32 percent of total expenditures.[23] In 1982, DGSS reported that the state had given them 7,869 million new pesos, equivalent to 48 percent of the total expenditures to cover the deficit of that year (employers contributed 27 percent, and the insured 22 percent).[24] But there is no precise information to determine whether VAT revenues really covered the total cost of this transfer.

Financing Methods

Although there is no information on this subject, it appears certain that the DGSS uses the pure assessment method, possibly with a small contingency reserve. (In 1982 a reserve equivalent to 3 percent of total expenditures was reported.) The occupational risks program operated by the BSE and private independent funds use some capitalization method, but the exact type is unknown. The armed forces' funds apply a pure assessment method. It is not known whether recent actuarial studies have been done of the DGSS and of other programs.

Measures to Increase Revenues

This section has mentioned several measures introduced in recent years by DGSS to reduce evasion and payment delays, such as rationalization and better control of collection. It has also been seen that, in 1969–84, the insured's contribution in rural–domestic service increased from 5 to 13 percent, while the employer's contribution doubled, from 5 to 10 percent. In addition, in 1982 the self-employed rural workers and employers became obligated to contribute. But this increase in revenues did not make up for the sizable reduction caused by cutbacks in the insured's contribution in the other two groups as well as the reduction of the employer contribution in industry-commerce and the elimination of family allowances and unemployment contributions. The most important source of social security financing appears to be the VAT, but it is unknown whether this compensates for the reduction in revenues and the increase in expenditures. The economic crisis that deepened in 1982–83 provoked an increase in unemployment and evasion, as well as a fall in real salaries and sales, all of which probably reduced social security revenues.

If the government decides not to increase wage contributions and if the revenues generated by VAT are insufficient to balance the system, it will be necessary to increase the VAT rates. In any case, the government should consider the incorporation of the independent funds, which generate surplus, into the DGSS (in order to further the principle of solidarity). Contributions of the insured could also be increased in the funds that cover higher income groups and in the independent funds with a deficit (military and police), whose contribution is relatively small, to finance their generous benefits.

BENEFITS, EXPENDITURES AND COSTS
Benefits and Entitlement Conditions

In spite of the unification and standardization process, there are still notable differences in benefits and entitlement conditions; the only completely standardized program is that of occupational risks. Even within the DGSS there is standardization in only part of the private sector (workers in industry-commerce and rural workers in some programs), as the public sector has a different system, and the independent funds in the private and public sector aggravate the differences. This diversity impedes comparison of benefits in Uruguay with those in other countries.

In spite of these limitations, Uruguay is one of the top countries in Latin America in terms of the number of risks covered, including unemployment and family allowances, both of which are available in only half a dozen countries. For a comparison of benefit entitlement conditions, we have used the group that encompasses the majority of insured in Uruguay (industry-commerce). This has stricter entitlement conditions than both the civil service–education and the independent funds and less stringent conditions than only rural–domestic service. In the health and maternity programs, entitlement conditions are some of the most generous in Latin America, with the sole exception of the contribution period for obtaining health entitlement. In terms of pensions, Uruguay occupies an intermediate position in the region in retirement eligibility (sixty years of age for men and fifty-five for women, with thirty years of contribution). This requirement is stricter than in Costa Rica, similar to those of Cuba and Peru, and less than those in Chile and Mexico. On the other hand, Uruguay grants unemployment and welfare pensions (available in very few countries) and, in spite of high inflation, has followed a moderate policy of pension adjustments. The average total wage contribution in 1984 (35 percent in industry-commerce) is the second highest in Latin America, and to this must be added the significant contribution of the VAT. The burden of benefits is nevertheless very heavy and exhibits a tendency to increase.

Table 70 records Uruguay's progress in health services and levels in 1960–81. It must be noted that the table does not include the total number of practicing physicians but instead shows generally the active members of the university professionals' fund; a more accurate estimate made by the author in 1983 showed a ratio of 22:1.[25] On the other hand, the number of hospital beds in 1980 includes those in "short stay" institutions but excludes beds in mental hospitals and tuberculosis sanatoriums. In both doctor and hospital bed ratios, Uruguay ranked first in Latin America, while in life expectancy, it ranked third and in infant mortality fifth. The general mortality index is relatively high and stable, in large part a result of Uruguay's having the oldest population in the region.

It should be noted that Uruguay's health levels in 1950 were already first or second in Latin America. For example, Uruguay was ahead of Cuba in

TABLE 70

HEALTH SERVICES AND LEVELS IN URUGUAY, 1960–1981

	Hospital Beds per 1,000 Persons	Physicians per 10,000 Persons[a]	Mortality Rate		Life Expectancy[b]
			General	Infant	
1960	5.5	12.2	10.0	50[c]	67.2
1965	5.1	11.4	9.6	49	68.4
1970	5.9	10.9	9.6	48	68.6
1975	**	14.1	10.0	41	68.8
1980	6.0	17.5	10.3	38[c]	69.6
1981	**	18.5	9.4	31[c]	**

Sources: General mortality to 1975 and life expectancy from CELADE, *Boletín demográfico* (July 1983). The remainder from: ECLA, *Statistical Yearbook of Latin America, 1981;* PAHO, *Health Conditions in the Americas, 1973–1976;* República Oriental de Uruguay, *Anuario estadístico, 1970–1978* and *1983;* WHO, *World Health Statistics, 1982;* UN *Statistical Yearbook, 1981,* and information from the Ministerio de Salud Pública and from the Caja de Profesionales Universitarios, 1984.

a. Does not include the total number of practicing physicians.
b. Values for five-year periods (e.g., 1955–60 = 67.2).
c. Annual figure.

**Not available.

three of the five indicators shown in the table and ahead of Costa Rica in four (in general mortality, Costa Rica had a lower rate because of its younger population). Nevertheless, in the last two decades, progress in these levels has been very low or stagnant. Life expectancy rose rapidly until the end of the 1950s. Later its growth rate slowed and reached almost a complete stand-still in 1964–76. In part, the reason was the relatively high level that Uruguay had already reached, which made each subsequent increase more difficult. However, in the same period, other countries with a similar life expectancy or an even higher one achieved increases above those reached by Uruguay. Other countries have been closing the gap as a result and even managed to surpass Uruguay's life expectancy (for example, Costa Rica and Cuba).[26]

The infant mortality rate fell rapidly until 1955, remained almost stagnant until 1965, and renewed its fall in the 1970s but at a slower rate than would have been expected, given the health levels and development of the country. In 1980, the infant mortality rate was relatively high, the cause being the neonatal rate (infants less than four weeks old); this rate, which accounts for more than 60 percent of the total, was higher than the 1963 rate. Neonatal mortality is a major health problem in Uruguay; to solve it the country would need to know the number of pregnancies controlled, to follow up high-risk cases, and to ascertain the quality of institutional care for delivery and for newborns.[27]

Inequalities in Benefits

The distribution of public health expenditures has to do with the revenue of the users and not necessarily with their needs. In 1982, the expenditure per person covered was highest in the autonomous agencies, followed by the mutual aid societies, and the lowest in MSP. Apparently, the distribution of these expenditures has become more regressive in the last years. While in 1972 MSP received 94 percent of expenditures and the military and police 6 percent, in 1982 the MSP share had been reduced to 66 percent (in spite of the fact that many more people were cared for by MSP), and that of the armed forces had risen to 10 percent.[28]

Geographic disparities in health services and levels, as has been seen, are particularly large between Montevideo and the rest of the country. In 1981, Montevideo had 33.9 doctors per 10,000 inhabitants, while the department of Rivera had 5.9 and Flores had 3.8. The comparison of hospital beds per 1,000 inhabitants is less precise, as it is based only on the MSP's facilities, excluding those of mutual aid societies, which are concentrated in Montevideo and other urban centers. Even so, in 1981 Montevideo had a ratio of 3.2, while Rivera's was 1.8. Surprisingly, the infant mortality rate in Uruguay exhibits a pattern different from that in the other countries studied, as in 1980 Montevideo had a rate of 40.1 (above the national average), while the lowest rate was registered in Colonia, with 25.5. The highest rates in the country were in Salto (54.7), Flores (53.5), and Cerro Largo (44.6), departments that are less developed than the previous two.[29]

In pensions, the inequalities are notable among the diverse insured groups. At the beginning of the 1970s (before standardization), the following legal pension regulations were compared for most insured groups: retirement age, required contribution to the seniority pensions (existence of the contribution and years for which it had been made), basic salary on which pension was calculated, cost-of-living adjustments in pensions, and average time required for processing the pension. The study found that the armed forces, with the best benefit package, occupied first place; funds for workers in civil service-education, professionals, public notaries, and bank employees were second; industry-commerce came third; and rural-domestic service was last and far behind the first.[30]

Table 71 proves that, in spite of the standardization process, inequalities in pension amounts continue, although they are somewhat less accentuated and show interesting changes in order. In 1965, bank workers received the highest average pension, almost thirteen times the lowest average pension,

TABLE 71

DIFFERENCES IN ANNUAL AVERAGE PENSIONS AMONG INSURED
GROUPS IN URUGUAY, 1965 AND 1982

	1965		1982	
Average Pension	*Average Pension*[a] *(thous.)*	*Ratio*[b]	*Average Pension*[a] *(thous.)*	*Ratio*[b]
Rural–domestic service workers	4,487[c]	1.0	12,177	1.0
Industrial–commercial workers	9,422	2.1	14,612	1.2
Civil service–education workers	14,707[c]	3.3	29,896	2.5
Jockeys	16,803	3.7	21,746	1.8
Military	28,751	6.4	72,175	5.9
Police	**	**	66,050	5.4
Notary publics	28,571	6.4	53,111	4.4
University professionals	30,463	6.8	50,148	4.1
Bank workers	56,703	12.6	68,638	5.6

Sources: Calculations by the author based on *Anuario estadístico, 1964–1966,* and *Uruguay, 1983: Anuario estadístico,* except for military and police, which in 1982, are based on *El día,* Montevideo, March 3, 1984.

Note: 1 new peso = 1,000 old pesos.

   a. Arithmetic average of all pensions (including retirement and old age).
   b. Taking rural–domestic service average pension as a base (1.0).
   c. Grouped to permit comparison.

   **Not available.

which was received by those in rural work and domestic service. In 1982, the highest pension was received by the military, almost six times the lowest pension that the rural-domestic service continued to receive, while that of banking had passed to second place, with a ratio of 5.6:1.

The Growing Cost of Social Security and Its Causes

In 1965 the cost of social security in Uruguay reached almost 15 percent of GDP, which had historically been surpassed in the region only by Chile in 1971 (17 percent) and which, in 1965, was higher than the percentages in the United States and other developed countries. Table 72 shows that social security expenditures as a percentage of GDP in Uruguay fell dramatically in 1969–80 to 8.3 percent but later rose to reach 12.8 percent in 1982. At the beginning of the 1980s, Uruguayan social security expenditures as a percentage of both GDP and central government expenditures were the highest in Latin America (with Chile and Argentina either tied or taking second place). I analyze the causes of the high cost of social security below.

General causes. As in the cases of Chile, Costa Rica, and Cuba, the universalization of population coverage is an important source of increased costs. In addition, Uruguay is one of the few countries in the region to cover all social risks, and it also has a generous benefit package with more liberal entitlement conditions than in the majority of countries.

Information on administrative costs is scarce. According to calculations

TABLE 72
THE COST OF SOCIAL SECURITY IN URUGUAY, 1965–1982
(MILLIONS OF NEW CURRENT PESOS)

	GDP	Total Central Govt. Expenditures	Social Security Expenditures		
			Total[a]	% of GDP	% of Central Govt. Expenditures
1965	52	13	8	14.5	61.5
1969	499	118	70	14.2	59.3
1975	7,108	1,878	872	12.3	46.4
1980	81,429	20,812	6,797	8.3	32.6
1981	106,384	30,969	12,192	11.4	39.4
1982	112,564	41,274	14,398	12.8	34.9

Sources: 1965–69 from Carmelo Mesa-Lago, *Social Security in Latin America* (Pittsburgh, Pa.: University of Pittsburgh Press, 1978); 1975 from ILO, *The Cost of Social Security, 1975–1977,* and IMF, *Government Finance Statistics, 1982;* 1980–82 from DGSS, *Memoria, 1982,* and *Uruguay 1983: Anuario estadístico.*

Note: Figures are billions of old pesos in 1965 and 1969; 1 new peso = 1,000 old pesos.

a. Excludes expenditures for occupational risks and smaller programs.

based on official figures, the administrative cost of DGSS, as a percentage
of total revenues, rose from 6 percent in 1976 to 7 percent in 1980, but fell
to 5 percent in 1982. This percentage is slightly lower than the regional
average, but it is very high for international levels. The number of DGSS
employees is not known, but in 1982 there were between 30,000 and 50,000
employees in the health sector alone, or from 1.7 to 2.8 per hospital bed. In
1976, 72 percent of DGSS administrative expenditures went to employees'
remuneration, although the percentage fell to 67 percent in 1982, a figure
similar to that for Costa Rica and much higher than that of Peru.[31]

Table 73 shows that the major component of Uruguayan social security
expenditures is pensions, which are responsible for a growing percentage of
the system's outlays: from 66 percent in 1970 to more than 82 percent in
1982. Not only is this percentage the highest in Latin America but, in addition,
it surpasses by 25 percentage points those of the closest countries, Argentina
and Chile. The percentages of health and family allowances expenditures
appear to be dropping.

The percentage dedicated to the unemployment program is the smallest
but with important fluctuations; its decline in 1979–81 was due to the fall in
the unemployment rate from almost 12 percent to 7 percent, while the increase
in the expenditure percentage in 1982 resulted from a new increase in the
unemployment rate to 12 percent in that year because of the economic crisis.
With the jump in unemployment to almost 16 percent in 1983,[32] the expenditure percentage for this program must have risen and may possibly have been
responsible for the second highest deficit within the social security system.

Causes related to the pension program.   In Uruguay the extremely high

TABLE 73

DISTRIBUTION OF SOCIAL SECURITY EXPENDITURES
BY PROGRAM IN URUGUAY, 1970–1982
(PERCENT)

Program	1970[a]	1975[a]	1979	1980	1981	1982
Pensions	66.3	73.6	76.1	78.8	81.5	82.5
Family allowances	20.9	16.9	14.8	13.4	11.8	8.9
Health	3.9	3.6	7.0	5.9	5.0	4.8
Unemployment	5.4	4.0	2.1	1.9	1.7	3.8
Occupational risks	3.5	1.9	**	**	**	**

Sources: 1970 and 1975 from ILO, *The Cost of Social Security, 1975–1977.* 1979 to 1982 from DGSS, *Boletín estadístico* 4:10 (March 1983).

Note: Includes all programs in 1970–75, but in 1979–82, only those of DGSS are included.

a. Distribution of benefits; excludes other expenditures that are included in each program in 1979–82.

**Not available.

percentage of expenditures in pensions and their tendency to increase can be explained by some of the oldest legislation in Latin America; universality of coverage, generous pensions, and relatively liberal entitlement conditions (especially for certain groups); the oldest population in the region, with the third highest life expectancy; and a policy of adjusting pensions (albeit not fully) to the cost of living.

According to table 66, the quotient of demographic burden rose from 0.256 in 1960 to 0.822 in 1983, the latter being the highest in Latin America, almost double the quotient for Chile and more than triple that of Cuba. The growth rate of the EAP has averaged 0.5 percent annually since the end of the 1960s, while the active contributing insured show a declining tendency that was accentuated in 1982–83.

In 1960–80 the percentage of the population in Uruguay over sixty-five years rose from 8 percent to more than 10 percent, and it is expected to reach 12 percent in the year 2000. These are the highest percentages in the region (see table 74). It has been estimated that, in 1980, 66 percent of men and 79 percent of women reached the age of sixty-five; life expectancy at birth for women is four years more than that for men, and as women can retire at fifty-five (five years earlier than men), they have an average of twenty four years of life after retirement (men have sixteen years).[33] It must be taken into account that the retirement ages cited are those for industry-commerce, but in many of the independent funds the insured can retire earlier, in some cases at forty-five years of age.

As pensions take four-fifths of social security expenditures, cost-of-living-adjustments of pensions is a primary factor in the behavior of these expenditures. According to table 75, the real value of pensions fell to less than half in 1963–68 but recovered somewhat in 1969–70. A new reduction in the real value of pensions occurred in 1971–79; in the last year pensions were at the same level as in 1968. This explains the decline in social security expenditures as a percentage of GDP in the 1970s (see table 72). A new readjustment of pensions occurred in 1981–82 such that, in the last year, these approximated the 1971 level. This significant increase in pension expenditures largely ex-

TABLE 74

DISTRIBUTION OF POPULATION BY AGE GROUP IN URUGUAY, 1960–2010
(PERCENT)

Age Group	1960	1970	1980	1990	2000	2010
0–14	27.9	27.9	27.0	26.2	25.0	23.8
15–64	64.0	63.2	62.6	62.5	62.9	64.4
65 and over	8.1	8.9	10.4	11.2	12.1	11.8

Source: Based on CELADE, *Boletín demográfico* 16:32 (July 1983); calculations by the author.

TABLE 75
REAL VALUE OF ANNUAL PENSIONS IN URUGUAY, 1963–1982

	Pensions (millions of new pesos)[a]	No. of Pensioners (thous.)	Average per Capita Pension (new pesos)[a]	Index (1970 = 100)[b]		
				Nominal Pension	Inflation[c]	Real Pension
1963	2.1	328	6.4	7.0	5.4	129.6
1964	2.7	346	7.9	8.7	7.5	116.0
1965	3.4	358	9.6	10.6	11.8	89.8
1966	5.4	368	14.6	16.1	18.2	88.5
1967	9.9	408	24.2	26.6	42.8	62.1
1968	17.4	426	40.8	44.9	71.0	63.2
1969	34.0	451	75.4	83.1	85.2	97.5
1970	40.5	447	90.7	100.0	100.0	100.0
1971	56.7	464	122.3	134.7	135.7	99.3
1972	86.9	489	177.8	195.9	239.5	81.8
1973	155.0	500	309.9	341.5	469.4	72.8
1974	285.2	508	561.5	618.7	831.8	74.4
1975	492.9	494	997.7	1,099.4	1,509.0	72.9
1976	770.6	502	1,535.1	1,691.6	2,272.5	74.4
1977	1,180.5	529	2,231.6	2,459.2	3,595.1	68.4
1978	1,777.4	547	3,255.3	3,587.3	5,194.9	69.1
1979	2,798.0	567	4,934.7	5,438.0	8,665.1	62.8
1980	4,972.3	596	8,342.8	9,193.8	14,167.5	64.9
1981	9,439.1	616	15,323.3	16,886.3	18,984.5	88.9
1982	12,093.8	634	19,075.4	21,021.1	22,591.5	93.0

Sources: Number of pensioners and pension amount from the Dirección General de Estadísticas y Censos, *Anuario estadístico, 1961–1963, 1964–1966, 1967–1969, 1970–1978,* and *Uruguay, 1983: Anuario estadístico.* Inflation rates from ECLA, *Economic Survey for Latin America, 1963* to *1982.* Averages and indexes calculated by the author.

Note: Old age, disability, and survivors' insurance; excludes the armed forces from 1970 on.

a. 1 new peso = 1,000 old pesos.
b. Average pension calculations and the corresponding pension indexes were done by taking the total sum of pesos.
c. 1963–68 and 1971 are December to December variations; the others are average annual variations.

plains the increase in the cost of social security/GDP in 1981–82 and the enormous growth of the deficit of the pension program and the general system in these two years (see table 69).

Causes related to the health program. Table 73 underestimates health expenditure as a percentage because it reports only the sector covered by DGSS. But even if the total expenditure of the health sector were included, as a percentage it would probably be very small compared with that in Costa Rica, Mexico, and Peru. These countries have younger populations; in 1980 the percentage of the population fourteen years old or less was between 43 percent and 66 percent greater in these three countries than in Uruguay. On

the other hand, Uruguay has the highest percentage of its population at productive age—a group with a relatively low health risk—of any country in
Latin America. This figure is 8 and 11 percentage points above the percentages
for Peru and Mexico, respectively. Granted, Uruguay has a higher percentage
of its population over sixty-five (a group with a high health risk) than these
countries, but this is more than compensated for by the high percentage of
the population at productive age and the low proportion of the population
under fourteen years of age (a high health risk group). In 1980 Uruguay had
the lowest dependency index in Latin America (59.8 percent) after Argentina,
while the Peruvian index (83.2 percent) was average and that of Mexico (93.4
percent) was the fourth highest in the region.

On the other hand, Uruguay—like Chile and Cuba and even more than
Costa Rica—has changed its pathological profile and is confronting the high
cost of the "diseases of development," made worse by the aging of its population and the high life expectancy. Nevertheless, here as in other countries
in the region, part of the health cost is due to administrative inefficiency,
especially in the MSP. Approximately 65 percent of the hospital beds belong
to the MSP, and its occupancy index, 75.8 percent in 1979, fell to 68.7
percent in 1980, although it rose to 73.8 percent in 1981. The latter was
below the indexes for Chile, Costa Rica, and Cuba. The average occupancy
index for hospitals in the interior was even lower—67 percent in 1981—
fluctuating between 33.3 percent and 88 percent. The occupancy index in the
Montevideo hospitals, however, ranged between 29 percent and 99 percent,
but in almost half of the hospitals, the index was below 60 percent. The
figures for installed capacity show that the hospitals are fairly old; only 2
percent were built after 1963 and 37 percent are older than 1930. Another
indication of inefficiency is the extremely high number of days per average
hospital stay, 20.9 in 1980, which is more than twice the average for Chile,
Costa Rica, and Cuba.[34]

A characteristic of Uruguayan health care that is common to the greater
part of the region is the high priority given to curative medicine and the little
emphasis placed on preventive medicine (save for immunizations). The MSP,
which is responsible for preventive medicine (and for curative medicine for
about two-fifths of the population) has received a decreasing proportion of
public health expenditures as a percentage of the central government expenditures: 95 percent in 1974 and 63 percent in 1982.[35]

Measures to Reduce Expenditures

Uruguay is in a much more difficult position to reduce social security
expenditures than the other countries studied here (with the possible exception
of Chile) because of the previously discussed demographic factors and the
irreversible generosity of the past, which has largely contributed to the current
high quotient of demographic burden. There is only a limited possibility of

avoiding cost-of-living adjustments in pensions, which are already low for the majority of the pensioners, and doing so would cause political tensions.

The DGSS has taken some positive steps to increase administrative efficiency and to reduce costs. These include: the introduction of an accounting and auditing system with mechanization of payments; the affiliation of family members of the insured to improve the control of payments; the reorganization of the medical files to eliminate double histories; and the unification and simplication of benefit processing. But these measures cannot correct the principal problems of Uruguayan social security, and more drastic measures are needed to counteract the errors of the past and to establish the basis for gradually reducing future costs and balancing the system.

With this objective, retirement ages should be raised. The retirement age for women should be made equal to that for men (sixty years), and, ideally, both should increase to sixty-five years. Also, the social security system should be totally unified and standardized, with stricter legislation to eliminate seniority pensions and other generous conditions, to emphasize the payment of basic benefits, to integrate the health system and improve its efficiency, and to give greater emphasis to preventive medicine. It should also be possible to complement basic benefits with others financed by the insured through mutual aids societies and private insurance. In the five cases previously discussed, other policies to reduce administrative expenditures have been mentioned that could also be applied in Uruguay.

THE IMPACT OF SOCIAL SECURITY ON DEVELOPMENT

Uruguay is one of the few Latin American countries to have substituted the VAT for part of the wage contribution. There are several studies on this subject, on which I will now focus. At the end of 1983, a survey of public social expenditures was being planned that, by gathering information on social security and income, would make it possible to analyze the impact of the former on the distribution of the latter. Unfortunately the processing of the survey's results had not been finished at this writing.[36]

Savings and Investment

As we have already seen, the bulk of Uruguayan social security uses the pure assessment method, and there is only a small contingency reserve with an insignificant impact on investment. The system has suffered from financial disequilibrium for many years and has thus required large state transfers, hence its impact on investment is probably negative.

Employment

Until the end of the 1960s, the unemployment rate in Uruguay was low, as were the rate of population growth and the ages for retirement. Labor was therefore not abundant, and as social security coverage was universal, the country appeared to approximate the inelastic labor supply model described in chapter 1. On the other hand, wage contributions varied significantly among economic activities. The state intervened to a great degree in the regulation of salaries and other labor and social security conditions as well as in the control of prices. Trade unions were strong and influential. This scenario indicates that the supply of labor was not perfectly inelastic. Wage contributions for social security legally placed on the employer were among the highest in the region and ranged from 10 percent to 44 percent, approximately twice the contribution of the insured. With such a complex situation and without adequate studies, it is impossible to reach a conclusion about the incidence of the employer's contribution, but possibly it could not be transferred completely to either the workers or the consumers and hence had some negative impact on employment.

The VAT and its theoretical effects.   Since the beginning of the 1970s up at least to the time in Uruguay's government began to be democratically elected, there were important changes in the above-described situation: unemployment increased, the power of the unions declined, the state intervened less in the economy (and assumed, as in Chile, a subsidiary role), trade was liberalized, price controls diminished, and the employer contribution was significantly reduced to 15–25 percent. (If the state sector is eliminated, the reduction was 15–19 percent.) To compensate for the fall in social security revenues that resulted from cutting the employer's wage contribution (and part of the insured's contribution), the state increased the rate of the VAT in 1980, earmarking these resources for social security.

From 1967 to 1980 the VAT was adopted in seven Latin American countries, including Uruguay in 1972. But only two countries substituted this tax for the social security wage contribution, and these have done so only partly: Argentina and Uruguay. In the latter the VAT generated more than half the total tax revenues at the end of the 1970s.[37]

From a theoretical standpoint, if the VAT were established in a country without social security wage contributions, its impact on employment would be neutral, as it would favor neither capital nor labor. But the VAT has been introduced in two countries with an existing and high social security wage contribution. Hence in these countries the tax is assumed to have had a positive impact on employment, as it eliminated the discrimination against the labor factor or, in other words, the incentive to substitute capital for labor. If the VAT also substitutes for part of the cost of the insured's contribution, it must act to increase real salaries. This could also occur in the short run if the employer contribution were cut but as an alternative to the positive impact on employment (in which case there would be no change in the cost of production). It could also occur in the long run if the increase in the demand for labor neared a situation of full employment.[38] By reducing the cost of production in labor-intensive industries, the VAT would also increase the competitiveness of exports. These effects are based on the following assumptions: (1) that such effects are considered in the long run; (2) that there is elasticity in the substitution of factors of production; (3) that there is competition among enterprises; and (4) that the worker does not perceive at least one part of the employer's contribution as an integral part of his remuneration (given that the entire contribution, if it were perceived as part of the remuneration, would be absorbed by the insured and there would be no negative impact on employment).[39] Hypothetical studies on the impact of the VAT have been conducted by various specialists, as we saw in the cases of Chile and Mexico.

The VAT has been the object of criticism for its allegedly regressive impact on income distribution, for the possible low elasticity of factor substitution, for the difficulty of collecting it, its possible effect of feeding inflation, and for its ideological-symbolic implications.[40] Below I will analyze the criticism of the VAT effect on distribution. If the elasticity of factor substitution is really low, the VAT could still produce positive effects on employment though to a lesser degree. It appears to be relatively easy to collect VAT revenues (except in countries with a very poor tax payment infrastructure) if there is an equal rate, but collection is complicated if exemptions and discriminatory rates exist. If the VAT replaces a preexisting tax (for example, the wage contribution) with an equal sum, its impact on inflation must be neutral. In the short run, however, there could be an inflationary effect if there is insufficient competition, as monopolistic or oligopolistic enterprises could maintain the same production costs and pocket the wage contribution cut as profit. Finally, the VAT has at times provoked criticism from unions because it eliminates or reduces employer contributions and is therefore considered to erode an old social gain and supposedly to increase the burden on low-income consumers. I leave the analysis of this last argument, inasmuch as it refers to redistribution, for the last section of this chapter. In terms of union criticism, if the VAT is applied and functions correctly, it should have a positive impact on employment and, in the long run, on real salaries.

The effects of the VAT in Uruguay.   As noted above, the increase of the VAT rate for social security began in 1980 in Uruguay: the first stage of substitution was initiated in January and the second in July (but afterward certain changes occurred in the employer contribution). The only study on the effects of the VAT in Uruguay covered the year 1980 and is thus limited to the very short term. Another problem of this study is that the information on certain variables, such as real salary and occupation, apparently suffered from methodological deficiencies.[41] But the principal defect is that the study does not isolate the effect of the VAT from that of other economic measures taken before it or from circumstantial factors.[42]

The study affirms the hypothetical, beneficial effects of the VAT: increases in employment and real average salary in the short run (the latter by reducing the insured's contribution, at least in industry-commerce), decreases in production costs, and greater competitiveness in exports. It maintains that Uruguay should export labor and land-intensive products, which are relatively abundant, and that the heavy tax on labor induced a selection of production technologies that discriminated against labor-intensive activities and reduced the competitiveness of exports. Ideally, the VAT should have completely substituted for the employer wage contribution, but this change was not made—according to the study—as the existence of the income tax on industry and commerce (IRIC) would have provoked an inverse discrimination—that is, the substitution of labor for capital to avoid the IRIC payment. Thus an optimal rate of substitution is said to have been fixed, favoring neither capital nor labor.[43]

According to the above-mentioned study, all of the first-degree effects envisioned materialized: (1) unemployment was reduced from 8.1 percent in the second half of 1979 to 7 percent in the second half of 1980, while employment rose 1.2 percent in this period; (2) real salary rose almost 12 percent in the same period; (3) the relative participation of labor income in total income rose from 30.2 percent in 1979 to 32.8 percent in 1980; and (4) the competitiveness of local production in the domestic and international markets improved (the study presents no figures on this aspect). In addition, it is maintained that real benefits rose 3 percent in 1980 and that the increase in prices caused by the VAT was only 1.7 percent and occurred only once.[44] But the analysis of tendencies prior to 1980 (on the basis of information from the ECLA) does not always reinforce these conclusions. For example, the unemployment rate fell gradually from 12.7 percent in 1976, and in fact, the reductions experienced in 1978 and 1979 were greater than that of 1980. Employment increased after 1975 (except in 1978), although at lower rates than that in 1980. The volume of exports also increased after 1973, and in 1973–76 the rates were greater than in 1980. The increase in real salaries in 1980 was reported as 0.5 percent, instead of 12 percent, and the participation of labor income in total income was 41.4 percent in 1971 and 29.7 percent in 1977. To these tendencies must be added an average growth rate of real GDP per capita of 4 percent in 1975–79. This improvement in the Uruguayan economy largely reflected external variables: the increase in exports (mostly to Argentina because prices were lower in Uruguay) and the increase of foreign investment (fundamentally from Argentina and for construction).[45]

The positive performance of the Uruguayan economy continued until approximately mid-1981, and then the recession broke loose. In large part external factors were again responsible: the devaluation of the Argentine peso, which eliminated Uruguay's comparative advantage and produced a reduction in exports to and investment from Argentina. According to information from the ECLA, in 1981, unemployment was further reduced to 5.5 percent, the employment rate rose by 3.2 percent, real salary rose by 7.5 percent, and the volume of exports grew by 7.1 percent. But with the recession, all of these indicators deteriorated in 1982 and 1983; the unemployment rate rose in the second half of 1981 to 6.7 percent and later reached 15.7 percent in 1983: real salaries fell by 0.3 percent in 1982; the volume of exports continued to grow in 1982, but at half the 1981 rate and abruptly fell 12 percent in 1983. Finally, the inflation rate, which had fallen in 1980–82, rose to 62.7 percent in 1983.[46]

As it is not possible here to isolate the factors related to the crisis associated with the VAT factor, it cannot be concluded that the deterioration of employment, real salary, and exports resulted from the VAT. But for the same reason, it cannot be maintained that the study cited proves that the substitution of the VAT for the wage contribution positively affected these variables in 1980. It is necessary to carry out an analysis that adequately evaluates the effects of the VAT—isolating them—given that the Uruguayan experience is important as an alternative in the future design of policy for social security in Latin America.

The Distribution of Income

Although no studies measure the impact of social security on the redistribution of income in Uruguay, there is some evidence that in 1963–79 a general deterioration in distribution occurred.[47] I offer the following speculations on the possible specific impact of social security, but a thorough study on this subject is needed.

Universal population coverage, apparently including part of the critical poverty group through welfare pensions, is a progressive aspect of the Uruguayan social security system. Conversely, the continued existence of groups with independent pension programs, in spite of the unification process, is regressive, as is the direct relationship between income and entitlement to institutional health coverage and, within this category, entitlement to the better institutions (mutual aid societies, and military health services). With respect to the wage contribution (I discuss the impact of the VAT below), the progressive elements are the absence of wage ceilings, the process of standardizing contributions, and the reduction in the employer contribution. On the opposite side are the reduction of the contribution from the middle-income insured (industry-commerce and civil service–education) vis-à-vis the increase in the contribution from the low-income insured (rural–domestic service) as well as the maintenance of the highest wage contribution by the state employer for its employees (including the autonomous agencies) and the generous state subsidies to the highest income groups.

In terms of benefits, the welfare pension is positive but at a very low level. Furthermore, four-fifths of benefit expenditures go to pensions, and there are significant inequalities in amounts among different groups. These inequalities are based not on salary differences alone but on more generous entitlement conditions and the substantial support of the state to medium- and high-income groups such as university professionals, public notaries, banking employees, and the armed forces. In the health area there are notable inequalities in medical services between Montevideo and the interior (and among departments in general), although at least one health indicator, infant mortality, appears not to reflect these inequalities.

The introduction of the VAT in a system of universal coverage such as those in Uruguay and Argentina should eliminate or at least reduce its possibly regressive impact, as the entire population is covered and contributes (although possibly in a manner disproportionate to income). Conversely, in the countries with low population coverage, the introduction of the VAT would have a clearly regressive effect on distribution, as the majority without coverage would be contributing to the system through it. The partial replacement of wage contributions by the VAT may have had cross-effects in Uruguay. As the low-income groups were not exempt from the contribution (with the exception of indigent pensions), nor was there a progressive scale, the VAT probably did not produce any important changes in distribution although the VAT revenues earmarked for social security did not exempt the low-income group from payment and did not discriminate in terms of goods and services taxed. But the increase in the low-income group contribution is probably regressive. This group does not benefit from the partial replacement of wage contributions by the VAT and, in addition, must contribute to the tax.

Finally, the VAT has noticeably reduced the insured's direct contribution (except for the low-income group) to finance benefits, for which the VAT now largely pays. This eliminates all justification of the relationship between salaries and monetary benefits, which should now consist of a basic amount, varying only in accordance with the number of the insured's dependents. As I suggested above, the basic amount could be supplemented by the insured through mutual aid or private insurance companies.[48]

8

The Needed Reform:
Strategies and Obstacles

COMPARISON OF PERFORMANCE
AMONG THE CASE STUDIES

I WILL NOW compare the performance of the six countries in terms of fulfillment of objectives and the application of social security principles. I will also verify the hypotheses established in chapter 1.

Unity and Standardization of the System

Within the top group, the three pioneer countries (Chile, Uruguay, and Cuba) developed highly stratified systems that were eventually reformed when the state's power was strengthened (under governments with different ideological orientations) with regard to the pressure groups but with varied results in terms of the degree of unification and standardization.

Cuba has the most standardized and unified of the present systems not only among the pioneer countries but among all six case studies. It achieved these goals by having the most powerful state, the most significantly weakened pressure groups, an economic model of central planning, and an ideology that emphasizes equality. Nevertheless, the Cuban system is neither totally standardized nor unified inasmuch as there is still an independent pension subsystem for the armed forces and discriminatory treatment of some groups.

Under the military government, Uruguay unified and partly standardized the three major insured groups but without merging their respective pension funds and thereby eliminating differences in contributions and benefits. In addition, various independent pension subsystems (for example, for the armed forces, police, university professionals, and bank employees), along with independent family allowances subsystems, have been maintained. In the health sector, myriad administrative agencies operate with very little coordination. As a result, the Uruguayan system today remains the most stratified system after the Chilean one.

The Chilean system was originally the most stratified. The reform started by the military government standardized certain benefits and entitlement conditions and also grouped several subsystems together under a common administration. But these subsystems' funds have not been merged, differences among them persist, and some maintain independent administrations. The latter group includes the armed forces and police, which have been practically unaffected by the reform. Parallel to the old system—still the most stratified in the six countries—a new system has developed that promotes the coexistence of various administrative agencies and diverse contributions and benefits in pensions and health even though entitlement conditions are standardized.

The tardy appearance of social security in Costa Rica (a transition country but placed in the top group), saved it from the initial acute stratification that occurred in the pioneer countries. As a result, the present system is the second most unified and standardized of the six case studies with a high degree of integration in the health sector. Because Costa Rica does not have an armed force, it was freed from the difficult task of incorporating this group into the general system. But various independent pension subsystems cover influential groups in the public sector (for example, the judicial branch, Congress, and the treasury) that resist unification.

Within the middle group, Peru and Mexico have relatively unified subsystems, Peru's being probably more unified than that of Mexico. Peru's original system was not as stratified as those of the three pioneer countries, but it did appear early and generated enough multiplicity and diversity to require reform. The reform, facilitated by the concentration of power under the military government, was able to establish a unified and standardized general system. But there are still various independent subsystems (for the armed forces, for civil servants hired prior to the establishment of the general system, and for two groups of blue-collar workers) as well as special regulations within the general system. In addition, the health sector has not reached the level of integration that was achieved in Cuba and Costa Rica.

Like the Costa Rican system, Mexico's appeared late and, in addition to the general system, created independent subsystems—not only in pensions but also in health and other programs—for the powerful groups in the public sector (for example, the federal government, the armed forces, and petroleum industry). The majority of these still exist. Within the general system there are also special regulations for insured groups, and the health sector shows much less integration than in Cuba and Costa Rica.

Universality of Coverage

The four countries in the top group have attained superior levels of population coverage. In 1981 the percentage of coverage in Cuba was the highest, at least in legal terms: 100 percent of the total population (in health) and 93 percent of the EAP (in pensions). This figure included social welfare. Totally or partly excluded from insured monetary benefits were the owners of small farms, self-employed workers, unpaid family workers, and the unemployed, but if these people lacked means, they were eligible for social welfare benefits. Although a direct measurement of possible differences in coverage between provinces in Cuba was not possible, a surrogate method showed that the capital and the most-developed provinces have health services and insured monetary benefits superior to those in the less-developed provinces; the extreme ratio (between the best and the worst province) is 2.5:1.

In 1983 the Uruguayan insurance system statistically covered 70 percent of the total population and 82 percent of the EAP, but if welfare pensions and welfare health care are included, the system approaches universality. Nevertheless, a fall in EAP coverage as a result of the economic crisis was registered in the 1980s. Unpaid family workers and the unemployed lack insurance coverage (as do rural workers, although they do have health coverage), but if these lack means, they are eligible for social welfare. Even though a direct measurement of differences in coverage by department was not possible in Uruguay either, a surrogate method proved that health services and certain monetary benefits in the capital are superior to those in the rest of the country.

In 1980 Chile's insurance system statistically covered 67 percent of the total population and 62 percent of the EAP—although there are no statistics, possibly both percentages were similar in 1982—and if one adds welfare benefits, it approached universality. Since the beginning of the 1970s, there appears to have been a decline in coverage. The majority of the self-employed as well as all unpaid family workers and the unemployed are not covered by the insurance system (although they are covered under welfare programs if they lack means). The highest coverage is registered in the most-developed regions and the lowest in the least-developed ones (with an extreme ratio of 2.3:1). Economic sectors with the best coverage are mining and public utilities, and the sector with the worst coverage is agriculture (with an extreme ratio among sectors of 2.4:1).

The acceleration of insurance coverage expansion in the 1960s and 1970s permitted Costa Rica statistically to cover 77 percent of the total population and 68 percent of the EAP in 1982, thus surpassing the level of Chile. In addition, those without insurance and lacking means were entitled to health care and welfare pensions. The self-employed (who had decided not to affiliate themselves) and unpaid family workers, as well as the unemployed, were not covered by the insurance system (although they were covered under the welfare program if they lacked means). There also appears to be significant evasion among salaried agricultural workers. The capital and the most-developed provinces have higher coverage than the less-developed provinces (with an extreme ratio of 2.2:1), while among economic sectors the best coverage is found in services, public utilities, and industry, and the worst coverage is in agriculture (with an extreme ratio of 2.6:1).

The two countries in the middle group have lower population coverage than the pioneer countries. Mexico statistically covered 60 percent of the total population (including the welfare health program of the COPLAMAR) and 42 percent of the EAP in 1983; there are no welfare pensions in Mexico. The economic crisis caused a slight decline in EAP coverage in 1982–83. Excluded from mandatory coverage are the self-employed, unpaid family workers, domestic servants, unassociated *ejidatarios,* small producers and employers (all of whom can voluntarily be affiliated), and the unemployed. A high number of salaried rural workers, especially seasonal ones, also apparently lack effective coverage. Some of these without insurance coverage can receive welfare health care. The federal district and the most-developed states have much higher coverage than the less-developed states (with an extreme ratio of 20:1). The economic sectors with the best coverage are the federal government, public utilities, and the petroleum industry, while the sector with the worst coverage is agriculture (with an extreme ratio of 17:1).

Peru has the lowest population coverage: in 1983 only 18 percent of the total population and 38 percent of the EAP were statistically covered. In spite of its low level, Peru occupies an intermediate position in Latin America, because the rest of the countries of the region (with a couple of exceptions) have lower coverage. As in almost all the other cases, the self-employed and unpaid family workers as well as the unemployed are not covered. In addition, a very low number of Peru's dependent family members are insured (a fact that explains the extremely low coverage of the total population). Because of the high percentage of noninsured, the welfare health services are clearly inadequate, and there are no welfare pensions. Coverage in the capital and the most developed departments is far greater than that in the least-developed departments (with an extreme ratio of 11:1).

Financial Equilibrium

In the top group the three pioneer countries have the highest deficits because of virtually universal coverage, the oldest pension programs, the most generous benefit packages, and the highest costs. These three countries (and Costa Rica) appear to support a social security burden that exceeds their economic capacity. Uruguay, Chile (in the old system), and Cuba use pure assessment in the pension program, while the rest use partial capitalization methods.

Uruguay, the second country to introduce a pension program, heads the list with a deficit of 81 percent of revenues in 1982, although at least part of this deficit was covered by VAT revenues, which compensated for the reduction in the wage contribution (still, the latter continued to be one of the highest in the region). The cost of Uruguayan social security reached 14.5 percent of GDP in 1965, and even though it fell to 13 percent in 1982, it was the highest in the region. This country was probably the pioneer in changing to the pure assessment method in the pension program.

The Chilean system was the first to introduce a broad pension program in the region, but that program generated a surplus until 1980. Still, the role of state contributions in the system's equilibrium is a point of debate, and in any event, the total percentage wage contribution was the highest in Latin America. The scarce data available on the old system after 1980, although not strictly comparable with previous data, indicate that in 1983 there was a deficit equivalent to 297 percent of revenues. On the other hand, the new system accumulated a surplus similar to the amount of the deficit in the old system. The cost of the total system in 1980 (prior to the introduction of the new system) was 11 percent of GDP, the highest in the region after that of Uruguay. The old pension program changed to the pure assessment method, while the new pension program uses full capitalization.

The system of the third pioneer country, Cuba, yielded a total deficit equivalent to 33 percent of revenues in 1982. This deficit was covered through transfers from the state budget. Wage contributions, paid entirely by employers, are too low to finance the benefits. The cost of the system reached its zenith in 1971 at 12 percent of GDP but declined to 9 percent in 1980, so it was still the third highest in the six countries. Since the 1960s a sort of pure assessment method has been used.

The systems of Costa Rica, Mexico, and Peru are more recent and have generated cash surpluses. Nevertheless, the Costa Rican system (at the bottom of the top group) has almost universal coverage and a generous benefit package. These factors and the state's failure to fulfill its financial obligations have resulted in a surplus that, as a percentage of revenues, has been the smallest in the three countries since the mid-1970s (0.8 percent in 1982) in spite of a fairly high contribution percentage. The cost of the system has risen gradually, reaching 9 percent of GDP in 1980, similar to the figure for Cuba. The pension program in the general system uses, at least de facto, the scaled-premium method.

The Peruvian system, older than those in Costa Rica and Mexico, generated a surplus, albeit a decreasing one, equivalent to 4 percent of revenues in 1982. Nevertheless, substantial deficits in 1983 and 1984 were expected because of the economic crisis. It must also be taken into account, however, that if the state had fulfilled its financial obligations, past surpluses would have been greater and the present imbalance could possible have been avoided. The cost of the system has been stagnant at somewhat more than 3 percent of GDP since the middle of the 1970s, a percentage similar to the average for the region and one that appears adequate for the economic capacity of the country (the wage contribution percentage is also average). The pension program of the general system is based on the scaled-premium method, but consideration is being given to replacing it with assessment of constituent capital.

Finally, Mexico combines a newer system, with somewhat more than half of the population covered, and a benefit package that is slightly above the average. Also, the state has fulfilled all of its financial obligations. Thus, although the wage contribution percentage is relatively low, the system has generated the largest surplus of the six countries, equivalent to 17 percent of the revenues in 1981. Nevertheless, because of the economic crisis, the surplus appeared to have been significantly reduced in 1982–83. The pension program of the general system has, since 1973, used the scaled-premium method but may switch in the near future.

The financial equilibrium of the last three countries may have been affected by the economic crisis (and the state debt to social security in Costa Rica and Peru), but this appears to be a circumstantial problem rather than the chronic problem suffered by the pioneer countries.

Completeness, Adequacy, and Equality of Benefits

Among the countries of the top group, Uruguay and Chile cover all social risks (including unemployment and family allowance programs). The other four countries have essentially three basic programs (pensions, health-maternity, and occupational risks). In terms of the generosity of the benefit package and entitlement conditions, Uruguay, Chile (at least in the old system), Cuba, and Costa Rica occupy similar positions, at the head of the region, while Mexico's system is slightly above the regional average and the Peruvian system is average.

In 1981 the four countries of the top group exhibited the highest health services and levels. Cuba and Costa Rica occupied very similar positions in terms of the principal indicators: an infant mortality ratio of 18 per 1,000 inhabitants and life expectancies of seventy-three and seventy-two years, respectively, the best in Latin America. Costa Rica has made a more significant effort than Cuba, as its levels in 1960 were lower; thus the closing of the gap has been greater. Chile and Uruguay occupy second place with similar positions: infant mortality ratios of 27 and 31 per 1,000, respectively, and life expectancy of sixty-eight and seventy years. Nevertheless, Chile has made the greatest effort to close the gap of any country among the six with a reduction of 93 percentage points in 1960–81 as compared with 51 in Costa Rica, 19 in Uruguay, and 18 in Cuba. (It must be recalled that, when infant mortality ratios become very low, it becomes increasing difficult to reduce them further.) Mexico stands in third place with an infant mortality ratio of 39 per 1,000 and a life expectancy of sixty-four years; in terms of closing the breach in infant mortality, Mexico registers a reduction of 36 percent. Peru comes last, with an infant mortality ratio of 100 and a life expectancy of fifty-eight years, but in closing the gap in infant mortality (42 percentage points) Peru is surpassed only by Chile and Costa Rica.

In terms of cost-of-living adjustments in pensions, the performance of the pioneer countries has been less good. If we take 1970 as a base year, the real value of the average pension in 1981 was equivalent to 198 in Costa Rica, 141 in Mexico, 90 in Uruguay, 82 in Chile (1980), 64 in Peru, and 61 in Cuba. This ranking, however, does not measure the purchasing power of the pensions; a more profound investigation of this subject is needed.

In all of the countries, the availability of health services among geographic areas parallels the degree of population coverage: the more developed, the better the coverage and services, and vice versa. The disparities in the number of physicians per inhabitant are always sharper than those for hospital beds per inhabitant. It is difficult to compare the extreme differences in these services among the six countries because of the number and size of the geographic areas involved and because of differences in the scope of the figures. Nevertheless, this book suggests that the smallest disparities exist in Chile and Cuba (although Cuba's lowest and highest health levels are higher than those in Chile) and the greatest disparities are found in Peru. The comparison among countries in terms of disparities in pensions is even more fraught with complexity, yet in general the disparities are greater in the stratified systems than in the standardized or relatively standardized ones. For example, the extreme ratio between the highest and lowest average pensions received by groups of insured is 8:1 in Chile (old system) and 6:1 in Uruguay but 4:1 in Costa Rica.

Impact on Development

A simple correlation between the percentages of total population coverage and the ratios of infant mortality in the six countries give a coefficient of − .9313. A similar exercise between total population coverage and life expectancy resulted in an even higher coefficient: .9691. Social security thus appears to have had a positive impact on health standards in all countries. Nevertheless, variables other than social security could have been determinants of health standards, such as house access to sewerage and potable water or nutritional levels. These two variables, as well as social security coverage, tend to relate to economic development, and further research on the subject is needed to identify the most important independent variable.

The impact on development is the most difficult question to evaluate because of the absence of studies in almost all of the countries. In terms of savings, the hypothesis appears to be confirmed that the greater the development of the social security system, the lower the generation of saving and investment and vice versa. Thus in Uruguay, Chile (under the old system), and Cuba, there is apparently a neutral or negative impact on savings, whereas in Costa Rica, Mexico, and Peru (as well as under the new system in Chile), the effect is apparently positive. But the sole existing study concerns Chile; hence I am making only an educated guess.

In terms of employment, the elimination of the employer contribution in Chile and its reduction and substitution by the VAT in Uruguay should have had a positive impact, but the existing studies were made very soon after this reform was introduced and thus do not adequately evaluate its effect. As there are no studies on the other countries, it is impossible to reach any conclusions concerning this issue.

Studies of the impact of social security on the distribution of income have been made only in Chile and Costa Rica. In the former case, the evidence is contradictory. The majority of observers conclude that the effect has been regressive, but the last two studies registered a slight progressive impact under the old system and a more marked, progressive impact under the old health program. Two studies on Costa Rica agree that the net effect of the system has been slightly progressive. The absence of studies on the other countries impedes any evaluation of them.

SUMMARY OF THE KEY PROBLEMS CONFRONTED BY THE COUNTRIES

Top Group

Within the top group, it is necessary to distinguish between the pioneer countries (Uruguay, Chile, and Cuba) and Costa Rica, the country in transition between the two groups.

The pioneer countries.   The principal problem of the pioneer countries is not to expand coverage, as universality has already practically been reached, but an effort must be made to avoid any decline in coverage. During the economic crisis a fall in coverage did occur in Chile and Uruguay. The health levels and services of the pioneer countries are among the highest in the region and should not be a matter of immediate preoccupation.

The key problems that these countries confront are the financial imbalance and the extremely high costs of social security, which appear to surpass the countries' economic capacity. The highest percentage of social security expenditures is in pensions: 83 percent in Uruguay, 53 percent in Chile, and 44 percent in Cuba. The second highest percentage is in health: 42 percent in Cuba, 22 percent in Chile, and 5 percent in Uruguay (the percentage for Uruguay would be much greater if all health expenditures were taken into account).

The pioneer countries have the highest quotients of demographic burden: Uruguay's (0.822 in 1983) is almost twice that for Chile (0.458 in 1980), four times that of Cuba (0.211 in 1981), and about ten times greater than those for the other three countries. As the pioneer countries have already left the demographic transition stage, their population growth rate has slowly declined. This drop, combined with the process of universalization, has also resulted in a decline in the rate of the growth of the active insured. The active insured's growth rate has declined faster than the population growth rate, and the two are now about equal. In Uruguay this phenomenon occurred at the end of the 1960s, in Chile at the beginning of the 1970s, and in Cuba at the end of the 1970s. The economic crisis caused an increase in unemployment and growth in the number of self-employed and unpaid family workers, which in turn provoked negative rates in the growth of active insured in Chile and Uruguay (in the latter the negative rates began at the end of the 1960s but reflected the elimination of duplication in coverage). The above-mentioned factors, combined with the extreme age of the pension program, the relatively low retirement age, and high life expectancy, are responsible for the high quotients of demographic burden. None of the three countries has completely adjusted the value of pensions to inflation, but the partial adjustment (in 1981 the real value of pensions fluctuated at between 63 percent and 82 percent of the 1970 value) has constituted a very heavy burden because of the high percentage of social security expenditures that goes to the pension program.

The pioneer countries have the lowest figures for demographic dependency (from 60 percent to 63 percent): the productive age group is the largest population group, and as this group has a relatively low health risk, health expenditures should also be low. Yet, on the other hand, the pathological profile of the pioneer countries is similar to that for the developed countries—that is, the principal causes of death are cardiovascular and degenerative diseases, which are difficult to eradicate and expensive to treat. Also, the emphasis is on curative and capital-intensive medicine; health-maternity benefits are the region's most generous; and health expenditures are relatively high and, in Cuba, practically equal pension expenditures.

The systems of the three countries (except for Chile's new system) suffer from large deficits that, if they are not resolved, will further erode the real value of pensions and, in the long run, will negatively affect the high health levels. The present economic recession has not caused the social security crisis but has aggravated previous imbalances. Most reforms introduced in the pioneer countries are positive, but more drastic measures are needed to reestablish equilibrium.

The transition country. Costa Rica, as the country in transition from the intermediate group to the top group, at least temporarily combines positive aspects of both groups: coverage is almost universal, health levels are very high, pensions have been adjusted above the level of inflation, and all these results have so far been achieved without a chronic financial imbalance. But the cost of the system is very high and appears to exceed the economic capacity of the country. Fundamentally, this cost results from the health program's expenditures (75 percent of social security expenditures), which have been kept in equilibrium through transfers from the pension program. As a consequence, the pension program has been gradually decapitalized.

Costa Rica is leaving the stage of demographic transition, but its mortality rate has declined faster than its fertility rate. Thus the population growth rate is still high, though it is declining. The figure for demographic dependency (23 percent) is the fifth lowest in Latin America and puts Costa Rica just behind the pioneer countries. Costa Rica echoes the syndrome of the pioneer countries: it shows a pathological profile similar to that in the developed countries, with emphasis on curative and capital-intensive medicine and excessively generous benefits. But in Costa Rica the bulk of social security expenditures are devoted to the health program; hence the problem is magnified.

The rapid expansion of coverage in the pension program during the past two decades resulted in a very high ratio between the growth rates of the active insured and the EAP (15:1 in 1965–70), but as the population rate decreased and the system neared universal coverage, an abrupt fall in the active/EAP ratio occurred (it was 1.4:1 in 1975–80). Later the ratio became negative as a result of the economic crisis. Yet the general pension program in Costa Rica is relatively recent (although retirement conditions are very liberal), and the average age of the population is very young, so that the quotient of demographic burden is very low. Unlike the pioneer countries, the real value of pensions almost doubled in Costa Rica in 1970–81, but as the percentage of social security expenditures devoted to the pension program is very low, this readjustment presents a less heavy burden. The crucial problem that confronts the pension program is its decapitalization through transfers to the health-maternity program. Even though some steps have been taken to reestablish equilibrium, the losses have been large.

The economic crisis and state debts have created a difficult but probably temporary financial situation; it is hoped that economic recuperation and negotiation of the state debt will resolve the problem. But the present model, if it is retained, will eventually give Costa Rica the chronic disequilibrium typical of the pioneer countries. Therefore, Costa Rica should exploit the current respite to undertake the needed reform of the system.

Intermediate Group

The fundamental problems of the two countries in the middle group are how to obtain universality (in spite of structural obstacles), how to improve health levels, and how to maintain the real value of pensions without provoking a future financial imbalance. As in Costa Rica, the bulk of social security expenditures in Mexico and Peru (65 percent and 63 percent) go to the health program. This program has been kept afloat with resources from the pension fund, which has been gradually decapitalized in both countries. The cost of social security in Peru appears appropriate in relation to the country's economic capacity, but the expansion of coverage would elevate the burden significantly. Mexico has the reverse situation; its burden is apparently below its economic capacity, and population coverage is three times that of Peru. Thus Mexico has greater space and more time than Peru to cope with its problems.

Both countries are in demographic transition (Mexico has been for some time and Peru is just beginning). As a result, their population growth rates are very high, although in Mexico growth has declined since the mid-1970s. Mexico's figure for demographic dependency (93 percent) is the fourth highest in Latin America and the highest for the six case studies, whereas the figure for Peru (83 percent) approaches the regional average. Thus the percentage of the population under fourteen years of age is very high in both countries (42 percent in Peru and 45 percent in Mexico), while the population at productive age in both countries, expressed as a percentage, is the smallest. Although the pathological profile of both nations is changing, the majority of deaths are still caused by perinatal, intestinal, and respiratory diseases. The emphasis is nevertheless on curative medicine and, especially in Peru, on care for the population with the lowest health risk. In Mexico the ratio of health expenditures for curative medicine versus preventive medicine is 9:1, and in Peru, social security covers only dependent children under one year of age. This explains the relatively high infant mortality rates, especially in Peru. It appears financially impossible to reach universal coverage with this model.

In Mexico the high population growth rate and the acceleration in the expansion of coverage during the last two decades resulted in a high ratio between active/EAP rates (3.5:1 in 1960–65). Although this ratio later declined (it was 2.1:1 in 1965–80), it was still the highest of the six countries. But in 1981–83 the economic crisis resulted in stagnant or negative rates in the growth of active insured. In Peru, coverage was paralyzed in the 1970s; hence the ratio of active/EAP rates decreased from 3:1 in 1960–65 to 1.8:1 in 1980 and later to 1.3:1 in 1982. The sharpest fall in the ratio was caused by the economic crisis, but earlier the growth rate of active insured rose almost twice as fast as population growth. Because the pension program in Peru is the oldest and has more liberal retirement conditions than that in Mexico, the quotient of demographic burden of the former (0.107) is higher than that for the latter (0.089). In any case, both quotients are very low in comparison with those of the pioneer countries. Pensions have seen far more adjustment in Mexico than in Peru (198 versus 64 in 1981, if we use 1970 as base), but in Mexico the percentage of social security expenditures dedicated to pensions (21 percent) is the lowest of any for the six countries, and thus the burden of the adjustment is less than in the pioneer countries. As in Costa Rica, the crucial problem for the pension programs of both countries is their decapitalization by the health-maternity program.

The economic crisis, combined with the state debt in Peru and the freezing of the pension program's contribution percentage in Mexico, has created financial difficulties that could be resolved (at least temporarily) with economic recovery and the correction of the above mentioned problems. But in the long run, both countries must change the present model if the indicated objectives are to be achieved and if the financial imbalance that has occurred in the pioneer countries is to be avoided.

GENERAL STRATEGY AND SPECIFIC POLICIES

Three different strategies could be adopted to address the problems just described. The first strategy expounds the notion that social security reflects society and thus cannot be asked to be better than the society that it serves. According to this strategy, in the sixty years of social security's existence in Latin America, significant progress has been achieved in terms of what is possible in each of the countries. Again, according to this argument, social security must evolve in a gradual manner, as society evolves; its progress cannot be forced.

The second strategy coincides with the first inasmuch as it assumes that social security is determined by the socioeconomic structure of the country. Rather than accepting the correspondence between the two, however, it proposes structural change in order to transform social security. The scope and degree of intensity of this change can vary. In its most radical version, a different economic system is needed. Other versions propose a modification of production, consumption, and distribution patterns and the design of an integrated development policy to promote full employment and the satisfaction of basic needs, including social security.

The first strategy could lead either to prolonged stagnation or to very slow development of social security, especially in the countries in the bottom group. The second strategy could also postpone the solution of the problem until there were structural changes of diverse magnitude. A third proposed strategy combines aspects of the other two: to create incentives in the short and medium term to promote the maximum possible change of the present social insurance model, taking into account the realities and limitations of each country; and, in the long run, to pursue the ideal of social security.[1] Those countries with social security that has ceased to be economically viable have probably paid a price in economic growth and have compromised the financial stability of the social security system and have created pernicious mechanisms by which benefits are adjusted to the economic reality. One of the pioneer scholars in the study and reform of Latin American social security has recently stated that the excesses that have pushed social security beyond reasonable limits in some countries have provoked a swing in the pendulum in the direction of privatization; hence a search for an intermediate point between the two extremes is necessary.[2] Thus the advance of social security should be planned carefully, taking into account the economic capacity of the country and other basic, more pressing needs (for example, employment, sanitation, and nutrition).

My analysis of the six cases has demonstrated that—contrary to the gradualist strategy—it is possible to by-pass some structural obstacles to social security and to advance on various fronts. For example, the barrier to expansion in the old social insurance model has been eroded by innovative measures such as the programs that protect indigents and low-income groups in Uruguay, Chile, and Costa Rica; the IMSS-COPLAMAR program in Mexico; and the comprehensive national health system in Cuba.

The following recommendations reflect the ideal, long-run principles of social security: unity, standardization, universality, completeness, adequacy, solidarity, and so forth. When for economic or political reasons such an ideal is not feasible, I suggest other policies for the short and medium term. The notion of compromise is implicit, and there is usually a need to sacrifice some of the above-stated principles for the sake of others with higher priority.

Organization

Planning.   In view of the need to coordinate social security and economic growth, as well as existing conflicts between national objectives, and taking into account the high cost of social security in various Latin American countries, surprisingly few have included social security in their national plans. One of the reasons cited is that planners are interested only in the reserves of social security and then only as potential for investment, and in many countries these reserves are small or nonexistent. Another explanation is that only part of social security revenues comes directly from the public resources that planners must assign.[3]

But the impact of social security goes beyond fiscal payments and investment potential, since—as we have seen—it affects the costs of the factors of production, employment, distribution, prices, inflation, and the competitiveness of exports. Planners are in the best position to coordinate the policies of social security, health, sanitation, nutrition, employment, distribution, and so forth. The implementation of goals such as expanding coverage, unifying the system, integrating health services, improving the distribution of services and benefits, and finding alternative sources of financing requires a national effort, setting priorities, and implementing technical decisions that can succeed only through careful planning.

Unity and standardization of the system.   Unifying and standardizing the social security system should simplify affiliation, individual accounts, collection of contributions, and the processing of benefits. It should also eliminate duplication in coverage and the lack of continuity among subsystems, thereby permitting the accumulation of work time in occupations covered by different subsystems. Finally, it should cut administrative costs, reduce inequality, and facilitate transfers among groups (solidarity) and the progressive redistribution of income.[4]

Standardizing the social security system does not always mean that all insured contribute the same sum and receive the same monetary benefits. Instead it means that legislation prescribes equal treatment for all insured (with exceptions justified by the type of work) in terms of: contribution percentage (if this financing method is maintained), type of benefits available, entitlement conditions, and method of computing benefits. Standardization, combined with the expansion of coverage, should necessitate the elimination of certain benefits and the reduction of excessively generous conditions enjoyed by the most privileged groups (for example, seniority pensions, retirement at a young age, housing loans, and so forth). In other words, universalization of coverage plus massification of privilege is not financially viable. The decrease in benefit levels should reflect the available resources and economic capacity of the country, and an effort should be made to avoid reducing benefit levels for the lowest population group. Moving from a stratified system to a standardized one poses the problem of how to deal with acquired rights; this difficulty could be resolved by guaranteeing these rights to those who already enjoy them (for example, to retired persons) or who have begun the process of retirement or will retire within a short transition period. But it is not possible to guarantee the entitlement rights of the previous systems to all of the insured, as doing so would destroy the objective of the reform, prolong the present situation of inequality, and mortgage the future of the standardized system.[5]

In the last twenty years there has been significant progress in this respect, with the total or partial unification of the social security systems of Cuba, Chile, Peru, and Uruguay (as well as those of Argentina and Brazil). In Mexico, several independent subsystems have been incorporated into the general system. In addition, health services have been integrated or coordinated in some countries. But the analysis of the six case studies showed that all of them maintain independent subsystems, special regulations within the general system, and significant inequalities.

Even in Cuba, the most unified and standardized system of the six, the armed forces pension subsystem and the special regulations for small private farms and self-employed workers should be unified and standardized. In Costa Rica the independent pension subsystems should be integrated into the general system and standardized. In Peru it would be advisable to integrate the independent subsystems of the armed forces, civil servants, and blue-collar groups into the general system. Mexico should integrate federal civil servants, the armed forces, and the petroleum subsystems into the general system as well as standardize both these subsystems and the diverse special regulations within the general system. Uruguay should complete the unification and standardization of the three groups under the general system and integrate the independent pension subsystems into it. Finally, Chile should complete the unification and standardization process in the old pension system.

Integration/coordination of health services.   Equally important is the integration, or at least coordination, of health services of the social security institutions, the health ministry, and other administrative agencies. In the case studies, examples of successful integration have been seen in the Cuban Ministry of Health or under the Social Security Institute of Costa Rica. The fundamental question is not which organization should be responsible for the integration but how the integration is to be achieved. Chile has integrated and coordinated the public sector with the private sector, taking the free choice approach, while in Mexico the first step has been the establishment of a national health system coordinated by the Ministry of Health. In Peru and Uruguay, integration or greater coordination among the diverse administrative agencies is badly needed.

Coverage

Ways of reaching universal coverage.   The most important priority for social security should be to expand coverage to the entire population, subject to a ranking of priorities in terms of risks so as to protect benefit levels. This step should precede the addition of new programs and benefits to the sector already covered. Coverage of the rural sector and the less developed regions, as well as self-employed and unpaid family workers, domestic servants, the unemployed and other low-income groups, would thus have to be achieved. It is impossible to attain universal coverage with the same benefit package, entitlement conditions, and level and quality of health services now enjoyed by the privileged groups, as the cost would be prohibitive. There are two ways of coping with this problem.

The first option would ideally combine universalization with standardization. To achieve both goals it would be necessary to eliminate the most generous benefits, tighten entitlement conditions, suppress the less essential programs (for example, loans, subsidized housing, and "social benefits"), and extend the reduced system of benefits to the whole population. But the cost of even this reduced benefit package might possibly be so high as to exceed the economic capacity of the country. In this case the establishment of basic benefits, sufficient to cover the minimum necessities and equal for the entire population, could be considered.

If existing economic/political obstacles make the first alternative impractical, a second one could give priority to universalization rather than standardization. A dual system could be instituted that would maintain the benefits to the sectors already covered and would grant coverage for limited risks (for example, only health care) at a lower level to the sector targeted for incorporation. This course of action is pursued by the countries with social solidarity or welfare programs that cover part of the rural sector (for example, in Mexico) or cover indigents or low-income groups who are not entitled to social insurance benefits (for example, those in Costa Rica, Cuba, Chile, and Uruguay). In some of these countries, however, the nonmonetary health benefits are uniform and only welfare pensions are at a lower level.

It should be noted that in market economies the operation of a universal social security system (with either standardized or dual benefits) does not preclude the existence of complementary insurance systems (privately or publicly operated) that would offer additional benefits financed either exclusively by both the insured of by the insured and the employer.

Registry, identification, and statistics.   With few exceptions, the countries studied have a deficient system for registry, identification, and statistics. As a result there is underestimation and duplication of coverage, so that it is difficult to estimate the sectors that do and do not have coverage, and evasion is easier than it would otherwise be. Costa Rica was planning to introduce a unique national identification system in 1983, and similar efforts were under way in Chile and Uruguay. Coverage statistics show ample room for improvement. Costa Rica reports coverage of the general system but not of the pension subsystems. Cuba publishes no coverage statistics at all. Chile has not published statistics of the old system since 1980, and the statistics for the new system were frozen in 1983, allegedly because of the need to eliminate overestimation. Mexico has very good series for IMSS and ISSSTE but not for the other two subsystems. Peru does not publish coverage statistics and has only estimates. And in Uruguay there are no precise statistics on the number of active insured. All of these countries must try to improve their performance in this important respect.

Financing

Measures to increase revenues.   It is extremely difficult to finance the expansion of coverage to the self-employed and unpaid family workers as well as to the rural sector by means of the wage contribution. However, if it were decided to continue with this method of financing, an effort should be made, at least, to eliminate wage contribution ceilings (in Mexico and Peru), apply the contribution percentage to all remuneration for labor, establish a progressive contribution rate on wages, and combine the wage contribution with other sources of financing. As I have already mentioned, in Brazil coverage was expanded to the rural sector through taxes on the payroll of urban enterprises and on agricultural production. Direct state transfers have been used in all six case studies (except in Peru), and in Mexico state transfers have been combined with contributions in the form of work in the community.

Although the social security burden is already very heavy in the majority of the countries, wage contributions can still be increased. In Mexico the contribution to the pension program has not increased since the program's creation, a fact that may have contributed to the financial imbalance in that program. In Cuba the total wage contribution is very low, and the insured do not contribute at all. In the majority of the countries, the contribution of the insured in the subsystems is usually insufficient to finance their excessively generous benefits. The insured's contribution should therefore be increased, or benefits should be proportionally reduced. A better system for registry, identification, and coverage statistics, combined with more efficient inspection, stricter penalties (considerably above the rate of inflation), and prosecution of violators would considerably reduce evasion and payment delays. Payment agreements with delinquent insured persons must be monitored for compliance, and those who do not fulfill the agreed-upon obligations must be prosecuted.

Systems that use capitalization methods of financing should avoid transferring resources from the pension to the health-maternity program, as well as loan and housing programs to the insured, and their reserves should be invested so as to generate yields that are at least equal to those in the financial market.

State contributions should be set at a reasonable level and should be paid without delay. The state debt of Costa Rica and Peru has been a principal cause of the financial imbalance of social security, and even though the state is paying off its debts, the losses from inflation and lost capital yields can never be recovered.

Alternative sources of financing.   Within the ideal of social security and to facilitate universality, to avoid the negative effect on employment, and to promote the progressive effect on distribution, the wage contribution should be replaced by a neutral or progressive type of tax. The possibilities include a progressive income tax (exempting the lowest income group) or a VAT (exempting articles of primary necessity). Such a change in financing would eliminate all pretense that entitlement reflects the contribution made by the insured and would facilitate the integration of social insurance and social welfare programs.

Another possible source of revenues could be a minimum fee for the use of physicians' services and medicines, exempting the lowest income group. This measure would also discourage unnecessary or excessive use of these services. It might also be possible to establish varied levels of care (above a minimum level that would be free) and to fix a contribution scale for the insured.

Equilibrium and financing method.   The three pioneer countries are based on a pure assessment method (an exception is Chile under the new system), and all of them run deficits. Costa Rica, Mexico, and Peru use the scaled-premium method in their pension programs, but the latter two will probably make modifications in the near future. The change in capitalization methods creates an illusion of equilibrium but in reality only temporarily postpones the day of judgment. If the countries could balance their systems financially, much less actuarially, when they were newly created and in the stage of accumulation of reserves, they will hardly be able to do so when their systems mature. In the final analysis, equilibrium must be established by increasing revenues or reducing benefits and/or making entitlement conditions more rigorous. The countries in the intermediate and bottom groups have more room than those in the top group to achieve equilibrium; the burden in the pioneer countries is so heavy already that equilibrium will have to be accomplished mainly through reductions in expenditures.

Benefits

Risk priorities. Health-maternity should be the first risk covered, and nonmonetary benefits should be equal for the whole population, with emphasis on preventive medicine and primary health care. When existing obstacles block this strategy, the alternatives explained in the section entitled "Coverage" above may be followed. A second priority could be the pension program; ideally a minimum, adequate, and equal benefit would be established. Another option could be to establish a basic minimum and maximum (the latter not at a very high level). The amount of the pension could then be fixed between the two, according to previous income levels. In both cases pensions should be adjusted to the cost of living. The occupational risk program should be merged with the social security system. Special treatment should be eliminated, and cases should be cared for through the health-maternity and pension programs. Nevertheless, in countries without universal coverage, these programs would have to be kept separate, as the occupational risk program has greater coverage than the other two. Family allowances could be fixed according to a minimum or existing wage and would ideally be equal, limited to low-income groups, and preferably given in kind, using supplies of milk and other basic nutrients. Unemployment compensation programs make little sense in Latin America, as unemployment is usually a chronic phenomenon, more structural or seasonal than cyclical. Furthermore, open unemployment is high, there is a considerable proportion of self-employment, and underemployment tends to be more important than open unemployment. The cost of unemployment compensation at the national level would be prohibitive, and it would be preferable to use the resources in question to promote employment or to provide health care and family allowances for the unemployed and their families, at least for a period following dismissal. Finally, nonessential programs such as personal loans, subsidized housing, stores with subsidized prices, and cultural and sport services should be eliminated.

Benefit level. As indicated above, if the alternative of a universal basis, adequate, and equal benefit is pursued, this basis benefit could be supplemented with additional benefits. It should be noted that this course of action would not substitute for the general system but instead would complement it, being financed totally or partly by the user. In some of the countries studied, the social security system itself envisions this type of benefit, which can also be organized by the private sector. This strategy would satisfy the basic needs, especially for the low-income group, and—as market economies exist in practically all countries of the region—would permit members of the middle-income group to receive additional benefits in accordance with their income. As an incentive, these contributions might be exempted from income tax until retirement, when the insured's income is generally lower than when s/he was active. The slight regressive effect of this exemption on income distribution could be balanced by the healthy effect it would have on savings, inflation, and the capital market.

It must be recalled that under the current financing structure in almost all countries, the insured legally contributes one-third or less of the cost of benefits. Therefore, no party can claim—at least from a juridical point of view— a right to benefits that are often excessively generous. The basic benefit would correspond more to the insured's contribution, and this feature would work to strengthen the principle of solidarity among different income groups, accentuating the progressive impact of the system.

Changing the health model.   A common characteristic of the six case studies is the overwhelming allocation of resources to curative, capital-intensive medicine rather than to preventive medicine, with a ratio that fluctuates from 4:1 in Costa Rica to 15:1 in Chile. (Although there are no figures for Cuba, it is probable that its ratio is similar to or lower than that for Costa Rica.) No only is this health care model very costly, but it is also inefficient, especially in the countries where there has been no change in the pathological profile, and hence a large percentage of the deaths are caused by diseases than can be largely prevented through immunization or can be controlled through measures relating to basic sanitation, nutrition, and health education.

To reduce social security expenditures, facilitate universalization and financial equilibrium, and improve the health levels of the population, the present health model should be replaced by one based on prevention and primary health care, with preference going to the mother-infant and high health risk groups and to immunization, sanitation, nutrition, and health education. More use should be made of paramedical and auxiliary personnel rather than medical personnel, and mobile health care units and clinics should be emphasized over hospitals (although the hospital base necessary for a referral system should be established).

Growing costs per hospital bed must be reduced through maximizing the use of existing facilities and reducing the average stay. In the six countries, the national average for hospital utilization ranges from 69 percent in Uruguay to 81 percent in Cuba (with significant differences among specialties and regions), and the average hospital stay ranged from five days in Mexico (IMSS) to twenty-one days in Uruguay. In some countries (for example, Costa Rica and Cuba), there would be no need for new investments in hospitals for a long period if existing capacity were more fully used.

Finally, medicines take a large share of the health cost. Several of the countries have introduced a list of basic medicines, but some still have quite a long list. I have already mentioned the possibility of charging a minimum fee to reduce overmedication and medicine expenditures. Also, several of the countries have shown some progress in developing a domestic pharmaceutical industry; this effort should be increased and further regional integration promoted.

Restricting the generosity of pensions. The majority of the six countries have seniority pensions, if not in the general system, at least in the subsystems, which sometimes permit retirement at age forty-five. This type of pension should be eliminated in all cases. Furthermore, the retirement age for old age pensions is usually low, especially in relation to life expectancy, and is often lower for women than for men, even though women have a higher life expectancy. For example, it is fifty-seven years for both sexes in Costa Rica; fifty-five years (women) and sixty years (men) in Cuba, Peru, and Uruguay; and sixty years (women) and sixty-five years (men) in Chile. On the other hand, Mexico, which has a lower life expectancy than the pioneer countries, fixes its retirement age at sixty-five years for both sexes. The retirement age for men and women should be the same. Although differences in life expectancy among countries should be taken into account, in general terms the minimum age should be sixty years for both sexes and sixty-five in the most-developed countries. I have already shown that the result would be a large saving for the pension program.

Reduction of administrative expenditures. The percentage of administrative expenditures over total expenditure in the system is very high, fluctuating from 7 percent in Costa Rica, Chile, and Uruguay to 10 percent in Peru and 18 percent in Mexico, percentages far above those in the developed countries. The majority of administrative expenditures relate to the remuneration of personnel, which is excessive in practically all of the countries. For example, the number of employees per 1,000 insured is 12 in Costa Rica and, per hospital bed, is 7 in Mexico.

Social security personnel generally receive wages and fringe benefits that surpass the average for the insured; in some countries, personnel are also exempted from social security contributions or pay lower contributions. It is necessary to reduce surplus personnel, pay reasonable salaries, and eliminate special benefits for the privileged. Dismissal of personnel is politically, economically, and socially difficult, but it should be taken into account that the cost of unnecessary personnel negatively affects passives, who at times receive insufficient pensions, and that the objective of social security is not to be a source of employment but to attend to the need created by social risks.

Finally, it should be mentioned that community participation can be a way of reducing personnel expenditures and a way of involving the insured so that they feel part of the system. The following cases are examples: the experiences of Mexico with the IMSS-COPLAMAR program; Cuba with community participation in immunization, sanitation, and health education campaigns; and Costa Rica with rural health clinics.

Possible Obstacles to the Reform

The proposed reform, especially if it attains the ideal goals of social security, could achieve universal coverage with financial equilibrium and could exert positive effects on employment, distribution of income, and savings. But implementation of the reform could encounter both economic and political obstacles.

The cost of the reformed system may be an obstacle. The social security systems and economies of Latin America show significant differences, and this book proposed a varied menu of options, so that it would be difficult to offer any concrete calculations, even rough, of the cost. Nevertheless, the financial key to the reform is to compensate for the cost of expanded coverage with a reduction in the levels of privilege and expenditures, combined with increased resources through alternative, additional sources of financing. Obviously, this is a generalization, and it is necessary to study the possible means and costs of reform in each country. The least-developed countries are often those with lowest coverage and weakest taxing power. It will therefore be difficult for them to balance universal coverage with reduced expenditures and increased revenues. In these cases, it is important to exercise greater care in assigning risk priority and in deciding how best to expand. It is also important to resist the temptation to create a legally perfect system that in practice offers monetary benefits insufficient to supply even the basic necessities of the lowest income group.

Political obstacles are perhaps as important as economic ones. The reform could meet with opposition from the privileged insured groups, who usually also wield powerful influence in society. On the other side, the sector without coverage is dispersed and unorganized and lacks sufficient education to understand and support the reform. The state has promoted change in all of the countries with social security systems that have seen total or partial reform. It is thus important to inform people regarding the experience of the countries that have reformed their systems and to educate the political leadership on these issues.

The social security bureaucracy in some countries with relatively unified systems (for example, Costa Rica) stands at the vanguard of the expansion process, but in countries with stratified systems the bureaucracy fears reform, as it could be accompanied by a loss of employment and privileges. Employers do not always take a negative attitude toward reform (especially if it will simplify "red tape" without increasing contributions), but some entrepreneurs fear that the loss of privileges enjoyed by their employees will encourage them to recover lost advantages through collective bargaining, so that the burden shifts to the employer.

Last but not least, international social security and health organizations and associations hold a favorable position on reform. The International Labour Office (ILO), the World Health Organization (WHO), Pan American Health Organization (PAHO), the International Social Security Association (ISSA), the Interamerican Permanent Committee on Social Security (CPISS) and the Iberoamerican Organization of Social Security (OISS) have played a fundamental role in promoting the development of social security in Latin America. Recently this effort has met with support from other international and regional organizations such as the World Bank, the Economic Commission for Latin America, the U.S. Agency for International Development, and the Inter-American Development Bank, which have carried out various studies and/or have extended the scope of several missions or technical assistance projects to include social security. The significant impact of social security on development is a convincing reason for these economic agencies to expand their involvement and assistance in this area. It would also be advisable to establish long-term goals for social security, similar to those adopted in the health sector for the year 2000. The experience of several countries such as Costa Rica and Mexico indicates that establishing these goals at a national level is crucial in setting priorities and allocating resources, educating the government and the public, and mobilizing international aid.

A Research Agenda for the Future

This book has drawn attention to gaps in both the statistics and the research on social security. Future work should take several directions.

A study similar to this one could usefully be prepared for other countries in the region. (1) *Argentina,* a pioneer country occupying second place in the top group, has replaced part of its wage contribution with the VAT and is in a political stage that favors reform. (2) *Brazil,* also a pioneer located in the top group, has valuable experience with unifying a highly stratified system and developing an innovative strategy for the expansion of coverage to the rural sector. (3) *Colombia,* in the intermediate group, still has a relatively stratified system with low coverage yet a relatively high cost. (4) *Venezuela,* which in spite of its abundant resources is at the bottom of the intermediate group, has half of its population covered by a system with a relatively low cost. (5) *Guatemala,* with the highest coverage in the bottom group (and greater EAP coverage than some countries in the intermediate group) has a relatively new and low-cost system. (6) *Nicaragua,* a country that integrated the health sector, is expanding coverage rapidly but because of scarce resources could face financial imbalances in the immediate future.

The following are suggested topics for further research: (1) estimating the cost involved in attaining universal coverage in several countries; (2) surveying the real access to social security and health services among geographic regions and income groups; (3) evaluating statistical series of coverage, contrasting them with the results of surveys on real access; (4) studying the economic capacity of a country and its social security burden to determine its potential tolerance; (5) evaluating the feasibility of substituting the VAT for wage contributions, also evaluating its impact on employment and isolating this impact from those produced by other factors; (6) studying administrative efficiency in health services, comparing the public sector (with the ministry of health separate from the social security institute) with the private sector; (7) measuring the impact of preventive and curative medicine on health levels; and (8) evaluating the impact of social security on savings/investment and on the distribution of income.

Appendix Tables

Notes

Index

APPENDIX TABLE A: STANDARDIZED SCORE OF THE ELEVEN VARIABLES AND AVERAGE

	1	2	3	4	5	6	7	8	9	10	11	Unweighted Average of the 11 Variables
Argentina	1.35	1.23	0.98	2.94	1.55	1.72	1.26	0.63	0.99	1.91	1.01	1.42
Bolivia	-0.78	-0.39	-0.79	0.48	-0.52	-0.72	0.43	-0.23	1.05	-0.50	-1.81	-0.34
Brazil	1.35	1.75	1.92	0.59	0.07	1.72	0.70	0.39	0.13	-0.12	0.23	0.79
Chile	1.35	0.87	0.74	0.95	1.85	1.11	1.15	-0.60	1.85	0.61	0.85	1.98
Colombia	-0.07	-0.78	-0.65	-0.11	-0.22	-0.11	-0.68	0.43	-0.67	-0.36	-0.09	-0.30
Costa Rica	-0.07	1.20	0.95	0.71	1.26	1.52	-0.62	0.10	-0.61	-0.31	1.32	0.50
Cuba	1.35	1.87	1.82	-1.29	1.26	-0.82	0.65	1.99	0.31	1.48	1.64	0.93
Dominican Republic	-0.07	-0.91	-0.93	-0.82	-0.81	-0.51	-0.62	-0.06	-0.55	-0.65	-0.40	-0.57
Ecuador	0.64	-0.91	-0.61	0.01	-0.52	-1.12	0.87	-1.38	-0.06	-0.36	-0.40	-0.34
El Salvador	-0.78	-0.97	-1.00	-1.05	-0.81	-0.92	-0.79	-0.84	-0.48	-0.41	-0.09	-0.74
Guatemala	-1.49	-0.72	-0.27	-0.11	-0.81	-0.72	-1.00	-0.02	-0.61	-0.65	-0.71	-0.65
Haiti	-1.49	-1.12	-1.34	-1.05	-1.11	-0.61	-1.23	-0.51	-0.73	-0.36	-1.81	-1.03
Honduras	-0.78	-0.94	-0.96	-0.82	-0.52	-0.92	-1.40	-0.68	-0.85	-0.74	-0.87	-0.86
Mexico	-0.07	0.42	0.05	-0.35	-0.52	-0.31	-0.62	-0.60	-0.48	-0.31	0.23	-0.23
Nicaragua	-0.78	-0.88	-0.75	-0.58	-0.81	-0.21	-0.90	-1.29	-0.48	-0.89	-1.18	-0.80
Panama	-0.07	0.36	0.18	0.01	0.66	0.20	0.10	0.55	-0.24	0.08	1.17	0.27
Paraguay	-0.07	-0.60	-0.93	-0.11	-0.81	0.10	-0.07	-0.51	-0.55	-0.41	1.23	-0.34
Peru	0.64	-0.63	-0.13	0.01	-0.52	-0.61	0.15	-0.39	-0.42	-0.31	-0.71	-0.27
Uruguay	1.35	0.93	1.40	1.42	1.85	1.82	2.58	2.57	3.00	2.98	1.16	1.92
Venezuela	-1.49	0.21	0.32	-0.82	-0.52	-0.61	-0.04	-0.96	-0.61	-0.70	0.54	-0.42

Source: Table 6.

Note: The standardized scores have an average of zero and a standard deviation of 1.

APPENDIX TABLE B
RANKING AND GROUPING OF LATIN AMERICAN COUNTRIES BASED ON AVERAGE OF THE ELEVEN VARIABLES

Group	Average
Top	
1. Uruguay	1.92
2. Argentina	1.42
3. Chile	0.98
4. Cuba	0.93
5. Brazil	0.79
6. Costa Rica	0.50
Middle	
7. Panama	0.27
8. Mexico	−0.23
9. Peru	−0.27
10. Colombia	−0.30
11. Bolivia	−0.34
12. Ecuador	−0.34
13. Paraguay	−0.34
14. Venezuela	−0.42
Bottom	
15. Dominican Republic	−0.57
16. Guatemala	−0.65
17. El Salvador	−0.74
18. Nicaragua	−0.80
19. Honduras	−0.86
20. Haiti	−1.03

Source: Appendix table A.

APPENDIX TABLE C: CORRELATION COEFFICIENTS AMONG THE ELEVEN VARIABLES

	1	2	3	4	5	6	7	8	9	10	11
1	1.00	0.68	0.71	0.57	0.73	0.60	0.77	0.54	0.62	0.71	0.61
2	0.68	1.00	0.96	0.48	0.81	0.70	0.60	0.62	0.50	0.64	0.78
3	0.71	0.96	1.00	0.48	0.79	0.68	0.66	0.66	0.53	0.67	0.77
4	0.57	0.48	0.48	1.00	0.65	0.79	0.66	0.34[a]	0.64	0.59	0.35[a]
5	0.73	0.81	0.79	0.65	1.00	0.74	0.71	0.67	0.73	0.82	0.79
6	0.60	0.70	0.68	0.79	0.74	1.00	0.57	0.48	0.57	0.59	0.57
7	0.77	0.60	0.66	0.66	0.71	0.57	1.00	0.56	0.88	0.81	0.52
8	0.54	0.62	0.66	0.34[a]	0.67	0.48	0.56	1.00	0.56	0.81	0.57
9	0.62	0.50	0.53	0.64	0.73	0.57	0.88	0.56	1.00	0.82	0.35[a]
10	0.71	0.64	0.67	0.59	0.82	0.59	0.81	0.81	0.82	1.00	0.62
11	0.61	0.78	0.77	0.35[a]	0.79	0.57	0.52	0.57	0.35[a]	0.62	1.00

Note: The results are significant with a 95 percent degree of confidence except where specified.

a. Not significant with a 95 percent degree of confidence. N = 20.

Notes

INTRODUCTION

1. For a summary of social security advances in Latin America in the twentieth century, see Giovanni Tamburi, "Social Security in Latin America: Trends and Outlook," in *The Crisis of Social Security and Health Care: Latin American Experiences and Lessons,* ed. Carmelo Mesa-Lago (University of Pittsburgh: Latin American Monograph and Document Series, no. 9, 1985), chap. 2. See also Beryl Frank, *La seguridad social en América Latina* (Washington, D.C.: OEA/CIESS, 1982).

2. On the concepts of social insurance and social security and the latter's principles, see Carmelo Mesa-Lago, *Planificación de la seguridad social* (Madrid: OISS, 1959).

CHAPTER 1
The Evolution of Social Security in Latin America

1. Felix Paukert has attempted to prove that the financial burden of social security results from economic development and that the heavier the burden, the greater the redistributive effect of the system; see "Social Security and Income Redistribution: Comparative Experience," in *The Role of Social Security in Economic Development,* ed. Everett M. Kassalow (Washington, D.C.: GPO, 1968). Dieter K. Zschock, in "Review of Medical Care under Social Insurance in Latin America," Washington, D.C.: USAID, March 1983, argues also that social security expands and becomes less unequal in tandem with economic development and growth in the size of government. Henry Aaron has provided evidence countering this assertion and favoring the thesis that the system's age is the most important explanatory variable in terms of the level of social security expenditures; see "Social Security: International Comparison," in *Studies in the Economics of Income Maintenance,* ed. Otto Eckstein (Washington, D.C.: Brookings Institution, 1967), pp. 13–48.

2. See David Collier and Richard E. Messick, "Prerequisites versus Diffusion: Testing Alternative Explanations of Social Security Adoption," *American Political Science Review* 69 (December 1975): 1299–1315.

266 Notes to Pages 4–18

3. See Carmelo Mesa-Lago, *Social Security in Latin America: Pressure Groups, Stratification, and Inequality* (Pittsburgh, Pa.: University of Pittsburgh Press, 1978), pp. 14–16, 264–91.

4. See James M. Malloy, *The Politics of Social Security in Brazil* (Pittsburgh, Pa.: University of Pittsburgh Press, 1979).

5. For a summary of the debate, see C. Mesa-Lago, "Comparative Research on Social Security in Latin America," *Social Science Research Council ITEMS* 30:2 (June 1976): 18–21.

6. See Silvia Borzutzky, "Politics and Social Security Reform" in Mesa-Lago, ed., *The Crisis of Social Security and Health Care*, chap. 9.

7. ILO/UNDP, "Previsión social del Brasil: Politica social," Geneva, ILO/UNPD, 1981.

8. Mesa-Lago, *Social Security in Latin America*, pp. 265–66.

9. Aldo Isuani, "Social Security and Public Assistance," in Mesa-Lago, ed., *The Crisis of Social Security and Health Care*, chap. 3.

10. See chapters 2, 4, and 5; for Colombia, see Ministerio del Trabajo y Seguridad Social, Instituto de Seguros Sociales, *Informe de actividades, 1981* (Bogota: ISS, 1981). For rural coverage in nine countries in the second half of the 1970s, see Alfredo Mallet, "Social Protection of the Rural Population," *International Social Security Review* 33:3/4 (1980): 366.

11. See chapters 2, 4, 5 and 6; Ernesto Isuani and Carmelo Mesa-Lago, "La seguridad social en Panamá: Avances y problemas," Santiago, ILPES, 1981; and José Rómulo Sánchez, "La sequridad social en Guatemala," *Revista Centroamericana de ciencias de la salud* 6:15 (January–April 1980): 103–14.

12. Gonzalo Arroba, "La financiación de la seguridad social en los países en desarrollo," *Estudios de la seguridad social* 29 (1979): 5–31; and Isuani, "Social Security and Public Assistance."

13. Programa Regional del Empleo para América Latina y el Caribe, *Dinámica del subempleo en América Latina* Estudios e Informes de la CEPAL, no. 10 (Santiago: PREALC, 1981), pp. 35–54; Victor Tokman, however, takes a more optimistic position in the long run, concentrating on the expansion of the formal sector and arguing that, if the past repeats itself in the future, it will be necessary to examine the system carefully to finance the rapid expansion of the covered population. See "Comment," in Mesa-Lago, ed., *The Crisis of Social Security and Health Care*, chap. 8.

14. Isuani, "Social Security and Public Assistance." A similar argument is advanced for all basic necessities in COPLAMAR, *Macroeconomía de las necesidades esenciales en México: Situación actual y perspectivas al año 2000* (Mexico City: Siglo, XXI 1983), pp. 105–10.

15. Francisco León, "Comment," in Mesa-Lago, ed., *The Crisis of Social Security and Health Care*, chap. 3.

16. Dieter K. Zschock, *Health Financing in Developing Countries* (Washington, D.C.: American Health Association, 1979), and "Health Care Financing in Central America and the Andean Region: A Workshop Report," *Latin American Research Review* 15:3 (1980): 149–68. According to different viewpoints, the unequal distribution of resources between social security and public health does favor global health policy, in macroeconomic terms and in the long run. See Milton Roemer, "Does

Social Security Support for Medical Care Weaken Public Health Programs?'' *International Journal of Health Services* 6 (1976): 69–78.

17. Arroba, "La financiación''; Jorge Brenes, "Costo e investigación económica aplicados a los seguros de enfermedad y maternidad,'' *Seguridad social* 89 (1974): 65–112.

18. See Peter Thullen, "The Financing of Social Security Pensions: Principles, Current Issues, and Trends,'' in Mesa-Lago, ed., *The Crisis of Social Security and Health Care*, chap. 5; and International Social Security Association, *Methods of Financing Social Security: Their Economic and Social Effects*, ISSA, Studies and Research, no. 15 (Geneva: ISSA, 1979).

19. See Jean Bourgeois-Pichat, "El financiamiento de judilaciones mediante capitalización,'' *Notas de población: Revista latinoamericana de demografía* 10:29 (August 1982): 43–69. Gonzalo Arroba et al., *El impuesto al valor agregado en el financiamiento de la seguridad social y el proceso de integración latinoamericano* (Washington, D.C.: BID/INTAL, 1980), 1:49. See also the comparison of financing methods in seven countries, which reinforce the argument of this section (p. 202).

20. ILO, *The Cost of Social Security, 1975–1977* and *1978–1980* (Geneva: ILO, 1981, 1985).

21. Mesa-Lago, *Social Security in Latin America*; and Mesa-Lago, "Financing Health Care in Latin America and the Caribbean,'' Washington, D.C.: World Bank/ PHND, March 1983.

22. Mesa-Lago, *Social Security in Latin America*, pp. 283–89.

23. William McGreevey, "Brazilian Health Care Financing and Health Policy: An International Perspective,'' Washington, D.C.: World Bank/PHND, August 1982.

24. Caja Costarricense de Seguridad Social, "Financiación pluralista de las prestaciones médicas en la seguridad social costarricense,'' VII Congreso Americano de Medicina de la Seguridad Social, Quito, June 2–5, 1981.

25. James Malloy and Silvia Borzutzky, "Politics, Social Welfare Policy, and the Population Problem in Latin America,'' *International Journal of Health Services* 12:1 (1982): 77–98; Mesa-Lago, "Financing Health Care in Latin America.''

26. ILO, *The Cost of Social Security, 1978–1980*. For other administrative problems, see Beryl Frank, *La seguridad social*, pp. 58–75.

27. Marshall Wolfe, *El desarrollo esquivo* (Mexico City: Fondo de Cultura Económica, 1976), pp. 256–57.

28. See chapters 2 and 5.

29. Fernando Rezende et al., "Os custos da assistencia médica e a crise financiera da previdência social,'' *Dados* 25:1 (1982): 25–43; McGreevey, "Brazilian Health Care Financing.''

30. Antonio Ugalde, "The Integration of Health Care Programs into a National Health System,'' in Mesa-Lago, ed., *The Crisis of Social Security and Health Care*, chap. 4; Zschock, "Health Care Financing''; McGreevey, "Brazilian Health Care Financing.''

31. ILO, *The Cost of Social Security, 1978–1980*, p. 7.

32. Zschock, in *Health Financing*, has studied the problems that distort international comparisons of health expenditures.

33. See Philip Musgrove, "The Impact of Social Security on Income Distribution

in Latin America," in Mesa-Lago, ed., *The Crisis of Social Security and Health Care,* chap. 6.

34. For summaries of this theme, see José Pablo Arellano, "The Impact of Social Security on Savings and Development," in ibid., chap. 7; Christine Wallich, "Savings Mobilization through Social Security: The Experience of Chile, 1916–1977," Staff Working Papers no. 553, Washington, D.C., World Bank, 1982, pp. 1–28.

35. Arroba et al., *El impuesto al valor agregado,* pp. 319–20.

36. Arellano, "The Impact of Social Security"; and Musgrove, "The Impact of Social Security."

37. For a good summary of the debate in the United States, see George F. Break, "The Economic Effects of the OASI Program," in *Social Security Financing,* ed. Felicity Skidmore (Cambridge, Mass.: MIT Press, 1981), pp. 59–71. For a study of the OECD countries, see Erkki Koskela and Matti Viren, "Social Security and Household Saving in an International Cross Section," *American Economic Review* 73:1 (March 1983): 212–17.

38. See Wallich, "Savings Mobilization," pp. 29–77; Arellano, "The Impact of Social Security."

39. ILO, *The Cost of Social Security, 1978–1980.*

40. Hector L. Diéguez, "La seguridad social en América Latina: Reflexiones sobre sus características y problemática," Centro de Investigaciones Económicas, Instituto Torcuato di Tella, no. 84, 1978, pp. 29–32.

41. ILO, *Papel de la seguridad social y del mejoramiento de las condiciones de vida y de trabajo en el progreso social y económico* (Ottawa: ILO, 1966), pp. 76–83.

42. Carmelo Mesa-Lago, "Social Security and Extreme Poverty in Latin America," *Journal of Development Economics* 12 (1983): 83–110. For analysis and projections for the years 1890–2000, see Enrique de la Piedra, "Conceptos y medidas de la pobreza: Una síntesis," Santiago, CEPAL, March 29, 1983, and "La pobreza en América Latina: La situación actual, las perspectivas, y el marco global de políticas," Santiago, CEPAL, December 1982.

43. Musgrove, "The Impact of Social Security."

44. For a good summary of the incidence of the employer contribution, see Arroba *El impuesto al valor agregado,* pp. 320–30.

45. See ibid.; Musgrove, "The Impact of Social Security"; and Break, "The OASI Program," pp. 71–72.

46. In Musgrove's view, even in developing countries, skilled labor is not abundant, and in negotiations with the state or employer the employer contribution is included as part of the wage package. Thus supply is not perfectly elastic, and the employee probably pays part of this contribution.

47. See Alejandro Foxley, Eduardo Aninat, and José Pablo Arellano, *Efectos de la seguridad social sobre la distribución del ingreso,* Estudios CIEPLAN, no. 8, (Santiago: CIEPLAN, 1977), pp. 23–24; and Richard R. Wilson, "The Impact of Social Security on Employment," in Mesa-Lago, ed., *The Crisis of Social Security and Health Care,* chap. 8.

48. See Christian Kornevall, "Un cambio en el financiamiento de la seguridad social y sus efectos en el empleo," *El trimestre económico* 44:2 (April–June 1977): 455–82.

49. Tokman, "Comment."

50. Musgrove, "The Impact of Social Security."

51. Mesa-Lago, "Social Security and Extreme Poverty," pp. 94–95.

52. CEPAL, *Economic Development and Income Distribution in Argentina* (New York: United Nations, 1969), pp. 262–64.

53. Hector L. Diéguez and Alberto Petrecolla, "La distribución funcional del ingreso y el sistema previsional en Argentina, 1950–1972," *Desarrollo económico* 55 (October–December 1974): 423–40.

54. Fernando A. Rezende, "Redistribution of Income through Social Security: The Case of Brazil," presented to the Thirty-first Congress of the International Institute of Public Finance, 1974; Rezende and Dennis Mahar, *Saude e previdencia social: Uma analise econômica* (Rio de Janeiro: IPEA, 1974).

55. Dianne W. Green, "Some Effects of Social Security Programs in the Distribution of Income in Costa Rica," Ph.D. diss., University of Pittsburgh, 1977. See Musgrove's critique of this study in "The Impact of Social Security."

56. Edgar A. Briceño and Eduardo A. Méndez, "Salud pública y distribución del ingreso [familiar] en Costa Rica," *Revista ciencias económicas* 1:2/2:1–2 (1982): 49–69.

57. For details see Mesa-Lago, *Social Security in Latin America*, pp. 54–55.

58. Foxley, Aninat, and Arellano, *Efectos de la seguridad social*, p. 38.

59. José Pablo Arellano, "Gasto público en salud y distribución del ingreso," in *Salud publica y bienestar social*, ed. Mario Livingston and Dagmar Raczynski (Santiago: CIEPLAN, 1976), p. 166.

CHAPTER 2
Costa Rica

1. The best history of the creation of CCSS is that of Mark B. Rosenberg, *Las luchas por el seguro social en Costa Rica* (San Jose: Editorial Costa Rica, 1980). For a summary, see Rosenberg, "Social Security Policy-making in Costa Rica: A Research Report," *Latin American Research Review* 15:1 (1979): 116–33.

2. Interview with Guido Miranda Gutiérrez, presidente ejecutivo of CCSS, San José, May 6, and Pittsburgh, June 27–29, 1983; interview with Juan Jaramillo Antillón, Ministro de Salud, San José, July 12, 1983.

3. Ministerio de Planificación Nacional y Política Económica, "Plan nacional de desarrollo, 1982–1986," San José, 1982, p. 49.

4. Based on figures from the CCSS, División Estadística, Dirección Técnica Actuarial de Planificación Institucional, and the Ministerio de Salud, San José, July 1983.

5. Interview with Gerardo Arauz, jefe de la Dirección de Seguros Solidarios, INS, San José, July 7, 1983.

6. Figures for 1978–80 from table 12; ILO *Yearbook of Labor Statistics*, 1981; and PREALC, *Dinámica del subempleo en América Latina*, p. 26.

7. See Carmelo Mesa-Lago, "Financing Health Care in Latin America," pp. 60–65; and "Social Security and Health: Final Report to the World Bank Structural Adjustment Loan Mission to Costa Rica," July 1983, p. 6.

8. CCSS, *Anuario estadístico, 1981* (San José: CCSS, 1982); "Situacion presupuestaria de la Caja Costarricense de Seguro Social," San José, 1982; and information from the Sección Financiera, July 1983.

9. CCSS, Sección Financiera, July 1983.

10. Ibid.; ILO, *The Cost of Social Security, 1975–1977.*

11. Jorge Montt D., "Pensiones por jubilaciones en Costa Rica," Instituto de Estudios en Población, Heredia, 1982; and interview with Jorge Arturo Hernández, jefe, Sección Financiera, CCSS, July 6, 1983.

12. Ibid.; WHO/PAHO, "Análisis integral de la Caja Costarricense de Seguro Social: Informe final," San José, WHO/PAHO, 1980, and information provided to the author in visits to hospitals on July 7 and 8, 1983.

13. Sección Financiera, CCSS, July 1983. According to the IMF, the general balance of the CCSS in 1983 generated a surplus of more than 1,000 million colones, 12 percent of revenues. See IMF, *Costa Rica* (Washington, D.C.: IMF, 1984).

14. Interview with Roger M. Aguilar, actuary, CCSS, July 6, 1983.

15. Montt, "Pensiones."

16. CCSS, *Plan de emergencia* (San José, 1982).

17. Interview with Jorge A. Hernández, jefe, Sección Financiera, CCSS; interview with Thomas McKee, chief, General Development Division, USAID, San José, July 6, 1983; interview with Eduardo Lizano Fait, director, Escuela de Economía de la Universidad de Costa Rica, July 5, 1983.

18. Interview with Ricardo Fallas, director, Departamento de Servicios Médicos, CCSS, July 5, 1983.

19. Interview with Aquilar.

20. The calculations of doctors and hospital beds are based on Direccion General de Estadística y Censos, "Población de la República de Costa Rica por provincias, cantones y distritos," no. 43, San José, DGEC, 1979, and CCSS *Anuario Estadístico, 1981*. See also Mesa-Lago, "Financing Health Care," pp. 75–76; Antonio Casas and Hermán Vargas, "The Health System of Costa Rica: Toward a National Health Service," *Journal of Public Health Policy,* no. 1 (1980): 273; and Fernando Naranjo et al., "Desarrollo de los programas de seguridad social en Costa Rica: Universalización y extensión de los servicios médicos asistenciales," *Seguridad social,* nos. 105–06 (1977): 59–138.

21. Montt, "Pensiones"; legislation and interviews by the author with functionaries of the independent funds, San José, July 6–12, 1983.

22. CCSS, *Memoria, 1981*; Montt, "Pensiones"; and Naranjo et al., "Desarrollo."

23. Interview with Aguilar and Jaramillo; interview with Saeed Mekbel, subgerente médico, CCSS, July 11, 1983; Casas and Vargas, "Health System"; WHO/PAHO, "Análisis integral."

24. CCSS, "Financiación pluralista de las prestaciones médicas."

25. Edgar Mohs, "Infectious Diseases and Health in Costa Rica: The Development of a New Paradigm," *Pediatric Infectious Disease* 1:3 (1983): 212–16.

26. Juan Jaramillo Antillón, *Los problemas de la salud en Costa Rica: Políticas y estrategias* (San José: Litografía Ambar, 1983), p. 77.

27. Visits of the author to various hospitals in the provinces of Alajuela and San José, July 1983; and interview with Lizano Fait.

28. CCSS, *Anuario estadístico, 1979* (San José, 1981); Mohs, "Infectious Diseases."

29. Interview with Hernández.

30. Ibid.; interview with Arauz.

31. CELADE, *Boletín demográfico* 17:33 (January 1984): 64, 69.

32. See CELADE, "Costa Rica," in *Estudio económico de América Latina, 1982,* Santiago, October 1983; and "Síntesis preliminar de la economía latinoamericana durante 1983," Santiago, December 20, 1983.

33. CCSS, *Plan de emergencia*; interview with Fallas.

34. Ibid.; Víctor M. Gómez, "Pautas de atención médica y estimación de características de la demanda futura: Los servicios médicos en la perspectiva demográfica," San José, CCSS, 1981; Ministerio de Planificación Nacional, "Plan nacional de desarrollo."

35. Interviews with Hernández and McKee; interview with Emidgio A. Balbuena and José M. Marin, San José, PAHO/WHO, July 11–12, 1983.

36. Interviews with Fallas and Arauz.

37. Interview with Edgar Mohs, former minister of health, San José, July 7, 1983; Lenin Sáenz et al., "El recurso humano médico en Costa Rica entre 1970–1980: Informe de subcomisión a comisión para el estudio de recursos humanos para el sector salud," San José, Ministerio de Salud, 1981.

38. Interview with Guido Miranda, president, CCSS, San Jose, May 6, 1983, and Pittsburgh, June 27–29, 1983.

39. Green, "Some Effects of Social Security." See the critique of this study in Musgrove, "The Impact of Social Security."

40. José Pablo Arellano, discussant in the "Seminario sobre Seguridad Social y Desarrollo," celebrated in CEPAL, April 26, 1984.

41. Based on ideas of Enrique de la Piedra, División de Desarrollo Económico, ECLA, March 1984.

CHAPTER 3

Cuba

1. See Carmelo Mesa-Lago, *Planificación de la seguridad social: Análisis especial de la problemática cubana* (Havana: Editorial Librería Martí, 1960); Grupo Cubano de Investigaciones Económicas, *Un estudio sobre Cuba* (Coral Gables, Fla.: University of Miami Press, 1963), pp. 725–53, 1180–1230, and idem, *Social Security in Cuba* (Coral Gables, Fla.: University of Miami, 1964).

2. International Bank for Reconstruction and Development, *Report on Cuba* (Baltimore: John Hopkins Press, 1951), chap. 22.

3. Comisión de Aportes Estatales a la Seguridad Social, *Bases técnicas para la reforma de los seguros sociales* (Havana: Editorial Lex, 1957).

4. The text of the current law was published in Central de Trabajadores de Cuba, *Sistema de seguridad social: Régimen de asistencia social, régimen de seguridad social* (Havana: CTC, 1980). Other laws are compiled in Ministerio del Trabajo, *Principales disposiciones vigentes de la seguridad social cubana* (Havana: MT, n.d.) and Central de Trabajadores de Cuba, *Sistema de seguridad: Anexo* (Havana: CTC, 1980). Ac-

counts of social security progress under the Revolution include: Basilio Rodríguez, "La seguridad social en Cuba," *Cuba Socialista* 6:64 (December 1966): 14–30; CETSS, *La seguridad social en Cuba* (Havana: CETSS, 1977); and CETSS, *24 años de revolución en la seguridad social cubana* (Havana: CETSS, 1983; the latter is the most extensive and documented of the studies.

5. CETSS, "Investigación sobre evolución y tendencias de la seguridad social en el trienio, 1974–1976," *Seguridad social* 26:105/106 (May–August 1977): 171. The present section is based on this article and especially on CETSS, *24 años de revolución.*

6. The first statistical series on social security published by CEE in *Anuario estadístico de Cuba 1982* (Havana: CEE 1983) refer to occupational accidents and expenditures on monetary benefits by social security and do not include coverage figures.

7. The analysis of legal coverage is based on existing legislation and CETSS, *24 años de revolución.*

8. CEE, Oficina Nacional del Censo, *Censo de población y vivienda de 1981, República de Cuba* 16:1–2. (Havana: CEE, 1983).

9. See Centro de Investigaciones de la Economía Mundial, *Estudio acerca de la erradicación de la pobreza en Cuba* (Havanna: CIEM, 1983); and C. Mesa-Lago, "Seguridad social y pobreza," in Sergio Molina, ed., *Se puede superar la pobreza?* (Santiago: CEPAL/ILPES, 1980), pp. 163–89.

10. Calculations by the author based on CEE *Anuario estadístico de Cuba, 1982,* p. 127.

11. Comisión de Aportes a la Seguridad Social, *Bases técnicas.*

12. CETSS, *24 años de revolución.*

13. The private sector consists less than 20 percent of agricultural property, 2 percent of transportation, and a tiny percentage of professional and personal services.

14. Karl Marx, "Critique of the Gotha Programme," in *Selected Works,* ed. Marx-Engels-Lenin Institute of Moscow (New York: International Publishers, 1936), 2:562–66; Gregorio Ortega, "El salario en la sociedad socialista," *Trabajo* 4:9 (June 1963): 20; and Carmelo Mesa-Lago, *The Labour Sector and Socialist Distribution in Cuba* (New York: Praeger, 1968), chaps. 1 and 4.

15. CETSS. "Investigación sobre evolución y tendencias," p. 166.

16. See Mesa-Lago, *The Economy of Socialist Cuba: A Two-Decade Appraisal* (Albuquerque: University of New Mexico Press, 1981), pp. 102–07.

17. Fidel Castro, "Discurso en la sessión de clausura del 4° Congreso de la Unión de Jóvenes Comunistas," *Granma resume semanal,* April 18, 1982, p. 4; and "Discurso en la sessión de clausura del 6° Congreso de la ANAP," *Granma resumen semanal,* May 30, 1982, pp. 3–4.

18. CETSS, "Investigación sobre evolución y tendencias," p. 166.

19. Cuban Ministry of Labor, "Seguridad social y economía nacional," *Revista international de actuariado y estadística de la seguridad social* 11 (1965): 213.

20. Author's calculations based on sources of table 25 for the increase in the cost of social security, and on José Luis Rodríguez Guerra, "La economía cubana entre 1976 y 1980: Resultados y perspectivas," *Economía y desarrollo* 66 (January–February 1982): 137; and other figures on labor productivity reported in *Granma* for 1981 and 1982.

21 Cuban Ministry of Labor, "Seguridad social," p. 212.

22. CETSS, *24 años de revolución*, p. 66.

23. For a reconstruction of the budget series in 1962–65 and 1978–82, see Carmelo Mesa-Lago and Jorge Pérez-López, "Study of Cuba's MPS, its conversion to SNA, and Estimation of GDP/Capita and Growth Rates," Project on CPE's National Income Statistics, Washington, D.C.: World Bank, November 1982, p. 12.

24. CEE, *Anuario estadístico de Cuba, 1980* (Havana: CEE, 1981).

25. Mesa-Lago and Pérez-López, "Study of Cuba's MPS," pp. 1–13.

26. Seminario Latinamericano de Cuentas Nacionales y Balances de la Economía, *Cuba: Conversión de los principales indicadores macroeconomicos del sistema de balances de la economía nacional (SBEN) al sistema de cuentas nacionales (SCN), 1974* (Havana, March 1982), table 1.

27. National Bank of Cuba, *Informe económico* (Havana: NBC, 1982), p. 31.

28. Orlando Peñate Rivero and Ismael Lugo Machado, "Acerca del financiamiento de la seguridad social en Cuba," in *Modelos y estrategias financieras: Conferencias* (Mexico City: CEISS, 1985), pp. 58–75. The estimate of 20 percent of the wage fund was given by Lugo in his oral presentation in CIESS, June 25, 1985.

29. Gretel Castellanos, an official of CETSS, maintained this criterion in the international conference "Social Security and Health Care in Latin America and the Caribbean in the 1980s," University of Pittsburgh, June 29, 1983.

30. CETSS, *24 años de revolución*, p. 28.

31. Oficina Nacional de los Censos Demográfico y Electoral, *Muestreo sobre empleo, subempleo, y desempleo* (Havana: ONCDE, 1959–61): JUCEPLAN, *Censo de población y viviendas 1970: Datos fundamentales de la población* (Havana: JUCEPLAN, 1981), author's calculations based on pp. 1, 3, and 13; and CEE, *Censo de Población y viviendas, 1981, República de Cuba* 15:1 (Havana: CEE, 1983), p. cciii.

32. For a study of unemployment in Cuba, see Mesa-Lago, *The Economy of Socialist Cuba*, pp. 121–32.

33. Orlando Peñate Rivero, "Información sobre el sistema de seguridad social cubano," Havana, CETSS, March 21, 1984, pp. 2–4.

34. For an analysis of health in Cuba under the revolution, see CEE *Cuba: Desarrollo económico y social durante el período 1958–1980* (Havana: CEE, 1981), chap. 10; CEPAL, "Apreciaciones sobre el estilo de desarrollo y sobre las principales políticas sociales de Cuba," Mexico City, CEPAL, November 1978, pp. 162–67; Ross Danielson, *Cuban Medicine* (New Brunswick, N.J.: Transaction Books, 1979); and Sergio Díaz-Briquets, *The Health Revolution in Cuba* (Austin: University of Texas Press), 1983.

35. Legislation, and CETSS, *24 años de revolución*, pp. 82, 106.

36. Central de Trabajadores de Cuba, *Sistema de seguridad social*, p. 18; armed forces social security law, in *Gaceta oficial*, November 30, 1976; CETSS, "Investigación sobre la evolución y tendencias," p. 162.

37. Peñate Rivero, "Información sobre el sistema," p. 4.

38. Ibid.

39. Mesa-Lago, *The Economy of Socialist Cuba*, p. 167; CEE, *Anuario estadístico de Cuba, 1982* (Havana: CEE, 1983), p. 480.

40. MINSAP, *Informe anual, 1978* (Havana: MINSAP, 1979); CEE, *Anuario estadístico de Cuba, 1982*.

41. CETSS, *24 años de revolución*, pp. 28, 80.

42. Helen Matthews Smith, "Cuban Medicine: An Eyewitness Report," *MD* (May 1983).

43. For sources and more details, see Mesa-Lago, *The Economy of Socialist Cuba,* pp. 170–72.

44. A four-peso increase was planned for those who receive pensions of less than eighty pesos monthly; the official estimate of the increase in prices for an average family of four people was eight pesos; if a pensioner's family consisted of two people, the increase in the pension would compensate for the increase in the cost of living (based on *Granma,* December 14, 1981, p. 2).

45. Frank Hidalgo Gato, "De los precios y su función redistributiva en la economía socialista," *Economía y desarrollo* 59 (September–December 1980): 41–53. In 1965, however, it was maintained that the cost of social security was not charged to prices; see Cuban Ministry of Labor, "Seguridad social" p. 213.

46. Claes Brundenius, *Economic Growth, Basic Needs, and Income Distribution in Revolutionary Cuba* (Lund, Sweden: University of Lund, Research Policy Institute, 1981); Arthur MacEwan, *Revolution and Economic Development in Cuba* (New York: St. Martin's Press, 1981), pp. 229–31; and Mesa-Lago, *The Economy of Socialist Cuba,* chap. 7.

CHAPTER 4
Chile

1. For a summary of the evolution of the Chilean system from 1882 to 1973, see Carmelo Mesa-Lago, *Social Security in Latin America: Pressure Groups, Stratification, and Inequality* (Pittsburgh, Pa.: University of Pittsburgh Press, 1978), pp. 22–33. More recent accounts, which encompass the beginning of the 1980s decade, are Silvia Borzutzky, "Chilean Politics and Social Security Policies," Ph.D. diss., University of Pittsburgh, 1983, and Sara Cofre Yánez, "El sistema previsional chileno," Tesis de Grado, Universidad de Santiago, 1984.

2. Comisión de Estuidos de la Seguridad Social, *Informe sobre la reforma de la seguridad social chilena* (Santiago: Editorial Jurídica de Chile, 1964, 1965). Another important study was *El sistema de previsión social chileno: Informe de la Misión Klein y Saks* (Santiago: Editorial Universitaria, S.A., 1958).

3. Borzutzky, "Chilean Politics," chap. 8; Cofre Yanez, "El sistema previsional chileno," pp. 65–70; and Carmelo Mesa-Lago, "Alternative Strategies to the Social Security Crisis: Socialist, Market, and Mixed Approaches," in Mesa-Lago, ed., *The Crisis of Social Security and Health Care,* chap. 10.

4. Interview with José Pinera, former minister of labor and social insurance, Santiago, September 29, 1983.

5. Interview with Pablo Izquierdo, director, SSS and EMPART, Santiago, August 17, 1983; interview with Joaquín Echenique, director, Instituto de Normalización Previsional, Santiago, August 26, 1983.

6. Interview with Luis Larraín, director, Superintendencia de Seguridad Social, Santiago, August 24, 1983.

7. Interviews with Izquierdo and Echenique.

8. Interview with Izquierdo; Cofre Yánez, "El sistema previsional chileno," pp. 67–68.

9. Interviews with Larraín and Echenique.

10. Joseph L. Scarpaci, "Public and Private Health Care Delivery in Chile," Department of Geography, University of Florida, December 1983. Scarpaci carried out numerous interviews in the Ministry of Health and its subunits and shared this information with the author.

11. Mesa-Lago, *Social Security in Latin America,* pp. 42–43.

12. Superintendencia de AFP, *Boletín estadístico mensual,* nos. 1–32 (May–June 1981–January 1984).

13. Interview with Larraín.

14. It is possible that the EAP figures in table 31 and those given in the text for 1982 are somewhat overestimated. Chilean official figures for EAP in 1980 and 1982 were 3,635,500 and 3,503,600, which would raise the coverage figures to 64.3 percent in 1980 and 76.5 percent in 1982. See INE, *Compendio estadístico, 1983.*

15. Interview with Juan Ariztia, director, Superintendencia de AFP, August 3, 1983; interview with Izquierdo.

16. Interview with Izquierdo. In mid-1984, Eugenio Camus, head of the financial division of the superintendencia de AFP, gave an even lower figure for affiliates of 1.1 million (*El mercurio,* June 9, 1984, pp. A-1 and 12).

17. Scarpaci, "Public and Private Health Care Delivery," tables 3 and 4.

18. Ibid., p. 14 and table 7; and *El mercurio,* October 19, 1983, p. B-2, and December 14, 1983, p. B-2.

19. The figures come from table 3; PREALC, *Dinámica del subempleo en América Latina*; and INE, *Compendio estadístico, 1982.*

20. Per capita GDP and urbanization figures from CEPAL, *Distribución regional del PIB sectorial en los países de América Latina* (Santiago: Cuadernos Estadísticos de la CEPAL, 1981), and INE, *Compendio estadístico, 1982.*

21. See Mesa-Lago, *Social Security in Latin America,* pp. 46–47.

22. The estimate of insured in the old system made by Izquierdo during my interview, and that of insured in the new system comes from the Superintendencia de AFP, *Boletín estadístico mensual,* no. 19 (December 1982). The calculation of self-employed workers was carried out by applying the corresponding percentage of the 1978 distribution to the employed population in 1982 given in the *Compendio estadístico, 1983.*

23. The calculation of unpaid family workers was carried out as for self-employed workers. The number of unemployed comes from *Compendio estadístico, 1983.*

24. Mesa-Lago, *Social Security in Latin America* pp. 48–52.

25. See José Pablo Arellando, "Elementos para el análisis de la reforma previsional chilena," *Colección Estudios CIEPLAN,* no. 6 (December 1981): 5–44.

26. Felipe Larraín Buscunan, "Cuatro aspectos de la reforma previsional," *Economía y sociedad,* no. 5 (September 1982). The figures in the text are the author's calculation based on Superintendencia de AFP, *Boletin estadístico mensual,* no. 6 (November 1981) and no. 28 (September 1983).

27. Arellano, "Elementos para el análisis."

28. *El Mercurio,* June 10, 1984, p. B-1; and author's calculations based on Superintendencia de AFP, *Boletín estadístico mensual,* no. 32 (January 1984) and *El Mercurio,* April 21, 1984, p. 1, and May 31, 1984, pp. B-2.

29. Sergio Baeza Valdés, "Radiografía de la nueva previsíon," *Economía y sociedad,* 17 (September 1983): 20.

30. Interview with Larraín.

31. Interview with Izquierdo. The director of one AFP has considered that evasion is not too important and has estimated that payment delays amount to no more than 5 percent of revenues. Sergio Baeza Valdés, "Dos años de operación del nuevo sistema previsional," conference in the Primera Jornada Previsional, Santiago, August 31, 1983.

32. Information from Fanor Larraín Verdugo, Santiago, December 21, 1983.

33. Interviews with Larraín and Echenique; interview with Alfonso Serrano, subsecretario de prevision, *El Mercurio,* June 10, 1984, p. B-1.

34. Author's calculations based on the source for table 35.

35. José Pablo Arellano, "Sistemas alternativos de seguridad social: Un análisis de la experiencia chilena," *Colección Estudios CIEPLAN,* no. 4 (November 1980): 133–40; and Arellano, "Elementos para el análisis." The figures for 1980 were calculated by the author on Superintendencia de Seguridad Social on the basis of *Seguridad Social: Estadísticas, 1980* (Santiago, 1982).

36. *El Mercurio,* February 8, 1984, p. B-2, and April 14, 1984, p. B-1.

37. AFP, *Boletín estadístico mensual,* no. 31 (February 1983) and no. 32 (January 1984); interview with Pinera.

38. Interview with Ariztía; and *El Mercurio,* August 7, 1983, p. D-4.

39. Interview with Ariztía.

40. José Pablo Arellano and Raúl Eduardo Sáenz, "Reforma de la previsión y la salud," in *Desarrollo social y salud en Chile,* ed. H. Lavados (Santiago: Corporación de Promoción Universitaria, 1982), pp. 160–61.

41. *El Mercurio,* September 21, 1983, p. B-2, and December 14, 1983, p. B-2.

42. Tarcisio Castañeda, "Contexto socioeconómico y causas del descenso de la mortalidad infantil en Chile," Departamento de Economía, Universidad de Chile, May 1984.

43. Scarpaci, "Public and Private Health Care Delivery," p. 12.

44. 1980 figures are from INE, *Compendio estadístico, 1982 and 1983.* The comparison of health services by province is based on Mesa-Lago, *Social Security in Latin America,* pp. 65–66.

45. Author's calculations based on figures for SSS and EMPART from the interview with Ariztía; figures for CANAEMPU and other agencies from the interview with Larraín; and AFP from Baeza Valdés, "Dos años de operación del nuevo sistema previsional."

46. Castañeda, "Contexto socioeconómico y causas," pp. 23–24, 40.

47. Interview with Izquierdo; and Bascunán, "Cuatro aspectos."

48. Castañeda, "Contexto socioeconómico y causas," pp. 2–3.

49. Thus in 1983 the AFP Habitat offered the lowest commissions and contributions and the highest average yield of the twelve, yet it ranked fifth in number of affiliates, while AFP Invierta had the highest commissions and the third highest contributions plus a low yield yet ranked fourth in the number of affiliates, and AFP Provida offered average conditions yet had the greatest number of affiliates. (My comparison of information from the *Boletín estadístico mensual,* and *Tercera de la hora,* August 8, 1983, p. 2.)

50. Juan Ariztía, discussant in the Primera Reunión Previsional, Santiago, August 31, 1983; and statements by Benjamin David, Ignacio Cousina, and Virgilio Perreta in *El Mercurio,* August 7, 1983, p. D-4.

51. Tecnología Investigación de Mercado, "AFP y sistema de comisiones," Santiago, TIME, 1982.

52. The passive figure was obtained in the interview with Larraín.

53. My calculations based on *Seguridad social: Estadísticas, 1980.*

54. Carmen Arretz, "Efectos en los aportes al sistema de seguridad social de cambios en la edad de jubilación," Santiago, CELADE, Serie A, no. 102, May 1970.

55. Arellano, "Sistemas alternativos," pp. 135–36.

56. The calculations from table 41 include welfare pensions; other calcuations that exclude the welfare pensions show a slight decline in the real value of pensions. See René Cortázar, "Chile: Resultados distributivos, 1973–1982," *Desarollo económico* 23:91 (October–December 1983): 371.

57. Castañeda, "Contexto económico y causas," pp. 8–9.

58. Ibid., pp. 3–4, 23–37.

59. Scarpaci, "Public and Private Health Care Delivery," p. 19.

60. The different estimates in the text are from Scarpaci, "Public and Private," table 6; and Castañeda, "Contexto económico y causas," pp. 2, 23, 24, 40.

61. José Pablo Arellano, "The Impact of Social Security." This section is based on Arellano's study except where a different source is cited.

62. *El Mercurio*, May 31, 1984, p. B-2; Ariztía, in Primera Jornada Previsional.

63. Hernán Aldabe, "Comment," in Mesa-Lago, ed., *The Crisis of Social Security and Health Care*, chap. 7.

64. See note 28 and *El Mercurio*, May 14, 1984, pp. B-1, 2.

65. See the debate over this aspect between Víctor García (article forthcoming in the *Revista de la facultad de economía de la Universidad de Chile*) and the Superintendencia de AFP (*El Mercurio*, December 26, 1983, p. B-3).

66. *El Mercurio*, December 1, 1983, p. B-1.

67. Interview with Ariztía.

68. Interview with Piñera.

69. *El Mercurio*, April 20, 1984, pp. B-1, 2: interview with Juan Ariztía, *El Mercurio*, May 14, 1984, pp. B-1, 2; and interview with Serrano.

70. The three studies are: Eduardo Aninat, "La eliminación de las cotizaciones previsionales: Estimación de su impacto sobre el empleo," *Estudios de planificación* (CIEPLAN), no. 9 (1971); PREALC, *Acción de los ministerios del Trabajo en la política de empleo del Grupo Andino* (Santiago: PREALC, 1975); and N. Villagran, "Proposición de un nuevo sistema de financiamiento de los fondos previsionales y sus implicaciones sobre el nivel de empleo en el sector agrícola," Tesis de Postgrado, Departamento de Economía Agraria, Universidad Católica de Chile, 1976. A comparison and evaluation of the three methods is made in Arellano, "Sistemas alternativos," pp. 146–49.

71. Arellano, "Sistemas alternativos," pp. 137, 149–53.

72. Carlos Briones et al., "Antecedentes básicos y análisis del estado actual de la seguridad social en Chile," *Seguridad social* 98 (July 1968): 98.

73. José Francisco Pizarro Blancaire and Juan Gutiérrez Vistozo, "Bases para un sistema integrado de pensiones: Estudio del costo," *Memoria*, Facultad de Ciencias Económicas, Universidad de Chile, 1967.

74. Comisión de Estudios de la Seguridad Social, *Informe sobre la reforma*, pp. 827–38; Briones et al., "Antecedentes básicos," pp. 95–103; ODEPLAN, *Informe económico anual 1971*, p. 821.

75. Foxley, Aninat, and Arellano, *Efectos de la seguridad social,* table 10.

76. José Pablo Arellano, "Gasto público en salud y distribución," p. 166.

77. A family survey conducted on a national scale in 1983 by the Instituto Latino-americano de Doctrina y Estudios Sociales on the redistributive impact of social expenditures included the impact of social security, but the results of the survey were not available at the time of this writing.

78. Interview with Ariztía; interview with Piñera, presentation at the Primera Jornada Previsional, Santiago, August 31, 1983.

CHAPTER 5
Mexico

1. For an account of Mexican social security history up to 1973, see Mesa-Lago, *Social Security in Latin America,* pp. 208–21.

2. For a comprehensive history of the IMSS, se IMSS, *Instituto Mexicano del Seguro Social 1943–1983: 40 años de historia* (Mexico City, 1983).

3. Ibid., pp. 47–49.

4. *Programa IMSS-COPLAMAR,* Mexico City, 1983.

5. This section is based on Mesa-Lago, *Social Security in Latin America,* pp. 224–28; IMSS, "Contestación a la encuesta anual sobre la evolución y tendencias de la seguridad social," AISS, Geneva, 1983; IMSS, *Instituto Mexicano*; and interview with Gabino Fraga, secretary general, IMSS, Mexico City, February 28, 1984.

6. The analysis of legal coverage is based on IMSS, *Ley del seguro social* (Mexico City, 1982); Ley del ISSSTE de 1983, *Diario oficial,* December 27, 1983, and laws and agreements in existence for the armed forces and Pemex.

7. COPLAMAR, *Necesidades esenciales en México: Situación actual y perspectivas al año 2000—Salud* (Mexico City: Siglo XXI, 1982), p. 146.

8. The original figures are from Coodinación General del Programa IMSS-COPLAMAR, "Informe mensual de población y servicios otorgados," 1980–83; the revised figures are from "Ambito geográfico del programa IMSS-COPLAMAR," November 4, 1983. In an effort to account for the discrepancies, the author consulted José M. Gutiérrez Trujillo, coordinator of IMSS-COPLAMAR (interview, March 3, 1984 and private correspondence).

9. COPLAMAR, *Necesidades esenciales,* p. 148; and sources of table 43.

10. SPP, Instituto Nacional de Estadística, Geografía e Informatica (SPP/INEGI), *Agenda estadística 1983* (Mexico City, 1984), p. 91.

11. PREALC, *Dinámica del subempleo en América Latina,* p. 26; CEPAL, "Síntesis preliminar de la economía latinoamericana durante 1983," Santiago: CEPAL, December 20, 1983, p. 34.

12. Based on CEPAL, *Distribución regional del PIB sectorial en los paises de América Latina* (Santiago: CEPAL, 1981), p. 36; and COPLAMAR, *Necesidades esenciales,* pp. 146–53.

13. Data for 1969 are based on Mesa-Lago, *Social Security in Latin America,* pp. 237–39; and for 1980 on the author's calculations using figures from SPP, *Anuario estadístico de los Estados Unidos Mexicanos, 1981;* IMSS, *Memoria estadística, 1981* and ISSSTE, *Anuario estadístico, 1981.*

14. COPLAMAR, *Necesidades esenciales*, pp. 172–79.
15. This section is based on ISS, "Contestación a la encuesta"; and interview with Fraga.
16. COPLAMAR, *Necesidades esenciales*, pp. 195–96, 253–55.
17. Peter Thullen, "The Financing of Social Security Pensions," chap. 5.
18. IMSS, *Memoria estadística, 1981*.
19. Interview with Carlos Soto Pérez, subdirector of actuarial services, IMSS, February 28, 1984.
20. ISSSTE, *Agenda estadística 1982*.
21. Mesa-Lago, *Social Security*, pp. 240–41.
22. IMSS, *Memoria estadística 1981*; ISSSTE, *Agenda estadística 1982*; information from the Subdireccion de Actuaría y Estadística, February 1984.
23. IMSS, "Informe financiero y actuarial del IMSS al 31 de diciembre de 1982," September 1983, p. 8.
24. This section is based on the 1982 actuarial study and the interview with Soto Pérez.
25. In mid-1983, Peter Thullen predicted that the capitalization method of the IMSS pension program would gradually change to pure assessment with an emergency reserve; this shift appears to have occurred much sooner than he anticipated ("The Financing of Social Security Pensions").
26. The real value of the reserves in the pension and occupational risk programs was calculated by the author using the figures in the 1982 actuarial study and the inflation rates reported by CEPAL.
27. COPLAMAR, *Necesidades esenciales*, pp. 62–71; and interviews with Marco A. Michel Diaz, Director de Servicios, Secretariado Técnico del IMSS, February 28 and March 3, 1984.
28. COPLAMAR, *Necesidades esenciales*, p. 64.
29. Ibid., p. 174; and SSP/INEGI, *Anuario Estadístico Compendiado 1970*, p. 70.
30. Mesa-Lago, *Social Security in Latin America*, pp. 248–50.
31. SSP/INEGI, *Agenda estadística*, p. 67.
32. Author's calculations based on IMSS, *Anuario estadístico, 1981* and information provided in February 1984; ISSSTE, *Agenda estadística, 1982*, and SSP/INEGI, *Agenda estadística*, p. 63.
33. IMSS, "Informe financiero y actuarial," pp. 21–22; "Reporte de Auditoría a la valuación financiera y actuarial al 31 de diciembre de 1982," October 14, 1983.
34. SSP/INEGI, *Agenda estadística*, pp. 28, 30.
35. *Programa IMSS-COPLAMAR*, table 3; interviews with Michel Diaz.
36. Author's calculations based on SSP/INEGI, *Agenda estadística*, p. 67; table 43, and *Program IMSS-COPLAMAR*, budget.
37. Richard R. Wilson, "The Corporatist Welfare State: Social Security and Development in Mexico," Ph.D. diss., University of Pittsburgh, 1981; and Antonio Ugalde, "Public Health in Latin America," seminar held at the University of Pittsburgh, March 2, 1983.
38. Author's calculations based on SSP/INEGI, *Agenda estadística*, pp. 63, 80–81; IMSS, *Anuario estadístico, 1981* and information provided February 28, 1984; ISSSTE, *Agenda estadística, 1982*; *Programa IMSS-COPLAMAR*, table 8.

39. Thullen, "The Financing of Social Security Pensions," table 13.

40. IMSS, *Instituto Mexicano*, pp. 49, 135; and information from IMSS, February 1984.

41. COPLAMAR, *Necesidades esenciales*, pp. 249–55.

42. Richard Wilson, "The Impact of Social Security on Employment," in Mesa-Lago, ed., *The Crisis of Social Security and Health Care*, chap. 8.

43. Ibid., esp. tables 7 and 8.

44. Victor Tokman, "Comment," in ibid., chap. 8.

45. "Evaluación de los efectos redistributivos derivados de las operaciones del IMSS," Mexico City, 1984. In February 1984 this study was still in the preliminary design stage (interview with Michel; and interview with Enrique Hernandez Laos, February 29, 1984).

46. COPLAMAR, *Macroeconomía*, pp. 105–10.

CHAPTER 6
Peru

1. For the years until 1973, this section is based on Mesa-Lago, *Social Security in Latin America*, pp. 113–32.

2. Francisco Ipiña Gondra, "Estructura financiera, recursos económicos, causas del desequilibrio financiero, conclusiones y recomendaciones," Lima, OISS, 1962, and "Estudio actuarial de pensiones," Lima, OISS, 1963; Alfredo Pérez Armiñán, "Informe sobre la situación administrativa del seguro social del empleado del Peru," Lima, OISS, 1965; a study prepared by Peter Thullen and Giovanni Tamburi for the ILO in 1965. The four independent blue-collar funds were created at the beginning of the 1970s under the military government.

3. A legal compilation of these dispositions and other prior ones still in force is IPSS, *Legislación de seguridad social en el Perú* (Lima: IPSS, 1980).

4. "Dictamen de la Comisión Bicameral Investigadora del sistema de Seguridad Social," Lima, Cámara de Senadores, November 16, 1983, p. 7.

5. See the social security program of Acción Popular in Octavio Mongrut Muñoz, "La seguridad social en Peru," *IPSS* 1:1 (October–December 1982): 4–16.

6. The commission initiated its activities in December 1980 and its investigations, covering the period November 1973–June 1982, spawned fifty technical reports and one final report. "Dictamen."

7. This section is based on IPSS, *Legislación*; Jorge Rendón Vázquez, *Manual de Derecho de la Seguridad Social* (Lima: Ediciones Tarpuy, 1981); and interviews with Frank Griffiths Escardó, executive president of IPSS, Lima, March 5, 1984, and César San Román, gerente financiero, IPSS, Lima, March 6 and 8, 1984.

8. On the defects of insured participation in administration, see Javier Slodky F., "Seguridad social: La participación de los asegurados," Lima, Fundación Friedrich Ebert, 1984.

9. Mongrut Muñoz, "La seguridad social en Perú," pp. 7–10; interview with Griffiths.

10. Rendón Vázquex, *Manual*, pp. 84–86; Luis Aparicio Valdez, "Situación de

la seguridad social," *Análisis laboral* 7:78 (December 1983): 4–5; interview with San Roman; and "Dictamen," p. 15.

11. I formally requested coverage figures for 1970 and 1983 from the armed forces to no avail, so I extrapolated from the existing figures for 1961–69 (Mesa-Lago, *Social Security in Latin America*, p. 135). For pension coverage for fishermen, I used the coverage figures for occupational risks.

12. Based on figures from the statistical office of IPSS, December 1983.

13. INE, *Producto interno por departamentos* (Lima: INE, June 1983).

14. Mesa-Lago, *Social Security in Latin America*, pp. 136–41.

15. In April 1984, IPSS conducted a survey of insured that might provide this information, but in spite of various efforts, it was not possible to obtain it.

16. Information on the composition of the labor force is from ILO, *Yearbook of Labour Statistics, 1983* (Geneva: ILO, 1983).

17. Interview with Griffiths; interview with San Román.

18. The text of the Ley Orgánica de Seguridad Social appears in *Análisis laboral* 7:78 (December 1983): 19–24.

19. IPSS, *Legislación*; Aparicio Valdez, "Situación de la seguridad social," pp. 3–4; interview with San Roman.

20. Interview with Alfred Jalibie, gerente general, Departamento de Finanzas, Banco de la Nación, Lima, March 9, 1984.

21. "Dictamen," pp. 17, 27, 31.

22. Mongrut Muñoz, "La seguridad social," p. 11.

23. "Dictamen," pp. 24–26; Rendón Vázquez, *Manual*, pp. 106–07.

24. IPSS, *Legislación*; Rendón Vázquez, *Manual*, pp. 137–38; Mesa-Lago, *Social Security in Latin America*, pp. 142–43.

25. Rendón Vázquez, *Manual*, pp. 98–99. See also "Dictamen," pp. 16–20; Aparicio Valdez, "Situación de la seguridad social," pp. 4–5; interview with Griffiths; interview with San Román.

26. "Dictamen," p. 22.

27. Interview with Griffiths; Mongrut Muñoz, "La seguridad social," p. 11; quotation from "Dictamen," pp. 20–23. In comparing these figures, remember the rapid inflation of the recent years.

28. Ibid.

29. "Dictamen," p. 13.

30. The estimate of the 1983 deficit is taken from Aparicio Valdez, "Situación de la seguridad social," p. 5; the 1984 deficit is taken from interview with Griffiths.

31. "Dictamen," pp. 28–33; interview with Giffiths.

32. The information in this section comes from interviews with San Román and Griffiths.

33. Ley Orgánica de Seguridad Social, *Análisis Laboral* 7:78 (December 1983): 19–24.

34. INE, *Perú: Compendio estadístico, 1982* (Lima: INE, 1983).

35. IPSS, *Legislación*; for a historical analysis of the differences in benefits of the diverse groups in Peru, see Mesa-Lago, *Social Security in Latin America*, pp. 147–56.

36. Information supplied by IPSS, November 1983.

37. "Dictamen," pp. 9–10.

38. Figures from the executive budget provided by the Contaduría General of IPSS, March 1984.

39. Interview with Joaquín Leguía Gálvez, minister of labor, Lima, March 6, 1984.

40. "Dictamen," p. 36.

41. Ibid., pp. 11–13.

42. Ministerio de Salud, *Proyecciones de población por regiones de salud y utilización de indicadores del sector: Período 1980–1985* (Lima: MS, 1983), pp. 50–51.

43. Interview with Griffiths; "Dictamen," pp. 38–40.

44. Ibid.

45. Interview with Griffiths.

46. INE, *Informe estadístico, cuarto trimestre 1983* (Lima: INE, 1984); "Dictamen," pp. 35–40.

47. "Dictamen," p. 30.

48. Interview with Griffiths.

49. Interview with professors from the Universidad del Pacífico, Lima, March 5, 1984.

CHAPTER 7
Uruguay

I am grateful for the valuable support of Ariel Gianola Margegani in compiling legal and statistical information for this chapter.

1. For a historical study of the evolution of social security in Uruguay in 1829–1973, see Arturo C. Porzecanski, "The Case of Uruguay," in Mesa-Lago, *Social Security in Latin America*, pp. 70–84.

2. ILO, *Informe al Gobierno de la República Oriental del Uruguay sobre Seguridad Social* (Geneva: ILO, 1964); *Comisión de Inversiones y Desarrollo: Plan nacional de desarrollo económico y social* (Montevideo: CCEA, 1966).

3. An unpublished document by Oscar Hermida, Montevideo, 1984, was used in the preparation of this section.

4. For each sector's facilities in 1980 and 1983, see Dirección General de Estadística y Censo, *Uruguay, 1983: Anuario estadístico, 1983* (Montevideo: DGEC, 1983), and Ministerio de Salud Pública, information from 1984.

5. For more details concerning the organization of the health sector, see UNICEF/CIESU/ILPES, "Elementos para un diagnóstico social del Uruguay," Montevideo, March 1984, sec. 3.

6. Current legislation and DGSS, *Memoria, 1982* (Montevideo: DGSS, n.d.).

7. UNICEF/CIESU/ILPES, "Elementos para un diagnóstico," p. 50.

8. Porzecanski, "The Case of Uruguay," pp. 89–90.

9. Cited by UNICEF/CIESU/ILPES, "Elementos para un diagnostico," p. 33.

10. See table 2; ILO, *Yearbook of Labour Statistics, 1981;* PREALC, *Dinámica del subempleo en América Latina*, Estudios e Informes de la CEPAL, no. 10 (Santiago: PREALC, 1981); *Mercado de trabajo en cifras, 1950–1980* (Santiago: ILO, 1982); ECLA, "Síntesis preliminar." In Montevideo the proportions of the EAP in 1979

were even more favorable to the extension: 80 percent salaried, 13 percent self-employed, and 1 percent unpaid family workers (PREALC, *Mercado*).

11. Based on ECLA, Distribución regional del producto internosectorial en los países de América Latina, Cuadernos Estadísticos de CEPAL, no. 6 (Santiago: ECLA, 1981); and Dirección General Estadistica y Censo, *Uruguay, 1983*.

12. UNICEF/CIESU/ILPESA, cited by "Elementos para un diagnóstico," pp. 39, 44–45, 49.

13. Author's calculations based on DGSS, *Memoria, 1982*, and *Boletín estadístico* 4:10 (March 1983).

14. Porzecanski, "The Case of Uruguay," pp. 88, 93.

15. Ibid., pp. 96–97; UNICEF et al., "Elementos para un diagnóstico," p. 52.

16. UNICEF et al., "Elementos para un diagnóstico," pp. 52–53.

17. Author's calculations based on DGSS, *Memoria, 1982*.

18. Porzecanski, "The Case of Uruguay," p. 98.

19. Ibid., p. 94.

20. DGSS, *Memoria, 1982*.

21. Dirección General Estadística y Censo, *Uruguay, 1983*.

22. Unofficial estimates from DGSS, 1984.

23. Jorge Caumont, "Efectos económicos del cambio en el financiamiento de la seguridad social: El caso uruguayo," *Integración Latinoamericana* 6:63 (November 1981): 17 and table 3.5.

24. DGSS, *Memoria, 1982*.

25. Based on information from the Caja de Profesionales Universitarios and the Ministerio de Salud Pública, 1984.

26. UNICEF/CIESU/ILPES, "Elementos para un diagnóstico," pp. 56–58.

27. M. Mutarelli, "Tendencia de la mortalidad infantil en Uruguay: Periodo 1961–1980" (Montevideo: MSP, n.d.), pp. 2–4, cited in UNICEF/CIESU/ILPES, "Elementos para un diagnóstico," pp. 63–64.

28. UNICEF/CIESU/ILPES, "Elementos para un diagnóstico," pp. 51, 55.

29. Dirección General Estadística y Censo, *Uruguay, 1983;* Alfredo Picerno and Pablo Mieres, *Uruguay: Indicadores básicos* (Montevideo: CLAEH, 1983).

30. Porzecanski, "The Case of Uruguay," pp. 99–105.

31. Information based on DGSS, *Memoria, 1982*; and *Boletín estadístico* 1:1 (June 1980) and 4:10 (March 1983).

32. ECLA, "Síntesis preliminar," p. 34.

33. CELADE, *Boletín demográfico* 17:33 (January 1984).

34. Dirección General Estadística y Censo, *Uruguay, 1983*; Picerno and Mieres, *Uruguay: Indicadores básicos*; UNICEF/CIESU/ILPES, "Elementos para un diagnóstico," p. 32.

35. UNICEF/CIESU/ILPES, "Elementos para un diagnóstico," p. 56.

36. BID/ECIEL/CIESU/CINVE, "Encuesta de gasto público social" (questionnaire), Montevideo, October 1983.

37. Arroba et al., *El impuesto al valor agregado en el financiamiento de la seguridad social y el proceso de integración latinoamericano* (Washington, D.C.: BID/INTAL, 1980), pp. 211–13.

38. See Jorge Macón, "Financiamiento de la seguridad social: IVA o contribucion sobre salarios?" *Integración Latinoamericana* 6:63 (November 1981): 7.

39. In the theoretical analysis of the IVA and its effects, the author benefited from the help of Joseph Ramos, from the Division of Economic Development, ECLA.

40. For several of the criticisms against VAT made by social security specialists, see Giovanni Tamburi, "Social Security Financing: What Next?" *Benefits International* (July 1981): 7–12; and Alvaro Castro Gutiérrez, "Consideraciones preliminares para un estudio del financiamiento de la seguridad social en América Latina," *Estudios de la seguridad social,* no. 40 (1982): 5–28.

41. Caumont, "Efectos económicos," pp. 9–10.

42. This problem is noted in a study of the adoption of the IVA in Argentina, which—unlike the comparable development in Uruguay—coincided with a strong recession; thus the author warned that the recessive factors should be separated from the effects of the adoption of IVA. See A. Atchabarian, "Reformas en el financiamiento de la seguridad social: Efectos económicos: La experiencia argentina," *Integración Latinoamericana* 6:63 (November 1981): 24.

43. Caumont, "Efectos económicos," pp. 10–12.

44. Ibid., pp. 12–17.

45. Joseph Ramos, *Estabilización y liberalización económica en el Cono Sur,* Estudios e Informes de CEPAL 38 (Santiago: ECLA, 1984), chap. 5.

46. Ibid.; ECLA, "Uruguay," in *Estudio económico de América Latina, 1982;* ECLA, "Síntesis preliminar."

47. Picerno and Mieres, *Uruguay: Indicadores básicos.*

48. See Arroba et al., *El impuesto al valor,* p. 347; and Macón, "Financiamiento," pp. 7–8.

CHAPTER 8
The Needed Reform: Strategies and Obstacles

1. The original idea comes from Anibal Pinto, "Un itinerario realista para la reforma previsional," in *Inflación: Raíces estructurales* (Mexico City: Fondo de Cultura Económica, 1973), pp. 237–45.

2. Peter Thullen, "El financiamiento de regímenes obligatorios de pensiones bajo condiciones dinámicas y las nuevas matemáticas actuariales," *Seguridad Social,* 31:135–36 (May–August 1982): 234.

3. See Paul Fisher, "Seguridad social y planificación nacional," presented to the Conferencia Interamericana sobre Planificación de la Seguridad Social, Buenos Aires, 1974; and Wolfe, *El desarrollo esquivo,* pp. 246–50.

4. See Carmelo Mesa-Lago, *Planificación (1959),* chaps. 1 and 2.

5. Alfred Mallet, "Diversification or Standardization: Two Trends in Latin American Social Security," *International Labor Review* 101:1 (January 1970): 76–80.

Index

Wage contribution (*Continued*)
  guay, 229–34; to Uruguayan social security, 214–16
Wage contribution. *See also* Employer's contribution; Insured's contribution
Women: and Chilean social security, 134;
  and Cuban social security, 94, 99, 102;

and Peruvian social security, 199; and
  Uruguayan social security, 226
Worker's compensation program: administration of, 6; benefits of in Costa Rica, 59–
  60; organizational structure of in Chile,
  112; population coverage of in Costa Rica,
  49; sources of financing of, 16

Pitt Latin American Series

COLE BLASIER, EDITOR

ARGENTINA

Argentina in the Twentieth Century
David Rock, Editor

Argentina: Political Culture and Instability
Susan Calvert and Peter Calvert

Discreet Partners: Argentina and the USSR Since 1917
Aldo César Vacs

Juan Perón and the Reshaping of Argentina
Frederick C. Turner and José Enrique Miguens, Editors

The Life, Music, and Times of Carlos Gardel
Simon Collier

The Political Economy of Argentina, 1946–1983
Guido di Tella and Rudiger Dornbusch, Editors

BRAZIL

External Constraints on Economic Policy in Brazil, 1899–1930
Winston Fritsch

The Film Industry in Brazil: Culture and the State
Randal Johnson

The Manipulation of Consent: The State and Working-Class Consciousness in Brazil
Youssef Cohen

The Politics of Social Security in Brazil
James M. Malloy

Urban Politics in Brazil: The Rise of Populism, 1925–1945
Michael L. Conniff

COLOMBIA

Gaitán of Colombia: A Political Biography
Richard E. Sharpless

Roads to Reason: Transportation, Administration, and Rationality in Colombia
Richard E. Hartwig

CUBA

Cuba Between Empires, 1978–1902
Louis A. Pérez, Jr.

Cuba, Castro, and the United States
Philip W. Bonsal

Cuba in the World
Cole Blasier and Carmelo Mesa-Lago, Editors

Cuba Under the Platt Amendment
Louis A. Pérez, Jr.

Cuban Studies, Vols. 16–19
Carmelo Mesa-Lago, Editor

Intervention, Revolution, and Politics in Cuba, 1913–1921
Louis A. Pérez, Jr.

Lords of the Mountain: Social Banditry and Peasant Protest in Cuba, 1878–1918
Louis A. Pérez, Jr.